AF584539

NIGHTS AT THE RED STEINWAY

NIGHTS AT THE RED STEINWAY

Adventures in Jazz Piano, from the Wall Street Journal *and Elsewhere*

WILL FRIEDWALD

Foreword by Bill Charlap

Bloomsbury Publishing Group, Inc.
Backbeatbooks.com

Distributed by NATIONAL BOOK NETWORK

British Library Cataloguing in Publication Information available

Library of Congress Cataloging-in-Publication Data
Names: Friedwald, Will, 1961- author.
Title: Nights at the red Steinway : adventures in jazz piano, from the Wall Street Journal and elsewhere / Will Friedwald.
Description: Essex, Connecticut : Backbeat, 2024. | Includes index. | Summary: "NIGHTS AT THE RED STEINWAY: ADVENTURES IN JAZZ PIANO, FROM THE WALL STREET JOURNAL AND ELSEWHERE" —Provided by publisher.
Identifiers: LCCN 2024013809 (print) | LCCN 2024013810 (ebook) | ISBN 9781493084128 (cloth) | ISBN 9781493084135 (epub)
Subjects: LCSH: Pianists—Biography. | Jazz musicians—Biography. | Piano music (Jazz)—History and criticism.
Classification: LCC ML397 .F75 2024 (print) | LCC ML397 (ebook) | DDC 786.2/1650922 [B]—dc23/eng/20240327
LC record available at https://lccn.loc.gov/2024013809
LC ebook record available at https://lccn.loc.gov/2024013810

∞™ The paper used in this publication meets the minimum requirements of American National Standard for Information Sciences—Permanence of Paper for Printed Library Materials, ANSI/NISO Z39.48-1992.

To Tony, who loved a great piano player more than anybody.

CONTENTS

Acknowledgments ix

Alphabetical List of Performers xi

Foreword by Bill Charlap xiii

Introduction xv

Founding Fathers 1

Royalty 11

Masters and Monsters 27

Leading Men 37

Transitional Figures 43

Superstars 55

Beyond Compare 71

Mr. Gershwin, Mr. Wilson, and Dr. Zeitlin 83

Fellow Travelers 89

Rugged Individuals 103

Postmodern Poster Children 115

World Jazz and Ethno-Piano 135

Pianoforte Africanus 149

Class of 1970 167
Three of a Kind 177
Contemporary Masters 195
Ensembles 211
Pan-Generational, Pan-Stylistics 225
More than Accompanists 239
The Next Generation (*Pianoforte Millenianus*) 247
Index 259

ACKNOWLEDGMENTS

John Cerullo, Alan Nahigian, William Clark, David Hajdu, Bill Sando, Raymond DeFellita, John Seeley, Eric Gibson, Brian Kelly, and Tom Buckley, and especially to Bill Charlap, both for his wonderful playing and his wonderful foreword.

ALPHABETICAL LIST OF PERFORMERS

Abrams, Muhal Richard (1930–2017)
Akiyoshi, Toshiko (born 1929)
Alexander, Joey (born 2003)
Alexander, Monty (born 1944)
Allen, Geri (1956–2016)
Barron, Kenny (born 1943)
Basie, Count (1904–1984)
Bley, Carla (1936–2023)
Bley, Paul (1932–2016)
Brubeck, Dave (1920–2012)
Charlap, Bill (born 1966)
Chestnut, Cyrus (born 1963)
Childs, Billy (born 1957)
Cohen, Emmet (born 1990)
Cole, Nat King (1919–1965)
Corea, Chick (1941–2021)
Diehl, Aaron (born 1985)
Dyer, Bokani (born 1986)
Ellington, Duke (1899–1974)
Evans, Bill (1929–1980)
Firth, Tedd (born 1976)
Fortner, Sullivan (born 1986)
Garner, Erroll (1921–1977)
Glasper, Robert (born 1978)
Hancock, Herbie (born 1940)
Harris, Barry (1929–2021)
Hersch, Fred (born 1955)
Hines, Earl "Fatha" (1903–1983)
Hyman, Dick (born 1927)
Ibrahim, Abdullah (born 1934)
Iverson, Ethan (born 1973)
Iyer, Vijay (born 1971)
Jamal, Ahmad (1930–2023)
Jarrett, Keith (born 1945)
Jones, Hank (1918–2010)
Keezer, Geoffrey (born 1970)
Kellaway, Roger (born 1939)
King Cole Trio
Levant, Oscar (1906–1972)
Lewis, John (1920–2001)
Mehldau, Brad (born 1970)
Miller, Bill (1915–2006)
Miller, Mulgrew (1955–2013)
Mintun, Peter (born 1950)
Modern Jazz Quartet
Monk, Thelonious (1917–1982)
Moran, Jason (born 1975)
Morton, Jelly Roll (1890–1941)
O'Donnell, Bill (born 1953)
Pérez, Danilo (born 1965)
Peterson, Oscar (1925–2007)
Powell, Bud (1924–1966)

Ra, Sun (1914–1993)
Reed, Eric (born 1970)
Rosenthal, Ted (born 1959)
Rosnes, Renee (born 1962)
Shearing, George (1919–2011)
Solal, Martial (born 1927)
Stritch, Billy (born 1962)
Tatum, Art (1909–1956)
Taylor, Cecil (1929–2018)
Taylor, Dr. Billy (1921–2010)
The Bad Plus
Thompson, Isaiah J. (born 1997)
Tristano, Lennie (1919–1978)
Tyner, McCoy (1938–2020)
Waller, Thomas "Fats" (1904–1943)
Walton, Cedar (1934–2013)
Weather Report
Weston, Randy (1926–2018)
Williams, Mary Lou (1910–1981)
Wilson, Teddy (1912–1986)
Zawinal, Joe (1932–2007)
Zeitlin, Denny (born 1938)

FOREWORD

Will Friedwald is in the house. I have seen him countless times over the years from my vantage point on the bandstand, *and* in the audience, from every club to every concert hall and performance space throughout New York City. Always stylish, always engaged, always thoughtfully and intensely checking out the scene. Friedwald's writing on music captures the excitement and vitality of the art as it's being created in the moment . . . not from an ivory tower but rather, smack dab in the middle of the action. With his vast knowledge of the players art and his love of singers and the song, Will Friedwald always homes in on the drama, personality, and unique charisma of each musician he profiles. His columns for *The Wall Street Journal* and *The New York Sun* have been a gift to the city's culture. Will is a champion. Will is singularly perceptive. Will is watching, listening, learning, and delivering. Will Friedwald is in the house.

—Bill Charlap

INTRODUCTION

There's a famous joke among keyboard players: A pianist shows up for a gig at a restaurant where he's never worked previously. When he sits down at the piano, he immediately realizes that the instrument is in terrible shape, badly out of tune, and missing several keys and the action is severely damaged and the sustaining pedals aren't working. He complains to the proprietor of the joint: "Hey! You gotta get this piano fixed before anyone can play it." The owner, absolutely clueless as to what the pianist is talking about, responds, "What do you mean? I just had it painted!"

The joke is, of course, that having a piano painted has absolutely no effect on how the instrument actually sounds; the visual element should not have any effect on how we experience the music itself.

And yet I wonder.

Have you ever seen a bright red Steinway piano? I did, for several nights' worth of piano recitals in June 2008. This was near the end of the long and satisfying history of the Newport Jazz Festival (then in its final phase as the JVC Jazz Festival) in New York. It had been the tradition of impresario George Wein, for many years, to hold a special series of keyboard evenings, some solos, some trios, and other piano-centric formats. This year, the piano evenings were held at the New York Society for Ethical Culture, which includes a charming midsize auditorium, off Central Park at 2 West 64th Street. As usual, Mr. Wein's second-in-command, the redoubtable Charles Bourgeois (1919–2014), took care of the nuts-and-bolts details.

As he had a thousand times before, Charlie contracted for a nine-foot Steinway piano from one of his usual sources. Imagine everyone's surprise when the instrument delivered was unpacked and, lo and behold, turned out to be encased in bright orangey red enamel, with a bright red bench to match. From a distance, it looked like a chariot of fire.

Yet here's the funny thing: obviously the red color had nothing to do with the way the instrument actually sounded, but it was the visual effect, the surprising color, that inspired us to pay attention to the instrument in a whole new way. And that apparently extended to the players as well as the audience. Perhaps for that reason, the three specific concerts I heard that week, by three very different players—the modern jazz stylist George Cables, the swing and bebop pioneer Hank Jones, and the uncategorizable but undeniably extremely avant-garde Cecil Taylor—were among the finest hours in the whole history of George Wein's Festival production shows, indeed, three of the greatest piano concerts I have ever attended. The red Steinway turned out be a magical piano, with the power to transform itself into an entirely new instrument each time a different master touched it.

In this book, I use the adventure of the red Steinway as the jumping off point for a collection of writings about jazz piano. These come from over a period of almost 40 years from some of my earliest professional assignments up to my more recent stories.

A caveat—sort of—this book is an anthology, not a comprehensive history of jazz piano, although I herewith admit that such a volume is sorely needed. As will be obvious, the current work is a very personal and informal survey of jazz piano from the earliest days in New Orleans at the turn of the twentieth century up to the major players of the current generation. There is, admittedly, a bias toward contemporary players (i.e., musicians who have been active in the time that I have been writing).

Nights at the Red Steinway serves as an unorthodox history of the piano in jazz, from the legendary piano professors of the New Orleans red-light district, such as Jelly Roll Morton, and such jazz-age piano pioneers as the great Thomas "Fats" Waller and Earl "Fatha" Hines as well as swing masters such as Teddy Wilson and Joe Bushkin. Along the way, we also encounter masters and monsters endowed with sheer, overwhelming technique, such as Art Tatum and Oscar Peterson. There's also a special section on musicians so talented that they were nicknamed after royalty: Duke Ellington, Count Basie, and Nat King Cole. A section on "Transitional Figures" talks about those players who were a key part of the evolution of swing into bebop and modern jazz, such as Mary Lou Williams and her student, Thelonious Monk, as well as the legendary Bud Powell.

Piano players, often leading distinctive small combos, became superstars in the 1950s, such as George Shearing, Dave Brubeck, and Ahmad Jamal, while Erroll Garner was in a class by himself as a headliner in clubs and concert halls all over the world, the first jazz musician to be presented like a classical artist. There are unique players such as Lennie Tristano and Bill Evans, who found a personal style within the larger vocabulary of modernism. We eventually wind up in the millennial era, in which piano is dominated by pan-generational stylists such as Dick Hyman and Bill Charlap, as well as such uniquely modern, consistently exploratory players as Chick Corea, Fred Hersch, and the bad boy of the piano (in the way he treats his audiences, not his playing), Keith Jarrett.

Along the way, there are all sorts of fascinating detours and side streets, for example, a look at master accompanists, such as Frank Sinatra's longtime piano partner Bill Miller, and the contemporary Billy Stritch and Tedd Firth. We also examine a unique subgenre that we might call world jazz piano or "ethno-piano," which includes unique players from all over the world, from the great French stylist Martial Solal to the Brooklyn-born Afrocentric master Randy Weston, to Panama's Danilo Perez and Jamaica's Monty Alexander, all of whom combine jazz with their local musical traditions. (The critic Stuart Nicolson has described this as "Glocal" music.)

For better or worse, there are two perspectives that have dominated nearly every serious look at jazz, but it may well be that both are ultimately dead ends. Sometimes we look at the music in terms of "tradition," which links to the past, and sometimes we think about "innovation," which is supposed to point to the future.

But what if we choose to celebrate the music for its own merits? My goal is to make the argument for a common humanity that pervades all of the best jazz—from all styles and all eras—which transcends era, genre, and vogue. An unspoken thesis underlies all this work: that the music covered herein speaks of the human experience in a way that transcends both of the traditional viewpoints—it checks every box. This music is always timely because it defies time. In other words, the goal is to look at the music for its own sake.

I've written extensively about singers, songs, and the myriad uses of the human voice. I try to keep the concept of a "voice," whether literal or metaphoric, at the heart of my writing about instrumental jazz as well. The idea is to look for the most distinctive voices in all the various subgenres across the breadth and scope of jazz piano, to listen to what they're saying and look at how they're saying it.

The millennial era differs sharply from previous periods in the music's history in the ways that both the music itself and information about it are disseminated—or not. From the 1950s to the turn of the new century, there was frequent coverage of jazz in all the major newspapers, such as, to name just three in New York: *The New York Times*, *The Village Voice*, and *The Wall Street Journal*. They all regularly covered the music, both in terms of new performances and current releases of classic and historical albums.

Also, there was always something more social about going to record stores, where one could hang out—at the old J&R or Tower (where I worked in the mid-1980s for the princely sum of $3.85 an hour). You could always ask the salesclerks for recommendations or explanations, and there were always more knowledgeable fans and collectors coming in. Plus, of course, back when we were taking in the music via physical media, LPs and CDs, there were always liner notes to illuminate the music things.

Now, all of that is gone, and it's harder for anyone interested in the music to be able to learn about it. The ironic thing is that much of the music is readily available; between Spotify, Apple Music, and YouTube audio and even video, virtually all of jazz history is accessible in less time than it takes to type out a name such as "George

Shearing." Thirty years ago, for instance, it was easier to read about Erroll Garner than it was to actually find his music, and now the situation has reversed itself—finding the music itself is relatively easy but putting it into context and making sense of it is the hard part. That's essentially what I'm going for here.

Much writing about jazz consists of what we might call polemics and "problem pieces": stories about something bad that happened, such as racism or sexism, or more often, griping that such-and-such an artist isn't as famous as he should be, controversies within the music, and other such problematic issues. *Nights at the Red Steinway* stresses the upbeat side of everything; it aims to present to the reader musicians, bands, and recordings that they should know about—it is almost entirely positive. *Nights at the Red Steinway* could be subtitled *The Joy of Jazz Piano*.

These pieces were written primarily for *The Wall Street Journal* between 2008 and 2023 as well as *The New York Sun* between 2003 and 2008 and then again from 2022 to 2024; in some cases, they have been slightly revised, updated, and in some cases, expanded as much as they need to be. I'm hoping that this book will become an essential read for everyone who loves the quintessential American art form known as jazz piano.

FOUNDING FATHERS

JELLY ROLL MORTON (1890–1941)

It was Wynton Marsalis who once articulated what made Jelly Roll Morton so special and put it in terms that followers of 21st-century politics could relate to. Most of the early jazz giants from New Orleans, such as Joe "King" Oliver, as the JALC artistic director put it, were all about "states' rights." Morton, contrastingly, represented the musical equivalent of a "strong federal government." What Wynton means was that the first jazzmen rarely thought to give the music any form beyond a simple playing of the blues or popular songs, usually for dancers, with brief solos strung together. Morton, on the other hand, was the first to give the music a larger sense of form—and also to write music specifically for the jazz ensemble—and thus became the music's first great composer and bandleader.

Morton's detractors, and there are many, would argue that it would hardly be surprising that he created a music in which one figure—the composer/arranger/bandleader—was at the center because Morton has an unshakable reputation as perhaps being the biggest egomaniac and one of the least lovable individuals in the history of jazz. Even a century after his first inarguable breakthrough—the publication of "Jelly Roll Blues" in 1915—Morton's self-centeredness and ego are as much a part of his legend as his remarkable music.

Still, the music speaks for itself: as jazz's first great "auteur," he can lay claim to having been the spiritual inspiration for a huge part of the music's history, from Fletcher Henderson (who reorchestrated Morton's music for the swing era) and Duke Ellington to Gil Evans (who reworked Morton's music for the modern era) and Maria Schneider. Yet as it's also been pointed out (by Martin Williams, among others), Morton himself remains *sui generis*: he showed the world how to capture lightning in a bottle when he proved that the music could be written down, annotated, and played by ensembles of virtually any size, yet no one ever dared to try to sound like him whether in his own time or since.

Morton's achievements are a continual source of controversy: he spent the second half of his life exaggerating what he had done in the first half, most famously on a legendary series of oral history recordings made at the Library of Congress in the spring of 1938. He loudly proclaimed, to everyone who would listen, that he was the sole creator of jazz, blues, stomps, all of hot music—apparently, he wasn't willing to share credit with anyone.

Even his birthdate is a source of controversy; since Morton claimed to have invented jazz in 1902, he had to make himself out to be at least five years older than he was to help substantiate the claim. However, he is now believed to have been born in New Orleans in 1890; he was a Creole of Color and as such, bragged that "My folks were all Frenchmen," rather than Americans, and regarded themselves as several steps higher on the social ladder than Negroes. The Creoles considered themselves a cultured and privileged class, and as such, music education was de rigueur for their young, although it was somewhat shocking when, at the age of 14, Morton (born Ferdinand Lamothe) took his education in classical piano and went to work playing blues and jazz in the Crescent City's infamous red-light district.

The young Ferd was working in "sporting houses" under the name "Morton" to shield his family from scandal, he said, but when they found out, they sent him packing just the same. It no longer mattered; even by his teens, Morton was already one of the founding fathers of the new music and one of the first New Orleans musicians to travel widely, even to the West Coast. He played in touring minstrel shows and for blues singers and vaudevillians, and he led his own bands; he was a literal superstar in Chicago at the height of the jazz age. To describe "Mr. Jelly Lord," as he referred to himself, as "highly competitive" would be an understatement: he bragged about being a pool shark and a pimp as well as nothing less than a piano predator, the musical equivalent of a marksman and sharpshooter, who relished not only being able to outplay virtually all of his fellow keyboardists but also humiliating them in the process. You go up against Jelly Roll at your own risk.

The recordings he made, especially the legendary Red Hot Peppers sessions from Chicago and then New York, are among the greatest jazz sessions ever, comparable with Louis Armstrong's Hot Fives or the best of Duke Ellington or Charlie Parker. Morton's classics, such as "King Porter Stomp," which went on to become a virtual national anthem during the swing era; "New Orleans Bump," a long-standing favorite of Wynton Marsalis and Jazz at Lincoln Center; the piano tour de force "The Pearls"; "Wild Man Blues," which inspired one of Louis Armstrong's greatest solos; and the blues-drenched wit and humor of "Sidewalk Blues" and "Dead Man Blues," are all an unimpeachable part of the American musical canon.

Like the hero of an ancient Greek tragedy, Morton was ultimately brought down by his own arrogance—what the Greeks called *hubris*—as well as changing tastes in music, the Great Depression, the deeply entrenched biases against people of color (Creole and Negro alike), and the inability of Americans to take their own culture seriously. He died broke and alone in Los Angeles at the age of 50 in 1940. Yet what he gave to music, the systems he created and the foundation he laid for the future, makes him nothing less than the Alexander Hamilton of Jazz.

(Program notes for Jazz at Lincoln Center, 2017)

THOMAS "FATS" WALLER (1904–1943)

To hear even a little of Fats Waller is to want to hear everything, and to that end, I highly recommend a series of CDs from the JSP label in England, collected in six boxed sets of four discs and titled *Fats Waller: Complete Recorded Works, Volumes One through Six*. It's rather amazing to realize that Waller recorded 24 CDs' worth of material in just 39 short years, a total of 832 tracks. However, if you don't want to make the major investment in 24 CDs' worth of music, there's a decent sampling of Waller's greatest, released by BMG (formerly RCA, formerly Victor Records) in 2002, possibly in anticipation of the great man's centennial two years hence. It's titled *At the Piano*, and since it is readily available on Apple Music, Spotify, and the other streaming platforms, it's as good an introduction to Waller's playing and singing as any.

***

When we talk about the history of a genre of music or any kind of innovation, we tend to think in terms of firsts. Who was the first great jazz improviser? Who led the first great jazz big band? Who was the first to play something that sounded like bebop? Yet sometimes the *last* great musician to work in a genre or style is even more impressive.

Thomas "Fats" Waller was not the first stride pianist. The claim has never been made that he invented the style. Rather, it makes more sense to think of Waller as the last great stride pianist—that he did so much with the style, over the course of 832 tracks' worth of music, that after his tragically young death, no one else wanted to do anything with stride. It was felt that everything had been done with it and there was nothing left for anyone else to do. Players who came after Waller, such as Joe Sullivan, were determined to keep the style alive rather than do something new with it.

Waller was hardly a "revivalist," like, say, the younger stride acolyte Dick Hyman. But he was born considerably later than the other acknowledged pioneers and masters of stride, such as James P. Johnson, Willie "The Lion" Smith (both born in 1893), and Lucky Roberts (1887). With the evolution of jazz happening on such a fast-paced scale, that essentially meant that Waller was a whole generation younger than the other stride masters. Earl "Fatha" Hines, born in Pittsburgh in 1903, was actually a year older than Waller, and he was enthusiastically described by his own disciple, Nat King Cole, as the first major player to move beyond the stride school. (It's kind of startling to realize that at the time of Waller's death in 1943, futurists such as Thelonious Monk and Lennie Tristano were already moving jazz piano into a whole other era.)

Waller was, in fact, revitalizing stride: throughout the 1920s, up through the classic solos of 1929, he's playing the more traditional form of the genre, with lots of speed and energy. But by the great years of the "Rhythm" ensembles of the mid-1930s and onward, he has refined the basic stride technique into something more personal, more elegant, what pianist and scholar Raymond DeFellita describes as more graceful, "still using the left hand in stride motion but in a slow, gentle and dreamy manner." I'm particularly fond of his treatment of an eminently forgettable song from 1941, "Come Down to Earth, My Angel," on which he does everything: plays piano in this nouveau stride manner, sings (without comic asides, for once), and throws in a solo on organ.

At the Piano starts with an iconic performance of an iconic song, "Ain't Misbehavin'," which as Waller liked to tell people, he had written while residing in jail after a failure to pay his alimony. Probably his best-known composition, he performed and recorded it many times, but one of the very last occasions, from January 23, 1943, is the best known. This was the soundtrack recording session for his final film appearance, the 20th Century Fox all-Black musical *Stormy Weather*. Waller is leading an all-star edition of what was essentially "His Rhythm," the six- or seven-piece band that he worked with for most of his career, featuring Benny Carter on trumpet, guitarist Irving Ashby, bassist Slam Stewart, and New Orleans drummer Zutty Singleton, along with trombonist Alton Moore and saxophonist/clarinetist Gene Porter.

There's a jaunty intro, and Waller slides into the famous melody extremely relaxed; the track is four minutes long, considerably longer than most standard 10-inch 78s at the time, which might explain why Waller feels less rushed than on customary commercial recordings. Fats is 4/4 swing time but with something of a two-beat feel, and the phrasing is low key and elegant. He throws in flourishes while approaching the bridge, and the bridge itself is rendered in descending, cascading lines. His singing is equally low key; this is the version people remember, where, at the end of the first eight bars, "saving my love for you," he repeats those two words, "for you, for you, for you," as if transferring his attention from one woman in the crowd to another.

After the vocal, the piece immediately shifts gears into a faster 4/4 episode in which Waller and the rhythm section interact with drummer Singleton; it builds to an ecstatic line with the three horns that comes to the bridge. Waller slows down as he sings the last eight in kind of a vaudeville half-time climax.

The second tune on *At the Piano* is "Smashing Thirds," a piano solo from 1929. The more obvious choice for a Waller solo piano composition would have been "A Handful of Keys" or "The Viper's Drag," but "Smashing Thirds" will do nicely. It's much jauntier and even more nervous than the 1943 Fats session, but the playing is strong and confident. The piece knows exactly where it's going to go and how it's going to get there. It unrolls logically and orderly, more evidence, indeed, that

Waller, like many artists and musicians, had considerably more control in his art than in his life.

"Don't Let It Bother You" was written as Fred Astaire's opening number in the 1934 movie version of *The Gay Divorcee*, although it's sung by the chorus girls rather than Astaire himself. This is the kind of song that jazz historians would complain about in the 1960s, typically referring to them as dog tunes foisted upon artists such as Waller and Billie Holiday. If you ever come across a sentence like that in a book or a liner note, my advice is to skip it. "Don't Let It Bother You," like the vast majority of songs recorded by Waller in particular, is a wonderful song.

According to a note on the official RCA recording session ledger, it begins with "a conversation between FATS WALLER & TRAPMAN," and in fact, the song starts with dialogue between Waller and drummer Harry Dial.

Fats: Boy, what's the matter with you?

Dial: Ah man, everything's wrong! My old lady done run off with the iceman!

Fats: What?

Dial: Fats! And my daughter run off with the undertaker! And I'm about to die, and I ain't got nobody to bury me.

Fats: Son, don't let it bother you! Listen here.

And at this point, he starts into the song, a typical cheer-up song of the Great Depression era. After the vocal, we hear a tenor saxophone solo by Gene Sedric, making his first appearance with Waller and launching a long collaboration, with bassist Billy Taylor taking the bridge. ("Then I'll Be Tired of You," also on this collection, comes from the same date.) To make sure his down-and-out drummer has gotten the optimistic message, Waller returns at the end, sings the last eight bars again, and concludes with "My my, yes, yes!"

Next comes an April 9, 1937, version of another Waller classic, the all-time jam-session favorite "Honeysuckle Rose." The epically complete Waller bio discography, *Fats in Fact* (researched and written by Laurie Wright and published by Storyville Press in 1991) informs us that this was originally recorded as a 12-inch master, which explains why it's all of 4:25 in length—again longer by a third at least than the usual 78. It was first released as part of one of the earliest jazz albums, RCA's 1937 *A Symposium of Swing*.

As it happens, Waller had also recorded this signature song only a week or so earlier on March 31, 1937, as part of an all-star group featuring Tommy Dorsey and Bunny Berigan. That version has much more of a two-beat Dixieland feeling than the April version with the Rhythm.

The April recording is not, however, the typical Fats-and-his-Rhythm side because it stresses individual solos, rather than the ensemble, and there's no vocal. Waller plays a chorus in double or triple time at the start, barely getting four bars into the melody before launching into variations. The second chorus features drummer Slick Jones soloing on vibraphone à la Lionel Hampton and turning the bridge over to guitarist Al Casey. Gene Sedric gets a lively solo on tenor, and then we come back to Fats, who plays a full solo, and then trumpeter Herman Autry has his say. There follows a drum solo by Jones, playing lots of press rolls, punctuated by Waller's piano, which actually anticipates the drum sequence on the 1943 "Ain't Misbehavin'." The track ends with a wild, jammy finish by the ensemble.

"A Porter's Love Song to a Chambermaid" is the first ever song cut by Waller and what would be his longtime touring-and-recording group, billed on labels and marquees as "Fats Waller and his Rhythm." The song itself might have been dismissed by one of the old-guard jazz critics as a dog song, and more likely, it would be viewed in a dim light by the 21st-century PC police as a song demeaning to African Americans because it presents the protagonists as lowly domestics. Both charges might be nullified by the larger truth that the song was written by two great Black songwriters, the two men closest to Fats, James P. Johnson and Andy Razaf. Both Johnson's melodies and Razaf's metaphors are resplendently juicy. Waller truly exalts both, and it's sheer rapture to hear him digging into both. "I will be your clothes pin/Be my pulley line/We'll hang out together/Wouldn't that be fine?"

"Sweet and Slow" was written by Hollywood's greatest songwriter, Harry Warren, with his major partner of the 1930s, lyricist Al Dubin, for a Dick Powell musical titled *Broadway Gondolier*. This is the same project for which they wrote "Lulu's Back in Town," which also became a Fats Waller classic; conveniently, the two Waller–Warren sides were issued back-to-back on Victor 25063. The main difference between the two is that "Sweet and Slow" was barely included in the final movie; it's only heard as background music and never sung onscreen. But even more than "Lulu," it was Waller who made what would have been an obscure song into something of a jazz standard. Waller really croons the lyric here, all the while engaging in a back-and-forth with Autry's trumpet obbligatos—you see why he was so influential as both a pianist and singer. It's a rare example of a 1930s 78 that following the instructions of the lyric really does take its time.

"Keepin' Out of Mischief Now" is another major Waller–Razaf standard, but he wrote the song in 1932, before the start of his Rhythm series and the Victor contract. Somehow he only recorded it once, at a 1937 solo piano session. That said, it's a singularly lovely performance. Surely, it's no coincidence that the most infamous party animal in the history of American music—who essentially partied himself into a very early grave—wrote two of his most famous songs about avoiding mischief and NOT misbehaving. Waller phrases the melody tellingly; he plays the main phrases lightly and sweetly, looking like a character in a 1930s cartoon harkening to the angel on his shoulder but punctuating those lines with bass notes in his left hand as if he were deliberately undermining the text. So is he keeping out of mischief and not misbehaving, or is he musically illustrating how he's going to fall off the wagon?

"Willow Tree" is a bluesy tune Waller wrote in 1928 and also recorded only once, on a brilliantly experimental session from that year. For starters, there are two keyboards: Waller's mentor, James P. Johnson, is playing piano, and Fats himself is playing pipe organ. We know that he learned the organ playing for services in his father's church and that on occasion, a young man of his own age, Bill (not yet "Count") Basie, learned the instrument from hearing and watching Waller play it—and helping out with the requisite pumping. The two keyboards give the recording a wide, spacey sound, only partially filled in by two horn players, the trumpeter Jabbo Smith, playing muted here, and multireed player Garvin Bushell. Bushell plays clarinet on "Willow Tree"—elsewhere on the date, he plays bassoon, even as he would on John Coltrane's *Africa Brass* album from 1961. Waller's first recordings for Victor were as a featured soloist playing jazz on the pipe organ, and they are lovely enough, but the combination of Waller's organ with Johnson's piano, plus Bushell and Smith weaving in and out of them and around each other, is fairly magical.

On *At the Piano*, we go from one Waller pipe organ classic to another, from 1928 to the 1942 masterpiece "Jitterbug Waltz." The pianist's son, Maurice Waller, who was 14 in 1942, remembered how one night his father arrived home in the middle of the night and woke him up. The boy's mother said, "Leave him alone—let him sleep!" But Fats insisted, "No, no, he's gotta hear this. It's a killer diller!" According to Maurice, Waller Sr. then "sat at the organ and played 'Jitterbug Waltz' with great gusto. A tremendous smile of self-satisfaction wrapped around his happy face." Fats asked Maurice what he thought of it, but before the young man could even answer, Fats stated, "Good as anything Gershwin's ever written."

"Jitterbug Waltz" is one of Waller's last great compositions, a beautiful melody, which he had the novel idea of setting in 3/4 time. Dance bands had occasionally played waltzes in the 1920s and early 1930s, but during the swing era, they were hardly ever heard, at least as played by jazz ensembles. Waller's composition may be the most famous waltz in jazz at least until 1959–1960 when Miles Davis and John Coltrane popularized jazz in 3/4, 6/4, and 6/8 time—around the same moment that Dave Brubeck was experimenting with jazz in 5/4 and other nutso time signatures. The original 1942 recording is an all-time jazz classic; in later years, there would be lyrics added, both for Dinah Washington on her Fats Waller songbook album and for the 1978 Broadway revue *Ain't Misbehavin'*, but these are ultimately unnecessary—the song is perfect as an instrumental.

Between his earlier sessions on the traditional pipe organ and his later work on the new electric organ, Waller must be credited as the original pioneer on the instrument—a generation before such innovators as Bill Doggett and Jimmy Smith. Maurice Waller's telling of the origin of "Jitterbug Waltz" also implies that Waller was fond enough of the electric organ to actually keep one of the early models in his apartment—surely not a common thing in 1939.

"Your Feet's Too Big" (1939) is also in *Ain't Misbehavin'*, one of a number of songs associated with Waller that he didn't actually write. Even so, this song, written by Fred Fisher and introduced by the Ink Spots in 1935, is one of Waller's comedy classics; it's hard to imagine a Waller tribute without it. As an entertainer, Waller is somehow very broad and very subtle at the same time. There's actually less overt clowning around on a song like this, which is already funny on its own, as opposed to something like "Until the Real Thing Comes Along," in which he takes a "straight" love song and makes it funny. Here, Waller's asides are all the funnier for being so understated in terms of his usual gargantuan standards, especially his opening line over the piano intro, "Who's that walkin' around out there? Sounds like baby patter. Baby elephant patter, that's what I calls it!"—some of his most quotable. The song was popular enough to join "Ain't Misbehavin'" and "Honeysuckle Rose" as one of Waller's three Soundies jukebox movie shorts.

"Squeeze Me" is one of Waller's first songs, if not his very first notable success, which according to legend, he created by reworking an old-time dirty ditty titled "The Boy in the Boat." He first documented it as a piano roll in 1926 but thankfully, recorded a full-on version with his Rhythm in 1939, the session immediately prior to "Your Feet's Too Big." "Squeeze Me," like "Willow Tree," is a popular song with elements of the blues; the jazz-and-blues singer Mildred Bailey recorded fairly definitive versions of both. Waller's piano chorus at the start is followed by his vocal chorus and then equally lovely and croony solos from Sedric and Autry. They're not just jamming; but no less than the leader's playing and singing, they're perfectly capturing the mood of the piece and extending the romantic feeling established by Waller.

"Then I'll Be Tired of You" comes from the second session by Waller's Rhythm, the one immediately following "Porter's Love Song"—the same date as "Don't Let It Bother You." The song became both a jazz and a pop standard, thanks not least to this wonderful performance; it was written by two major Broadway songwriters who rarely collaborated, lyricist Yip Harburg and composer Arthur Schwartz, although it was apparently an independent pop song, not intended for a specific musical or revue. Truly it's one of the loveliest performances Fats ever made with the Rhythm ensemble, in both his playing and singing; he's just serious enough, just silly enough, just emotional enough, and just showbiz-y enough that he keeps everything in perfect balance. (And so again are Autry and Sedric, as mentioned, on his first session with Fats.) To me this is a major Fats Waller classic, and I'm very glad it's included here. (In 1947, the King Cole Trio recorded a lovely ballad treatment of "Then I'll Be Tired of You"; Cole never cited Waller as a direct influence, but it's hard to believe he didn't learn this song from Fats.)

We end with Irving Berlin's "Mandy," from the third session by Waller's Rhythm, September 1934. It was always associated with minstrel shows, but it was not written for an actual minstrel show but for an elaborate Florenz Ziegfeld–style re-creation of an old-time minstrel show in the 1919 *Ziegfeld Follies*. In 1934, Ziegfeld veteran Eddie Cantor included it in his big movie that year—another elaborate, affectionate tribute to the old-time minstrel shows—*Kid Millions*, produced by Samuel Goldwyn, a Ziegfeld successor if ever there was one. (That same production number also includes "Minstrel Man," by Burton Lane, which was later rewritten as "You're All the World to Me" in *Royal Wedding*, 1951.) Therefore, the vintage 15-year-old song was essentially reintroduced and recorded by bandleaders Claude Hopkins, Joe Haymes, and others. (The song would be re-reprised in the very odd whiteface minstrel show sequence in the 1954 movie *White Christmas*.)

Waller's version, not unexpectedly, is a total joy, beginning with a brief piano flourish of an intro and then lunging into a playful, growling, muted solo by Autry. We expect bands large and small to state the melody straightforwardly in the first chorus, but Autry is gloriously playful, making animal noises that we might interpret as an African American musician telling us exactly what he thinks about the entire minstrel show tradition.

Waller's choruses are even more so; here's the fat one at his most full of fun. He enjoys one of his favorite gambits, commenting on his own solo from the third person, "oh the tickling is so terrific . . . oh stop it, baby!" After the vocal per se, he improvises some scat choruses and enjoys some interplay with the horns. Al Casey gets a guitar solo, which doesn't happen very often, as Waller exhorts the band, "swing it, swing it," an expression that had not yet become common currency in 1934. He ends with an exuberant scat phrase, a vivid flourish expressed as a vocal rather than on piano or trumpet, very much in the style of such contemporaries as Louis Armstrong and Leo Watson.

He then concludes with "and this is the end of the record!" And that must be why, in 2002, the compilers of Fats Waller *At the Piano* chose to end the album with it here.

***

PS: As mentioned above, *At the Piano* is an excellent single disc (14 tracks) to sample some representative Fats Waller. And at the other end of the size spectrum, there's the epic complete recorded works package on JSP—24 CDs. If you're looking for something somewhere in between, I highly recommend *Fats Waller and his Rhythm: If You Got to Ask, You Ain't Got It*, a three-CD package issued by Sony-BMG in 2006. The set is divided into three sections, one per disc: "Fats Waller Plays and Sings Fats Waller," including not only such obvious faves as "Ain't Misbehavin'" and "Honeysuckle Rose" but also lesser-known Fats works such as "Ol' Grand Dad" (somehow the more senior I get, the more I like that one). Disc two is another inspired idea, "Strictly Instrumental," containing not only piano solos but band numbers, too, and lots of additional Waller compositions. The third CD is "Fats Waller Sings and Plays Around with Tin Pan Alley." Some of my favorites are not in there, such as "Until the Real Thing Comes Along" and "Then I'll Be Tired of You," but in general, I can't complain—no two Fats Waller fans could possibly agree on a selection that could please everybody. *Fats Waller and his Rhythm: If You Got to Ask, You Ain't Got It* (admittedly, that's a rather awkward title) also boasts a splendiferous booklet with excellent, comprehensive liner notes by Dan Morgenstern. Sixty-six tracks by Waller is hardly enough, but this is an excellent and highly recommended start.

(*Slouching Towards Birdland*, Substack, 2023)

ROYALTY

DUKE ELLINGTON (1899–1974)

Money Jungle at 60

Sixty years ago, Duke Ellington released one of his most controversial albums, *Money Jungle*, a once-in-a-lifetime collaboration with two much younger masters of modern jazz, bassist Charles Mingus and drummer Max Roach. A lifetime later, it's still impossible to get a consensus on the music, but nonetheless, it has become one of the most widely heard and well-regarded projects of the Maestro's long career.

There are two relevant stories regarding Ellington's reaction to two of the most prominent jazz composer–bandleaders of the generation after him. One was somewhat complimentary, albeit arguably in a backhanded way, and the other less so. The story goes that Ellington happened to hear one of Thelonious Monk's very first recordings, and as trumpeter Ray Nance recounted, "Duke was passing by in the corridor, and he stopped and asked, 'Who's that playing?' I told him. 'Sounds like he's stealing some of my stuff,' he said."

The second incident occurred during Ellington's South American tour in 1968. The orchestra is in Tucuman, a province in the north of Argentina, and it is here that Ellington was giving a press conference. (And, yes, it says something that Ellington was still popular enough this late in his career to be asked to give a press conference, especially in this rather out-of-the-way part of the world.) Someone asks Duke a question about Charles Mingus and describes the bassist–composer as a "member of the Ellington school." Ellington answers, "that's what he says," placing the emphasis on the word "he" in such a way as to suggest that Ellington might not agree with this assessment.

Much of Ellington's reaction can be attributed to the way he was asked these questions: without being prompted, he does suggest that Monk learned something from him, but when directly asked the question, he seems to want to put some distance between himself and Mingus. My own feeling is that, in the abstract at least, Ellington knew that both Monk and Mingus had learned a lot from him and that this made him proud.

There was a moment in September 1962, when Ellington was called upon to put his feelings about young and allegedly more "modern" musicians to the test, when, back-to-back, within less than 10 days, he recorded two of the most unusual but, ultimately, most highly regarded albums of his career, *Money Jungle* and *Duke Ellington and John Coltrane.*

Money Jungle has grown over the years, both in the general esteem of listeners and in the size of the work itself—the original album, issued 60 years ago in 1963, was a mere seven tracks. There have been three subsequent reissues on LP and CD, each at least slightly larger, adding additional material; the most recent issue, from 2002, includes 15 tracks and now includes almost 70 minutes' worth of music.

There are two conflicting stories about the backstory of *Money Jungle*: some say it was Ellington's idea, while others say it was brought to him by the producer Alan Douglas—who would go on to become both famous and infamous for his work with Jimi Hendrix. As a young man, Douglas had been kind of a "go-fer" for Duke during certain gigs in Douglas's native Boston, and in 1962, he was producing jazz for the United Artists label. Douglas does seem to be the one who thought to use Charles Mingus, who had also just signed with UA Records for the purpose of taping the epic Town Hall concert that was to come about a month later, and Mingus apparently suggested that they bring in Max Roach.

Mingus biographer Krin Gabbard, in his excellent book *Better Git It in Your Soul*, reports that Ellington initially presented himself to his two young collaborators with great humility. First, he tells them, "Think of me as the poor man's Bud Powell." Then, he informs them, apparently sincerely, that he doesn't intend to dominate the project and that he was open to playing compositions other than his own. In the end, however, that's not the way it worked out: it's an Ellington project through and through, and all the tunes are his.

There have been four major releases of *Money Jungle*, two LPs (the 1963 original and a 1986 reissue) and two CDs (1987 and 2002). More importantly, it has been issued both in the original album sequence, which is presumably the way Ellington intended, with the title track, "Money Jungle" coming first, and also in the actual recording sequence, with "Very Special" coming first.

Sequencing makes a major difference in that the tension between the three musicians has been well documented. Although both Mingus and Roach, who were by then well-established bandleaders in their own right, deferred to Ellington's leadership, there was still a degree of contentiousness between the two younger men. Famously, at one point, Mingus got furious—possibly at Roach, possibly at how the session was going—and stormed out of the studio. Duke had to be the bandleader again, going after Mingus and telling him how wonderfully he'd been playing and generally, calming him down. As some, including scholar Tom Cunniffe, have suggested, when you listen in recording sequence, you can hear the tension building.

By that standard, the first tune recorded, "Very Special," is one of the gentlest and least radical. Despite its title, this is a fairly standard Ellington blues of the sort that he might have played in a more customary trio project, such as his 1961 album, *Piano in the Foreground*, with the band's regular rhythm section, Aaron Bell and Sam Woodyard.

Indeed, the album is full of blues. Recorded later in the session, "Switch Blade" is a more angular blues with a prominent part for Mingus—and, yes, Ellington wasn't merely flattering the bassist; he really is playing spectacularly well here. "A Little Max (Parfait)" gives equal time to Roach and features the drummer in a series of stop-time breaks similar to what Ellington wrote for himself in "Dancers in Love." Two more such blues tunes, "Backward Country Boy Blues" and "REM Blues" were only added in the later editions—Ellington and Douglas probably felt that they had enough such numbers in the original release.

But the original album opened with "Money Jungle," which must have knocked listeners for a collective loop in 1963. It's not necessarily that it sounds like Cecil Taylor or some other state-of-the-avant-garde pianist of the early 1960s; Duke never sounds anything like other than himself, but it is a rougher, more aggressive, and even dangerous Duke than we've ever heard anywhere else. Mingus and Roach support him indirectly, not playing in the customary supporting role or comping, odd as it sounds, but supporting him by antagonizing him and even irritating him. At first, it sounds like a chaotic free-for-all, but it gradually makes more and more sonic sense as it progresses.

Ellington obviously didn't want to challenge longtime fans with a program of all new music, and so there are three of his songbook standards, "Solitude," "Warm Valley," and "Caravan." They are each conventional by Ellington standards, and they, too, could have been on *Piano in the Foreground*. Gabbard suggests that Duke might have included "Caravan" as a way of teasing Mingus since the bassist had played very briefly in Ellington's band in 1953, and in Mingus's own account, he had to leave after getting into a knife fight onstage with trombonist and "Caravan" composer Juan Tizol.

Still, the album's acknowledged masterpiece is "Fleurette Africaine (Little African Flower)," the second track on the album and the third to be recorded. Even the title is arresting; Duke, a self-described "race" man, included many allusions to Africa in his music titles, but he was also enough of a self-parodying sophisticate to employ a lot of parlor French. Here, he does both. "Fleurette Africaine" is the major new composition here, and though he never recorded it in a studio again or expanded it beyond the trio format, the tune does recur on several later Ellington concerts wherein the maestro is working in a piano-centric context. "Fleurette Africaine" figures prominently in the dual lineage of Ellington works inspired by Africa as well as his long history of floral and garden–inspired works. It's also the forerunner to another, more elaborate but similarly titled piece, "La Plus Belle Africaine" from 1966.

Douglas had vaguely hoped to reunite this trio for a second session, and Mingus himself wanted to do a date of piano–bass duets with Ellington in honor of Duke's pioneering duos with bass innovator Jimmy Blanton. Neither happened. In fact, no one made much of a fuss about *Money Jungle* in 1963; Miles Davis himself pooh-poohed it: "Mingus is a hell of a bass player, and Max is a hell of a drummer. But Duke can't play with them, and they can't play with Duke." And though Mingus and Ellington later became two of the most conspicuous autobiographers in jazz, neither mentioned it in their memoirs.

Yet the album grew in everyone's estimation over the decades; when I conducted a critic's poll for *The Village Voice* in 1985, more critics named *Money Jungle* and the Coltrane album than any "standard" Ellington project. Ten years ago, on the occasion of the 50th anniversary, drummer Terri Lynn Carrington released a tribute project, *Money Jungle: Provocative in Blue*, which has its moments; the flutes are groovy on "Fleurette," but Clark Terry's familiar "Mumbles" routine seems unnecessary. In general, the 2013 album can't lay a glove on the original. *Money Jungle* is that rare work of art, imperfect yes, but the kind of art that you love not just in spite of its flaws but to a large part, because of them.

(*The New York Sun*, 2023)

EARL "FATHA" HINES (1903–1983)

"Say, Earl Hines, why don't you let us in on some of that good music, Pops?" Louis Armstrong asks at the start of the 1928 classic "A Monday Date," and Hines answers, "C'mon here! Let's get together then."

Lately, the world has been sadly slow to get in on some of that good music. Hines was a superstar even into his final decades but since then, has hardly received the attention he deserves.

I can think of no obvious reason that the 100th anniversary of a man so important to jazz as Earl "Fatha" Hines was all but ignored. There were no memorial concerts, no comprehensive box-set reissue packages—the Mosaic package arrived nearly 10 years later. (The major release commemorating this event is *Fatha's Day: An Earl Hines Songbook*, by the fine modern jazz pianist John Hicks [High Note 7110].)

Yet it's impossible to imagine the evolution of jazz piano without the influence of Earl Hines. Before Hines, there was stride piano, ragtime piano, and blues piano, but Hines was among the first to play in a style that resonates in contemporary ears as unhyphenated jazz piano. Earlier masters, such as Jelly Roll Morton, viewed the piano as a microcosm for an entire jazz orchestra, and they replicated a whole set of brass, reeds, and rhythm with their fingertips. Hines, contrastingly, figured out how the piano would fit in with the other instruments in the modern jazz ensemble and developed an approach with which the keyboard could hold its own against any horn soloist. He called it "trumpet-style piano," and when we listen to Hines today, he sounds less like his predecessors, such as James P. Johnson, and more like his successors, such as Teddy Wilson or Art Tatum.

Hines himself may have helped prevent a proper centennial celebration by messing around with his birth date. He claimed December 28, 1905, although contemporary sources state 1903. There is no formal biography of Hines; however, the late Stanley Dance put together a collection of interviews with Hines and his key associates and called it *The World of Earl Hines*, and this stands as the key reference source on the great pianist. He was born in Duquesne, Pennsylvania, a small suburb of Pittsburgh. His mother and then his stepmother played keyboards, and his father was an amateur trumpeter, which might have preordained him to come up with a style that combined piano and brass traditions. His early experience was playing light classics on the piano, accompanying a slightly older singer who sang arias and lieder. When he first discovered jazz in his late teens, his first impulse was to learn to play the new music on trumpet, but he said, "then the idea came to me to do on the piano what I wanted to do on the cornet."

Hines would spend most of his career in Chicago and in the mid-1920s, established his reputation via collaborations with two pioneers from New Orleans, clarinetist Jimmie Noone and trumpeter Louis Armstrong. Hines and Noone co-led the Apex Club Band, where the underaged Nat (the future "King") Cole hovered outside the window, soaking up every note—when Cole later played and sang his hit "Sweet Lorraine," it was in homage to Hines and Noone.

Hines's work with Armstrong was even more memorable: together, they created the 20 sides that climax the legendary "Hot Five" series and changed the course of Western civilization. Hines played a key role in such masterpieces as "West End Blues," which did more than any other to establish the primacy of the improvising soloist in jazz. Their duo, "Weather Bird" is easily the most famous pairing of a horn and a keyboard in all of the music, a meeting of the minds that is rife with humor, energy, and swing—camaraderie and musical one-upmanship. "When we were playing together, it was like a continuous jam session," Hines later said. "When people talk about my 'trumpet style,' they usually mean when I play in octaves like a trumpet player. But I used tremolo to give an effect like Louis's vibrato too."

Throughout the 1930s and 1940s, Hines led one of the greatest of all jazz big bands, holding forth at Chicago's most prominent Black nightclub, The Grand Terrace. Thanks to a virtually uninterrupted series of recordings and radio broadcasts that reached the entire country, Hines was a national celebrity and a role model for the Black community, musicians in particular. His early big bands anticipate the coming of the swing era, and his 1940s bands foreshadow both the rise of bebop (Charlie Parker, Dizzy Gillespie, and Wardell Gray were all in his orchestra) and of singers, as he launched the careers of Billy Eckstine, Sarah Vaughan, and Johnny Hartman.

Hines led a dual life in the recording studio in these years. Apart from his great big-band series, he also guest-starred with Sidney Bechet and created a brilliant run of solo sides (which have been gathered on a much recommended Danish CD, "The Earl Hines Collection," Collector's Classics 11). Hines's solos, with their rhythmic complexity and remarkable swing, seem to belong to a different era: the more harmonically dense passages foreshadow Tatum or Erroll Garner, and his use of space and silence points to Thelonious Monk.

With the decline of the big bands, Hines became a founding member of Louis Armstrong's well-named All Stars. However, conflicting egos—it was too late for him to go back to being a sideman—led Hines to resume leading his own groups. After holing up in San Francisco for most of the next decade, he reemerged as a major presence on the national and international jazz circuit in the mid-1960s, working in the solo format as well as the leader of a strong quartet that costarred the underappreciated tenor giant Budd Johnson. No other elder statesman of jazz was as active as Hines, who toured and recorded constantly and usually brilliantly in his 1960s and 1970s. He recorded dozens of albums, including teaming up with all manner of musicians and songbooks representing the whole spectrum of the American songbook.

Of his many later recordings, two of my personal favorites are *Once Upon a Time* (A-9108, 1966) and *Grand Reunion* (Verve 3145281372, 1965). The first has the Fatha working with an all-star horn section from the Duke's band, including Johnny Hodges, as well as Pee Wee Russell and Elvin Jones. The second, a double disc set, offers copious amounts of the Earl Hines Trio live at the Village Vanguard and samples of interplay with two of his fellow colossi, Coleman Hawkins and Roy Eldridge.

Over the years, Hines's best-remembered showpiece was his often-performed "Boogie Woogie on St. Louis Blues." This was ironic, since by his own admission, Hines was less of an authentic blues player than the Southern and Southwestern pianists who specialized in the form. Yet by superimposing two subgenres of the blues on top of each other, he thus crafted a wildly entertaining set piece that the crowds cried for, night after night. In the end, it was gloriously typical of an artist who embraced everything that jazz had to offer.

(*The New York Sun*, 2003)

***

With his outsize helmet of hair, razor-sharp mustache, shield-like spectacles, and confident grin, Earl Hines in the 1970s (and his 70s) commanded attention even before he sat down at the piano. His playing showed boundless energy, invention, and an unstoppable desire to entertain a crowd.

Although born in 1903, Fatha, as he was always known, adapted to the modern era without missing a beat. I don't only mean that he played superfast rhythms or the more celestially boppish chord changes. He also adapted to a music that was primarily played by soloists who toured on an international circuit of jazz clubs and concert halls—so effortlessly that you'd think he'd been working that way all of his life. This Hines was easily reconcilable with the infamous egomaniac who had a hard time playing sideman to anyone, even the almighty Louis Armstrong when he was a member of Armstrong's All Stars.

Yet a recent seven-disc boxed set containing nearly all of the pianist–composer's early work under his own name, *Classic Earl Hines Sessions 1928-1945*, shows that the early Earl was a very different animal. As Brian Priestley observes in the liner notes, during these years Hines primarily "regarded himself as a group pianist rather than a soloist," and "his concern was for the overall impact of the group." Back then, Hines was primarily a bandleader rather than "just" a piano player, a purveyor of dance music and a pop entertainer as much as a jazz musician.

The cover of the Mosaic Records box shows Hines in 1938, leaning over the piano, his smile reflected in the polished lacquer. This conforms to the later Hines we remember, but a better image might have been of him leading his band, where he's only one of 15 men in the picture. Around the time of his 25th birthday, Hines was asked to lead a full-size dance band at The Grand Terrace, a new ballroom being launched in Chicago, and there he would remain in residence (except for the occasional tour) until the end of the big-band era in 1945.

Naturally, there are piano solos in many of the big-band arrangements, as well as 11 numbers where Hines plays unaccompanied piano (including two on an early electrified keyboard), but the piano is almost never in the foreground: Hines is the leader but never the whole show.

The first thing one notices on the majority of the 171 tracks is the way the band swings as a whole, whether in the syncopated two beats of the 1929–1930 sessions, which employ a banjo and tuba in the rhythm section, or in the more smoothed-out solid-four grooves of the band in the war years, propelled by guitar and bass in addition to Hines himself.

In both eras, Hines is all over the place—his piano is a major factor in sparking the band, driving the beat, and shaping the overall phrasing. The Earl of Hines (as Bugs Bunny referred to him in a 1955 cartoon) is a much more proactive pianist–leader than his fellow royals Duke Ellington and Count Basie. And when Hines does place his piano in the foreground, the results are often spectacular, as on "Piano Man" and "Pianology."

Hines is playing more piano than most bandleaders, but he's also giving his sidemen plenty of room to shine, particularly saxophonist and arranger Budd Johnson, who first appears in the band's reed section in 1937 and would continue to work on and off with Hines for the rest of Hines's life (Johnson died a year after Hines, in 1984). Johnson's inventive soloing is especially well featured on "Honeysuckle Rose," done on a quartet session in 1937. Hines was also quite fortunate in his choice of band vocalists: Valaida Snow, later known as a trumpeter, takes a memorable vocal in the style of Ethel Waters on "Maybe I'm to Blame"; Herb Jeffries, who later became famous with the Ellington band (and is still going strong at 99), is heard on three tracks. Most effective are 10 excellent vocals by the young Billy Eckstine.

Mr. Priestley shows how several recordings, including Eckstine's "Jelly, Jelly," point to the burgeoning R&B movement, and Hines's employment of Charlie Parker and Dizzy Gillespie was a key moment in the birth of bebop or modern jazz. The most surprising musical movement that Hines foreshadowed, remarkably, was rap. In 1929, Hines himself performed a monologue in minstrel-show Ebonics that could easily be done by Mos Def today. Even more surprising, in 1945, the band recorded Mary Lou Williams's catchy novelty tune "Satchel Mouth Baby"—a track being released for the first time in the current package—in which an unidentified entertainer delivers a full-blown rap, which includes lines such as "I laid a sound on this little quail that busted her nappy patch!"

In later years, on stage, Hines rarely spoke about his big band, instead preferring to talk about what he called "trumpet-style piano" in which he followed the lines of a horn soloist rather than approximating a full orchestra, as the ragtime and stride pianists were then doing. Two of Hines's most prominent self-confessed devotees were Teddy Wilson, who performed a marvelous two-piano duet with Hines in 1965 (available on YouTube) and Nat King Cole, both of whom were nearly as influential as Hines himself. Cole famously said, "Everything I am, I owe to that man, because I copied him." Several generations of piano players could have easily said the same thing.

(*The Wall Street Journal*, 2013)

COUNT BASIE (1904–1984)

Jazz Casual

Count Basie sits down at the piano and plays some jazz.

Ralph Gleason asks, "Was that the way they played the blues in Kansas City when you took over the band 30 years ago?"

Basie answers, "Well, no, that wasn't the way they played the blues, Ralph, because if that was the way they played the blues, then it would have been a pretty bad start of the blues, I think. We'll get further down the line—on them blues—later on."

We're barely two minutes into the program, and already Basie has found a way to denigrate his own playing. Basie's opinion of his own skills as a musician was unique to him; he might have been the only one who didn't consider him one of the best pianists in all of jazz. In fact, along with his colleague Duke Ellington, Basie was regarded as one of the greatest accompanists in all of the music, someone who always knew how to give a soloist or a singer exactly what they needed. (As it happens, Basie is also informing Gleason that the brief piece he played at the opening was not, in fact, based on the blues—although I have made that mistake myself, especially since it's always been listed as "Untitled Blues" in most discographies.)

Count Basie, piano; John Clayton, bass; Landmark Theater; Syracuse, NY; October 27, 1978

This conversation and performance were taped during the summer of 1967, when Basie and his orchestra were touring on the West Coast. For two nights, August 20 and 21, Basie and his crew were in San Francisco—literally ground zero for the "Summer of Love," playing the Fillmore Auditorium, which was soon to become a legendary rock-and-roll venue. On the afternoon of Monday, August 21—the Count's 63rd birthday—Basie stopped in at the local public television station to give an informal performance and interview with renowned jazz critic and TV host Ralph J. Gleason.

He brought along Freddie Green, his career-long collaborator whose guitar was the linchpin of what was called Basie's "All American Rhythm Section," along with bassist Norman Keenan and drummer Sonny Payne.

Gleason's question refers to the generally accepted notion that Basie started as a bandleader by taking over the older Bennie Moten Orchestra when that pianist and leader died in 1935. That's the way we were taught in many of the earlier jazz histories, but more recent scholarship, including Basie's own memoir, reveals that it was somewhat more complicated than that and that Basie had begun leading early editions of his own orchestra even while Moten was still alive.

Gleason asks Basie, "What were they playing when you took over the band?"

He answers, "Well, they were playing swing. I call it swing because truly that's what Bennie Moton was playing was swing." That's a good answer—it underscores the larger truth that even though Moten died in the year that is officially considered to be the start of the swing era, many Black bands were already playing pure swing well before Benny Goodman lit the fuse that ignited the era in 1935. Basie continues, "And I don't know whether he called it Western style or not, but it was sort of a Western swinger, I guess, if we would describe it that way." When he says, "Western style," we have to assume he means midwestern Kansas City style, not "Western swing" in the sense of Bob Wills and his Texas Playboys. Basie adds, "Because it suddenly had a beat! It's real foot-pattin'."

Gleason asks if the music has changed much. "Well, yes, beats change quite a bit, because they've been experimenting on different styles, which have been very successful." He continues, "Basically, we haven't changed that much" [meaning his own playing] although we have some soloists that sort of lean toward the modern side. But we sort of remained the same."

They continue discussing the nature of the blues. "Truthfully, I really never heard the blues until I had the pleasure of visiting Kansas City, which was in the very, very early days, even before the Blue Devils and Bennie Moten's band, because we were traveling through there with a burlesque show.

"I got a chance to wander over on 18th Street [which] at that time was blazing. I mean, everything was happening there. Beautiful! I mean, you could hear the blues from any window or door and it's the most remarkable thing I've ever heard. That's when I first got a good taste of listening to a blues singer. I didn't know anyone's name, but I do know they were belting out these blues: wonderful trumpet players, clarinet players, banjo players, and great piano players, blues pianists. I had never seen anything like it."

He continues talking about piano players who had an influence on him, "[b]lues wise." "There's guys that I can remember, particularly one guy, Pete Johnson. Pete was the guy that I really idolized as far as blues playing was concerned."

Then he decides to talk about his number-one favorite keyboardist. "But really the main guy that really influenced me was Thomas—Fats Waller. That was the man that I really did idolize. Fats taught me how to play what little bit of organ that I do know. And I used to watch him and [hang] around him long enough to try to style a little piano after him, which was quite difficult."

He demonstrates, with about 30 seconds of "A Handful of Keys," the finger-busting piano feature that Waller introduced in 1929. What's especially notable is that in replicating the style of his idol, Basie really does stop sounding like Basie; even though he can keep it up for only half a minute, he truly becomes Fats for that half a minute.

But then Basie moves back into his comfort zone in playing his second impromptu blues of the set. This one is slower than the first, though anything would sound slow after the breakneck tempo of "A Handful of Keys." As Dick Hyman has observed, stride piano, of the sort that Fats Waller played, was essentially a soloist's art; when Basie emulates Fats, the bass and the drums don't have much to do. But when he switches gears into the blues improvisation, the rest of the quartet becomes much more engaged. That's one of the key differences between Waller's and Basie's styles—Basie shares the musical responsibilities with the rest of the rhythm section much more democratically.

Gleason then asks, "So did Pete Johnson and other piano players turn you more into the blues?"

Basie responds, "I think so, but they really played the blues. That's just my thought of it—and it's a pretty good thought at that! But the influence was there. I never heard anybody quite playing like Pete and Albert and Lux. These guys really did it right."

Basie's attention turns to Fats Waller again, and he plays a lovely two-minute rendition of Waller's blues-influenced ballad, "Squeeze Me," starting with the verse but then treating us to two brief choruses of the tune. His playing here is sort of a hybrid of Waller and Basie. Just enough of the rhythmic phrasing and the note placement is completely faithful to Fats, but the overall texture, with Freddie Green's signature emphasis on the afterbeats, is much more Basie-esque.

Gleason then asks about one of the most famous and frequently played 12-bar blues numbers in the Count's history, his theme song of the previous 30 years, "One O'Clock Jump."

> Well, this happened in Kansas City while we were broadcasting from the Reno Club. In those years, you didn't have to program a number. You could just play anything that you'd like to play, and it would be perfectly okay. . . . Each Sunday night, we used to have a two-hour broadcast and we would sort of run out of tunes. I guess we must have had about a half hour and we'd light out and play one, and the announcer would ask, "What's the name of that?" And we'd say, "Well that's bing-bing-bing." Then we'd do another one. "What's the name of that?" "That's so-and-so." So now we still got about 15 minutes left. And so I just started something in there and then we went to D flat for a solo. And so he said, "You have a title for that?" Once I looked at the clock was about 10 minutes to one, so I said, "Yeah, that's the 'One O'Clock Jump.'" And it sort of stuck because the guys remembered it, more than the rest of the things that they were doing and it stayed there.

Basie adds that it hasn't changed much over the years but that "I think everybody else has got a better arrangement than we do on it really, actually," referring to so-called cover versions and variations by the likes of Benny Goodman and Harry James.

Gleason next asks why he plays so few piano features with his own orchestra, and Basie offers one of his more thoughtful responses. "Time marches, Ralph. See, that's just the reason why, in those years, I invented this"—he plays three notes reminiscent of the famous Basie tag—"because I knew there was going to be days when guys were going to have me running all over this piano," in other words, just to keep up with them. "And so I just did a little something, which I hope would sort of identify us. So, as far as I'm concerned, my piano playing is sort of dated and I'm just in the rhythm section. Which I'm very happy about, that the guys will allow me in there. And that's as far as my piano playing will go."

Basie feels like he's been talking too much, so he quickly launches into another improvised blues, which he spontaneously titles, in the tradition of the "One O'Clock Jump," "20 Minutes After Three." This piece again demonstrates the interplay between Basie and the guitar, bass, and drums. Together, Green and Keenan lay down the beat, and Basie is already improvising variations even while he's barely had a chance to lay down a single 12-bar chorus. At different points, the trio behind sounds like they're outlining a boogie-woogie pattern but played much more slowly and dance-ably than a fast boogie. Basie plays whisper soft at parts, laying down a three-note pattern that he repeats several times, each time landing on a different third note.

Gleason asks Basie about how he chooses tempos. "Oh, I don't know. I guess it's trying to make it easy on myself, possibly. But I do dig something that is sort of in a mood where you can pat your foot, if possible. And I think it's easy to listen to too, really. I sort of like to simplify things, which is the only way that I can do it. But even if I really could play a lot of piano, I would try to simplify it for myself because this is the type of thing I like. Although I like to listen to the giants and the fast ones, like Pete Johnson, Oscar Peterson, and all those guys. But this is me. This is what I like. I like tempos that are danceable."

"You started as a drummer?"

Basie's answer involves that other great jazz musician from his own hometown of Red Bank, New Jersey, Sonny Greer, who had served as Duke Ellington's drummer for most of the band's great years. "Yes, but I was discouraged by the wonderful gentleman who was with the master, Edward Ellington's band, Sonny Greer. And when we were back home, I used to have my little gigs, little piano gigs, and I'd try to sort of switch to the drums because of course that was my first love. And that in that intermission, Sonny would fall in from Long Branch somewhere and sit down on them drums. And that was all for me for the evening. So I said, 'This is not for me, this is going to happen all my life!' So that sort of turned me back to the piano."

"Is the blues as much fun to play after all these years?"

"Oh yes, Ralph. I can never get tired of playing the blues or listening to the blues. As a matter of fact, if I start to make an original thing, I mean, it's always based on the blues. And to me, the blues is a starting of an awful lot of things." At this point, surprisingly, instead of playing another full-on blues, he essays a delightfully spare, minimal—and unfortunately, very brief—rendition of "As Long as I Live," a somewhat blues-inflected popular song by Harold Arlen.

"You've heard so much good music back over those years, any particular things stand out?"

Basie clarifies, "As far as any band is concerned?" and then answers, "Yes. It still will linger with me is, of course, you know just what I'm going to say and who I'm going to say it to. And it's from, I think, the Dean of all, that's Edward Ellington. It's a little thing called 'Warm Valley.' I shall never forget that. Of course, I shall never forget this band, because I think this man is just the end of everything. Duke's been going back for 20 years"—although both Gleason and Basie were well aware it was over 40 years by 1967—"and ain't nobody got near him yet."

We would love for Basie to try his hand at Ellington's "Warm Valley" but instead, he treats us to a single chorus of a 1926 jazz standard "If I Could Be with You (One Hour Tonight)" by James P. Johnson, another iconic stride piano master. Like the other standards on this show, it's only a minute long and far too brief. Basie sort of hums or sings along, but you have to listen closely to hear it.

Gleason claims not to be aware of how much time has passed, but he then suggests that Basie and company conclude the program with something that they will agree to call "late birthday afternoon educational TV blues." This is a slightly faster 12-bar blues to end on, with Basie once again playing as little as possible, his piano notes serving more as a guideline for telling Green, Keenan, and Payne where to play, even as they would likewise serve as a marking point for instructing dancers when to put their feet down if, indeed, there were any dancers. Basie and the rhythm section continue to play even as the credits scroll across the screen.

"A Conversation with Count Basie," as this episode of *Jazz Casual* was titled, is a remarkable example of Basie doing two things he almost never did, featuring himself at the piano and talking. It emphasizes what we already knew, that Basie might be the only major pianist in jazz who didn't play like he was being paid by the note.

(*Slouching Towards Birdland*, Substack, 2023)

NAT KING COLE (1919–1965)

Cool King Cole: The Trio Days

The great schism in Nat King Cole's career didn't involve his not-at-all-incongruous identities as one of jazz's most brilliant piano players and one of pop music's biggest breadwinners—only the most myopic and biased of observers could overlook the direct continuity from Cole's early triumphs, such as "Sweet Lorraine" (1940), to later masterpieces, such as his Sinatra-inspired suicide album, *Where Did Everyone Go?* (1962). The really significant rift in Cole's art occurs primarily in the first half of his career: how do we reconcile the hell-for-leather improviser—with echoes of Earl Hines and Teddy Wilson in his left hand and Bud Powell, John Lewis, and other futurists in his right—with the mastermind behind the King Cole Trio, too often dismissed as a pop novelty group?

John Zorn has described Carl Stalling's scores for the Warner Bros. cartoons of the 1940s as the great avant-garde music of that period. By that standard, the King Cole Trio ranks as one of the era's great performance art ensembles. Nat Cole, guitarist Oscar Moore (later Irving Ashby), and bassist Johnny Miller (previously Wesley Prince, later Joe Comfort) didn't strictly extemporize their arrangements night after night, but they tinkered with them to perfection, much like a comedian works over a monologue, in the uniquely phrased ensemble "head" sections during Cole's vocals (or early on, the Trio's unison singing) and in the individual solos.

Nat King Cole did not single-handedly invent the combination of piano, guitar, and bass plus vocals; at least two earlier units come to mind, the Three Peppers and the Three Keys. But Cole and Co. so effectively perfected and popularized what became known, somewhat pejoratively, as a "cocktail combo" that even Art Tatum formed one in his search for mass acceptance.

The Trio had much in common with Ellington and the major jazz orchestras: Cole pared down the standard big-band instrumentation as Moore and Miller riffed behind him like brass and reeds; the fills they played between Cole's phrases on "Come to Baby Do" were comparable to those the Basie band supplied for Jimmy Rushing on "Goin' to Chicago."

On his first recording, in 1936, with a more conventional six-piece band co-led with his brother, Eddie, the presence of drums encouraged Cole to sound like his first idol, Earl Hines. But Cole's mature style developed directly out of his avoiding the trap of traps. In a drummerless trio, he wanted to make sure that the beat was keenly felt and not just taken for granted. So by 1939, when Cole and company cut four sides for the Ammor label, with drummer Lee Young, they used his drums for color rather than timekeeping. Young's shining moments came when he burst in at the stop time–styled breaks Cole usually set up for Moore.

With sublime perversity, Cole's self-imposed need to play more led to his developing new ways to play less, chiefly by reassigning major melodic responsibilities to the bass while playing single lines in the right hand and only the occasional accent from the left—two striking earmarks of bebop piano. When he accompanies a lesser vocalist, he compensates for their inadequacies by filling up the keyboard to carry them along. Conversely, when he plays behind a real singer, such as Kay Starr ("Stormy Weather," with the Capitol Jazzmen) or Frank Sinatra (on two radio shows), he treats them with the same respect he affords his own vocalizing or for that matter, the instrumental crooning of saxists Willie Smith or Lester Young.

Cole's penchant for trimming off excesses peaked with his "Calypso Blues," for which he was accompanied only by Jack Costanzo's bongos. He so exquisitely sustains the mood, pitch, rhythm, and narrative that he could justifiably claim, in an argument with business partner Harry Belafonte, that he had sung calypso long before the open-shirted showman, and better.

Cole maintained economy at all costs, even when the subject matter was "Mona Lisa" (the "touring" Trio version), which begged for artsy classical music–style filigrees, or when he adapted for the Trio Rachmaninoff's Prelude in C-sharp minor and "Vesti la giubba," which he called "Laugh, Cool Clown." The jazz and classical elements fit smoothly, and the pieces swung with Modern Jazz Quartet subtlety. Even Oscar Peterson, who cited Tatum and Cole as his major inspirations, could never match Cole's breathless economy—when Peterson accompanies Cole on "Sweet Lorraine" (when the Jazz at the Philharmonic troupe appeared on Cole's TV show), Peterson's fingers are much busier than Cole's ever were.

But Cole's technique isn't nearly as remarkable as the content of the King Cole Trio's material, which more successfully than any other jazz-based pop organization, created an art music that will last forever using the building blocks of pop culture, a total commitment to the temporal, the trendy, and the faddish. Again, like 1940s Warner Bros. cartoons, the Trio's records constitute an amazing amalgam of topical references, expressions, gags, and phrases both musical and verbal. Defending his career as a vocalist from commentators who accused him of "forsaking" jazz, Cole pointed out that even on its strictly instrumental records, the Trio made its living from ballads and novelties. The same observers paint a picture of money-hungry song pluggers forcing unworthy material on him, but Cole himself built a style on the most minimal kind of one-joke song, concocting many of his best-known novelties.

Cole plucked punch lines out of the air, built lyrics around them, and made them song titles. If the King Cole Trio were performing in the 1980s, they'd do titles such as "You Look Marvelous" and "Go Ahead, Make My Day." Many songs took on a format in which the first three lines of the lyric are a setup, and the fourth line delivers the payoff: "Now He Tells Me," "You Don't Learn That in School," and "Straighten Up and Fly Right."

The windup phrase is either the punch line to the joke or sometimes total nonsense. Take for instance, "But when you put your sweet, sweet lips to mine / Ooh kickeroonie" or when he employs Stan Kenton's artistry in cacophony and flying glass to underscore the "Flash! Bam! Alakazam!" that comes "out of an orange-colored sky!" With Cole, nonsense can assume all the potency of Louis Armstrong's scatting or Billie Holiday's "The Man I Love." Cole so tenderly intones the "magic" syllables of "Kee-Mo, Ky-Mo" that they couldn't possibly fail to make wishes come true, especially since the most important words of the spell are "I love you."

In 1951, Cole formally announced the end of the Trio; from now on, he was to be billed as "Nat King Cole" rather than the "King Cole Trio." Yet he never stopped playing the piano—there are, famously, three excellent all-new piano-centric albums between 1952 and 1956, and virtually every live recording that exists includes a segment of his playing piano.

In these later piano projects, *Penthouse Serenade* (1952), *The Piano Style of Nat King Cole* (1955), and *After Midnight* (1956), Cole conspicuously avoided the essential elements that made the Trio great. The King Cole Trio triumphed as a working band, which in Ellington's phrase, intuited each other's poker-playing habits, playing honed-to-perfection arrangements of anything-but-standard material. *After Midnight* is just the opposite: producer Lee Gillette round-robined Cole with one of four great soloists per cut, but they're in the studio cold, sometimes ad-libbing jam-session readings of standard tunes.

The piano and rhythm–only album, *Penthouse Serenade*, also removes Cole from the setting that originally distinguished him, though any full-length recital of his work at the ivories is to be treasured. Only one later piano record finally drops the other shoe and presents King Cole as superstar and monarch, with no pretensions to jazz's democracy: *The Piano Style of Nat King Cole.* Here, Nelson Riddle's orchestra provides a new backdrop for the Cole keyboard, and though its dramatic ballads are less successful, the swingers are magnificent. The "piano style" on the up-tempo tunes turns out to be identical to his vocal style, and Cole's linear phrases beautifully "sing" the melodies.

All of which barely describes one aspect of one part of Cole's career, hardly mentioning his magnificence as a strictly jazz pianist and one of our four or five most awe-inspiring mainstream vocalists, so popular that even his lesser achievements (the country-and-western albums) sold millions of copies. Like his predecessors, Armstrong and Waller, the King's royal celebration of the present justifies Kurt Vonnegut's observation that future historians will congratulate us only on our clowning and our jazz. His talent for both, especially as revealed in his performances with the Trio, is the kind that only those pessimistic characters who ain't got rhythm could possibly resist, and the kind of brilliance that comes along flash! bam! alakazam! out of an orange-colored sky.

(*The Village Voice*, 1989)

MASTERS AND MONSTERS

ART TATUM (1909–1956)

There's a remarkable photo in the booklet accompanying the new 10-CD boxed set of rare music by the legendary pianist Art Tatum (Storyville Records, 10 CDs + DVD).

We see the jazz icon at work, surrounded by three heavyweight keyboardists: Albert Ammons, the boogie-woogie pioneer; Teddy Wilson, a star of the swing era and master of the American songbook; and Hazel Scott, whose specialty was swinging the classics. All three of them are looking over Tatum's shoulder with a look in their eyes that seems to acknowledge that here is a musician who can do—all by himself—everything that the three of them can do collectively, who can play more piano than all of them put together and a great many others besides.

Tatum is unchallenged as far as sheer musical density is concerned: he played so many notes in a given performance that just counting them would be difficult and actually transcribing one of his solos, next to impossible. Just listening to Tatum at full blast can be overwhelming. (As Loren Schoenberg suggests in the booklet notes, Tatum is often best appreciated in small doses—playing all 10 of these volumes and bonus DVD—in one sitting is obviously not recommended.) Yet because Tatum cast such an enormous shadow over the entire history of the jazz piano and he died so young, at 47 in 1956, an odd dichotomy emerges in his oeuvre: he may have played millions of notes, yet every one of them is precious—the laws of supply and demand, not to mention physics, no longer seem to apply.

Commercial recordings, such as Tatum's classic series of solo and group recordings of the mid-1950s, only tell part of the story. The current set, issued in time for the pianist's centennial this October, encompasses a ragtag bag of mostly live performances from the complete scope of Tatum's 20-plus years in the major leagues, as collated over a lifetime of detective work by Tatum scholar Arnold Laubich. The package begins with a once-rare air check of the 24-year-old pianist in his native Ohio (playing the Busby Berkeley dance number "Young and Healthy" like Fats Waller on amphetamines).

The last volume is highlighted by a series of unique duets privately taped in a New York apartment, costarring guitarist Tal Farlow and then organist Joe Mooney. In both cases, the two partners play so pianistically that the results sound like four-handed keyboard duets, even though Tatum always sounds like he's playing with that many hands all by himself. (There are also a couple of impromptu duets with a pair of singers so out of tune and atrocious, they could almost be contestants on *American Idol.*)

When contemporary pianists illustrate Tatum's style, they invariably concentrate on his signature arpeggiated runs—when he waits for the end of a line in a popular standard before stuffing in a whole string of notes. The suspense he generates is inevitably amazing—a veritable movie serial cliffhanger as you wait breathlessly for him to finish his improvised line before he reaches the point where he has to start the next line of the written melody.

Yet this is only the beginning of what Tatum does, drawing on the vocabularies of stride, boogie, and Mozart all at the same time, all driven by an overwhelming flair for the dramatic—you use words like "adventurous" and "daring" when talking about Tatum. He's known for his damn-the-torpedo full-speed showpieces, such as "I Know That You Know" or the hell-for-leather second chorus of his operetta update "Song of the Vagabonds." Yet I actually enjoy him most on medium-fast treatments of familiar songs where he keeps both the melody and his own variations going at the same time, as if he were spinning multiple plates on *The Ed Sullivan Show*—or playing duets with himself.

Tatum's capacity for merging one tune into another adds yet another dimension to his music, and further, his penchant for inserting the classics into pop songs could be said to speak for a belief that Gershwin deserves to be taken as seriously—or as humorously—as Bach. Tatum blends "To a Wild Rose" seamlessly into "Memories of You," as if they were different parts of the same piece, and quotes "Narcissus" and "Stars and Stripes Forever" in the middle of "Sweet Lorraine," while "Vesti la giubba" rears its Italian head in "Body and Soul." It's in these quotes that Tatum's sense of humor rises to the surface, yet it's also present in other facets of his playing as well: he injects "Begin the Beguine" with so much warmth and wit that he lays the groundwork for the later career of Erroll Garner. He plays "Danny Boy" with so much tenderness that Tony Bennett was moved to name his son Danny.

A true prize in the box is Tatum's only known recording of Chopin's Waltz in C-sharp minor (Opus 64, No. 2), which he subjects to pumping rhythm that makes it sound like it was written by James P. Johnson. These classical showpieces—especially his often-played rearrangement of "Humoresque"—are important for another reason: they supplemented Tatum's reputation as perhaps the first jazz musician to be regarded by the larger culture as a serious virtuoso, comparable to Vladimir Horowitz or Van Cliburn. He anticipated the modern jazz movement not just in his advanced harmonies and breathtaking rhythms (it's said that the young Charlie Parker took a job as a dishwasher in a joint where Tatum was working just so he could listen to him all night) but also in the nature of his music itself: he wasn't an entertainer or singer, and he didn't play music for dancing.

On one 1956 show, critic Milton Cross talks about how the great classical pianists, such as Arthur Rubinstein, were already studying Tatum. No wonder. One chorus was enough to convince anyone that jazz was art and further, that Art was jazz.

(*The Wall Street Journal*, 2009)

OSCAR PETERSON (1925–2007)

The Importance of Being Oscar

The 1950s were probably even more of a great jazz age than the era that F. Scott Fitzgerald actually titled "The Jazz Age." It was the one decade when a handful of pure jazz instrumentalists became headliners who could fill clubs and even appear on TV variety shows. As jazz moved into concert halls, there were four superstars of the piano who brought a largely unprecedented combination of mass-market success and academic respect to the music: in order of appearance, George Shearing

Oscar Peterson, piano; Ray Brown, Bass; Herb Ellis, Guitar; Celebration; Town Hall; October 1, 1996

(1919–2011), Dave Brubeck (1920–2012), Erroll Garner (1921–1977), and Oscar Peterson (1925–2007).

Peterson is different from his colleagues in several ways: where Shearing, Brubeck, and Garner all have had at least one major hit record or album (Shearing's "September in the Rain" or "Lullaby of Birdland," Brubeck's "Time Out," and Garner's "Concert by the Sea"), Peterson is known more for his entire body of work. Where his three slightly older contemporaries all have a signature style that even a layperson can identify a mile away, it takes a more serious fan or a fellow pianist to pick out Peterson on a blindfold test.

Yet the drawback to having a trademark sound or a hit song, especially with a popular following, is that you run the risk of becoming tethered to it. Contrastingly, Peterson has always taken full advantage of the full range of possibilities open to him. On the 1950, "Salute to Garner," one of his first recordings made in America after settling here from his native Canada, he recaptures Garner's patented ebullience, bouncing rhythm, and cascading notes. On the 1964 "Goodbye J.D." (on *We Get Requests*), Peterson plays the opening head in a wacko time signature (don't ask me to count it), very much inspired by Dave Brubeck. On another original work, "The Music Box Suite," documented only once in a live concert in Vancouver from 1958 (not released until 45 years later), Peterson displays his knowledge of baroque fugal styles in a way that makes us think of Shearing.

Peterson sometimes seems to have as much chops as the other three put together—in addition to being as physically large as the other three combined. Tom Lord's *The Jazz Discography*, the standard work (www.lordisco.com) on the subject, lists 417 recording sessions by Oscar the great, more than half of which are as a leader. (One reason his output was so large was that he continued to record as a sideman and accompanist long after he established himself as a soloist.)

For nearly 60 years in the world of jazz and pop music, the name Peterson was synonymous with a keyboard technique that was so prodigious it was nearly overwhelming: He played more notes than any other pianist, more intense chords, and faster rhythms yet without ever descending into a quagmire of pure skill and speed. He also played with a supreme melodic logic: every one of the 80-zillion notes he played in every song was saturated with both feeling and swing.

As the pianist said in a 2001 interview with radio host Michael Anthony of WHPC Long Island, "Swing is the root of jazz. If you can't swing then you're not playing jazz. That is the impetus that drives the whole medium and has driven it throughout all these years. Swing is the infectious part of [jazz], the emotional end of it. If you don't have the swing element, then you're not operating in the jazz medium."

The contemporary pianist Bill Charlap describes Peterson as "one of the most profoundly important pianists in the history of the music. He straddles the entire history of jazz piano. Everything everyone says is true!"

Peterson, who was born in Montreal in 1925, was encouraged to play by his father, a sailor, and by his older brother, Fred, who began playing jazz piano at an early age. "He was just beginning to get into jazz," Peterson later said. "It was different from the studies that I was doing. All I knew was that I wanted to play like that. Ironically, if he was living today [Fred died at 16 years old], I would NOT be playing jazz piano, because he was better than me." Peterson earned his professional stripes with Toronto big-band leader Johnny Holmes and first recorded in that city in 1945. In 1949, he was invited by impresario Norman Granz to participate as a special guest at a Jazz at the Philharmonic concert at Carnegie Hall. In Granz, Peterson found a manager and producer whose appetite was as capacious as the pianist's talent was prodigious. From 1950 forward, Granz recorded Peterson continually, both in his own trios and duos and with all the best-known names in jazz.

Peterson once said that when he first heard the legendary Art Tatum, which he did on a record when he was a teenager, he was so overcome that he couldn't touch the piano for a week. (In some tellings, it was a month or more.) Peterson was sometimes described, occasionally by himself, as Tatum's heir, but he is no imi-Tatum; it's rare to hear Peterson re-creating a classically Tatum-esque set of runs and arpeggios. As Charlap puts it, "He assumed the mantle of Tatum, but Oscar doesn't play Art's stuff—it's Oscar's stuff." Part of the difference was also attitudinal, as clarinetist Buddy DeFranco has said (in an interview in All About Jazz): "I loved Tatum's playing but working with him could be difficult. It was his ball game. When I played with Oscar he had more sensitivity and he played for *you*."

Charlap also points out that "Oscar also has that churchy, bluesy feeling that he didn't learn from Tatum." In establishing his own style, Peterson became much more of a specialist in funky, church-influenced blues than Tatum was and also more of a balladeer—both were qualities that he probably absorbed from his other major role model, Nat King Cole, who was a much stronger blues player and a ballad singer (both on the piano and later, vocally). Partly through Cole's influence, Peterson's mature music was much more directly connected to the lyric and more emotional—Tatum couldn't break your heart the way Peterson does on "Tenderly."

Peterson said that the three pianists who influenced him most were Art Tatum, Teddy Wilson, and Nat King Cole. As he told Anthony, "I admired Teddy primarily for his beautiful touch on the instrument. Needless to say, he had a flawless technique. Art not only had great technique, but he was harmonically perfect. Nat Cole gave me the incentive to swing real hard." Both Peterson and Charlap were quick to point out that Cole's importance to the legacy of jazz piano has been underappreciated ever since he started landing hits as a singer. In fact, the influence of the King Cole Trio was so all pervasive in the 1940s that even Tatum himself worked for most of that decade with a Cole-inspired trio of piano, guitar, and bass. That, too, was the format when Oscar Peterson put together his first widely successful trio in 1952—Peterson even hired guitarist Irving Ashby, who had only recently left the King Cole Trio to fill the same role in the new Oscar Peterson Trio.

Given wide exposure by Granz (on recordings and JATP tours), the original Oscar Peterson Trio quickly became one of the great jazz groups of a great jazz era, thanks largely to the totally telepathic playing of Peterson, his equally formidable bassist

Ray Brown, and the brilliant guitarist Barney Kessel. When in 1958, Kessel had to leave the group, they decided to change the format rather than replace him. In 1959, Peterson introduced his second all-time great trio, with Brown remaining on bass and the superlative drummer Ed Thigpen creating a whole new roll in Peterson's musical universe.

The switching of drums for guitar did not make Peterson swing more—that would have been impossible—but oddly, gives the trio more of a relaxed feeling. Rather than pushing the piano and the bass harder, in the earlier group all three men sometimes seemed to be pushing as hard as they could to compensate for the absence of percussion. With Thigpen on board, they seem more inclined to lay back and let it go.

Two years into the group's existence, The Peterson–Brown–Thigpen trio made, what for me, is its definitive statement when Verve recorded the threesome at length at the London House in Chicago over a week in the summer of 1961. Although the company released some of the material at the time, more than four LPs (including Peterson's marvelous, bittersweet reconception of the *Bye Bye Birdie* showtune "Put On a Happy Face"), the whole works were finally released as the absolutely essential five-CD box, *The London House Sessions*, in 1996. (Pianist and singer Diana Krall once described these recordings as her favorite album ever.)

As Charlap has said, one of the trademarks of great jazz "is that you can hear everything in it, the past, the present, and the future." My single favorite performance by Peterson is his brilliant treatment of the standard "Sometimes I'm Happy" from *The London House Sessions.* He begins not with the original melody as written by Vincent Youmans but with tenor sax giant Lester Young's famous adaptation of that tune from 1943. Peterson introduces the tune with Young's closing riff (itself a paraphrase of "My Sweetie Went Away") and in this 11-minute romp through the changes, not a second of which is wasted, also detours through the blues (referencing Dinah Washington's "Lean Baby") and eventually gravitating toward an extended quote from Oscar Pettiford's "Swingin' Till the Girls Come Home." Ray Brown, who doesn't miss a trick, spends much of his solo quoting Slam Stewart's equally famous 1943 bass part. Even when the group builds to a big crescendo that sounds, for all the world, like the entire Count Basie Orchestra perfectly replicated by a mere three men swinging, the trio's playing never sounds forced or aggressive.

Peterson has worked mostly with the piano–bass–drum combination even after the Brown–Thigpen unit broke up in 1965. By the 1960s, Peterson was increasingly appearing in concert halls and garnering accolades, especially from his native Canada (although, remarkably, he was never named as an NEA Jazz Master), including 16 honorary doctorates and eight Grammy Awards, culminating in the NARAS Lifetime Achievement Award in 1997. From the 1960s on, Peterson worked more frequently as a composer; his most ambitious work was the album-length *Canadiana Suite* of 1964, of which the most performed movement was his "Hogtown Blues." He also frequently played his own "Blues for Big Scotia," another blues with a Canadian theme.

In the 1960s and 1970s, Peterson went beyond his famous trio to collaborate with such fellow jazz giants as Milt Jackson and Clark Terry and also to make several albums with full orchestral accompaniment (one of which was arranged and conducted by Nelson Riddle). At the opposite end of the spectrum, he recorded an exceptional series of solo albums in Germany in 1970. Peterson was slowed down considerably by a stroke in 1993, and although he eventually went back to work, he never completely recovered the remarkable proficiency he had earlier. Even so, I couldn't help but observe that when Oscar Peterson made what would be his final appearance in New York, at Birdland in August 2006, that even after the stroke and even at 81, Oscar Peterson still played more piano than any other three great pianists put together.

(*The New York Sun*, 2005 and 2007)

***

When one thinks of Oscar Peterson, the mind races, with a speed second only to the great pianist's flying digits, for superlatives: intense, powerful, forceful, brilliant, awe inspiring, and God Almighty fast. One rarely, however, thinks of Peterson as being relaxed. Just the opposite—it isn't that Peterson doesn't swing; it's just that he almost never seems to breathe. At times, he can just plain overwhelm listeners by playing more piano than the human ear can possibly absorb.

Peterson's most relaxed and swinging unit, however, was the remarkable trio he employed for a few years beginning in 1959, with drummer Ed Thigpen and virtuoso bassist Ray Brown. It was Brown, in particular, who was able to bring out a loose and laid-back quality in Peterson's work that he rarely achieved with other sidemen. Fortunately, this great group was extensively recorded, most notably between July 27 and August 6, 1961, when the trio played a two-week stand at Chicago's London House nightclub. The group was hardly as democratic as the trios of Bill Evans or Amad Jamal—on the contrary, Brown and Thigpen don't even need to take solos to make their presence felt—although Brown gets the chance to stand out on fellow bassist Oscar Pettiford's "Tricotism." (One highlight: "Sometimes I'm Happy," wherein Peterson transcribes Lester Young's famous solo on the tune, and Brown reprises that of Slam Stewart from the same 1943 disc.) The three men perform with so much warmth and swing, without forsaking Peterson's characteristic energy, that these six hours of music just whiz by.

(*Stereo Review*, 1996)

***

Once I was having a drink with the excellent singer and pianist Freddy Cole when the stereo system served up a sound that made me stop dead in my tracks: a recording I had never heard by the King Cole Trio, the legendary combo led by Freddy's late older brother, Nat King Cole. I pointed this out to Cole, and he shot me back a look that said "Gotcha!" It wasn't Nat Cole at all; instead, it was an early recording in the King Cole style by one of the King's most ardent subjects, the young Oscar Peterson.

Peterson was quite possibly the most celebrated and prolifically recorded jazz pianist of all time; even today, the size of the Peterson bin in any record store will dwarf that of virtually any other artist. It's hard to believe that any aspect of his prodigious catalogue has been neglected by reissue producers, yet Mosaic Records has just released a new seven-CD boxed set containing his least-heard music, from the very early period when the Canadian pianist's own North Star was Nat Cole.

In the wake of Cole's death in 1965, Peterson recorded a tribute album (*With Respect to Nat*), but it was always clear that the number-one influence on his music was the great Art Tatum. It was Peterson who did more than any other pianist to carry Tatum's torch into later generations. As we've noted, Peterson famously said that the first time he heard Art Tatum's playing (on a record), he was so blown away that he couldn't bring himself to touch the keyboard for a month. He later made up for it: over the course of his long career, virtually any night that Peterson performed, he played so much piano that it would take any other player a whole month to equal the quantity and quality of music Peterson produced in a single set.

In the pinnacle years of his fame, beginning with his high-energy trios of 1953–1958 (with bassist Ray Brown and guitarist Herb Ellis), and then of 1959 to 1965 (with Brown and drummer Ed Thigpen), up to his stroke in 1993, Peterson was known as a daredevil virtuoso. He often sounded like 10 Art Tatums playing at once, or like an acrobat who could walk a high wire at the same time that he was being shot out of a cannon.

To hear Peterson playing with the combination of economy and virtuosity that was the trademark of Nat King Cole is a startling thing, yet track after track finds Peterson, the man who would later be King, playing in the King's court. To start with, the instrumentation of Brown's bass and guitarist Barney Kessel was deliberately patterned after Cole's trend-setting piano–guitar–bass trio (a trend that Tatum himself even followed for a while in the 1940s—and so did many others, from Ray Charles to Red Norvo), and for one date in 1952, the guitarist was Irving Ashby, who had served with Cole for several years. And it's not just the format or the abstract mindset; the Oscar Peterson Trio closely follows the arrangement style, the chordal voicings, the approach to melody and harmony, and the back-phrasing employed on key parts of the tunes in the manner of the King Cole Trio.

It wasn't a coincidence. Cole had earlier been the star of producer Norman Granz's Jazz at the Philharmonic concert series but around this time, gave up his trio to become one of the most successful pop singers ever. John McDonough, in his excellent liner notes, quotes Granz as saying that he was looking for a replacement for Cole. "And then, when I found Oscar, he became my Nat Cole." As if the sound of the piano and the trio weren't close enough, Peterson even sings (on six titles here) in a high voice that sounds like a Canadian King Cole.

The music itself is consistently brilliant, and the set is more than a worthy sequel to Mosaic's long out-of-print complete 18-CD set of "The Complete Capitol Recordings of the King Cole Trio." Peterson shows that he already had his own voice on the keyboard on bassist Oscar Pettiford's more modernistic blues "Pettiford's Tune" (later known as "Swingin' Till the Girls Come Home") and especially in a series of six extra-long numbers, which pretty much toss formal arrangements aside in favor of raw, even competitive jamming, which fit the pianist's own description that "having an opposing force [like Kessel] shocked me. He came hungry to play, and the first night Barney nailed me to the cross six ways till Sunday."

Though these after-hours style recordings are exciting in the extreme, the meat of the set is a series of six early LPs instigated by Granz that were among the earliest jazz songbook albums, devoted to the works of Cole Porter, Irving Berlin, George Gershwin, Jerome Kern, Richard Rodgers, and Vincent Youmans. These projects signify the beginning of Peterson's reputation as something more than a jazz pianist; he was one of the definitive instrumental interpreters of the Great American Songbook. In years to come, he would be singing their melodies with his unmistakable touch at the keyboard rather than his throat. As Peterson himself once related, the first time Cole came to hear him, he told the younger man, "Look, I'll make a deal with you: you don't sing, and I won't play piano!"

(*The Wall Street Journal*, 2008)

***

About 30 minutes into the documentary *Oscar Peterson: Black + White*, there's archival footage of a television conversation between Peterson and the late Andre Previn in which both piano masters discuss their mutual admiration for the great Nat King Cole. They both agree that a major attribute of Cole's piano work was, as Previn says, that "he knew not only what to play, but what to leave out."

Peterson agrees. (He consistently said that the two biggest influences on his own playing were Nat Cole and Art Tatum.) But if there ever was a giant of jazz whose genius was predicated on not leaving anything out, it was Oscar Peterson. Indeed, he did everything at the same time: exalt the melody, plumb the depths of the chord changes, and swing like crazy with intellectual acumen as well as sheer emotion; he was a monster soloist who also excelled at interacting with others.

If *Oscar Peterson: Black + White* has a flaw, it may be that it tries to do too many things at once—it's almost like the director himself does *not* know what to leave out. Yet that approach somehow suits the subject matter. The new film, which like the keyboard giant himself, comes from Canada, is foremost a documentary profile of a great artist and as such, follows the general chronological and biographical format of such projects. But it's also a filmed record of a Peterson memorial concert, featuring a half dozen or so mostly younger Canadian pianists. The onscreen commentators fluctuate between older American living legends, such as Herbie Hancock, Ramsey

Lewis, and Quincy Jones, and young Canadian players. (The primary Americans under 60 on camera are *The Late Show*'s Jon Batiste and the *New York Times*'s Giovanni Russonello, both welcome presences.)

The general pace of the movie is exceedingly up-tempo; like most documentary filmmaking in the digital era, the incessant cross-cutting is almost schizophrenically frenetic. We watch and hear historical footage of Peterson in concert playing a few bars of a fast blues even as the soundtrack is overlaid with the voice of a talking head or as vintage imagery parades by: photos, posters, advertisements, and notices from old newspapers. Yet the tempo is appropriate to Peterson's own relentlessly fast playing—in a way that it wouldn't be with a more lyrical player, say Bill Evans, or one who never made a virtue of speed, say Thelonious Monk.

The director seems unwilling to let us hear Oscar play, other than in the briefest of excerpts. It's not that he doesn't trust the music itself but apparently because he has no faith in millennial attention spans. He also doesn't trust that most of his viewers will have even heard of Oscar Peterson—which is a logical starting point, to take nothing for granted. (To this end, the participation of rock-and-roll icon, singer–songwriter–pianist Billy Joel is especially valuable—hopefully, millennials will have heard of him at least.) Despite some missteps (we don't really need a detour into Black Lives Matter movement), *Oscar Peterson: Black + White* captures the jubilant spirit and exciting flavor of its subject and will inspire those viewers, both veterans and newbies, to want to hear more. That's what documentaries like this are supposed to do.

But *Oscar Peterson: Black + White* is aware enough of itself to realize that profiles such as this can and should never be the whole story. Ideally, when it is released on DVD, hopefully, it will include at least 60 or so minutes of uninterrupted bonus performances of the great man in concert—or failing that, much great footage is readily viewable on YouTube—in which the music can speak for itself.

(*The New York Sun*, 2022)

LEADING MEN

ERROLL GARNER (1921–1977)

The pianist Erroll Garner was one of the great improvisers of all time—and not exclusively in his music. A *New York Times* profile of Garner in 1959 by John S. Wilson observed that the pianist refused to make any kind of plan until the very last minute: he cooked elaborate dishes without the aid of a recipe book by simply throwing different ingredients together and tasting, and he taught himself to play golf without instruction. He also played thousands of songs entirely by ear, without ever bothering to learn to read music, and composed many original tunes that way, including the standard "Misty." Therefore, it shouldn't be surprising that Garner made his best album—the legendary *Concert by the Sea*—practically by accident.

On September 17, 1955, Garner (who is also represented on a marvelous new DVD of two concerts from Europe eight years later, *Live in '63 & '64*, as part of the Jazz Icons series produced by Reelin' in the Years) performed at Fort Ord, an army base near Carmel, California, at the behest of disc jockey and impresario Jimmy Lyons. Martha Glaser, who served as Garner's personal manager for nearly his entire career, happened to be backstage when she noticed a tape recorder running. As she told me in 2009, it turned out that the show was being taped—without Garner's knowledge—by a jazz fan and scholar named Will Thornbury strictly for the enjoyment of himself and his fellow servicemen. Ms. Glaser told him, "I'll give you copies of every record Erroll ever made, but I can't let you keep that tape."

She took it back to New York (carrying it on her lap), where she assembled it into album form, titled it *Concert by the Sea*, and then played it for George Avakian, who ran the jazz department at Columbia Records. Garner had actually left Columbia three years earlier, but as Mr. Avakian recently told me, "I totally flipped over it! I knew that we had to put it out right away."

When Columbia released *Concert by the Sea* a few months later, this early live 12-inch LP was a runaway sensation. It became the number-one record of Garner's 30-year career and one of the most popular jazz albums of all time. It's not hard to hear why: From the first notes onward, Garner plays like a man inspired—on fire even. He always played with a combination of wit, imagination, amazing technical skill, and sheer joy far beyond nearly all of his fellow pianists, but on this particular night he reached a level exceeding his usual Olympian standard.

Concert begins with one of Garner's characteristic left-field introductions—even his bassist and drummer, in this case Eddie Calhoun and Denzil Best, rarely had an idea where he was going to go. This intro is particularly dark, heavy, and serious—so much the better to heighten the impact of the "punch line," when Garner tears into "I'll Remember April." Originally written as a romantic love song, Garner swings it so relentlessly fast that you can practically feel the surf and breeze of the windswept beach image from the album's famous cover.

The sheer exhilaration of Garner's playing never lets up, even when he slows down the tempo on "How Could You Do a Thing Like That to Me" by trombonist Tyree Glenn (a tune also known as Duke Ellington's "Sultry Serenade"), the pianist shows that he's just as adroit at playing spaces as he is at playing notes. The bulk of the album showcases his brilliant flair for dressing up classic standards such as "Where or When" (when Garner plays it, he leaves the question mark out—you know exactly where and precisely when). But "Red Top" illustrates what he can do with a 12-bar blues, and "Mambo Carmel" comes out of his fascination with Latin polyrhythms.

Concert by the Sea has never been off my iPod—even though it wasn't released in a decent digital edition until 2015. If any audio of any classic jazz album called for a little tender loving care, this is it; the original tape was barely a professional recording, and the bass, for instance, was barely audible. Sony had issued a CD in 1991, which, alas, was just a straight transfer of the 1955 master, and the digital medium made it sound worse rather than better. In 2009, Avakian (who died in 2017) confirmed to me that the original tape included, in Ms. Glaser's words, "a whole album's worth of unissued tracks" (four of which are listed in Tom Lord's *The Jazz Discography* at lordisco.com) that still exist in the Sony vaults. "We didn't put them out at the time because Erroll had already done those songs for Columbia," says Mr. Avakian. "But ideally there should be a new, remastered CD that includes the complete concert."

Ironically, while it was Martha Glaser who was, to a large degree, responsible for the existence of the album to begin with, she was also very likely the reason that the Garner catalog was so badly treated over the years. In fact, it was after Ms. Glaser died in December 2014 that the canon was rejuvenated with the double-CD *Complete Concert by the Sea* in 2015 and followed by, a year later, the previously unissued material that became the *Ready Take One* album in 2016.

In the latter part of her life, the best release that Glaser did authorize was a spectacular DVD of two European concerts by Garner, the first from Belgium in 1963 and the second from Sweden a year later. Both shows are replete with Garner's famous bait-and-switch trick with tempos: "It Might as Well Be Spring" and "When Your Lover Has Gone," both normally slow love songs, here become rollicking and strident, while "Fly Me to the Moon," usually heard as an up-tempo swinger, shows Garner at his most tender and introspective. He plays "My Funny Valentine" with so much harmonic ingenuity and melodic originality, with cascading runs of notes that enhance, rather than distract from, the romantic mood that you don't even mind hearing this overdone chestnut yet again.

The most irreverent performance here is also Garner's most classically inspired. In his treatment of "Thanks for the Memory," he goes comically overboard with classical references: "To a Wild Rose," "Voices of Spring," Liszt's "Liebesträume," and Rachmaninoff's Prelude in C-sharp minor. In a 1983 interview on a liner note for a French LP, the pianist Martial Solal praised this aspect of Garner's artistry, likening his use of quotes "to telling jokes," adding, "The independence of [Garner's] hands was very seductive. I even transcribed his solo on 'The Man I Love'—that was one of the only pieces I've ever written out. For about three months I tried to play like Garner."

The concert in Belgium also includes a stunning reading of Garner's most durable original composition, "Misty," which had already proved a pop hit both for himself and for several singers. Garner looks particularly happy to be playing it; throughout the tune, he sits there drenched in perspiration but with a beaming smile on his face and an irresistible expression of joy. He looks like someone who has just enjoyed the single most pleasurable experience a man can have—at least while wearing a tuxedo.

(*The Wall Street Journal*, 2009)

***

There's a live recording from 1958 featuring a legendary jazz pianist who introduces his band, one member at a time, saving himself for last: "and my name is Erroll Garner." He then proceeds to play "On the Street Where You Live" with all of Garner's trademark stylistic devices: the rollicking melody, the rococo embellishments, the sense of adventure and swing, and the startling thumps to the bass with the left elbow. It's classic Garner, but it isn't Garner at all—it's George Shearing. Most imitations of this sort are a deliberate parody, as when Sammy Davis Jr. impersonated Nat King Cole, but Shearing's is a highly respectful homage in which he reveals how Garner's style is so effervescent, so full of life and energy, that one doesn't even have to actually be Erroll Garner to participate in it.

Garner himself died at age 55 in 1977, which was hardly enough time for him to fully explore all the implications of the piano style that he created. Though his recorded catalog is huge (143 sessions are listed in Tom Lord's *The Jazz Discography*), every new release of previously unheard Garner material is cause for celebration.

Ready Take One, being issued by Legacy Recordings and Octave Music, is especially valuable: Six of this collection's 14 studio performances from 1967 to 1971 are original Garner compositions not heard since he played them live. "High Wire" is particularly catchy, with Garner stating the melody in the treble against a funky groove laid down by the bass and bongos, while "Wild Music" opens with the pianist heightening the suspense by starting with a grandly Tchaikovsky-like intro before he lunges into the tune with an exuberance that's remarkable even for him.

But Garner's interpretations of standards were, if anything, even more compelling. Being familiar with the actual melodies allows us to look more closely at what Garner does with them—and often there's a sense of duality between tension and release, control and abandon. The most basic visual metaphor for Garner's playing is the act of dancing. Yet in the standards, in particular, one gets a sense of two figures moving, and not necessarily in a social–partner kind of dance—rather, one can always sense the melody and at the same time, another figure dancing around it. Garner isn't merely a solo dancer; he's a whole dance team all by himself.

In Garner's hands, "Night and Day" and "Sunny" trade places with each other. Cole Porter's 1932 classic becomes a bluesy riff that suddenly sounds completely contemporary, while Bobby Hebb's 1966 pop hit is treated with the respect usually reserved for the upper echelon of The Great American Songbook. Garner imbues "Sunny" with a significance it never had before and, indeed, renders it worthy to stand beside the work of Porter and of Duke Ellington (who's represented here with highly original treatments of "Caravan" and "Satin Doll").

The set ends with "Misty," Garner's most famous original. Johnny Burke's lyrics to the contrary, Garner's rendition is shinier than anything. He makes his own tune glitter and gleam as if it were sewn together out of sequins—and the piano itself even seems to glow with a kind of inner radiance.

(*The Wall Street Journal*, 2016)

OSCAR LEVANT (1906–1972)

Beats there a heart so dead that it doesn't love George Gershwin's "Rhapsody in Blue"? This is one of those pinnacle achievements, a work that makes you feel good to be alive. Whose soul doesn't soar at the sound of that remarkable opening, with its clarinet *glissando*. And even more so at the finale, with its fortissimo crashes, as Gershwin piles on the suspense and the drama with one great staccato burst of melodic energy after another? It's hard to imagine any work of art—musical, visual, literary, theatrical, or even cinematic—that moves us and thrills us like this extraordinary piece of American music from 1924.

The closest thing this Gershwin classic has to a flaw is the middle; it simply can't compete with the beginning or the ending. In the hands of lesser pianists, that middle section can be a meandering placeholder, a respite between two colossal moments of musical brilliance. I personally prefer the first recording, a truncated 1924 performance with the composer himself and Paul Whiteman's orchestra, because—at just nine minutes—it condenses the middle section. The only performance I've ever heard of the complete "Rhapsody" whose middle section justifies its existence is the brilliant 1945 recording by Oscar Levant; not for nothing was he the highest-paid classical artist in America in the 1940s and 1950s.

Levant, whose recorded work is the subject of *A Rhapsody in Blue: The Extraordinary Life of Oscar Levant*, a new eight-CD boxed set from Sony Classical, impels the middle section with amazing force and feeling—his piano propelling the entire Philadelphia Orchestra the way that a great drummer drives a jazz band. Levant has all the technique and volume of an orchestra unto himself, and thus, his pairing with conductor Eugene Ormandy often sounds like two full ensembles playing at once, both in cooperation and competition.

Making his work all the more remarkable, Oscar Levant wasn't even best known as a musician. He was also a songwriter (whose best-known number, "Blame It on My Youth," was sung brilliantly by both Frank Sinatra and Nat King Cole) as well as an actor and TV personality. No less than his contemporary Dorothy Parker, Levant with his hundreds of brief, quotable quips foreshadowed Twitter. And he was ahead of his more buttoned-up times, as well, in talking openly about his neuroses on national television during talk-show interviews in the 1950s and 1960s.

The new set contains 109 tracks recorded between 1941 and 1958—the final sessions are in stereo—and was produced by Robert Russ. Michael Feinstein supplied a biographical essay and many of the dozens of rare illustrations and photographs for the 124-page hardcover book that houses the whole package.

As a musician, Levant is best remembered for his interpretations of the Gershwin canon and the performances here of the "Piano Concerto in F," "Second Rhapsody for Piano and Orchestra," and "'I Got Rhythm' Variations," and the three remarkable "Preludes" can all be considered definitive. (He also appeared as actor and performer in two classic Gershwin-centric movies, the *Rhapsody in Blue* biopic and *An American in Paris*.)

Yet well beyond the music of his close friend, this set is an outstanding collection of epic showcases for classical keyboard. The eight discs contain dozens of virtuoso pieces that would have been very familiar to mainstream listeners in the 1940s and 1950s, like de Falla's "Ritual Fire Dance"; Lecuona's "Malagueña"; and the number that launched a thousand plate spinners on *The Ed Sullivan Show*, Khachaturian's "Sabre Dance." These works were ensured—as if by Lloyd's of London—to generate a tumult whenever Levant played them, and he delivers them with maximum muscularity and irresistible, driving rhythm.

Still, Levant played in other styles as well. He renders the famous "Liebestod" from *Tristan und Isolde* in a rather dramatic adaptation by film composer Franz Waxman that makes it sound like a vintage Hollywood romance or as if Levant himself were playing the leading man in the opera. He plays Brahms's Waltz in A-flat major (no. 15, Op. 39) and Schumann's "Träumerei" with uncommon tenderness. He's no less adept at interpreting the Impressionists than the Romantics: Here's a "Clair de lune" (Debussy) for the ages and two Ravel masterworks, "Sonatine" and parts of

"Le Tombeau de Couperin." These works were extremely influential among superior jazz and pop orchestrators of the 1950s, such as Nelson Riddle, who were especially inspired by Ravel's use of polyphony.

Two works here, the Bach "Partita No. 1 in B-flat major" and "Blue Plate Special," are previously unreleased; the latter, by Levant himself, is particularly fascinating in the way it combines stride-like techniques, quixotically repetitive patterns, and angular dissonances. In fact, they reveal nothing less than the same antic wit and humor as his talk-show appearances. As we hear on these discs, he channeled that energy into performances that changed the way we understand the classics. Levant famously said, "I don't want to be known as a wag, I want to be known as a serious musician." Could it possibly be that Levant wasn't quite as completely schizophrenic as he wanted us to believe? Any one of the performances on this set will leave the listener with no doubt as to what his most valuable legacy actually was.

(*The Wall Street Journal*, 2018)

TRANSITIONAL FIGURES

MARY LOU WILLIAMS (1910–1981)

In her lifetime and for decades afterward, generally, the first thing you read about Mary Lou Williams was that she was the greatest of all female jazz musicians. Even I have written about her as such, although from the perspective of the 21st century, her gender hardly seems to matter: she was one of the most important and influential pianist–composer–bandleader–educator–sages that jazz has ever known and in her lifetime, provided an all-important direct link from the jazz age to the swing era and then well into the rise of modernism and even well beyond that.

There are many titles we could bestow on Williams: She was a spectacular pianist but also a pioneering orchestrator in the development of big-band swing in the 1920s and 1930s. An era or two later, she played an equally key role in the emergence of bebop. She learned her trade from the great ragtime and stride players of the World War I era, and 60 years later, she shared a duo concert with the most extreme of avant-garde pianists, Cecil Taylor.

Mary Elfreda Scruggs was one of a disproportionate number of great jazz pianists from Pittsburgh; she became Mary Lou Williams after she married saxophonist John Williams in 1927. The Williamses recorded their first sessions with his band, and within a short while, both were playing with the increasingly popular Kansas City–based orchestra leader Andy Kirk. Williams came into her own as both a pianist and composer–arranger under Kirk's leadership, and in 1936, he paid tribute to her by recording the number "The Lady Who Swings the Band."

At the height of the swing era, Williams's music was played by all the major bands, including those of Benny Goodman, Casa Loma, Louis Armstrong, Bob Crosby, and both Dorsey Brothers. Roy Eldridge sang "Pretty-Eyed Baby," Nat King Cole sang "Little Joe from Chicago," and Dizzy Gillespie broke it up on "In the Land of Oo-Bla-Dee." Glenn Miller, Jimmie Lunceford, Anita O'Day, and many others essayed her popular blues, "What's Your Story, Morning Glory?"

Williams's biggest supporters were Benny Goodman and Duke Ellington. At the height of the swing era, Goodman had dozens of her charts in his band book, most famously his perennial "Roll 'Em." Then, as the age of modernism was dawning, he hired her to play in his new sextet, alongside Wardell Gray and Stan Hasselgård, essentially anointing her as his Virgil to lead him into the brave new world of bebop.

When Williams's second husband, trumpeter Harold "Shorty" Baker, joined Ellington's brass section, she began a long working relationship with that leader as well. Williams traveled with the Ellington band as an on-staff arranger for a year or so, working alongside Ellington and fellow Pittsburgher Billy Strayhorn. Her most famous pieces for Ellington were appropriately trumpet-centric: "Trumpets No End," her brassy variation on "Blue Skies," and "Otto Make That Riff Staccato," a novelty feature composed by Williams's one-time boyfriend Milt Orent for singing trumpeter Ray Nance. Ellington, who famously had a way with words, described her as "like soul on soul."

Williams gained a name of her own as a fashionable and elegant keyboardist, working at Café Society in the mid-1940s, at which time she also had her own weekly series on New York radio. She supervised a brilliant series of jazz small-group dates for the Asch label at this time (involving many of the biggest names in jazz) and began composing "Zodiac Suite."

Williams performed "Zodiac" work in three versions. First it was as an album of solo and trio performances (which were commercially released). Then at Town Hall in December 1945, she played it with a combination of jazz soloists plus a small chamber orchestra with woodwinds and strings. Finally, in June 1946, it got a full symphonic treatment at Carnegie Hall. Even Ellington, who established the precedent for suites and extended works in jazz, never attempted anything so ambitious. (For information about the first complete, full-scale studio recording of the *Zodiac Suite*, see elsewhere in this book.)

Williams herself never again attained the peak of celebrity she enjoyed during the years of the swing-to-bop transition. Like many other idiosyncratic jazz visionaries, she was, from the 1950s onward, forever scuffling from gig to gig, from composition to brilliant composition, trying to keep body and soul together. She had a devout belief in the supernatural and seems to have been somewhat paranoiac, always believing that somebody had it in for her. (She accused both Ellington and Monk of appropriating her themes—she had a better case with the pop song "Black Coffee," which bears a similarity to "Morning Glory" in its first few bars.)

Still, Williams was—with Ellington and John Coltrane—one of jazz's greatest exponents of the metaphysical and spiritual. Besides "Zodiac," there were later pieces, such as "The Black Christ of the Andes" and "Mary Lou's Mass," done after her conversion to Catholicism. In addition to being a composer, pianist, and bandleader, Mary Lou Williams was also a teacher and musical and spiritual mentor. But though William served the Church with all her heart and soul, she was always and ultimately the most effective evangelist for the cause of jazz itself that the music ever had.

(*The New York Sun*, 2004)

THELONIOUS MONK (1917–1982)

The land above 110th Street in Manhattan is a world of magical transformations where frogs become princes. This is where the lowly, nondescript Sixth Avenue assumes the more majestic moniker of Lenox Avenue and Central Park West, and the avenue formerly known as Eighth herewith becomes the mighty Frederick Douglass Boulevard. This is also a place where gypsy cab drivers try to get *your* attention when *they* think that they should be driving *you* somewhere. It's only fitting that music should be reinvented in the same mysterious way: that an old familiar standard like "Sweet Georgia Brown" should be reinvented as "Bright Mississippi," where "Blue Skies" is reborn as "In Walked Bud," and where "Tea for Two" becomes "Skippy" and "I Got Rhythm" is magically transformed into "Rhythm-A-Ning."

Thelonious Monk is generally described as a composer, a pianist, and a bandleader, but he brought all three of these activities together to devise a whole new approach to jazz in which nearly everything that previously existed in the music was alchemized into something entirely new. Perhaps no less remarkably, Monk was at the forefront of the Harlem-based revolution that transformed music, even though he never actually lived in that area. He was born in Rocky Mount, North Carolina; when he was a youngster, his family joined the massive Northern migration of African Americans and settled on West 63rd Street, which was then a primarily Black neighborhood known as San Juan Hill. He continued to live there as Harlem established itself as the focal point of creative Black musical expression and remained on 63rd although the area lost its earlier ethnic identity after the construction of Lincoln Center in the mid-1960s.

As a young pianist, Monk had mastered the Harlem stride style (the pianist Billy Taylor recalls a time when he and the young Monk hung out with Willie "The Lion" Smith, trying to learn what they could from him) and also immersed himself in the blues and spirituals, and even toured the Deep South as accompanist with a gospel music troupe. He helped lead the charge that brought forth bebop or modern jazz and along with Charlie Parker, Dizzy Gillespie, Charlie Christian, and Kenny Clarke, was one of the new music's most important founding fathers—and its first pianist. Their experiments created bebop in the late 1930s and early 1940s when the five (in various combinations) jammed together after hours at Minton's on West 118th Street, where Monk was the house pianist from 1939 on.

Playing a central role in the creation of modern jazz was only the beginning of Monk's evolution; even after bebop emerged and became the dominant form of jazz, Monk continued to develop and refine his music. When Monk recorded as a leader–composer for the first time, his own distinct brand of modern jazz was nearly perfected. In 1947–1948, on a classic series of sessions for Blue Note Records, he introduced a string of early masterpieces, such as "Off-Minor," "Misterioso," and "Epistrophy," yet like Billy Strayhorn (with "Take the 'A' Train"), his single most popular work was also one of his first, the ballad "'Round Midnight," introduced while he was still playing piano for trumpeter Cootie Williams's big band in 1944. Monk's music was at once denser and lighter than most archetypical bebop as played by Parker, Gillespie, and their legions of disciples and yet at the same time, more whimsical.

Monk's use of dissonance always had a capricious side to it, as if he were somehow making fun of the stereotype of "serious" composer, writing artsy, inaccessible music in an ivory tower. Monk's music was like Picasso's paintings: for all of its artfulness, it was inclusive, rather than exclusive, and while it was certainly appreciated by the intelligentsia, you didn't have to be an insider to dig it.

Like Picasso, he created fine art that was profoundly idiosyncratic without being in the least bit elitist; many of his compositions were inspired by and dedicated to his two children. Also like Picasso, here was a transparent quality to Monk's music—when Picasso gave you the image of a woman, you always had a clear sense of what the figure originally looked like as well as what he was doing with it. Much as Monk did with a familiar standard, such as "April in Paris" or "I Should Care," it was like the original melody and Monk's version of it existed side by side, like one of those Picasso figures who looks sideways and right at you at the same time. Like a Picasso figure, a Monk treatment of a song has everything you expect to find in it, only perhaps not where you expect to find it.

As he built toward his mature style, Monk continued to alchemize all manner of musical metals into gold. He could start with something as familiar as the old standard "Just You, Just Me" and give it new life, such as "Evidence," yet often his building materials were far simpler: "Bemsha Swing" takes as its point of departure a simple two-note interval, a step up a perfect fourth; it goes on from there, but essentially, those two notes are all you need to know. Another of his best-known pieces, "Blue Monk," is precisely that, a straight-up 12-bar blues in B flat, yet he could also offer more complicated variations on the form, such as "Straight No Chaser" and "Misterioso."

Monk himself had several more transformations in store, not all of them positive. For the last few years of his life, The Wizard became more like a mystical hermit who rarely left the cave-like confines of his 63rd Street apartment; later still, he confined himself to the Weehawken, New Jersey, home of his great friend and patron, the "Jazz Baroness," Pannonica de Koenigswarter. Yet since his death especially, Monk has become second only to Duke Ellington as easily the most-performed jazz composer of all time; in the 1980s and 1990s, almost every third CD seemed to be a Monk songbook album. Monk's history of reinventing himself—and everything else—is hardly over.

(*The New York Sun*, 2007)

***

My friend Loren Schoenberg, the dirty so-and-so, somehow got a hold of an advance copy of *Thelonious Monk Quartet with John Coltrane at Carnegie Hall* before I did. We were standing on 125th Street, around the corner from his office in the National Jazz Museum in Harlem, when he popped his iPod headphones in my ears and gave me my first sample of this newly discovered recording from 1957. I began listening to a track that had already started; I had missed the "head," the first statement of the central melody, so I didn't know the song was "Epistrophy." What I heard was astonishing: Coltrane begins his improvisation by blasting out a series of dense note clusters, not quite riffs, not quite licks, but brief flurries of ascending notes, stuck together like peanuts encased in brittle—each of which rises in pitch within itself before the next batch starts on a higher note. Coltrane plays about a dozen brief variations on this three- or four-note mini phrase before he moves to something more like a melody line, as one is used to hearing in a jazz solo. As he comes out of the bridge on his last chorus, he plays another variation on the idea, only this time these note clusters—sort of melodic speed bumps—have been somewhat smoothed out and fit more gracefully within the flow of the line.

I couldn't help but think that I had never heard Coltrane—or anyone else—play anything remotely like this before. But I would bet that even before this new CD (Blue Note/Thelonious 35173) is officially released on September 27, 2005, that I will have heard this phrase or some kind of variation on it come back at me from dozens of saxophonists and other instrumentalists. It won't be long before every note of this solo and this entire concert is transcribed and memorized by every musician, student, and/or professional in the world.

A previously unknown performance by the combination of Thelonious Monk and John Coltrane would be big news, even if it were disappointing (even geniuses can have an off night) or as in the case of the 1993 release, *Thelonious Monk Quartet Featuring John Coltrane Live at the Five Spot Discovery!*, an amateur recording in inferior audio quality.

For decades, the quartet that featured both Monk and Coltrane together has been one of the missing links of jazz history. In 1957, Coltrane had just spent two years with the Miles Davis Quintet, which ended when the trumpeter fired Coltrane for missing gigs and being wasted most of the time when he did show up. Davis had had enough of heroin junkies, having himself come of age in Charlie Parker's quintet and having kicked his own addiction only a few years earlier.

Monk, who was not known to be a user himself, nevertheless had been denied the legal right to perform in New York jazz clubs, as had Billie Holiday (who also sang at this same 1957 Carnegie Hall concert). This city law was a holdover from the ill-informed days when addicts were unilaterally regarded as criminals rather than victims of a disease. The idea was to punish the wretched by denying them their ability to make a living rather than help or cure them. Monk and Holiday were perhaps the two most famous targets of this disastrous law, which was finally repealed in the 1960s. Monk had not made a New York club appearance for many years but regained the right to do so beginning in 1957.

It was synchronicity—and not. Coltrane, who had spent several months, after leaving Davis, purging his system of narcotics and undergoing a spiritual transformation, happened to need a gig at the same time that Monk was putting together a new quartet. The pianist had already begun working at the Five Spot Café in Greenwich Village, and Coltrane joined him in the new Monk Quartet from July 1957 to the end of the year. Unfortunately, even though Monk was then under contract to Riverside Records and he was working on several albums at the time, until recently there has been virtually no recorded "Evidence" of what Monk and Coltrane sounded like together. Riverside's normally astute producer/co-owner Orrin Keepnews somehow did not send a tape crew down to the Five Spot, although he would a year later to document Monk's 1958 quartet with Johnny Griffin.

There are only three studio tracks by the Monk–Coltrane quartet, which offer a tantalizing taste of what they were creating nightly at the Five Spot. Coltrane also participates in the classic album *Monk's Music*, but here, he is one of several celebrity horn players, along with Coleman Hawkins, Gigi Gryce, and Ray Copeland, in this all-star showcase of some of the pianist–composer's best-known works. The following summer, Coltrane rejoined Monk's group for a one-night reunion at the Five Spot; luckily, parts of that performance were informally recorded by the saxophonist's wife, but even though that tape was officially released in 1993, the music is barely audible.

Only a few Coltrane scholars, among them biographer Lewis Porter, even knew that the Monk–Coltrane quartet had appeared at Carnegie (November 29, 1957) as part of an all-star benefit for the Morningside Community Center (a few blocks west of the National Jazz Museum in Harlem), which also featured the groups of Billie Holiday (not recorded), Ray Charles (presumably with his octet of the period), and Chet Baker with Zoot Sims and Sonny Rollins, not to mention the full Dizzy Gillespie Orchestra. Nobody knew for sure that the Voice of America had recorded this concert, not even the VoA themselves or the Library of Congress, which housed the tape. It was finally discovered this year by the LoC engineer and jazz scholar Larry Applebaum. The Monk portion, which runs 51 minutes, is the only set so far announced for commercial issue. (Alas, even 20 years later, none of that additional material has since been released.)

The music, which took nearly 50 years to be found but following that, less than eight months to be legally issued, is as revelatory as we could have hoped. Not every meeting of two jazz giants is as good as the sum of its parts, but this one is even better. Both men were feeling liberated by their circumstances—the newfound freedom from drugs and legal shackles—and more importantly, by each other. There's a joy in their playing together here that's even more pronounced than in what they had done and would do separately. For Coltrane, especially, this is the best playing he had yet done on record (with the possible exception of *Blue Trane*, recorded two months earlier in September); the mature masterpieces with Miles Davis (particularly *Kind of Blue*) and his own groups were still to come.

Thelonious Monk Quartet with John Coltrane at Carnegie Hall is the kind of CD that will immediately start turning up on top-10 lists, and not just for the best releases of 2005, but of all time. Critics and scholars compiling lists of the first 10 CDs anyone should buy for a basic jazz compilation will include it as a representation of both Monk and Coltrane at their best (killing two birds with one stone), the same way that *Kind of Blue* shows four giants, Miles Davis, Coltrane, Cannonball Adderley, and Bill Evans, at their absolute pinnacles.

The CD opens with applause being faded up as we hear the first few notes of Monk playing one of his major slow ballads, the 1947 "Monk's Mood" (which preceded both "Moody's Mood" and "Parker's Mood"). We hear his characteristic juxtaposition of wide-open spaces, mysterious portals to some other dimension of sounds, and those arpeggios and glissandos that sound like a wry parody of a cocktail pianist affecting an exaggerated imitation of Earl Hines or Art Tatum. As a keyboard stylist, Monk is equal parts Teddy Wilson and Jonathan Edwards.

Monk's melody solo here is by turns dark and optimistic, heavy and light, stark and opulent—there's a deep quality about Monk, even when he's enjoying a laugh, but also a refusal to take anything too seriously—his playing is full of humor, even when he's at his most somber. Just when we think "Monk's Mood" is going to be a full-track unaccompanied solo, Coltrane comes in; then, just when we think it's going to be a rubato sax-and-piano duo, the bass (Ahmed Abdul-Malik) and drums (former Basie-ite Shadow Wilson) enter. It turns out the rhythm section is only heard briefly: the opening track is, in fact, a formal showcase for the undiluted power of Monk and Coltrane together.

Supposedly, in the early nights of the Five Spot engagement, it took Coltrane a while to catch on to the means and ways of his leader; this was several generations before budding jazz students would be raised on Monk's tunes. After four months of working with him, however, Coltrane plays these tunes like he invented them. If there's any good reason *not* to like the Carnegie Hall concert, it might be because it makes Monk's other groups, even the classic quartet he led for 10 years with the fine tenor saxophonist Charlie Rouse, suffer by comparison.

Indeed, Coltrane is the perfect interpreter of Monk's music: he makes it sound more steadfastly Monk-ish than any other of the composer's collaborators: "Monk's Mood" is more moody; the other crucial ballad, "Crepuscule with Nellie," is more romantic; "Evidence" is more completely justified; "Nutty" is nuttier; the one non-Monk standard, "Sweet and Lovely," is sweeter and lovelier; "Blue Monk" is bluer (with Coltrane piling 10 ingenious 12-bar choruses on top of each other); and "Bye-Ya," Monk's ode to Calypso, is even more jaunty in its use of Caribbean rhythms. Coltrane, at this point in his development, is the perfect sideman and collaborator, able to carry out the leader's ideas and enhance them without taking over. He would do the same for Miles Davis when he rejoined the latter's group for a second—and considerably more sainted—tenure from 1958 to 1960.

As noted, "Epistrophy" is even more epistrophal than usual, not least because there are two versions. The first one has a hint of the clusters effect mentioned above, although Coltrane more characteristically solos with the dense style that Ira Gitler would soon describe "sheets of sound." There are two versions of "Epistrophy," probably because the full lineup of bands actually gave two shows that night at 8:30 p.m. and then 12:00 a.m. (although Monk did not play "'Round Midnight"). The second crowd must have been there until 3:00 or 4:00 a.m. (It makes more sense that the current CD is compiled from both sets; I can't imagine each group being on for 50 minutes two times around.) The second "Epistrophy" is incomplete, although, thankfully, the whole Coltrane solo is intact, the tape fades down in the middle of Monk's solo. We can be glad that producers Michael Cuscuna and T. S. Monk (the composer's son and a respected drummer and bandleader in his own right) included this fragment—and so will saxophonists from now to judgment day.

(*The New York Sun*, 2005)

***

In a 1948 interview, Thelonious Monk told critic George Simon that "most bebop bands sound like Dixieland to me." The pianist–composer explained that he meant that he was afraid modern jazz would descend to a lot of "everybody blowing for themselves," without regard to the tune dictated or even what the other guys on the stand were playing; contrastingly, Monk's own idea of jazz was a compositionally driven music. His statement was also taken as an indication that even though Monk himself was one of the founders of the new movement, along with colleagues Charlie Parker and Dizzy Gillespie, he had already moved beyond basic bebop into an even-newer idiom that was entirely his own.

The remarkable saxophonist and composer Steve Lacy (1934–2004) had both begun and ended his career playing Monk's music. In 1958, his second album was *Reflections: Steve Lacy Plays Thelonious Monk*, one of the first-ever Monk songbook albums, and in 2004, his last major performance in his hometown, New York City, was at the Iridium in a program called "Monksiland." The quintet featured his long-time collaborator, trombonist Roswell Rudd, and contemporary star trumpeter and composer Dave Douglas (who among his many ensembles, leads a quintet called "Four in One" that plays nothing but Monk tunes), plus bassist Jean-Jacques Avenel playing (who soloed almost as much as any of the horns) and drummer John Betsch.

Monk's ensemble sound jelled in the mid-1950s, from which point he rarely varied from the familiar approach of his quartet—the longest-running edition of which featured Charlie Rouse on tenor saxophone—playing a core group of the composer's favorites of his own tunes and the occasional standard. For all of the angularity of Monk's music and his astute use of what writer Kevin Whitehead calls "trapdoor silences," this was a subtle music. While not shortchanging his massive sense of humor, the classic Monk Quartet was decidedly cool.

Lacy and his cohorts, however, have chosen another approach to Monk's music, one that's more perverse than subtle, more extroverted than introverted, more in your face than intimate. Lacy is the perfect musician to be at the center of such an endeavor—not only did he work with Monk on several occasions (most famously the composer's 1963 big-band concert at Philharmonic Hall), but at various points in his career, he and Rudd have both played traditional jazz, bebop, and free jazz. The Monksiland band sounds like all three jazz subgenres at once.

One thing that Monksiland does *not* sound like is the classic Monk–Rouse quartet. At times, the ensemble suggests Monk's own more exuberantly boppish early recordings (heard in their entirety on the four-CD "Complete Blue Note Recordings," Blue Note 30363), as they did on "Skippy," in which Douglas underscored the song's harmonic similarity to "Tea for Two." Indeed, the idea of basing new melodies on standard chord changes is itself a bebop characteristic, one which Monk disavowed in the Simon interview. He claimed, "I make up my own chords and melodies," which was largely true, even though he himself did compose a significant number of jazz's most famous contrafacts.

The idea of reinterpreting Monk without a piano, the most obvious way to reproduce his signature dissonances, is itself a surprising one (reprised by Ben Riley and Don Sickler in the Monk Legacy Septet). By dispensing with its easy-to-follow harmonic road map, the Monksilanders evoke the earliest New Orleans brass bands, which used only instruments that could be easily carried, and here Lacy's soprano suggests the E-flat metal clarinets that such bands employed. Yet the absence of a conventional chordal instrument also points toward free jazz as Ornette Coleman defined it in the early 1960s, which downplayed harmonic improvisation and emphasized improvising off new melody lines. In that respect, the Lacy–Rudd–Douglas combination illustrates how Monk's music is a bridge between the oldest and the newest jazz.

Throughout, Rudd offered a trombone approach that seemed to be premodern and postmodern at the same time: he plays in a gruff, blustery style, and always seems to be ready to exchange phrases or ideas with anybody else in the band. He also seems perpetually poised for a musical battle, and his shaggy beard even makes him look a little like Bert Lahr in lion drag. While bassist Avenel was frequently joining the front line, Rudd was often playing at the bottom of the sonic food chain, resurrecting the tailgate days when the trombone was as much a rhythm instrument, filling much of the function that the tuba and the string bass later assumed. I had never thought of either Lacy or Douglas as inwardly directed players, but compared to Rudd, they both seemed positively withdrawn.

The band started off the first set on opening night with "Monk's Dream," which immediately established how they were going for the visceral rather than the cerebral They followed with "Let's Call This," and even the ballad "Pannonica" seemed more muscular than tender. After "Skippy" came "Bemsha Swing," with its familiar perfect fourth opening. Even "Introspection" was aggressively played, while "Eronel" was pointillistically constructed out of dots and squiggles.

The set's high point was the penultimate number, "Bemsha Swing," which found Rudd in a Christmassy mood, quoting both "March of the Toys" and "Waltz of the

Flowers" from *The Nutcracker*. The piece erupted in an almost comically cacophonic climax in which everybody seemed to be, in Monk's worst fear, going for themselves. Yet it ended with the three horns serenely restating the melody, once again all back together on the same page—Monk's page.

(*The New York Sun*, 2004)

***

Thelonious Monk, *The Classic Quartet* (Candid Records)

There's a story, possibly apocryphal, about Thelonious Monk and his 1956 composition "Ba-Lue Bolivar Ba-Lues-Are." Supposedly, Monk performed the number at a club and afterward, a rather dignified South American gentleman walked up to him and said, "Thank you for naming that composition for our great hero, Simón Bolívar." Monk responded, "Actually, I got the name from a hotel."

My father related that anecdote to me, and the only part of it that's verifiably true is that Monk did indeed name the song after Midtown Manhattan's Bolivar Hotel, the temporary home of his beloved patroness, Pannonica de Koenigswarter.

Still, my dad was close enough to the jazz scene at the time, and since I never heard that story anywhere else, even in Robin D. G. Kelley's definitive biography of the pianist and composer, I like to think he might have been there when it allegedly happened.

"Ba-Lue Bolivar Ba-Lues-Are" is one of Monk's best blues tunes along with the more famous and less treacherously titled "Blue Monk." Both are part of *The Classic Quartet*, a new release of an excellent, lesser known set from Monk's first visit to Japan, in 1963. It features what was then Monk's working group, with tenor saxophonist Charlie Rouse, bassist Butch Warren, and drummer Frankie Dunlop.

True or not, the story about Monk and the Bolivian *señor* is pertinent because it illustrates Monk's acerbic wit, which is somehow very subtle and very broad at the same time. It seems entirely in keeping with his music that the man who came up with such quirky, off-beat melodies as "Nutty," "Bye-Ya," and "Bemsha Swing" would have such a quirky, off-beat sense of humor.

The 1963 Tokyo performance captures Monk's humor, not to mention his amazing sense of melody, harmony, and rhythm. This was originally produced as a TV concert, with the quartet performing five numbers in a studio without an audience. There's a low-res copy available for viewing (https://www.youtube.com/watch?v=mDlUsTKvCkQ) on YouTube, but the audio on this new LP and CD release is superb.

Still, the video, it must be admitted, does add a lot. The first number on it is "Evidence" (on the album, it's "Epistrophy"), and it gives a wonderful if very murky glimpse of one of jazz's most legendary characters in action.

We begin with the distinctive opening notes of one of Monk's best-known jazz standards, famously a contrafact built on the harmonic bones of "Just You, Just Me." Rouse is in the foreground soloing, and Monk is accompanying him in the background, jabbing at the keyboard in a highly percussive way, almost as if it were a vibraphone, and producing exactly the right notes to accompany the saxophonist. In this group, it often seems like all four members are soloing all the time, even when only one is in the spotlight.

About three minutes in, as Rouse continues, Monk gets up from the piano bench and starts to whirl around the stage. You might call it dancing, but I would argue it has more to do with Cab Calloway than Rudolf Nureyev; yes, he's moving in step with the music, but it's equal parts conducting. He throws his body around in exaggerated, jerky movements that both inspire and capture the beat. Dunlop's bass solo is also exaggeratedly rhythmic, while Warren's drum solo is surprisingly melodic.

The one questionable aspect of the release is the title, *The Classic Quartet*. Monk hired Warren just before they left for Japan, and they worked together in this particular lineup for only a few months.

Still, "Epistrophy" further shows how this foursome breathe and move as one, much like a dance troupe—they all land on the beat at the exact right moment, like the Nicholas Brothers times two. Both the timing and the combined notes are also in perfect sync with each other; the quirky tonality of the harmony matches the slightly unexpected, offbeat nature of the rhythmic placement.

It's also a real treat to have one of Monk's solo standards—and yes, his selection of what hipster audiences considered to be hoary old chestnuts, such as "Just a Gigolo," was also regarded, at the time, as further evidence of his impish sense of humor. He doesn't distort the tune but leaves it clearly recognizable, even as he overlays levels of interpretation on top of it, the spacey chords and the even more spacey rhythms.

With anyone else, it would seem like a somewhat disingenuous attempt to take a sentimental old song and merely funk it up, but Monk makes it into something wholly different, something better than it was before, Louis Prima and Keely Smith notwithstanding.

In both sequences, the video and the album, *Gigolo*, lead into a blues, which also starts with Monk playing unaccompanied before the rest of the trio joins in. The title of "Ba-Lue Bolivar Ba-Lues-Are" has by now been shortened to the simpler "Bolivar Blues." The Bolivar Hotel, at 230 Central Park South, has long since been converted into a condo, but both the building and the tune are still with us—Monk's music even more so.

(*The New York Sun*, 2023)

SUPERSTARS

GEORGE SHEARING (1919–2011)

In Jack Kerouac's *On the Road*, Sal Paradise, Kerouac's narrative alter ego, talks about accompanying his friend Dean Moriarty (Neal Cassady) to Birdland to hear George Shearing. Referring to Shearing as "the great pianist," Kerouac vividly describes him as "a distinguished looking Englishman with a stiff white collar, slightly beefy, blond, with a delicate English-summer's-night air about him." In his account, the opener is "a rippling sweet number," but before long, the pianist and his bassist start to find a groove.

> [Then] Shearing began to play his chords . . . faster and faster. . . . [T]hey rolled out of the piano in great rich showers, you'd think the man wouldn't have time to line them up. They rolled and rolled like the sea. Folks yelled for him to "Go!" Dean was sweating; the sweat poured down his collar. "There he is! That's him! Old God! Old God Shearing! Yes! Yes! Yes!"

This is one of the most colorful descriptions of a jazz musician in action, but the label of "old" was somewhat facetious. At the time Kerouac wrote *On the Road* (sometime around 1950), Shearing was all of 41—only three years older than Kerouac. The pianist seemed much more like an old god in his later years. He was still hard at work at the time of his 85th birthday, with a rare, three-night engagement at the Le Jazz Au Bar and an autobiography (published by Continuum Books), as well as a new double-CD retrospective released by Concord Jazz.

Shearing was born in the Battersea district of London on August 13, 1919; sightless from birth, he studied music in a school for the blind and first played professionally with an all-blind big band in the late 1930s. He has said that his handicap was

George Shearing; Mashpee Commons; Cape Cod, Massachusetts; August 31, 1996

actually an asset during the war years—he was better able to get around blacked-out London than his sighted friends.

It was during the war that he established himself as the most remarkable pianist on the British scene. He worked with established dance-band leaders (Bert Ambrose), visiting foreign stars (Stephane Grappelli), and local talent (Benny Goodman–influenced clarinetists Harry Perry and Frank Weir). By the late 1940s, however, Shearing was ready to make a transition—two, actually—from swing to bop and from England to the United States.

Shearing's first American recordings, done in 1947 for the preeminent bop label Savoy, show the influence of such early piano modernists as Bud Powell and Lennie Tristano. His composition "Conception" was instantly picked up by first-generation boppers, including Powell and especially Miles Davis, who recorded various variations under such titles as "Deception" and "Enigma."

But it was his fellow countryman, the critic, composer, and producer Leonard Feather, who helped Shearing achieve his commercial breakthrough. In 1939, Feather had produced Shearing's first featured recordings (including the intriguingly titled but, alas, unissued "Nagasuckle Rose"); ten years later, he and Shearing conceived the sound that would make the George Shearing Quintet one of the most popular ensembles of the next half-century.

Since the early 1940s, a technique had existed among jazz pianists—arranger Phil Moore claimed to have invented it—known variously as the "locked hands," "mirror chords," or "block chords" technique. It was a very full-sounding approach, a way of making the piano sound more orchestral in which all 10 fingers were generally used and the player's hands paralleled each other. Although the style had been popularized by both Milt Buckner (with Lionel Hampton) and Nat King Cole (with his legendary King Cole Trio), Shearing and Feather did them one better. They built an entire ensemble around the locked hands technique.

So while vibraphonist Marjorie Hyams doubled what Shearing was playing in his left hand, guitarist Chuck Wayne (and later, Belgian Toots Thielemans, who doubled on harmonica) would match what he played with his right. Add to the mixture the agile bass of John Levy and the drums of Denzil Best, and all at once, modern jazz had its first pop crossover act.

Most of the world first heard the Shearing Quintet on its best-selling single of "September in the Rain," and the piano–vibes–guitar–bass–drums combination continued to be Shearing's primary vehicle for almost 25 years after that. But it was far from his only one.

Indeed, the scope and variety of Shearing's musical accomplishments are truly astonishing. He composed "Lullaby of Birdland," which provided an anthem for both the nightclub and the bebop era (as well as the title for both the upcoming autobiography and the Concord package). But he was also among the first notable jazz soloists on the accordion on such recordings as 1939's "Squeezin' the Blues" and 1949's "Good to the Last Bop." (He once defined a gentleman as "Someone who can play the accordion—but doesn't.") And after 1953, when the Shearing Quintet annexed the remarkable Latin percussionist Armando Peraza, it became one of the jazz world's leading exponents of first the mambo and then the bossa nova.

Along the way, Shearing worked with pop and jazz singers (Mel Torme, Peggy Lee, Carmen McRae, Nat King Cole, and Billy Eckstine), orchestra composer–arrangers (Billy May, Robert Farnon, and Tito Puente), and fellow instrumental giants (Cannonball Adderley, Wes Montgomery, and Marian McPartland). Shearing's music was so easy to love that even non-jazz fans could go for it in a big way, and he sold more records than virtually any other instrumentalist of the pre–smooth jazz era, appearing regularly in top-dollar nightclubs and concert halls.

In my earlier days, I was guilty—like many others—of thinking that his very popularity somehow compromised his achievement. But Kerouac's passage about the performer is an important corrective to this misguided notion. We tend to think that the beats identified with angst-ridden miscreants, starving in garrets, and venting their tortured souls. Kerouac's paean to the pianist shows that the stiff white collar never constricted nor hid the high-flying artist beneath.

Whether playing solo, with a standard modern jazz trio (with a bass and drums), or with his re-formed quintet, George Shearing continues to alternate between rhapsodic lyricism and blistering bebop and continually reminds us that there's no God like an old God.

(*The New York Sun*, 2004)

***

A few years back, at a piano jazz concert at the 92nd Street Y, Bill Charlap played a particularly strong solo, one that so obviously thrilled the gentleman sitting next to me that he responded with delighted laughter and a strong cry of "Yeah!"

It was then that I noticed his thick South London accent and closed eyes (he wasn't wearing his trademark Ray-Bans) and realized I was mere inches away from George Shearing, a living legend of the jazz piano if ever there was one. His lifelong blindness aside, Shearing is regarded as a musical visionary by generations of pianists, including, as Charlap has pointed out, Bill Evans and Herbie Hancock. While Shearing opted at that moment to express his admiration for Charlap in a loud and forthright manner, on Wednesday Charlap honored the ongoing legacy of what he called "the George Shearing Sound" in a formal concert that served as the climax of the second week of the Y's Jazz in July series.

The obvious focal point for the show was the George Shearing Quintet, one of the most popular acts in the entire world of jazz for roughly three decades, beginning in 1949. The host alternated at the keyboard with Renee Rosnes (an exceptional pianist who, in 2008, became Mrs. Charlap), with the remaining roles being filled by the vibraphonist Joe Locke, the guitarist Peter Bernstein, the bassist Sean Smith, and the drummer Kenny Washington, with guests Danny Sadownick on Latin percussion and the vocalist Freddy Cole.

In a letter read by Charlap at the beginning of the show, the man of the hour, writing from his home in the Berkshires (he has not played in public in about five years), expressed his gratitude to the Y for re-creating the signature sound of his long-running quintet. He also acknowledged the assistance of the late critic–producer–composer (and fellow Londoner) Leonard Feather in helping to create the "sound," which they crafted by taking the block chord approach popularized by the Nat King Cole Trio and expanding it with the same notes repeated not only in the right and left hands of the piano but also by doubling, tripling, and quadrupling those notes with the guitar, vibraphone, and bass. In the letter, Shearing also gave Charlap a piece of advice that was new to all of us: turn off the electricity on the vibraphone, he wrote, thus giving it a dry, xylophonic sound that better blends with the rest of the ensemble.

The result was a thrilling experience—to hear a sound you know intimately from thousands of classic recordings but never thought you would encounter live—at least not since Shearing retired the quartet 30 years ago.

The opener, closer, and centerpiece of the concert was Shearing's most essential jazz standard, "Lullaby of Birdland," which was performed three ways: in its original incarnation as a medium-bop number, then sung tenderly (with George David Weiss's well-known lyrics) as a genuine lullaby by Cole, and finally revved up to maximum speed as a fast mambo. In addition to one of the composer's prettier ballads, "Enchanted," which was written for an album with the guitarist Wes

Montgomery in 1961, the group spotlighted the works of Shearing's great sidemen with the bassist Al McKibbon's blues number "Simplicity" and the drummer Denzil Best's polyrhythmic tune "Nothing but D. Best."

In 1949, the 30-year-old Shearing was one of the first high-profile leaders to employ a female instrumentalist, Marjorie Hyams, the original vibraphonist with the quintet. At the Y, Rosnes was a fitting choice as a second pianist, drawing attention to the classical aspects of Shearing's work in two unaccompanied solos: a surprisingly slow, impressionistic "Happy Days Are Here Again" and Kurt Weill's "My Ship," which was refloated with wavelike washes of melody from Debussy's "Sunken Cathedral."

Rosnes then joined the re-formed quintet on two numbers intended to showcase Shearing's Latin side—"Stranger in Paradise" and "The Lamp Is Low," for which Daniel Sadownick provided a strong *clave* beat on congas. Coincidentally, these two tunes also spotlighted the composer's classical leanings since the former is taken from a Russian opera by Borodin and the latter from a French *pavanne* by Ravel. Rosnes also shone on a trio arrangement of "Conception." Prior to 1952, when Shearing introduced "Birdland," this Lennie Tristano–esque line had been his most famous original composition.

Cole, standing in for the many great singers who recorded with Shearing through the decades (including Teddi King, Peggy Lee, Nancy Wilson, Mel Torme, and Mr. Cole's late brother Nat, who recorded a classic album with Shearing in 1961), opened the second half of the show with "Once in a While." He followed with two key numbers by his brother Nat—the ballad "I'm Lost," a classic 1961 encounter with the Shearing Quintet, and the innovative Cole–Shearing legato–staccato treatment of "Pick Yourself Up." This was the part of the evening that flew by the fastest; if Messrs. Cole and Charlap ever decide to re-create that brilliant album in its entirety, I will be first in line.

Charlap spoke glowingly of Shearing's harmonic genius. He could have also elaborated about his rhythmic brilliance, particularly on the Latin numbers, his amazing sense of dynamics, and his sensitivity as a vocal accompanist (not to mention his infamous penchant for puns, which, as he once said, ever since he turned 70 has become "an old age penchant").

Wednesday's concert did justice to nearly every aspect of the Shearing oeuvre, though I was slightly disappointed that the producer omitted what is probably Shearing's biggest pop hit, "September in the Rain," as well as "Mambo Inn," which I've always regarded as the quintet's most dazzling Cuban showpiece. Other than that, the only notable omission was the presence of a few of those busty models in tight dresses who were always lounging invitingly on Shearing's Capitol Records album covers.

(*The New York Sun*, 2008)

DAVE BRUBECK (1920–2012)

For some time now, Dave Brubeck, who is appearing tonight at Avery Fisher Hall with his octet, has used the word "time" as his calling card. His most popular album—in fact, one of the most popular in the entirety of jazz—is the 1959 *Time Out.* That led to four similarly themed follow-ups, all with "Time" in the title, which have just been collected for the first time in a five-CD box, *For All Time* (Columbia Legacy 87161). When Legacy released a four-CD retrospective of Mr. Brubeck's career 10 years ago, they called it *Time Signatures.* And to this day, no jazz group can use the word without evoking Mr. Brubeck; the contemporary pianist Joe Gilman recently released a tribute album titled *Time Again: Brubeck Revisited.*

But Mr. Brubeck does more than pay lip service to the concept of time; it is the key concept in most of his well-known music. While traveling on a world tour in 1958, Mr. Brubeck became fascinated with the time signatures of the music he heard in the Middle East. He was also struck by the ease with which the virtuoso drummer Joe Morello, who had been playing with Mr. Brubeck's quartet since 1955, caught on to the rhythms they were encountering.

Mr. Brubeck observed, at the time, that except for the earliest New Orleans jazz, which was originally in 2/4, nearly all of jazz since about 1930 was played in 4/4 time. Enterprising composers, such as Benny Carter and Max Roach, had experimented with 3/4 waltz time, but there was little if any use of signatures beyond three or four. (He probably wasn't familiar with "Off the Beat," a very obscure piece by 1930s bandleader Hal Kemp, or of a few little-known works by Duke Ellington in 5/4.) He conceived of a set of original compositions (all but one his own) in unusual signatures.

The resulting album, *Time Out,* included two of the quartet's best-known works: Mr. Brubeck's 9/8 "Blue Rondo a la Turk," which combined Mozartean and Middle Eastern influences, and the melody Mr. Brubeck had challenged his partner, alto saxophonist Paul Desmond (who was not nearly as prolific a composer as the pianist), to devise in 5/4, "Take Five."

Time Out not only sold a million copies—almost as unusual then as it is now for an instrumental, straight-ahead jazz package—but a 45-rpm single of the two songs was also a jukebox hit. And the album has virtues beyond its two hit tracks. Both "Strange Meadowlark" and "Three to Get Ready" shift tempos intriguingly. The first is an ornithological outing that merges bird songs (in both the zoological and the Charlie Parker sense), and the second moves back and forth between three and four.

Well before *Time Out,* Brubeck had established himself as one of jazz's preeminent pianist–composer–bandleaders. Two of his songs, "In Your Own Sweet Way" and "The Duke," had been recorded by Miles Davis, who played the first with both Coltrane and Sonny Rollins and the second with Gil Evans. "Sweet Way," more than any other of Mr. Brubeck's "Time" pieces, was perhaps his most popular composition with jazz musicians—its easy, graceful melody has been played by thousands, including Wes Montgomery, Stan Getz, and Bill Evans.

Dave Brubeck; Newport Jazz Festival; Fort Adams State Park; August 15, 1998

Likewise, the combination of Mr. Brubeck's piano and Desmond's alto was already established as among the most notable in American music. Mr. Brubeck's playing was influenced by European formal music, with overtones of both 19th- and 20th-century classicists. Mr. Desmond's tone was similar to such contemporaries as Lee Konitz and Art Pepper but if anything, even more light and lucid. Desmond's playing has been compared to "dry martinis," but anyone who could make such a statement is even more alcoholically illiterate than I; a Manhattan, maybe.

It's perhaps wrong to describe the other four "Time" albums as mere sequels to the first; they are further explorations of the worlds of rhythm that exist beyond three and four and never seem secondary to the original. *Time Further Out*, from 1961, contains the deceptively titled "It's a Raggy Waltz," which blends two and three in a way that you can still pat your foot to; on the Columbia Legacy CD, it can be heard both in the original studio treatment and a considerably looser live reading from Carnegie Hall two years later.

In 1962, the quartet released *Countdown: Time in Outer Space*, whose title track opens with a bombastic fanfare played by Mr. Morello on timpani and swingingly alternates between heavy classical passages and eight-to-the-bar boogie-woogie. *Time Changes*, from 1964, is highlighted by "Elementals," Mr. Brubeck's ambitious, 17-minute work in which a full symphony orchestra is employed as both a backdrop for the quartet and an extension of it. The last in the series, 1965's *Time In*, showcases yet more compositions in more unexpected meters (such as "Watusi Drums" in 6/4). The real kick of *Time In* is listening to the unison that the four men, including

Eugene Wright on bass, had achieved in the 15 years since Desmond and Mr. Brubeck began playing together in a quartet.

There are groups that come together for a relatively brief moment and leave their mark on the music immediately—for instance, the collaborations of Miles Davis and John Coltrane, or Gerry Mulligan and Chet Baker. And then there are others, such as those of John Lewis and Milt Jackson, or Dave Brubeck and Paul Desmond. The latter two first collaborated in college in the late 1940s and went on to create astonishing recordings for more than 30 years, continually upending the music until Desmond's death in 1997.

Had the two stayed together only as long as, say, Louis Armstrong and Earl Hines, they never would have produced their most celebrated innovations. As it is, it's a testament to their achievement that they could make Turkish- and Watusi-inspired originals sound just as much a part of jazz as the blues and standards. Dave Brubeck and Paul Desmond were one of the greatest collaborations in all of jazz, in their own sweet way.

(*The New York Sun*, 2004)

***

Dave Brubeck and his current quartet climaxed the 2005 JVC jazz festival with a concert at Carnegie Hall that still resounds in my memory. Where many jazz groups, including, alas, that of Ornette Coleman, were consistently defeated by the dodgy acoustics of Carnegie—don't get me started—the venue was a perfect spot for Mr. Brubeck's group, which has enough stage presence and musical acumen to more than fill the space.

Mr. Brubeck's final quartet was one of his best, thriving on the interplay between the leader and his star alto saxophonist, Bobby Militello, who enjoyed a rapport that never ceased to thrill audiences, especially when it encompassed bassist Michael Moore and drummer Randy Jones.

Militello is an enormous bear of a man, and in his hands, the diminutive alto looks like a toy instrument. And perhaps that was a key element in the group's music as well. Brubeck and Militello created an amazing contrast; the saxophonist was consistently soulful, playful, and highly expressive, whereas the pianist–leader was always heavier and more classically driven but no less swinging.

The opener, "Gone with the Wind" recalled the earlier days of the Brubeck Quartet, when the emphasis was on mostly swinging, boppish treatments of standards—way before they started monkeying around with all those nutso time signatures. Their second piece, an excerpt from Mr. Brubeck's brother Howard's *Dialogues for Jazz Combo and Orchestra*, was a reminder of the Brubeck family's classical proclivities: Mr. Brubeck introduced this work at Carnegie with Leonard Bernstein and the New York Philharmonic in 1960.

Most of the set consisted of blues and bop numbers, including the title track of his new album *London Flat, London Sharp* (Telarc 83625), which showcased Mr. Militello's effusive playing. The group wound up with its biggest hit, Paul Desmond's "Take Five," but for me, the climax was "Sleep," a 1923 standard employed equally by vaudevillians and swing bands—a catchy, zippy, and anything but sleepy melody well suited to tap dancers. Mr. Militello, Mr. Brubeck, Mr. Jones, and Mr. Moore couldn't have been more entertaining or compelling if they had started turning cartwheels.

(*The New York Sun*, 2005)

AHMAD JAMAL (1930–2023)

If you think of a jazz performance as a meal, it makes you wonder why most musicians serve dessert before the entrée. Considering that most listeners relish hearing the melody perhaps more than any other part of a particular song, why does the tune so often rush by at the very beginning, like an afterthought—or more precisely, a before thought?

The pianist Ahmad Jamal, who is appearing this week at the Blue Note and whose new album, "It's Magic" (Dreyfus), will be released next month, has some interesting answers. If the melody is the dessert, then he chooses not to serve it in a distinctly defined course but rather in small, tempting bites throughout the meal. Here's some steak for you, then some green beans, and wait, just a taste of ice cream.

That's the way Mr. Jamal, a 77-year-old Pittsburgh native, played "Wild Is the Wind" at the late show on Tuesday night (as on the new album). First, he begins with polyrhythmic background—part rhumba, part calypso—reinforced by the percussionist Manolo Badrena, who is armed with a Pan-American African percussion kit that I'm glad I don't have to get through customs. Mr. Jamal plays a bit of piano improvisation, then lays a little taste of the tune on us, then a brief bit of Idris Muhammad's drums, then more melody, then some bass from James Cammack, and so on. As they play, the leader stands up and turns away from his piano as if to project his star power onto his colleagues for their moments in the spotlight.

When he plays a standard, Mr. Jamal is brilliant at the old trick of delaying recognition of the melody, a simple enough move to heighten the drama. Before we're certain that we're hearing "Wild Is the Wind," he takes a side trip through the "Sesame Street" theme song, rendering it in a way that would scare the feathers off of Big Bird. He goes to an even further extreme with "The Way You Look Tonight," not allowing us to explicitly hear the melody until the coda—thus, dishing out the dessert at the end of the dinner, where it belongs.

Mr. Jamal is such a crowd-pleaser—the critic Martin Williams once famously accused him of "playing the audience" rather than the piano—that it's hard to imagine he spent the early part of his career known only to other musicians. Although

Jamal Ahmad, Iridium, 1998

he recorded as early as 1951 (tracks now available on *The Legendary OKEH & Epic Sessions*), his ideas were widely disseminated by Miles Davis long before Mr. Jamal was well known outside of Chicago. Born Frederick Jones in 1930, Mr. Jamal was one of a legion of heavyweight jazz pianists to rise out of Pittsburgh. He assumed the name Ahmad Jamal (which means "highly praised beauty" in Arabic) as part of his conversion to Islam at the age of 20.

Mr. Jamal's ideas regarding the use of melody—his contrast between a simple, clearly delineated tune and complex, modern jazz chords, as well as between sound and silence, rhythm, and even repertoire—were the major influence on Davis's classic quintet with John Coltrane in the late 1950s. The trumpeter not only employed Mr. Jamal's concepts but borrowed arrangements outright; "I Don't Want to Be Kissed" and the pianist's original "New Rhumba," from Mr. Jamal's *Chamber Music of the New Jazz*, were essentially transcribed into big-band format for *Miles Ahead* (1955).

Yet ironically, by the time Mr. Jamal finally landed his breakthrough hit, "Poinciana," in 1958, Davis was already on his way to something new, something cool, and something kind of blue. Coltrane also first heard "Pavanne" on one of Mr. Jamal's albums, which inspired him to transmute that Morton Gould tune into his own classic composition, "Impressions."

But 50 years later, Mr. Jamal no longer sounds like he did on his recordings of that era; rather, he is a much more assertive player today. His dynamics, much like Count Basie's, are wondrous to behold, making his Steinway live up to its full formal name, a pianoforte. He shows it's possible to swing and bop with considerable energy without drowning the listener in a torrent of notes; his ballads, mostly rendered only with Mr. Cammack, are models of economy, particularly Arthur Schwartz's "Then I'll Be Tired of You." Mr. Jamal establishes a serene mood, then disrupts his own tranquility with big, *fortissimo* distortions.

At the Blue Note, most of the faster numbers utilized island-centric beats, whereas most of the slower tunes were classic ballads. Some of Mr. Jamal's own tunes, such as the clave-driven "Fitnah," which closed the late set on Tuesday (as well as the album), are pure rhythm and special effects without much of a tune, but he can also write a gorgeous melody. "Whisperings" is lightly reminiscent of Jimmy Rowles's "The Peacocks" (and opens with a quote from "Lucky to Be Me") but is a strong original melody that was heard with a worthy lyric on the 2003 album *In Search Of.* If he hadn't introduced it as an original, one might have mistaken it for a work by one of the Old Masters.

Mr. Jamal is such a vital and contemporary player that even at 77, he seems to have come after, rather than before, nearly everyone playing the piano today.

(*The New York Sun*, 2008)

***

Can this really be the fifth season of Jazz at Lincoln Center at Rose Hall? Already there are young people filling seats at the Rose Theater who probably feel that JaLC has been around forever, and even take it for granted. They'd likely be amazed to learn that listeners in the 1940s thought it was a big deal whenever jazz made it to one of the major concert halls, such as Carnegie or Town Hall, and probably couldn't imagine a world in which American music was accorded the same respect as symphonies and chamber works. (It had, after all, only been a generation or so since ragtime was condemned by the pope and jazz itself was officially disowned by the city of New Orleans, where it had been created.) So if young fans want to act as though Rose Hall—the only jazz-specific multiplex in the country, if not the world—is no big deal, then that's a good thing, an illustration of how far we've come.

Last year, JaLC kicked off the fourth season at Rose with two of the best shows in its 20-year history in programs devoted to Benny Carter and Gil Evans. This year, it began equally auspiciously with a program on Thursday night built around the iconic pianist Ahmad Jamal. On paper, the idea looked dauntingly complicated: getting Mr. Jamal's famous trio to interact with the full Jazz at Lincoln Center Orchestra, led by artistic director Wynton Marsalis, would not be not an easy undertaking. Then again, there is a whole repertoire of modern jazz concertos (and concerto grossos) out there, from Sonny Rollins's 1958 "Big Brass," with charts by Ernie Wilkins, to George Russell's "Living Time" (1972) for Bill Evans.

In performance, the presentation turned out to be refreshingly simple. Mr. Jamal and his ensemble—a quartet, actually, with James Cammack on bass, James Johnson on drums, and Manolo Badrena on Latin percussion—held the stage for the first half of the evening, playing a condensed version of the sets they play in jazz clubs all over the world, beginning with his customary opener "Wild Is the Wind" and building to his signature hit, "Poinciana." Mr. Jamal is more of an interpreter than a composer: few of his own originals have caught on with other performers, but his touch at the piano and the sound of his augmented trio are so distinctive that he can make any melody sound like his own.

"Poinciana" is the archetype of the Jamal orchestration (which is not to say that his treatments of other songs follow it like a formula). He essentially downplays the original Brazilian melody and emphasizes a complex foundation of interlocking polyrhythms and an original, undulating vamp, which would make the song sound exotic even if it weren't South American. Mr. Jamal gives the actual melody of "Poinciana" less screen time than "I'm Glad There Is You," another 1940s pop standard that the pianist quotes throughout "Poinciana." Not only does the vamp get more attention, but Mr. Jamal stresses it so much that it eventually goes into business for itself and becomes the arrangement's central melody, rendering the "Poinciana" tune a fading counterpoint to itself.

Fifty years ago, when "Poinciana" was first heard on a live album recorded in Chicago's Pershing Room, it catapulted Mr. Jamal to the top of a food chain already rich with powerhouse pianists showcasing sheer chops (Oscar Peterson), sheer swing (Erroll Garner), and sheer style (George Shearing). Mr. Jamal was offering a thick yet translucent approach in which levels upon levels of melody and countermelody ran in and out of one another on top of multiple levels of rhythm, transforming the familiar into the exotic and vice versa.

Elsewhere in the first set on Thursday, Mr. Jamal played a melancholy original, "Papillon," which reflected his Francophile tendencies. (For the last decade or so, he's recorded for the French label Dreyfus Records.) "Melodrama," by friend Jimmy Heath, began with Havanese block chords and featured passages in which Mr. Jamal played on top of the rhythm section, rather like a horn soloist, and others in which he was completely integrated into it.

The second half of the performance consisted of three Jamal originals, arranged to include both his quartet and the 13 horns of the JaLC Orchestra. The orchestrations, by Byron Rooker and Trevor Kuprel, achieved the difficult task of integrating the big band into the quartet on Mr. Jamal's terms. After the first half of the show, when four men became a full orchestra, the second half saw an orchestra sublimate itself into a quartet. The first piece, "The Aftermath," set the pattern: Most big-band numbers begin with the full ensemble before breaking into individual solos. These Jamal works began with one of the pianist's characteristic introductions, which led into the trio playing the central melody or "head." The big band then stated its version of the melody in full force, which in turn introduced the individual horn soloists from the band. Finally, Mr. Jamal neatly concluded the works himself.

The meeting of the quartet and the horns seemed entirely natural and unforced, and the orchestra seemed like a direct, organic extension of the leader's piano, much the same way that the big bands of Duke Ellington and Count Basie seemed like extensions of their leaders' piano styles. The four trumpets, four trombones, and five saxophones introduced a world of new musical colors into a style that was already far from monochromatic.

The second orchestral piece, "Should I," had no connection to the standard of that title but was nonetheless a reference to vintage song styles: Set in 3/4 time, it combined the feel of a premodern jazz waltz, such as Fats Waller's "The Jitterbug Waltz," with a postmodern waltz, such as Miles Davis's "All Blues" (and reminded us that there are virtually no bebop-era waltzes). The final announced piece, "The Devil's in My Den," was a funk number dedicated to the late Stanley Turrentine (who recorded this song with Mr. Jamal in 1997) in which the horns swirled around Mr. Jamal like raging winds in a hurricane.

Commendably, the soloists, starting with Mr. Marsalis on "The Aftermath," absorbed Mr. Jamal's approach into their playing; the most notable part of alto saxophonist Sherman Irby's improvisation was his repetition of a simple phrase, varying only the most minute nuances of it, like a saxophonic equivalent of one of Mr. Jamal's piano vamps. The trumpeter Sean Jones played a Harmon-muted solo in which the motive seemed to be to leave as much space between the notes as possible, which again mirrored what Mr. Jamal would have played on his piano.

After a standing ovation from the sold-out opening-night crowd on Thursday, the quartet left the stage and returned to play the bouncy "You Can See," by the Jamaican pianist Monty Alexander, who was also in the house.

Although Mr. Jamal has not yet recorded these works, he and his quartet have performed them with the Chicago Jazz Orchestra and the Columbus (Ohio) Jazz Society Orchestra. The existence of a circuit of JaLC-like jazz orchestras around the world may be the best news of all. Younger jazz fans may take such things for granted, but I can't.

(*The New York Sun*, 2008)

***

My late friend and mentor, the *Journal*'s own Nat Hentoff, once made the mistake of dismissing Ahmad Jamal—and in the middle of an interview with Miles Davis no less—as "mainly a cocktail pianist." Davis immediately took umbrage, responding, "that's the way to play piano." On other occasions, Davis trumpeted his enthusiasm even more emphatically. "Ahmad is one of my favorites," he told Hentoff in a different interview. "I live until he makes another record. I gave Gil [Evans] a couple of his albums and he didn't give them back." Fans and critics were taken aback; here was a musician often written off as a lightweight at best, now being praised by the most highly regarded—not to mention the most serious—figure in all of jazz. For some, it was a distinct echo of when Louis Armstrong had spoken of his own love for Guy Lombardo a few decades earlier.

What Davis—and since then, several generations of jazz players and listeners—loved most about Mr. Jamal becomes crystal clear in two new sets of live recordings from a Seattle nightclub being released on the Jazz Detective label. *Emerald City Nights: Live at the Penthouse 1963-1964* and *Emerald City Nights: Live at the Penthouse 1965-1966* have both been produced by Zev Feldman.

Mr. Jamal, who is currently 92 and has described himself as retired, is often regarded as a musical minimalist. He has been praised for his silences as much as his notes, for what he doesn't play as much as what he does. But what these brilliantly recorded performances reveal here both supports and challenges that received wisdom.

Both packages open with Rodgers and Hart songs, "Johnny One Note" on the first and "I Didn't Know What Time It Was" on the second. The 1963 material starts with a very funky riff, which will soon reemerge as a countermelody and sounds like it's going to lead into the blues rather than a show tune. Mr. Jamal delineates the Rodgers melody with fanciful bursts of notes, placing staccato spaces between them; the harmonies themselves sound almost classical, but the rhythm is pure jazz. After stating the melody, there's a dramatic passage with big thunderous chords but still essentially in the same rhythmic pattern.

His subsequent choruses fly off in all manner of unexpected directions. There's a series of long runs where he seems determined to challenge the ability of listeners to breathe along with him. In another, he plays cat and mouse with drummer Chuck Lampkin in a set of improvised riffs that suggest an Afro-Cuban clave beat. Lampkin plays an extended solo in the center—unusual for an opening tune—yet it sounds more like a vaudeville turn or a dance break rather than like a drummer merely showboating.

Mr. Jamal ends the 10-minute track with a reprise of the melody as he played it at the start, although now the counter-riffs are even more insistent. There's a bass solo near the coda, then Mr. Jamal reenters hesitatingly as if teasing us with a note of piano here and there. This is supposed to be minimalist? There's so much going on here that this is probably the last term that would come to mind when trying to describe it.

The next tune, "Minor Adjustments," starts out rather baroque, but it quickly gets very bluesy. He keeps that duality going throughout the piece, playing a Bach-like phrase and then following it with something more earthy, and the track ends with a grandiose but swinging fanfare. Elsewhere, he spins 13 minutes' worth of variations out of another minor blues, this one titled "Minor Moods."

Mr. Jamal's capacity for endless invention comes through even more distinctly on the standard tunes, such as "All of You" and "Tangerine" and even the 1962 pop hit "Lollipops and Roses." The last is heard first slow and then faster, and Mr. Jamal plays both choruses in a fashion that's stylized but hardly distorted. As Cannonball Adderley described it, "Ahmad allows the tune to be the tune."

You can tell that these renditions are the product of the same mind that created his classic 1958 treatment of "Poinciana," which is heard here in a 1966 set. But Mr.

Jamal never repeats himself or even reuses any of the same devices. Which in itself is amazing. Over the past 65 years, musicians of every stripe have plundered that arrangement—the slow and steady, deliberate timing; the open spaces between the notes; the insistent percussion; the telltale use of mallets and polyrhythms; and the surprising detour through "I'm Glad There Is You." I could swear I've even heard entire sets at Birdland of young bands playing variations on "Poinciana" on one song after another. The only musician, in fact, who hasn't cannibalized "Poinciana" is Ahmad Jamal himself.

Note: A few months after this story ran in the *Journal*, Ahmad Jamal died at the age of 92 in April 2023, but not before the release of a third double-CD volume in the Jazz Detective series, *Emerald City Nights: Live at the Penthouse (1966–1968).*

(*The Wall Street Journal*, 2022)

BEYOND COMPARE

HANK JONES (1918–2010)

Hank Jones disputed this story, which was told to me in the early 1990s by the late Joe Williams, but I'm going to tell it anyway. In the early 1940s, Joe was playing through Cleveland when he stopped in at a club on Cedar Avenue and heard the most amazing piano player. It wasn't Art Tatum, and it wasn't Fats Waller; it was a sound completely new, coming from a young man the same age as Joe (both were born in 1918) named Henry Jones. Williams immediately made him an offer: "I said come to work with me, and I will split everything we get 50-50." Mr. Jones, Williams said, declined. "Hank and I laugh about that sometimes," said Williams. "He says that was still the best deal he was ever offered."

When I asked Mr. Jones about this incident, he would only admit that he did indeed meet Joe Williams in Cleveland at that time, but he stressed strongly that the singer would not have made him such an offer at that early stage of the game. "I wasn't ready to play professionally," he says. "That's ahead of my time! I was just doing a few little jobs here and there, but probably just still running scales and exercises—Joe must have been confusing me with somebody else." Yet Joe was sure it was Hank because he remembered seeing the pianist just a few years later. In a relatively short time, Jones had made the transition from obscurity to working with jazz royalty as the pianist with Ella Fitzgerald and the Jazz at the Philharmonic troop, and Joe remembered that this was the same piano player he'd seen just a few years earlier in Cleveland.

Which shows that Hank Jones—who is playing this year at the Lionel Hampton Jazz Festival—was already achieving legendary status even before he left his hometown. Jones was practically predestined to become one of the greatest pianists in the history of jazz, and today, he accepts his role as the elder statesman of jazz piano with dignity and swing. He is also the scion of one of the most prominent families in the history of jazz, his younger brothers (both now deceased) being cornetist and composer Thad Jones (best known for his work with Count Basie and the great Thad Jones–Mel Lewis Orchestra) and drummer Elvin Jones (one of the most powerful percussionists in jazz from his time with the classic John Coltrane Quartet onward).

Mr. Jones, like Joe Williams, his close friend the saxophonist Lucky Thompson, and many other musicians, was born in the rural Deep South (Vicksburg, MS) but grew up in the urban North, in Pontiac, Michigan, about 25 miles north of Detroit.

> In 1944, I was playing with Lucky Thompson in a territory band in Lansing, Michigan, led by a drummer Benny Carew, and doing a few little jobs here and there. Lucky went to New York a couple of years before me. One of the first bands he got a job with was Hot Lips Page, and he told Lips about me. Lips told me that I should look him up if I ever got to New York.
>
> Of course, New York was the center of everything. All musicians eventually want to come here. I came East in stages. First I went to Cleveland, where I worked in a band at a club called The Cedar Gardens for maybe six months or so. After that I came to Buffalo and worked in a little club called The Anchor Bar, with a trio that consisted of tenor sax and bass and piano, for maybe 6 or 8 months. I finally arrived in New York early in 1944. Soon after, I got a call from Lips, his piano player had left and he wanted to hear me. That was my first important band.

Within a short time, he had toured and recorded with Andy Kirk (his only major job with a traditional touring swing band), Coleman Hawkins, and John Kirby (on New York's famed Swing Street). He believes it was Hawkins who referred him to Norman Granz. In 1947, the impresario called him to work with Ella Fitzgerald, with whom he stayed for about four years, and the JATP organization. Jones was Granz's pianist in the early years (Oscar Peterson succeeded him) and under his aegis, performed and recorded with Fitzgerald, Charlie Parker, Lester Young, Coleman Hawkins, Gene Krupa, Flip Phillips, and virtually everyone else on the producer's early sessions.

In the 1950s, however, Jones spent less time on the road and more in the broadcast and recording studios. "CBS was the first to hire Afro-American musicians," he says. "A few years before me, CBS had hired Teddy Wilson and Ben Webster. But they all had left because they felt that they couldn't make any money, they couldn't make a living doing it, the studio scale was rather low at that time when they started, they felt they could make more money outside the studio. I was in the second wave." Mr. Jones became one of the most employed of all studio players, jazz or otherwise, on the same level as, say, Dick Hyman or Milt Hinton.

Yet he remained in the top rank of jazz players. Like Bill Clinton and Tony Blair, Jones is essentially a centrist—he was born in Mississippi but raised in the middle of the USA, in Michigan, and likewise came of age in the halfway point of the history of jazz, in the midst of the transition from swing to bebop. He explains, "[W]hen I first came to NY I wasn't playing anything like that, I was playing in the two-handed stride style, of Teddy Wilson, Fats Waller, that kind of thing. But when I heard the bop style, I was immediately attracted to it."

A year younger than bop pioneer Dizzy Gillespie—with whom he first recorded on a breakthrough modern session under Ray Brown's name in 1946—Jones was perfectly situated to distill all the prevailing elements of mid-century jazz, from East and West, premodern and modern. "I was attracted by the modern style, and I thought I would incorporate that style into my playing. But I never thought that I would abandon what I was doing before but incorporate the new style in, gradually. At that point in time, that was the only thing I could do, was to use the best of both worlds. So I played stride with my left hand, and tried to use the bop style with my right hand. George Shearing did the same thing when he came to NYC."

Two of his best albums, in fact, *Bop Redux* with trio, and *Groovin' High*, with a quintet featuring his brother Thad (two Muse albums reissued on the twofer CD *Master Class on 32 Jazz*), focus on 1940s compositions by Gillespie, Charlie Parker, and Thelonious Monk. Yet besides all his work with the modernists, he was also the pianist of choice for both Artie Shaw and Benny Goodman for many years.

Mr. Jones was most prolific in his 60s—from the mid-1970s to the mid-1980s, he turned out a steady stream of trio albums, more than at any other point in his career. One of the very best of these has just been reissued, *The Trio* (Chiaroscuro 188), which teams him with fellow studio veterans Milt Hinton, bass, and Bobby Rosengarden, drums. My ears were most agreeably detained by two numbers in unusual time signatures, Mr. Jones's unaccompanied solo on "Oh, What a Beautiful Morning" in 3/4 and "Queen of Hearts," a catchy original, somewhat similar to "That Old Black Magic," only in 5/4. It's a shame that this is the only time this particular trio ever recorded.

Hank Jones turned 85 in July 2003, an event that was celebrated with an all-star piano spectacular last night at The Blue Note—keyboardists on the bill included Oscar Peterson, Monty Alexander, Kenny Barron, Barry Harris, Eric Reed, Harold Mabern, Cedar Walton, McCoy Tyner, Marian McPartland, and James Williams—prominent nonpianists included Clark Terry, Abbey Lincoln, and Elvin Jones, among many others.

In the 1980s, Mr. Jones has collaborated with contemporary musicians, such as Joe Lovano and Charlie Haden, both of whom in working with him, declare their solidarity with the jazz tradition. "I first met Joe there at Idaho, but we hadn't worked together again until recently (on two albums for Blue Note and subsequent tours) and I have always known he's a great player," he says. In the near future, Mr. Jones has plans to continue recording for Justin Time, a Canadian label for which he has just made *For My Father*, with bassist George Mraz and drummer Dennis Mackrel. He has more concerts, festivals, and clinics lined up for many months to come. "I prefer to work in these formats, I rarely do night clubs these days," he explains. "You go out on the road for two or three weeks, come back and rest up, then do it again!" He has no plans to stop. It's a fitting state of senior citizenship for a man who has served for over 60 years as the house pianist for the whole of jazz.

(*The New York Sun*, 2003)

***

In her landmark play *for colored girls . . .*, the poet Ntozake Shange talked about "the craze that comes from too much choice." Sometimes in art, having too many options can be overwhelming, and it's often better to be as specific as possible.

That would appear to be the guiding philosophy in the music of saxophonist Joe Lovano and pianist Hank Jones, who are performing as a duo this week at Dizzy's Club Coca-Cola. Both of these master musicians have more than enough technique to play anything that they can think of: Mr. Jones has been a first-call professional since even before the start of the modern jazz era and has kept up with every change that has occurred since, and Mr. Lovano is the archetype of the contemporary jazzman who can work in virtually any style.

Yet narrowing the range of options sometimes produces a more substantial result: Mr. Lovano and Mr. Jones work within the classic jazz mold of written theme and improvised variations and stay more or less within the musical vocabulary of the late swing era. The playing of both men is driven by melody, and even when they go off on a harmonic tangent, the lines that they improvise are essentially melodic. They don't play anything that a casual listener would have a hard time following, with nothing that can be described as abstract and no free-form playing. Further, there's no grandstanding or cheap shots for attention or applause—everything each of them plays is directly relevant to what the other is playing. Further, the limited range of the two-man ensemble, which does not contain the expected bass and drums, somehow expands their possibilities rather than limiting them.

Mr. Lovano and Mr. Jones have spent much of the last three years in each other's company, having done two quartet albums together, *I'm All for You* (2004) and *Joyous Encounter* (2005). They have just returned from a tour of Europe as a twosome, and the Dizzy's gig is going to be recorded by Blue Note Records for release as the first Lovano–Jones duo album.

The saxophonist and the pianist first began working together earlier in the millennium at the Lionel Hampton Jazz Festival in Moscow, Idaho, but they have been connected to each other for at least 20 years, when the young Mr. Lovano joined the orchestra cofounded by Mr. Jones's brother, the late composer and trumpeter Thad Jones. Appropriately, most of the music played on the opening set on Wednesday night was by both Thad and Hank Jones. Many of these tunes were recorded by the pianist in the two outstanding tribute albums he has made for his younger sibling, the trio set *Upon Reflection* (1993) and the all-star octet album *One More: Music of Thad Jones* (2005), both on IPO Recordings.

At the same time, the music of the Lovano–Jones duet is highly grounded in the American songbook: even the originals by both men, and those of Thad Jones, are marked by singable melodies and have the feeling of popular standards. The opener, "Lady Luck," is a strong tune, at first reminiscent of "You Took Advantage of Me," while "Little Rascal on a Rock" boasts an attractive line that Mr. Jones gingerly delineates with something like the poststride approach I associate with Teddy

Wilson. Tadd Dameron's "Soultrane," for which the saxist switched to soprano, is best remembered from the composer's album *Mating Call* with John Coltrane, but Mr. Jones and Mr. Lovano gave it the sultry, melancholy feeling of an Ellington lament: if there were a lyric, it would say "you've left me, but I'll get along somehow."

Mr. Jones played two "Oh!" songs as solo features, "Oh, What a Beautiful Morning," the Richard Rodgers waltz, and "Oh! Look at Me Now." The latter was composed by the late pianist Joe Bushkin, who like Mr. Jones, continued to perform into his 80s; however, when Bushkin was still playing a few years ago, most of us were impressed that he could even do it at all, even though he was only a shadow of his former self. It's a reminder of how extraordinary Mr. Jones is: he turns 88 in July and his playing is at an all-time career pinnacle. There are precious few examples of performing artists in any genre who have achieved such a level of greatness at this point in their lives.

Mr. Jones then started what appeared to be a third solo feature, "Alone Together," but after the first chorus, was joined by his partner. Joe Lovano likes to use the term "organic" to describe music makers he admires and the goals he sets for himself. There are contemporaries of his—Michael Brecker comes to mind—who's playing invariably makes us focus on their awe-inspiring technique. Mr. Lovano has just as much chops as any of them, but when he plays, we don't think about his tools (which is, after all, what technique is) but about what he's communicating to us. His playing is always more about soul and feeling and ideas rather than drawing attention to the means by which they are transmitted. The medium is not the message.

The duo wound up the 75-minute set with two more standards, Victor Young's "Stella by Starlight," with Mr. Lovano stretching out the tune and providing an original coda, and Thelonious Monk's "Four in One," which the saxist opened with a solo cadenza. Though both men are capable of extreme virtuosity, this is some of the simplest and most effective music that either has ever created. It's not about knowing how to play but rather, to borrow a phrase from Abbey Lincoln, learning how to listen.

(*The New York Sun*, 2006)

***

In playing a horn, 90 percent of the work is done by the lips and the mouth. One can learn the basic fingering of the saxophone, in particular, in a couple of lessons, but mastering the breath control and embouchure to produce the right notes takes a lifetime of practicing. Sigurd Rascher, the great classical saxophonist and teacher, even demonstrated that all the notes could be played with just the mouth alone on a special instrument that had no valves or keys.

When we talk about the great saxophonists, we normally talk about their distinctive *tone*, but when we talk about the leading pianists, we talk about *touch*. Since there's no breath involved, every pianist could theoretically sound like every other pianist. The way Ben Webster plays E-flat sounds immediately different from the way Stan Getz played it, but a single note from Erroll Garner isn't necessarily different from the same note, in and of itself, as played by Hank Jones. It's the way in which they organize the individual notes, the context they place them in, and what they do with groups of notes that make all of the great keyboardists unique.

I know of no better way to demonstrate the concepts of "touch" and "tone," both in and of themselves and how they interact with each other, than in the remarkable music made by pianist Hank Jones and tenor saxophonist Joe Lovano. The two have a new album, their third overall but their first set of duets, *Kids: Duets Live at Dizzy's Club Coca-Cola* (Blue Note), and to mark the occasion, this week, Mr. Jones and Mr. Lovano are appearing together and separately at the same club where the CD was recorded a year ago.

Go and ask 9 out of 10 jazz buffs to name the greatest living pianist; if they don't say Hank Jones, then that immediately disqualifies them as experts. Mr. Jones, who turns 89 this July, has enjoyed a career that spans practically the entire history of the music: he was already playing (though not very well, he insists) at the start of the swing era in the mid-1930s and by the time of the birth of modern jazz a decade later, was well established as a veteran master. There is virtually no major musician he hasn't worked with on some level, no area of the music that he has not explored, no part of the jazz experience that he hasn't lived firsthand. More than practically anyone else in the history of jazz, Hank Jones has done most of his best work in the latter part of his career, the 1960s, 1970s, and 1980s. The appearances at Dizzy's mark an extra-special event in that they are his first performances since undergoing triple bypass surgery several months ago.

"Pauletta," the opener to *For My Father* (Justin Time) is a brilliant sample of Mr. Jones's amazingly lucid, sparkling touch. This is one of several Hank Jones albums recorded earlier in the decade but released last year, another being *Hank & Frank* (Lineage Records), a pairing with the marvelous tenor player Frank Wess. Mr. Jones is well known as the first-born and only surviving member of the most celebrated family in jazz, which included his younger brothers Thad (cornetist and composer) and Elvin (drummer), bandleaders all. The trio album *For My Father* is a project steeped in family, not only the actual father of the three Jones brothers, but fathers in a religious sense, as in the reverential "For the Grace of God," and in terms of musical inspiration, as in the works of Duke Ellington, Billy Strayhorn, and Thelonious Monk. In fact, it's playing works by these three major pianist–composers that Mr. Jones is more his own man than ever. His rendition of Monk's "Bemsha Swing" could never be confused with the composer's; he doesn't go near Monk's famously spooky silences and employs much more of a Pan-American rhythm, suggesting that the word "Bemsha" might even refer to a village south of the border somewhere.

Compared to the pairing with Mr. Lovano, *Hank & Frank* is a more predictable combination of touch and tone. This 2003 session teams Mr. Jones with one of the few great horn players of his approximate generation (3-1/2 years younger) who is still performing at his peak, and it also uses a full rhythm section rather than the more demanding duet format. Yet nothing about the music itself is remotely rote or formulaic. There are a number of well-stocked standards, including a Latinate treatment of "Autumn Serenade," a simmering "All or Nothing at All," and a reading of "The Very Thought of You" that seems to be taking the pianist back to the piano styles of his youth in the mid-1930s; when Mr. Wess steps in on flute, the track takes on a decidedly more modern feel. The two NEA Jazz Masters also utilize the opportunity to show what they can do with the blues, both on Mr. Wess's unusually structured original, "You Made a Good Move," and Charlie Parker's more exotic "Barbados."

The new album by Jones and Lovano, *Kids*, is also a perfect illustration of the interaction of touch and tone. I caught several of the sets at Dizzy's last April when the album was taped, but unfortunately, I missed the standout track of the set, "Lazy Afternoon." Yet I can well imagine that the crowd and the waitstaff were obviously as quiet as John LaTouche's lyric describes: "If you hold my hand and sit real still / You can hear the grass as it grows."

Playing soprano saxophone, rather than his customary tenor, Mr. Lovano sings the melody with an even more vocalized intonation than usual; he colors every pitch with the force and feeling of a great singer, and there's nary a note that you could confuse with that played by anyone else. In his solo spot, Mr. Jones runs light embellishments around the tune, dazzling the listener but never breaking the lazy mood. His touch at the keyboard is as perfect as piano playing can be. The tune, the only remembered remnant of the 1954 flop show *The Golden Apple*, is meant to convey a sultry, languid mood; nature abhors a vacuum, and when nothing else is happening, there's a window of opportunity for amorous activity. Mr. Lovano's first chorus is relaxed, though hardly lethargic, but obviously, thoroughly jazzed by Mr. Jones's statement; he conveys even more restrained passion and depth of feeling on his out chorus: erotic but somehow mournful, not only enjoying the moment, but in a sense, looking back on it from some future time. Mr. Jones's keyboard work is perhaps even more perfect underneath Mr. Lovano's playing, and the two transform the song into a romantic reflection on lazy afternoons past and present. Although as musician, Hank Jones has been anything but lazy, I would hope that he's enjoyed many lazy afternoons in his 89 years—so far—with us. May God bless him and grant him many more.

(*The New York Sun*, 2007)

BARRY HARRIS (1929–2021)

You can say what you like about the Village Vanguard, but its air-conditioning system works very well. One hot summer evening, as I descended from the sauna-like atmosphere of Seventh Avenue into what was now, on several levels, the coolest room in town, I was overwhelmed by a sense of giddy euphoria. Everyone in the room was feeling it too, particularly pianist Barry Harris.

What followed was one of the loosest—and most entertaining—sets of piano that I have heard in a long time. (And as readers of this column know, I have been hearing a lot of piano this month.) Mr. Harris is, along with Kenny Barron and fellow Detroiter Hank Jones, one of the great living exponents of bebop piano. I hadn't heard a whole evening with his trio in a while, however, and forgot how funny he can be.

The first time I had heard an entire evening by Harris and his trio had been about 1987 when my father and I caught him at his own venue, the Jazz Cultural Theater. I'll never forget that night for two reasons: it was a stunning set consisting entirely of tunes by Thelonious Monk and Bud Powell, and we were sitting at a table adjacent to the legendary jazz baroness, Pannonica de Koenigswarter. On this warm, low-key summer evening at the Vanguard in 2005, it was too hot to take anything seriously, so Harris spent the entire evening having fun playing around with standards with familiar lyrics.

By then, the Jazz Cultural Theater was long gone. But Harris had re-created its general atmosphere, and the entire audience at the Vanguard seemed to be Harris friends, fans, followers, and students. They needed no invitation to clap, snap, and hum along. At the end, one even spontaneously alighted on the Vanguard's tiny stage and began doing Bob Fosse dance moves. Lorraine Gordon, the room's majordomo, did not seem to approve of such shenanigans and would occasionally glower in Harris's direction.

Mr. Harris began by imitating an announcer offstage, introducing the trio: Earl May on bass and Leroy Williams, his collaborator for many decades, on drums. He spoke of himself in the third person: "Tonight's pianist, ladies and gentlemen, can actually take a Steinway and make it sound like an upright—there are not many pianists who can do that!"

Mr. Harris seemed unable to make up his mind whether he felt like playing "Like Someone in Love" or "My Heart Stood Still," so he played both—not exactly as a medley but more as a collage in that he alternated between eight and four bars of one and then switched to the other. He did this throughout all three major stages of the number: rubato intro, in-tempo chorus, and improvisation. The piece could have been called "Like Someone's Heart Stood Still."

Mr. Harris attempted to get a little more serious with the second number, a slow, unaccompanied treatment of Duke Ellington's "Prelude to a Kiss." He got about halfway through, having done the intro and most of the chorus, and we were all waiting to see where he would take it. Then, all of a sudden—*ring*—someone's cell phone went off! (Lorraine Gordon, the club's owner, does not suffer such intrusions, and this time, she stared accusingly at me—but no, it wasn't mine.)

If Mr. Harris had been playing an up-tempo or with a whole band, he probably would have been able to incorporate the rhythm of the ring tone into his solo. But considering that everyone was having a hard enough time concentrating as it was, he just stopped, telling the crowd, "If it's God calling, then you can pick up—otherwise throw it away!" And he left the prelude decidedly unkissed.

There was still plenty of great playing in store, however, and Mr. Harris continued to playfully use verses and introductions. He eased into the warhorse "Tea for Two" by starting with a luxuriant treatment of the verse. He also raced through "Star Eyes," with its famous Charlie Parker intro vamp. In both cases, even the ultrafast main chorus and improv were gentle—he had Erroll Garner, not Powell, on his mind. Following "Tea for Two," someone yelled, "Play that again!" and darned if he didn't lay another chorus on us.

Mr. Harris did succeed in putting down two absolutely gorgeous ballads without any extra-musical intrusions: "Some Other Spring," from the Billie Holiday songbook, and "My Devotion," written by Jimmy Dorsey's guitarist, Roc Hillman, but recorded by Powell. In between numbers, he launched into an unfamiliar melody that left both Mr. May and myself with puzzled looks on our faces. "Just a little something from Chopin," he explained. He wound up with two more bop fixtures, "Rhythm" (as in "All God's Chillun Got Wings") and Parker's B-flat blues, "Bird Feathers."

The set ended as it began, with a group of Barry Harris regulars humming along like the Swingle Singers. As I left, I looked at Ms. Gordon, who said rather sternly, "I could do without that anvil chorus!" But Mr. Harris, still seated at the keyboard and functioning as his own intermission pianist, began to play "Sweet Lorraine." "He's trying to win me over," she laughed. It was obviously working.

(*The New York Sun*, 2005)

KENNY BARRON (BORN 1943)

It was at a Jazz in July concert at the 92nd Street Y in 2003 that I found myself seated next to a fellow fan and writer, one who exemplified the breed once known as a "moldy fig"—someone who can't abide the direction music took after World War II and decries all contemporary players. I tried to carry on a civil conversation, but he was relentless in condemning virtually everyone who had been playing jazz in the second half of the 20th century. "Surely," I protested, "there's at least one young musician whom you like?" He thought for a second and said: "Kenny Barron."

Considering that Kenny Barron was turning 60 in 2003, it must have been a while since anyone had described him as a young, cutting-edge keyboard hotshot. Yet our moldy fig had a point in a certain sense: Mr. Barron plays with so much energy and imagination that it's hard to think of him as someone nearing retirement age, and it's only been about 10 years since he became a star.

Mr. Barron, after 35 years on the scene, enjoyed his first longtime relationship with a major label in the early 1990s. The series of albums he headlined for Verve—including *Spirit Song*, *Freefall*, and *Things Unseen*—represent some of the finest jazz to be recorded in that very busy decade. In the spring of 2005—still the first season of Dizzy's Club Coca-Cola—he presided over a three-week festival in which he led half a dozen different lineups.

Mr. Barron's story is characteristic of jazz piano in the contemporary era. While the postwar years were dominated by superstars, such as Bud Powell, Thelonious Monk, Errol Garner, Dave Brubeck, and Bill Evans, much of the best jazz piano of the 1980s and 1990s has been the work of incredible craftsmen who previously were hidden in plain sight—most notably Hank Jones, Barry Harris, the late Tommy Flanagan, and Kenny Barron.

For most of their careers, these men were somewhat taken for granted, regarded as great musicians, and the first guys you would call if you were doing a record date. But they were never given the star treatment. Now, they're getting their due.

Born in Philadelphia in 1943, Mr. Barron is the younger brother of another perennially underappreciated musician, the tenor saxophonist Bill Barron (1927–1989), a contemporary and colleague of John Coltrane. Kenny Barron, 16 years younger, played in R&B bands around Pennsylvania before he moved to New York at age 18, and he made his debut record appearance on his brother's 1961 *Modern Windows Suite.*

Even when Mr. Barron was barely known beyond the jazz world, he was one of the most recorded musicians in it—the new edition of Tom Lord's *The Jazz Discography* lists more than 450 sessions with Mr. Barron playing every kind of keyboard variation imaginable. He established himself among the bebop elite when he began working with the two most prominent boppers of the 1960s, James Moody and Dizzy Gillespie, and recorded and toured extensively with both of them.

Mr. Barron played with *Moody on Another Bag* (1962), *Comin' on Strong* (1963), and *Moody and the Brass Figures* (1966), among others, and with Gillespie on a particularly exciting series of albums from the mid-1960s that generally also costarred Mr. Moody. The Dizzy recordings ranged from straight-ahead bop (as on a 1965 Carnegie Hall concert) to several memorably goofy excursions to the calypso islands (*Jambo Caribe*) and tinsel town (*Dizzy in Hollywood*, aka *The Cool World*).

Mr. Barron recorded his first album as a leader in 1973 (*Sunset at Dawn* on Muse). But he first started to be recognized in his own right a decade later when he began an intense collaboration with Stan Getz, a saxophone colossus of roughly the same vintage as his older brother. Mr. Barron was the perfect partner for the great tenor's final years: Getz had both mellowed and matured in his early 60s, without having lost any of his youthful fire, and Mr. Barron both supported and challenged him.

The two made five official albums in the five years they worked together before Getz's death in 1991—although more previously unissued concerts (and one exceptional studio album, *Bossas and Ballads*) continue to be released. *People Time*, a set of duets, was the most remarkable perhaps because it was as much a Kenny Barron album as it was a Stan Getz album.

By the early 1990s, Mr. Barron was dividing his musical interests in three directions. First, he was getting more Pan-African, as he showed in the 1995 *Swamp Sally*, a disc of duets with the Martinique-born percussionist Mino Cinelu (who is costarring with him until Sunday). At the same time, Mr. Barron was also getting more European. He was at the center of the Classical Jazz Quartet, a group even more intent on combining bebop with baroque than the Modern Jazz Quartet, using the same instrumentation of piano, vibes (Stefon Harris), bass (Ron Carter), and drums (Lewis Nash).

On *The Classical Jazz Quartet Plays Bach*, their approach to the merger was relatively straightforward. They improvised over and swung six Bach opuses in a way that was simultaneously fun and tasteful. Mr. Barron's most recent quintet, which again featured Mr. Harris on vibes alongside flutist Anne Shelton, employed some of the same semiclassical techniques (as heard on Mr. Barron's most recent album, *Images*).

Yet most fans would agree that Mr. Barron's best music reflects his basic training in bebop, particularly 1995's *Things Unseen* and 1999's *Spirit Song*, which both feature the fine trumpeter Eddie Henderson (who will be part of Mr. Barron's sextet next week at Dizzy's). The former opens with an atmospheric, extended piece of swamp bop named after "Marie LaVeau" of New Orleans folklore. The latter leads off with "The Pelican," a memorable bop line that shows why Mr. Barron's tunes are increasingly being played by other bands (the ultimate test of mettle for a jazz composer).

Finally, there's *Freefall*, Mr. Barron's 2000 meeting with violinist Regina Carter (he plays on her 1998 *Rhythms of the Heart*), an exciting example of everything jelling beautifully in the studio. Ms. Carter is not a world-class improviser, but she has imagination and chutzpah. "Softly, as in a Morning Sunrise" combines every strain of Mr. Barron's music; he lays down a Cuban montuno pattern as she gives the swing treatment to this operetta-derived standard. Thelonious Monk's "Mysterioso," which opens with Mr. Barron laying down the essential three-note melody pattern while Ms. Carter accompanies him—before they reverse roles—is a wonderful example of their antic wit. I have no doubt that Monk himself would have dug it.

(*The New York Sun*, 2005)

MR. GERSHWIN, MR. WILSON, AND DR. ZEITLIN

TEDDY WILSON (1912–1986)

Teddy Wilson and His Trio, *Mr. Gershwin and Mr. Wilson* (1959)

In 1934, when Teddy Wilson was 21—and George Gershwin was 35—he recorded his first date as a leader, a set of four solos, two of which were songs by Gershwin, "Liza" and "Somebody Loves Me." "Liza," in particular, would be a Teddy Wilson perennial; there are at least 20 versions in his catalog, many from the 1930s alone. It would be Wilson's go-to Gershwin song. (There's an especially spiffy version from 1939, where he's backed up by his own short-lived big band; in this version in particular, you can really hear his roots in Earl Fatha Hines.)

In 1959, Wilson recorded what would be his only major songbook project, *Mr. Wilson and Mr. Gershwin*. What makes this album special is that it's a Gershwin collection from a great jazz musician who was playing those songs well within Gershwin's own short lifetime. This is important for two reasons: As we know, Gershwin was himself a jazz fan, who acknowledged freely his debt to the great African American piano giants. And also because, shamefully, although Gershwin lived in one of the great ages of sound recording and even sound film, he left a painfully small recorded legacy. He was the most public-facing songwriter of his day, who starred in his own radio show at several points in his career, and he was never shy to perform. Yet all that survives of his own playing are dribs and drabs.

It's not much to extrapolate that Gershwin heard Wilson playing at least some of his songs—certainly, if nowhere else, as pianist with Benny Goodman's trios and quartets. Even if Goodman hadn't been part of the especially jazzy pit orchestra on Gershwin's *Girl Crazy*, Goodman was the central figure in all of pop music and jazz by 1935–1936, and Gershwin would have been well aware of that.

When we listen to this 1959 album, I don't think it's much of a stretch to suggest that Gershwin himself would have loved it and that this was the way he might have wanted to hear his music played and even wanted to play it this way himself. Like Gershwin, Teddy Wilson (1912–1986) was a virtuoso player as well as a showman; Gershwin, unlike his close friend Oscar Levant, never worked as a sideman with one of the major dance bands of the era, but the syncopated sound of 1920s hot music was in his bones. More importantly, it was in his songs—every beat of his music in fact.

The modern piano trio—with bass and drums—didn't really come into its own until after World War II; as natural as it seems, for most of the 1940s, many keyboardists were so enamored of the King Cole Trio that they emulated its piano, guitar, and bass format. Wilson wouldn't have been working with the bass/drums trio until relatively late in his career. I personally enjoy *Mr. Wilson and Mr. Gershwin* not least because, other than adapting his playing to the relatively new format of the trio, this is fundamentally the way Mr. Wilson was playing these tunes when Mr. Gershwin was still with us.

Throughout, Wilson's style is firmly in the 4/4 swing tradition of the 1930s rather than the two-beat we associate with the Roaring '20s. Virtually every piece is in a swingingly staccato groove, and the image that comes to mind is dancing—the elegance and exuberance of one of the great African American tap dancers as well as that of fingers dancing across the keyboard. When Goodman and Wilson recorded a soundtrack for a Disney cartoon, the images included an abstract creature composed only of fingers for legs, literally dancing across an endless horizon of white-and-black piano keys.

The album opens with "Liza," from the 1929 Ziegfeld production *Show Girl*. For years, this was considered a classic Gershwin song, but it has been less frequently included in Gershwin projects over the last 60 years or so perhaps because it was originally written for a minstrel-style number and was conceived as a sort of zippier, more up-to-date version of an old-style "plantation" song. Wilson's version is particularly dance-centric; it's reminiscent of the great song-and-dance man Avon Long, who was supposed to sing it to Lena Horne in a cut number from the 1945 MGM movie musical *Ziegfeld Follies*. Close your eyes: it's hard not to visualize a dance act like the Step Brothers or the Berry Brothers going through their paces. Both bassist Al Lucas and drummer Bert Dahlander also seem to be dancing through their featured portions, which are more like breaks—dance breaks in fact—rather than full-out solos. An exchange with Dahlander (on brushes) sets up a series of false endings, which suggest, for all the world, a hammy dancer milking the applause and refusing to leave the stage, like Fred Astaire and Judy Garland at the end of "We're a Couple of Swells."

Speaking of Astaire, the collaboration between Gershwin and the great dancer—two Broadway shows and two classic films (not to mention the 1957 *Funny Face*)—is a major subset of the Gershwin catalog. Surprisingly, there are only two Astaire-associated songs here, and they're the next two tracks. Like "Liza," "Nice Work If

You Can Get It" (from *A Damsel in Distress*, 1937), and "Oh! Lady Be Good" are also highly dance driven. Lucas solos arco on the first, briefly quoting "Rhapsody in Blue," and summoning up the image of a dancing bear.

A standard jam-session icebreaker, "Oh! Lady Be Good," is one of many tracks where Wilson shows what he learned from Louis Armstrong, particularly after recording with the mighty man in 1933. He starts playing with the tune and improvising melodically from the very first note. Dahlander sets it up with brushes, and then Wilson is off to the races. He says all that needs to be said in a brief two and a half minutes, and there's even room for a solo by Lucas. Even the flourish at the coda again suggests a dance trio taking a bow.

Most of the other tracks frame the melody and then play with it in the same way. "Somebody Loves Me" shows what a great "singer" Wilson is—he captures the spirit of Buddy DeSylva's lyric as well as any vocalist ever has, optimistic but cautious, looking for "somebody" but slightly reserved and somewhat guarded. Conversely, "But Not for Me" is a cheerful song about a sad situation, delivered with the wry, self-mocking humor that was Ira Gershwin's trademark; his rationale seems to be, "well, I guess she's not for me—so I might as well dance and have a good time."

"I Got Rhythm" is a brief blowing number; at two minutes, including breaks by the bassist and drummer, it sounds like a "chaser," something he might throw in to quickly conclude a nightclub set—in fact, it concludes the album's side A.

We can't know if it was planned this way or not, but there are more ballads and concert-style numbers on the second side. "The Man I Love" has always heavily suggested Gershwin's concert pieces, in particular "Rhapsody in Blue," and Lucas has an especially compelling arco statement here.

There are also two numbers from another cornerstone of the Gershwin canon, *Porgy and Bess* (1935): "Bess, You Is My Woman Now" and "Summertime." Although swinging, they also sound like a 1930s notion of jazz chamber music, which seems to be how listeners regarded any small-group performance that wasn't an out-and-out freeform jam session. Wilson's phrasing on the former suggests the song's relationship to Gershwin's second prelude, and another arco bass solo further underscores the connection to classical music.

"Embraceable You" is sweetly melodic and vividly filled with ornamentation: cascades at the start, trills later. It's almost like he's accentuating lyricist Ira Gershwin's idea of the "many charms about you" by illustrating those charms musically. The way Wilson accentuates the high notes on the word "embraceable," then the lower notes on the bridge ("I love all those many charms about you") almost sounds like he's engaging in a duet or at least, a call-and-response pattern with himself. "Love Is Here to Stay" brings us back to what *Variety* described, back in the day, as "terp tempos," with more dancing-bear bass from Lucas.

The bassist opens "I've Got a Crush on You" in the same fashion, though somewhat slower; this is the song (first heard in the 1928 *Treasure Girl*) that the Gershwins had written as a bouncy foxtrot but that Ira famously later admitted sounded better as a slow ballad after hearing jazz singer Lee Wiley sing it that way. This version splits the difference, romantic enough, but with clearly delineated rhythm such that you can picture dancers pirouetting about the ballroom floor; there's a particularly precious pas-de-deux between Wilson and Lucas, again playing arco, as he does in most of his solo statements here.

"Summertime," which opens *Porgy and Bess,* is an arresting closer, wrapping up a great jazz album with a semiclassical note, particularly when Lucas, arco again, rephrases the melody to the accompaniment of Dahlander's mallets, which suggest Vernel Fournier with Ahmad Jamal. It's an effective synthesis of multiple strains of mid-century American music: jazz, opera, musical theater, and social dance music.

There's a famous story about George Gershwin going to 52nd Street at the pinnacle of "The Street"'s fame around 1936 and hearing the great jazz violinist, singer, and bandleader Stuff Smith. Smith and his men play one hot instrumental that has Gershwin particularly intrigued but also perplexed; when he asks Smith about it, the violinist responds, "Why, Mr. Gershwin, don't you recognize 'I Got Rhythm?'" Gershwin would have easily recognized all 12 of his classic tunes here, and to paraphrase what Ira Gershwin said about Ella Fitzgerald's songbook album of the brothers' music, Wilson would have made Gershwin appreciate his own work even more.

(*Slouching Towards Birdland,* Substack, 2024)

DENNY ZEITLIN (BORN 1938)

Crazy Rhythm: Exploring George Gershwin **(Sunnyside Records)**

I never thought I would hear "By Strauss" twice in the same month—in new performances, at least—and by two of the finest living jazz pianists, no less. It's one of George and Ira Gershwin's rarer standards and their most notable waltz. In fact, when Ehud Asherie announced a few weeks ago, in the middle of a splendid Monday evening trio set at Dizzy's, that his next tune was going to be a Gershwin waltz, everybody in the house knew there was only one song that it could possibly be.

And by coincidence, "By Strauss" is also a highlight of *Crazy Rhythm: Exploring George Gershwin,* the excellent new solo album from Denny Zeitlin.

Yet some might consider this more surprising: I tend to think of Mr. Zeitlin, who was 80 when he recorded *Crazy Rhythm: Exploring George Gershwin* in 2018, as more of a cutting-edge postmodernist and Mr. Asherie, 43, as more of a traditional player. Where Mr. Zeitlin is likely to go modal or freeform, Mr. Asherie is more likely to go stride or ragtime. Yet Mr. Asherie's arrangement of "By Strauss," which he recorded on his trio album *Music Makes Me* and and again with saxophonist Harry Allen on *For George, Cole and Duke,* is much more overtly "modern"—at points, he goes into 6/8 and uses "Valse Hot," Sonny Rollins's iconic framing of a bebop head in 3/4 time, as a countermelody.

Conversely, the interpretation by Dr. Zeitlin—yes, he is also a professor of psychiatry at the University of California—is rapturously tender and melodic. As he notes in the booklet, the song was most famously performed as a burlesque, a kind of sarcastic slap in the face to those old fuddy-duddies who preferred ancient Strauss waltzes to the more up-to-date music of Gershwin and his contemporaries. This must be a rare example of a modern musician challenging convention in such a fashion; it's the opposite of a parody: it's taking a funny song and making it sweet and romantic.

Dr. Zeitlin's new Gershwin album is the latest in his series of solo recitals that has so far included collections of music by Wayne Shorter (*Early Wayne*, 2016) and Miles Davis (*Remembering Miles*, 2019). Dr. Zeitlin starts with familiar Gershwin melodies and interprets them in a way that's playful and yet respectful; he never trashes or distorts the tunes or throws in so many quotes that one forgets what the original tune is. I've always regarded "The Man I Love" as one of the Gershwins' more classically styled, rhapsodic pop tunes; here, Dr. Zeitlin makes it sound as if it had been written for *Porgy and Bess* and shows what it has in common with that opera's introduction.

Sometimes, though, Dr. Z starts a track by dancing around the tune and doesn't coax it out of hiding until he feels good and ready, as on the opener, "Summertime." It almost sounds like warm weather waiting for the spring thaw: First, there's a kind of out-of-focus improvisation. We're not exactly sure where it's going, but a few minutes in, the familiar notes of the *Porgy and Bess* lullaby make their presence felt like flowers popping through the ice.

"Fascinating Rhythm" is perhaps even more literal. In 1924, this tune was a model of a Tin Pan Alley song that incorporated the very latest in jazzy syncopation; nearly a hundred years later, it becomes even more of a rhythmic manifesto.

Here, Dr. Z takes the Gershwins at their word: He starts playing the tune very fast, as indeed it was first heard, but then he slows down and crisscrosses the tune with Tatum-like runs and takes it through a series of variations and embellishments. He stretches the melody out, speeds it up, and slows it down as if he were playing with silly putty.

Yet in titling the album *Crazy Rhythm: Exploring George Gershwin*, Dr. Zeitlin is perhaps enjoying another joke. That title refers to a 1928 show tune with lyrics by Gershwin's one-time collaborator Irving Caesar and a melody credited to veteran composer Joseph Meyer and bandleader Roger Wolfe Kahn. The song "Crazy Rhythm" is frequently confused with the Gershwins' "Fascinating Rhythm" and "I Got Rhythm," and Caesar's lyrics are very similar to the former.

In both songs, the concept of rhythm is anthropomorphized as a sentient entity who won't leave the hapless protagonist alone; in the first, he pleads, "Fascinatin' rhythm, won't you stop pickin' on me?" and in the second, he insists, "Crazy rhythm, from now on, we're through!" Then, too, I hope that this song—which isn't included on this album since it isn't a Gershwin number—would be the only instance when a professor of clinical psychiatry would describe something or someone as "crazy."

(*The New York Sun*, 2023)

FELLOW TRAVELERS

LENNIE TRISTANO (1919–1978)

The legendary singer Bing Crosby, with characteristically extravagant eloquence, once referred to Dixieland jazz fans as a "cult." He was being at least slightly ironic: Traditional and New Orleans–style jazz was hugely popular at the time he employed the phrase. If there's any specific subgenre of jazz that always suggested a cult to me, though—at least from the outside looking in—it's that area of the music that gathered around the remarkable pianist, composer, bandleader, pioneering educator, and genuine iconoclast Lennie Tristano.

I have no memory of hearing Tristano live—there remains a likelihood that my father carted me along to one of his performances at a point when I was too young to remember—but I do know that Tristano-ites were all over the jazz scene in the 1970s and 1980s both in terms of musicians and fans.

His influence is still very much out there, including among contemporary musicians who picked up on Tristano directly, such as the fine and highly interesting pianist Virg Dzurinko and the saxophonist Mark Turner, who knows well the work of Tristano collaborator Warne Marsh.

There are also legions more who know Tristano through the profound effect he had on such subsequent piano giants as Bill Evans and Dave Brubeck. Further, although Tristano essentially stopped performing by the age of 50, his most celebrated collaborator, alto saxophonist Lee Konitz, kept playing, without a letup from the mid-1940s right up to the pandemic era, until his death at 92 in 2020. (It should be noted that both Tristano and Konitz would bristle at the latter being described, as he often was, as a Tristano "acolyte.")

For a titan of his stature, Tristano's recorded output is egregiously small, which is why the release of six CDs filled with previously unheard private recordings is a major event. The set owes its existence to the Tristano family, to Jerry Roche of Dot-Time Records, who has already released several collections of Tristano music, and to musicians such as guitarist Billy Bauer, who saved the music—on acetates, tape, and the short-lived technology of wire recording.

A particularly essential contribution was made by saxophonist and longtime Tristano sideman Lenny Popkin, who serves both as audio restoration engineer and annotator—and defender of the Tristano faith. In his function as annotator, Mr. Popkin informs us that most of the received wisdom concerning Tristano is flat-out wrong.

Perhaps it's because Tristano was one of the founding fathers of jazz education—among the first to demonstrate that improvisation could actually be taught—that his music is often described as cool, intellectual, and even academic. One of the most rewarding aspects of the many live performances in this package is how warm and even fiery Tristano's various duos, trios, quartets, quintets, and sextets are.

There's some especially inspired playing from the Orchid Room on Swing Street (West 52nd Street, where they shared the bill with a young Harry Belafonte) in 1950. Here, the six players—particularly the two saxophonists, Konitz (alto) and Marsh (tenor)—achieve a level of synergy that's remarkable, even for them. The "tutti" moments, following the individual solos, wherein the four rhythm and two reeds all come together, are both breathtaking and exhilarating, especially on the 10-minute "Sound-Lee."

The earliest material in the package, a set of trio sessions from various venues around New York from 1946 and 1947—possibly the first known recordings of a Tristano ensemble—are also exciting, even thrilling. The combination of piano, guitar (Billy Bauer), and bass (Arnold Fishkin) suggests that Tristano had, at some level at least, been listening to the King Cole Trio; the block chord passages on "Rhapsody" are particularly reflective of Cole's influence. Like much of the set, the music is variations on standards, with hints as to the source material in both the titles and the melodies.

The best-recorded music here is a series of completely solo performances taped in a studio rather than a club; the extra fidelity is appreciated because Tristano sounds like a four-handed piano duet even when he's playing by himself. "Lennie's Blues" and "Dusk" are dark and mysterious, but he's delightfully straightforward on "These Foolish Things."

The set ends with 42 minutes of live performances from the Half Note in the West Village, 1962, mostly in a duo format with bassist Sonny Dallas. The finale is a 10-minute "How Deep Is the Ocean," in which the two are joined by Konitz and in his only known appearance with Tristano, tenor sax giant Zoot Sims.

It's typical of Tristano's acumen that the climax is not the fastest or most exciting piece in the set but is the most personal and romantic. If there's anything cold or academic about the music of Lennie Tristano, you won't find it here.

(*The New York Sun*, 2022)

***

The back-to-school season is a good time to remember jazz's greatest pedagogue, pianist and composer Lennie Tristano. Last week, Birdland presented a quintet led by saxophonist Charles Krachy, featuring Virg Dzurinko (one of Tristano's younger students) and a Tristano-esque front line of two saxophones, alto and tenor, performing Lennie-style contrapuntal variations on standards. This week, tenor saxophonist Mark Turner—a young tenor saxophonist, who loudly trumpets his stylistic allegiances to Tristano and Warne Marsha—brings his outstanding trio, Fly, to the Village Vanguard.

Fly, which costars bassist Larry Grenadier and drummer Jeff Ballard, has also recently released their first CD, *Fly* (Savoy Jazz). After years of thinking of Mr. Turner as the most prominent latter-day Tristano-ite, the first thing I noticed is that as he ages (he'll be 39 in November), he steadily absorbs more and more influences. In fact, when I first heard tracks from his new album on WBGO—now there's a blindfold test for you—my best guess was that these tracks were by one of Joe Lovano's trios.

In a tradition we associate with both Ahmad Jamal and Bill Evans, all three players are equally important in Fly. The most exciting aspect of this trio is that it shows that three musicians can be playing essentially different things and all still be playing together. Mr. Grenadier plays mostly vamps on the bass. Mr. Ballard dispenses all manner of rhythmic patterns on the drums: marches, Latin, and funk. Mr. Turner sometimes plays with them, sometimes against them, but they're always on the same page, working in unison.

Ever since Benny Goodman's trio 70 years ago, the threesome of one horn (most often a reed) and two rhythm has generally been used as a vehicle for extended soloing. Fly, however, is a vehicle for the band's collective efforts as composers as well as players. Mr. Turner's composition "J. J."—a high point of the album, as it was on Wednesday night—exemplifies their approach. At times, Messrs. Ballard and Grenadier churn highly aggressive patterns of energy while Mr. Turner creates a contrast with cool intensity. His serene patterns focus one's attention, and he holds the stage without ever raising his voice.

The catchiest piece on the album, alas, wasn't heard on the set I attended, but undoubtedly, they'll play it over the weekend. "Piano Tune" (which is titled ironically, considering no piano was present) is an understated waltz reminiscent of the writing of John Lewis and Ornette Coleman's "European Echoes." It could be a hit single.

The set closed with "It's Magic," perhaps in anticipation of the Jule Styne Centennial next year. The Doris Day hit is well suited to Mr. Turner's style. Like many postmodern reed players, he likes to use the entire range of his horn, and here the opening line in itself descends a 14th from high E-flat to low B. It seems to be a trend in clubs lately for a group to close a program of very intense originals with a warm and familiar standard—the Ron Carter Trio did something very similar three weeks ago with "Autumn Leaves." I, for one, welcome it.

Messrs. Turner, Grenadier, and Ballard will be back at the Vanguard in two weeks in a quartet setting with Brad Mehldau (an appropriate point to play "Piano Tune"). It's been 10 years since Mark Turner released his first album, "Yam Yam" (Criss Cross). Since then he's progressed from a promising student to an emerging master. Lennie Tristano would be proud to claim Mark Turner as one of his own.

(*The New York Sun*, 2004)

BUD POWELL (1924–1966)

Complete Album Playlist

https://www.youtube.com/watch?v=dgErWGgCAjA&list=OLAK5uy_m9CYWhyx4vJD8JFSi4wNvVmnbi2k9OyzU

Bud Plays Bird opens with Bud Powell stretching out on "Big Foot," a 1948 blues by Charlie Parker that was also recorded by the composer under the title of "Drifting on a Reed." The first thing we notice is that it's fast but not killer fast; that in itself is a surprise or at least, a challenge to our preconceived notions of Bud Powell's music. Many listeners—most of all myself—tend to group pianists around their most obvious traits: I expect everything by Bud Powell to be fast, everything by Bill Evans to be lyrical, everything by Monk to be spacey, everything by Sun Ra to be outer-spacey, everything by Cecil Taylor to be weird, and everything by Oscar Peterson to sound like five pianists on five separate keyboards all playing at once. Needless to say, they wouldn't be real artists if they stuck to their calling-card approaches 100 percent of the time.

We associate Bud Powell with sheer speed because he was the piano poster child of the first generation of bebop, a music that distinguished itself from all the brands of jazz that had come before it both harmonically and rhythmically—as well as attitudinally. Part of the motivation for the creation of modern jazz was to devise a music that was so complex, so radically different from the swing and big-band styles that had come before it, that lesser musicians couldn't even understand it, much less play it. At first, the public couldn't make sense of it either, but gradually the music became so widely accepted that it became the dominant mode of jazz; when a friend invites you to a jazz club, this is what you expect to hear. When colleges teach young musicians how to play jazz, it's invariably bebop rather than swing or Dixieland.

"Big Foot" is fast, to be sure, but slower than a lot of Peterson or Art Tatum. Powell's playing has a remarkable clarity to it. You hear the melodic lines in the right hand loud and clear, and the chords and harmonic support in the left are never so dense as to distract from the improvised melody. In fact, that remarkable melodic transparency is as much a Bud Powell calling card as his usual sheer speed. And also, when the left and the right hands play in unison, that also suggests the single lines of a horn player—Charlie Parker in particular. And as with other keyboard players, Powell's humming—insomuch as the microphone picks it up—also adds another unison voice. He also benefits enormously from the very *sympatico* playing of his two trio associates, bassist George Duvivier and drummer Art Taylor.

Powell, Duvivier, and Taylor recorded the tracks that later become *Bud Plays Bird* over three sessions in October 1957, December 1957, and January 1958, under the supervision of Roost Records house producer Rudy Traylor. It was Powell's bad luck that somehow neither Roost nor Roulette Records got around to releasing them at the time; instead, they laid in the vaults until EMI acquired the Roulette-Roost catalog during the CD era and were discovered and released by Michael Cuscuna in 1996. *Bud Plays Bird* is such a strong album that it would have done a lot for Powell's already high reputation had it been released while he was still around to benefit from it, prior to his death at age 41 in 1966.

For one thing, *Bud Plays Bird* is virtually the only "concept" or songbook album of Powell's relatively short career—two of his final projects were tributes, respectively, to Thelonious Monk and Cannonball Adderley, but they're not nearly as specifically focused and continually excellent as these 1957–1958 sessions. Which is only natural: Powell was the pianist most associated with Charlie Parker, the one who did the most to help crystalize the ideas of Parker, Dizzy Gillespie, and company into keyboard form during Parker's even shorter lifetime. At 15 tracks and nearly 70 minutes, *Bud Plays Bird* constitutes an abundance of riches, enough for two LPs at least; it's almost as if Powell was somehow prescient enough to realize he was making a CD at least 30 years before the format was invented.

Drawing on works credited to Parker as a composer, the majority, starting with the opener "Big Foot" / "Drifting on a Reed," which is heard in two takes, were both recorded at the same January session, although Mr. Cuscuna rightfully placed them at the beginning and end of the CD. "Buzzy" from 1945, was also originally in B-flat but is, on the surface at least, a much simpler and more hummable piece—I imagine neophyte musicians at Minton's found it surprisingly complex. It was also part of the boppers' modus operandi to take a relatively straightforward tune as a point of departure and then weave all kinds of more complex lines in and out of it.

"Relaxin' at Camarillo," a blues in C from 1946, was almost the opposite of "Buzzy"; it sounds dense and complex at first but then swings in a relaxed way. The title was taken from Camarillo State Mental Hospital in California and was inspired by Parker's court-ordered six-month stay there in 1945–1946. Powell's treatment, however, is more "relaxin'" than anything else, with little to signify the presence of the inner demons that we know tormented both Parker and Powell. As Bill Sando puts it, "In order to give his right hand soloing clarity and a free rein, he uses chordally simple, limited and unintrusive comping techniques in his left."

"Billie's Bounce" is a much lighter tune with an appropriately lighter title and is, on the whole, a much more extrovertly swinging piece—like "Now's the Time," this is a Parker blues that could have been an R&B hit (as, indeed, "Now's the Time" was, albeit under another title and credited to another composer); I can readily imagine Louis Jordan playing either one. Powell plays it like the bouncing boppish blues that it is. As before, he makes creative use of both his hands together playing in unison. Also in F, "Barbados," has always sounded exotic to me and as such, is particularly ripe for Powell—here, he does more of his left–right unison playing, with a clean, uncluttered melody line—but then throws in a dash of spice via a major seventh leap upward in the right-hand melody line. "Barbados" is a close cousin to my favorite Powell original, his childlike calypso "Borderick" from his 1958 Blue Note sessions released as *The Scene Changes* album. Both tunes might be described as a halfway point between one of Bird's many blues and calypsos, such as "Sly Mongoose," which Parker also liked to play.

"Shaw 'Nuff," credited to Parker and Gillespie, has also always sounded exotic to me, especially in its florid, vivid opening, although this very early (1945) bop head is based on the chord changes to "I Got Rhythm" rather than the blues. Now this is Powell at full speed ahead, ripping through the chords so fast it's a wonder that even Duvivier and Taylor can keep up; just listening, I have a hard time taking it all in. At a certain point, he meanders through some different harmonies and some minor and flatted fourth colorings, and there's also a well-done trade of fours with Duvivier and Taylor toward the climax. The other "rhythm"-based tunes here, "Moose the Mooche" and "Salt Peanuts," are possibly even faster, with soaring, cleanly articulated lines from the pianist. Both pieces also heavily feature Taylor, the first in a vivid trade with Powell.

"Scrapple from the Apple," which uses an "I Got Rhythm" bridge (the A sections are based on "Honeysuckle Rose"), is another dense piece—heavy and light at the same time. Each note is actually a cluster, but there are crucial spaces between the notes, which are very clearly defined.

"Ornithology" is co-credited to the more obscure trumpeter "Little" Benny Harris and is based on "How High the Moon," a 1940 show tune that was already a jazz standard at the start of the transition into the modern jazz era just a few years later. It's a case where the contrafact melody is as good as the original; between the moon and the avian activity referenced in the title of this variation, Powell's interpretation is suitably high-flying and even soaring. "Ko-Ko," Parker's reworking of Ray Noble's "Cherokee," was a game changer in the development of modern jazz when first heard in 1945, and here, it's a vehicle for one of Powell's fastest and most fleet-fingered takes.

"Confirmation," as the indefatigable Phil Schaap once proved, was loosely based on "Twilight Time," a 1944 hit by The Three Suns (Artie Dunn, Al Nevins, and Morty Nevins) and quickly became one of Parker's most widely heard originals. It's another example of the lighter and brighter side of modern jazz. There's a nod to his buddy Thelonious Monk, with a few notes of "Well, You Needn't" at 3:40.

"Dewey Square" utilizes original changes; for all of Powell's much-publicized mental issues, the solos throughout here show the inherent logic of his conceptions; they sprawl out from the melody on a highly coherent basis and make perfect sense musically and otherwise. There's absolutely nothing here that suggests the product of a disordered mind. In fact, the whole album is like that—an album of bebop piano playing by one of the music's all-time masters and at the very pinnacle of his powers.

(*Slouching Towards Birdland*, Substack, 2024)

BILL EVANS (1929–1980)

Consider Robert Crumb. In 1981, a very zealous fan of the famous cartoonist (and jazz buff) compiled a remarkably thorough listing of everything that Mr. Crumb had ever done, which he modestly titled a "checklist." Crumb himself noted in his introduction to the book that such avid scholarship was rare in many fields but fairly common in the jazz world. There, as he put it, "a small army" of discographers and scholars followed the leading figures of the music, tracking their every note.

Several of these dedicated followers were also amateur recording enthusiasts, most famously, Dean Benedetti, whose homemade wires and tapes of Charlie Parker were long thought to be merely legendary but whose eventual discovery eventually led to a Mosaic box. We are fortunate indeed that major chapters of the legacy of two giants of the modern jazz piano, Bud Powell and Bill Evans, were preserved by fans and friends of these great musicians. Some of these private tapes have just been officially released in two new CDs from Fantasy: Bud Powell's "Parisian Thoroughfares" (Pablo 2310-976) and Bill Evans's "Getting Sentimental: Live at The Village Vanguard" (Milestone 9336).

Mike Harris was your typical incredibly devoted jazz fan. An optical physicist who left New York in the 1970s to work on the Hubble Telescope, he was also an amateur pianist. He and his wife began carting their barely portable Tandberg Model 64 to the Village Vanguard in 1966. Every time Bill Evans played there, the Harrises would tape—with the permission of Vanguard majordomo Max Gordon—the Friday and Sunday shows. Eight CDs' worth of the Harris tapes were released in 1996 as *The Secret Sessions* (Milestone 4421), but so far, neither Mr. Harris nor Fantasy has divulged a complete list of everything the couple taped or even what is likely to be released.

This new volume is being issued independently because Mr. Harris felt that it was a very special set that deserved to stand on its own. At the very least, this collection of 14 tracks from January 15, 1978, is unique: it seems to be the only recording of this particular Bill Evans Trio, with drummer Philly Joe Jones, his off-and-on cohort from the Miles Davis days onward, and bassist Michael Moore.

Mr. Moore had worshipped Evans ever since hearing the pianist's groundbreaking 1962 Village Vanguard album; the widely influential bass artistry of Scott LaFaro, who played on that album, had inspired him to take up the instrument in the first place. But Mr. Moore felt the pianist had reacted too strongly against fans and critics who thought of him only as romantic and lyrical. It was his opinion that Evans, in these years, was getting too self-consciously "hot" and "robotic" in his playing. His entire stint with Evans lasted only six months.

One doesn't get this impression from "Getting Sentimental." The tunes here are familiar ones that appear time after time in the dozens of discs of live recordings that have been released since Evans's death in 1980: Dave Brubeck's "In Your Own Sweet Way," Johnny Mandel's "Emily," and his "M*A*S*H Theme (Suicide Is Painless)," and the pianist's own "Turn Out the Stars."

Still, these are standout performances. "I Love You" opens with what Mr. Moore calls a "Chopinesque" introduction, before Evans launches into a brilliantly textured abstraction of Cole Porter's melody and a vivid illustration of the "rhythmic displacements" that Evans spoke of in interviews. Tommy Dorsey's theme, "I'm Getting Sentimental Over You," is a rarity in the Evans discography—he is known to have played it only a few times in the late 1960s. The way that he turns this ballad into a fast-moving butt-kicker (with a solo by Mr. Moore) supports the contention about Evans wanting to showcase his up-tempo playing. But Evans's work on the ballads, especially Jimmy Rowles's lovely, meandering, and Strayhorn-like "The Peacocks" (a song a lot of jazz singers are doing lately, though it works best as an instrumental) is as sublimely tender and sensitive as anything he ever recorded. He tried in vain to make the world regard him as a fighter; we all knew he was a lover.

Francis Paudras, like Mr. Harris, was born in 1935. He started as a classical pianist but had long since become a jazz convert by the time he met Earl "Bud" Powell in 1957. Between then and Powell's death in 1966, years in which the pioneer modern jazz keyboardist lived primarily in Paris, Paudras was more than a fan or even a friend: he helped sustain Powell, whose mental problems (the result of a racist attack in the mid-1940s) left him unable to care for himself. Their relationship inspired a highly regarded work of jazz fiction, the 1986 French film *Round Midnight*, in which jazzman (and Powell associate) Dexter Gordon played an amalgam of Powell, Lester Young, and other musicians he'd known.

Paudras, who committed suicide in 1997, also published a book, *Dance of the Infidels: A Portrait of Bud Powell* (Da Capo Press), and recorded dozens of hours of Powell's live performances. These were taped mostly in Paris at the Blue Note; the Club St. Germaine; and at least once, Paudras's own house. He also accompanied Powell on his return visit to New York's Birdland in 1964 and taped that as well. In 1979, Paudras bequeathed his private archive of Powell tapes to the pianist's daughter, Cecilia, and a decade later, a series of at least 11 now-scarce albums began coming out on Mystic Sound, an Italian label.

So far, Fantasy has released two CDs of this material, the first being *Paris Sessions* (2310 972). Although annotator Paul De Barros admits that "Powell is not at his best on these fugitive live recordings," there's enough here that I would encourage Fantasy to let us hear the entire stash. A rare meeting of American trumpeter Peanuts Holland and the fine French tenor Barney Wilen on Charlie Parker's blues "Buzzy" sounds murky. But a "Shaw 'Nuff" ("I Got Rhythm") from 1959 catches the pianist at his most inventive—and in fine fidelity. The climax is an outstanding meeting of the great tenor Zoot Sims with Powell's trio from 1961 in which both jazz legends stretch out for 12 minutes on Dizzy Gillespie's "Groovin' High."

Both in terms of performance and fidelity, this is an outstanding track, and one yearns to hear the other three tunes they cut that night at the Blue Note. Sims's first solo is disappointingly short, but he returns after Powell plays and more than redeems himself. Powell, relaxed and urgent at the same time, plays bebop like he invented it.

(*The New York Sun*, 2003)

***

Bill Evans was the last great romantic of jazz piano. Unendingly lyrical and supremely sensitive, Evans didn't play melodies or improvise so much as sail along on waves of pure feeling. Even his modal approach—which gave him access to a more expansive range of notes than possible in conventional harmony—seemed more driven by emotion than technique. Never merely sentimental, even with his predilection for ballads and waltzes, Evans's deft, light touch couldn't conceal an undercurrent of anguish.

But following a line of logic espoused by that eminent philosopher Yogi Berra—"Nobody goes there anymore, it's too crowded"—it was easy to pooh-pooh Evans by the 1970s precisely because he had become such an overwhelming influence. He had long since become the dominant icon of jazz piano—the keyboard counterpart to the shadow that Coltrane, his bandmate in Miles Davis's most celebrated quintet, cast over the tenor sax. Evans's influence was doggedly all pervasive; virtually every pianist one was likely to hear in that decade seemed to be either playing straight Evans or a kind of cocktail of Evans laced with McCoy Tyner, the former Coltrane pianist who paralleled Evans in his own highly individual application of modality and ballads. Evans's overwhelmingly introverted approach spoke to an era that valued the self above all, and perhaps it corresponded a little too conveniently to the ideals of the "me decade" for our comfort back then.

Evans has never been as influential since. One particularly irresponsible recent history of jazz shortchanges him completely, using the dubious excuse that since the blues were never one of Evans's strong points, he was therefore worthless as a jazzman. (When Stan Getz, at a 1974 concert released years later on the CD *But Beautiful*, surprises the pianist with an unplanned blues, an uncharacteristically uptight Evans reacts by refusing to play.) Worse, for such a dominant influence, Evans was hardly playing in a dominating fashion for much of the late 1960s.

While not all of the surreptitiously taped material on the boxed set *Secret Sessions* lives up to pianist Michel Petrucciani's assertion that Evans "was God on Earth," it does prove a number of points, the first being that the pianist's total self-absorption was partly a kind of deliberately cultivated persona. The familiar icon of Evans with his head slung so low it was almost buried in the keyboard equates with Miles Davis's insistence on turning his back on the audience. In comparison with the all-original studio set *The Bill Evans Album* (newly reissued with worthwhile alternate takes), Evans is more likely to phone it in when he doesn't know he's being recorded. Yet even at his most cursory, Evans still has more to say than most piano players at the top of their game.

And as the *Secret* box also shows, by the mid-1970s, Evans was gradually rescaling the heights toward the glories of his 1959–1961 trio with drummer Paul Motian and bassist Scott LaFaro. The chief assets of the early *Secret* discs are the oddball tunes, such as a haunting "Alfie" and a romping "Little Lulu," but by the time the package concludes, in 1975, Evans is back to giving us goose bumps with every number. There's also another collaboration with Stan Getz, this one from 1974 and one of only two recorded meetings between the two titans; here, they render Johnny Mandel's movie theme "Emily" with a veritable explosion of lyricism.

All of which was mere prelude to what Evans would achieve with his last great trio, which he formed in 1979 with bassist Marc Johnson and drummer Joe LaBarbera. At the time, Evans—hardly an underrecorded giant—was thought to have cut only one studio album (a quintet date) and an hour's worth of live material from Paris in that year, and nothing at all from 1980, even though the group kept performing through summer.

Now comes the avalanche: *Turn Out the Stars*, over seven hours taped in June 1980 with the last great Evans trio from the Vanguard—scene of many a past triumph—and two additional discs from London in July and August. Evans is as irrepressibly romantic as ever on these live recordings, but at the same time, there's an aggressive energy to his playing that makes these newly discovered documents some of the most exciting music of his career. Even at his most passive or classically beholden (as on three versions of "Nardis"), Evans always swings, and here, he proves that he can really tear into the keyboard and still sound like Bill Evans. Continually prodded by Johnson and LaBarbera, even as he's inspiring them, this is tenderness supported by strength and bite.

These 18 discs (with an additional 18 forthcoming in a complete Verve sessions box next year) make Evans the most reissued pianist since the King Cole Trio deluge of three years ago. (And there's still more: *Consecration*, an eight-CD live set from San Francisco, so far released only overseas, finishes just a week before Evans's cocaine-related death on September 15, 1980.) While these sets will probably not unleash a new wave of Evans imitators, they will reaffirm his position as one of American music's great poets.

(*Village Voice*, 1997)

***

Bill Evans's *Sunday at the Village Vanguard* is—like Miles Davis's *Kind of Blue* (on which Evans played)—Sonny Rollins's *Saxophone Colossus,* and John Coltrane's *A Love Supreme* is one of those masterpiece albums that is created only when the stars are properly aligned. Now that all 26 tracks recorded on June 25, 1961, alongside bassist Scott LaFaro and drummer Paul Motian have been reissued in a three-CD box, *The Complete Village Vanguard Recordings, 1961*, we can see the total picture of the threesome that redefined the essential notion of what a jazz piano trio could do.

The piano trio had become a standard format in the late 1940s and generally, featured a leader–star accompanied by two sidemen on bass and drums. Within a decade, both Ahmad Jamal and Evans were opening up the format so that the drummer and bassist had as many solo opportunities as the pianist. Even more important in the Evans trio was the way the three voices fit together and supported each other: Evans could never have flown out on his legendary lyrical flights of fancy had not LaFaro and Mr. Motian supported him so dependably.

Prior to forming the trio that played at the Vanguard, Evans had spent eight months in Davis's band; before that, he had been introduced to jazz's major leagues by the clarinetist Tony Scott. He played with LaFaro, and Mr. Motian from the winter of 1959–1960 until the 25-year-old LaFaro was killed in a car crash two weeks after that amazing Sunday at the Vanguard.

During this brief time, they recorded only two studio albums, *Portrait in Jazz* and *Explorations*—despite the efforts of Riverside Records producer Orrin Keepnews to corral the threesome into the studio more often. "I felt constantly in danger of having this marvelous source of creativity and imagination slip away from me," Mr. Keepnews writes in the booklet notes for the new set.

LaFaro had already collaborated extensively with free-jazz pioneer Ornette Coleman and had established himself at a very young age as one of the most remarkable soloists the bass has ever known. His playing was fast and imaginative, his tone distinctive. LaFaro's innovations left Mr. Motian with even more rhythmic responsibility; on the Vanguard recordings, the bassist at times seems to be playing his instrument like a second piano.

Bassist Jay Leonhart, a rough contemporary of LaFaro, has explained that LaFaro was never comfortable "comping" or merely accompanying whomever he was playing with but took it upon himself to accompany the main soloist with original melodies of his own rather than a mere chordal background. The one previously unissued track on the new box, a new take of LaFaro's "Gloria's Step" (heretofore withheld because an electric outage during the show caused a dropout) shows that here was one bass soloist whom no crowd would ever talk over.

Evans influenced a generation of keyboardists with his signature touch, which is generally described as expressively lyrical and intensely romantic. By the end of his life, however, he seemed to resent being known as a man who inspired introspection among more contemporary musicians than could possibly be numbered. When Evans appeared on Marian McPartland's *Piano Jazz* show on NPR in 1978, he made a point of talking about what was important to him, not the concepts of lyricism and romanticism but rhythm.

"[My] rhythmic construction [has] evolved quite a bit," he said. "Now, I don't know how obvious that would be to the listener but the displacement of phrases and the way phrases follow one another and their placement against the meter and so forth, is something that I have worked on rather hard."

You can hear what he means on Cole Porter's "All of You," which he played three times at the Vanguard on that fateful Sunday and then again for Ms. McPartland 17 years later. Even though he starts solo and in ballad time, he never quite states Cole Porter's melody. After the first chorus, where a jazzman would normally switch from melody to improvisation, the tempo intensifies, and Evans gets even more deeply into the changes, laying down long, cascading patterns that flow against the rhythmic grain. In the 1978 interview, Ms. McPartland compares this effect to "swimming against the tide."

Evans, LaFaro, and Mr. Motian played five sets that magical Sunday (two in the afternoon, three in the evening), resulting in 153 minutes of music. There are two sumptuous readings of Evans's most famous composition, "Waltz for Debby"; the exuberant "All of You"; another 3/4 beauty "Alice in Wonderland"; and touching readings of Evans's signature ballads "My Foolish Heart," "Detour Ahead," and "I Loves You Porgy." There are also two tributes to Evans's ex-boss Davis that the pianist would virtually never play again: "Milestones" and "Solar," the latter being a particularly valuable example of Evans playing pure bebop.

But the highlight of the box is Leonard Bernstein's "Some Other Time," which the bassist launches with a compelling vamp. This is essentially a slow, two-note pattern that becomes a backdrop over which Evans is free to state all manner of melodies in a feathery light piano dynamic. In his 1958 sessions for his second album, *Everybody Digs Bill Evans*, Evans used this vamp both as the intro to "Some Other Time" and as the background for a mostly free-form improvisation titled "Peace Piece."

The Vanguard "Some Other Time" begins with the "Peace Piece" vamp, which sounds even better with Evans stating the tune on top of it, graceful and light as can be, with an emotionality that's implied rather than directly stated. He picks up the tempo slightly in the bridge, which modulates up a sixth, and slightly varies his dynamic throughout the improvisation. He has long since figured out how to use his beloved rhythmic displacements, remarkable harmonic sense, and crystalline touch to enhance both the melody and the emotional message of whatever he's playing.

The pianist would later return to "Some Other Time" with two singers, Monica Zetterlund and more famously, Tony Bennett in 1975. As hauntingly beautiful as the Evans–Bennett version is, the presence of a vocalist with the Evans–Motian–LaFaro trio would have been redundant. Perhaps that's why both Evans albums with Bennett were strictly duets, sans bass and drums: it was impossible to improve on the Vanguard trio rendition of the Bernstein melody.

Listening to "Some Other Time," one can't help but wonder what Evans might have become if he had actually lived out something more like a normal life span. Evans was already using heroin in 1961, and it's as if he knew, even at the age of 32, that he wasn't going to have time to do half the things he wanted to. He wasn't apologizing, just telling us that we should be glad for what we had and what was to come.

(*The New York Sun*, 2005)

***

We hear an exquisitely beautiful string background, reminiscent of a late 19th-century symphonic tone poem depicting a peaceful forest or a woodland scene. It's lovely, mostly out of tempo, but though light in tone, by classical music standards at least, it's somewhat serious. A few minutes in, we can make out the woodwinds vaguely sketching out the contours of a familiar melody; then the piano enters, just in time to play half of a chorus. For about 40 seconds, we get the distinct mental image of a little girl scampering through the trees, and then, when she's departed the scene, the strings come back in as if playfully chasing after her.

This track is labeled "Intro/Waltz for Debby." The "intro" is the new orchestral part that frames the jazz standard composed by the legendary pianist Bill Evans. In this case, it's notable how the new material, the music for the intro and the orchestration for the entire track, supports and enhances what was already Evans's best-known work in ways that are both expected and not.

This session, with Evans and his trio, bassist Eddie Gomez and drummer Marty Morell, working with a string orchestra arranged and conducted by the composer Palle Mikkelborg, was recorded in 1969 in Copenhagen for Danish television. It's merely the most remarkable part of a new package of previously unheard live performances now being released as both a two-CD and a three-LP set.

The "Intro/Waltz for Debby" track turns out to be a kind of an overture; a fuller version of the waltz occurs a few tracks later. This one, conversely, starts with the piano as the pianist lays out his melody in as few notes as possible. The little girl is playing in her room. Gradually, the real-life settings of her house fade away, and as the horns come in around her, they represent the forest of her imagination. A few minutes in, she's surrounded not merely by dolls and teddy bears (as mentioned in Gene Lees's vibrant lyric) but by friendly forest animals or maybe even fairies and woodland sprites.

A few years earlier, Evans played a key role in Miles Davis's breakthrough album, "Kind of Blue," which, among other things, helped christen the birth of the modern "jazz waltz." Yet "Waltz for Debby" isn't to be compared to Davis's "All Blues"—most so-called jazz waltzes of the period are in 6/8 or 6/4, but "Waltz for Debby" is a deliberately old-school 3/4. The melody was inspired by Evans's young niece, and he was deliberately using the same time signature of many a nursery rhyme or children's song. Clearly, the time signature signifies the innocence of childhood. But this 1969

"Debby" is even more whimsical and capricious; this Debby doesn't merely waltz, she whirls and cavorts through the trees and with the dancing bears in this nocturnal forest of her dreams. It ends gradually and quietly, with the other instruments receding until only the piano is heard, as if Debby is slowly falling asleep—or perhaps waking up from this dream.

There are six tracks (28 minutes) of Evans accompanied by Mr. Mikkelborg conducting the large ensemble, a combination of the Danish Radio Big Band and the Royal Danish Symphony Orchestra, and they are a highlight of this new set. Another highlight is a lovely Mikkelborg original, "Treasures," in which Mr. Mikkelborg plays a Harmon-muted trumpet solo in a way that anticipates "Aura," the composer's inspired 1985 collaboration with Miles Davis.

There are also six tracks of Evans playing live and solo, and copious amounts of the pianist working in his preferred format, the trio with bass and drums—including an entire album costarring the Danish bass virtuoso Niels-Henning Ørsted Pedersen. The unaccompanied solos are swinging as well as introspective and the trio numbers are introspective and personal as well as highly swinging.

Treasures: Solo, Trio & Orchestra Recordings from Denmark (1965-1969) is the 10th such release of previously unheard live recordings by Bill Evans to be produced by Zev "The Jazz Detective" Feldman. It seems almost impossible to imagine that we'll ever reach the point of saturation—not when the "new" music we are hearing for the first time is as good as this.

(*The New York Sun*, 2023)

RUGGED INDIVIDUALS

CEDAR WALTON (1934–2013)

Cedar Walton was the man who *wood* be king.

In 1959, Walton, then a 25-year-old pianist from Dallas, did a single session with the emerging tenor saxophonist and composer John Coltrane, who was then gradually establishing himself as the leader of his own quartet. (This March 26 session for Atlantic with Walton was made in between the two dates in which Miles Davis, Coltrane, and company recorded *Kind of Blue*.) Although the Coltrane–Walton session was not issued for many years, it turned out to be one of the most important dates in the history of the music in that it included the first-ever recordings of three future Coltrane classics: "Giant Steps," "Naima," and "Like Sonny." The saxophonist would then audition several other pianists, among them Tommy Flanagan, before embarking on a long-term partnership with his fellow Philadelphian, McCoy Tyner.

From the 1970s onward, both Walton and Tyner were now primarily leaders themselves, with their own trios, quintets, and other ensembles, and they were frequently both working in New York. On one such week in 2002, Walton was playing the Vanguard at the same time that Tyner and his big band were at the Iridium. It occurred to me at that time that even the names of these pianist–composers were the very stuff that jazz is made of—can you imagine an accountant named "Cedar" or "McCoy"?

(In terms of their attitudes toward their names, Walton also had a lot in common with the late Lee Konitz, another NEA Jazz Master, in that they both had an irrepressible appetite for puns on their names (i.e., "Solid as Cedar" and "Ice Cream Konitz"; two of the pianist's best later albums were titled *Seasoned Wood*, 2008, and *Cedar Chest*, 2001).

Walton was such a prolific and accomplished composer that he was hardly willing to wait until he was in a position to lead his own groups before he started writing like crazy. He served as pianist for Art Blakey and the Jazz Messengers and succeeded the formidable Benny Golson as musical director for that essential ensemble. Where Golson had presided over the late 1950s edition with trumpeter Lee Morgan and pianist Bobby Timmons, Walton was responsible for most of what was played by the 1961–1964 edition of the group.

Even though Walton's edition of the Messengers included two future superstar instrumentalist–composers in tenor saxophonist Wayne Shorter and trumpeter Freddy Hubbard, the majority of the band's book was written by Walton, including such memorable album title tracks "Ugetsu" and "Mosaic." (Regrettably, Blue Note Records did not give him the opportunity to make albums of his own.)

In fact, he wrote so much for Blakey that when he finally launched his own groups in the late 1960s, their early recordings sound like a direct extension of the Messengers. Perhaps this is why, in the 1970s, Walton founded a new group called Eastern Rebellion; the sound was more Latin than Eastern, and whatever it was, it made a point to not sound like the Jazz Messengers. In the 1970s, Walton also led a more funk-oriented band called Mobius, which, among other things, made two well-received albums for RCA Records.

By the end of his life, Walton had risen to the rank of a true headliner bandleader and was one of the few who was able to command a two-week run at a major club in New York, which usually occurred during the summer months. In 2002, I caught him at the Village Vanguard; then, after Jazz at Lincoln Center opened up Rose Hall in 2004, he played every summer at Dizzy's Club Coca-Cola for the remainder of his life.

In many ways, the music that Cedar Walton made in his final decade was the best of his career, consolidating all the gains that he had made in his earlier phases, from the hard bop of the Messengers with a tinge of both 1970s funk and the notion of Eastern Rebellion. His annual stints at Dizzy's were more like pilgrimages, and the only difficulty was deciding whether I preferred his quintets, usually with Herring on alto and a brass player, such as trumpeter Jeremy Pelt or trombonist Steve Turre, or his increasingly iconic trio with Williams and Higgins, truly one of the greatest piano - bass - drums trios that I've ever heard.

The 2002 run at the Vanguard was a particularly memorable one, not least because he was spotlighting the repertoire from his album *The Latin Tinge* (2002). He played one week with his trio costarring bassist David Williams and drummer Kenny Washington plus guest percussionist Ray Mantilla and then joined forces with alto saxophonist Vincent Herring for the second week. He started his set with three trio numbers, beginning with "Raymond's Blues." Apart from a Coltrane-like vamp, it seemed to have no preset melody but went directly into an engrossing improvisation with lots of quotes ("Sweet and Lovely," "When Lights Are Low," "Jumping with Symphony Sid," and "Stumbling"). An aggressive bop number, "Simple Pleasures," and a ballad, "Dear Ruth," followed.

Then it was time for the *Latin Tinge* material, joined by Señor Mantilla, launching into Freddie Hubbard's "Little Sunflower." As good as the opening "pure" trio numbers were, the addition of Mantilla's congas brought the group to a whole new level; what had seemed good before now became great. On "Body and Soul," Walton opened with an unaccompanied chorus of the melody, replete with Art Tatum–like stops and starts. Then, he cagily contrasted Leroy Anderson's "Serenata" (which he probably learned from Nat King Cole and George Shearing), an American pop tune with Latin allusions, against "Perfidia," a Mexican song that became a pop hit and eventually, a jazz standard.

Here, Walton employed the Latin style of clave-driven keyboard chord voicings (which American jazz fans will recognize from the Shearing–Armando–Perrazza combination) and gave us a reading of "Perfidia" so pleasing that it could almost become a crossover hit. With or without Mantilla (who soloed on the closer, "Ojos de Rojos [Red Eyes]")—or for that matter, in any context whatsoever—Walton was irrepressible and never seemed to run out of ideas.

(*The New York Sun*, 2002)

***

Extending his self-kidding penchant for puns on his name, at the age of 74 in 2008, Cedar Walton released *Seasoned Wood*, and the title aside, the album itself was a serious reflection on who he was and where he was as an artist. The cover of the album is adorned with a photo of the wooden guts of a piano. Walton clearly suggested that his special affinity for the instrument stems from their both being made of wood. Wood implies a kind of sturdiness, a natural durability; likewise, the titles of Walton's compositions here, such as "Clockwise" and "Hindsight" (and Jimmy Heath's "Longravity"), refer to the passage of time and the steady force of life.

Indeed, time had been good to Walton, who had recently celebrated his 50th anniversary in the major leagues of jazz. He made his recording debut in 1958 (as a sideman with trumpeter Kenny Dorham) and earned his initial reputation as a pianist and more importantly, a composer with Art Blakey and the Jazz Messengers. But it wasn't until 1967 that Walton made his debut as a leader. Dorham returned the favor by guest starring on several tracks on the album titled *Cedar!*, the cover of which had the star's name displayed in big letters against a backdrop of wood paneling.

Walton's final decade was a rich and rewarding one: between 2001 and 2011, he made no less than nine new albums, most produced by Don Sickler for High Note Records, and he celebrated the release of most of these with a special annual two-week run at Dizzy's. *Seasoned Wood* costars Vincent Herring and Jeremy Pelt along with bassist Peter Washington and drummer Al Foster. At Dizzy's that August (2008), the group was trombonist Steve Turre; bassist David Williams; and the excellent drummer from the uptown club Smoke, Joe Farnsworth.

The centerpiece of both the album and Walton's set that summer was a stunningly stylish arrangement of Gershwin's "The Man I Love." One would expect the leader to retool the chord changes, and indeed, he did. But what was really arresting was the way he cast the tune itself. With the song set in a medium-up tempo, he subdivided the melodic line as if he were paying as much attention to the lyrics as the notes, playing the words "someday he'll come along" by himself with bass and drums, then having the horns play the rest of the line. As for Gershwin's beautiful bridge, Walton made it a gift to his bassist; no, you can't improve on Gershwin, but you can treat his music with a fresh take that honors the composer's own originality.

In the summer of 2008, Walton also performed as a soloist (without the rest of his band) on a Jazz in July concert at the 92nd Street Y at which he played a remarkable trio treatment of "Over the Rainbow," which was roughly in the same vein as his reading of "My Ship" on *Cedar!* It's not exactly irreverent, starting slow, with the bridge called into service as a verse. But even when he takes it into fast bop time, it's never disrespectful. Walton performs a service to the tune by showing that it doesn't lose its essential beauty even when recast in a radical new setting. On *Seasoned Wood*, he brings the same inspired touch to another standard, "A Nightingale Sang in Berkeley Square." He can play fast and loose with the melody and have fun with it, but he's laughing with it, not at it.

If brilliant recastings of standards were one aspect of Walton's wooden *oeuvre*, so, too, was a creative use of waltz time, which is a unique tendency among bebop and hard bop players. *Cedar!* included one original in 3/4 time ("Twilight Waltz"), and so does the new album, although it's a classic tune of Walton's creation, "Clockwise," which the composer first recorded in 1977. With "All Blues," Miles Davis had established the tradition of the modal waltz, and most jazz composers followed suit. The 3/4 time signature made them seem both rhythmically and harmonically ambiguous. Not so with this sharp tune. "Clockwise" is a solid and traditional number that owes more to Mozart than it does to Miles Davis. Walton also played this (in a double-Steinway treatment with Bill Mays) at 92Y that summer, but his new trio recording (one of three tracks on *Seasoned Wood* with just bass and drums) is a special one.

"Holy Land," which was first recorded by the tenor saxophonist Fathead Newman in 1967, was originally more of a gospel-y vehicle for soul jazz tenors such as Newman and Houston Person. Walton's quintet treatments of this tune have evolved through the years into something much more classical. At Dizzy's, he began with an elaborate, almost baroque introduction, which led into a bass solo. With this tune, one is never quite sure where the "head" is—and it doesn't help that it is only 12 bars long, and it's not a blues. The central portion of this performance of "Holy Land" was a series of exchanges among the piano, the trombone, and the saxophone that were linked by the drummer. It was hard to tell whether they were trading 12s or just playing a succession of single-chorus solos.

The Dizzy's set included two somewhat subterranean slices of Waltonia, "Underground Memories" and "Firm Roots." The first was a quintet expansion of a piece the composer recorded as a solo three years ago. When the leader dedicated the tune to the New York subway system, I expected it to be noisy, crowded, and relentlessly fast. Instead, it was sleek and stylish, efficiently traveling from one point to another in a manner that would have done the MTA proud, with Turre playing muted and Herring on tenor. The widely recorded "Firm Roots," another Walton classic with a tree-and-wood attitude, concluded the Dizzy's set. This memorable descending line has always struck me as a bebop equivalent of Tetris in which the notes fall into place and form patterns as they head downward.

No matter what the ensemble, the style, or the contest and whether he was playing Latin jazz, hard bop, soul jazz, or funk or solo, in his trio, or quartet, Cedar Walton was incapable of playing a note or a phrase that didn't resound with both melody and swing.

(*The New York Sun*, 2008)

DR. BILLY TAYLOR (1921–2010)

When I heard that Billy Taylor had died Tuesday at his home in Riverdale, New York, at the age of 88, it surprised me how fast I was able to think of my favorite performance by the brilliant pianist. It's a 1993 concert by Taylor and one of his favorite collaborators, the superlative baritone saxophonist Gerry Mulligan. The two of them are playing the jazz standard "Darn That Dream," and they're enjoying themselves so thoroughly that at one point early in composer Jimmy Van Heusen's melody, Mulligan just can't contain his joy and starts laughing right in the middle of the first chorus.

Over the course of a career that lasted 70 years, Taylor was one of the major figures who helped the world learn how to take jazz seriously. He was perhaps the first and greatest advocate for the whole of jazz as a teacher, broadcaster, producer, impresario, and all-around advocate. He was the composer of one of the great anthems of the civil rights movement, "I Wish I Knew How It Would Feel to Be Free," and he was the force behind Jazzmobile, which still brings jazz to uptown streets and residents 45 years later—and now 15 more years after that. His very visible dignity and decorum helped give jazz a degree of respect—particularly in education and political circles—that it had never known before. Yet Taylor's music itself was all about having fun. As a concept, fun is baked into the title of his most famous composition, "Capricious," and it's no surprise that while playing with Taylor, a major musician like Mulligan would burst out laughing.

Taylor was all these things and more. Before Wynton Marsalis, he was certainly the most famous spokesman that the jazz world ever had, a familiar presence on TV and radio as well as the force behind jazz at the Kennedy Center in Washington. If he had limited himself to being a pianist, composer, and trio leader—like most of his colleagues—he would still be celebrated as one of the major figures of the instrument. But Taylor went far beyond that.

Billy Taylor at Clark Terry recording session;
Chesky Records; St. Peters Episcopal
Church, NYC; December 1999

Billy Taylor was born in Greenville, North Carolina, in 1921 and grew up in Washington DC. His father played several horns and led the choir in church, and two uncles played piano. When one uncle played him a recording by Art Tatum, the teenage Taylor reacted by thinking, "Wow, who are those two guys?" As he told Marc Myers of JazzWax.com last year, he studied piano with the same teacher who had taught Duke Ellington. He also remembered seeing Ellington, Fats Waller, and others at Washington's Howard and Lincoln Theatres while still a student.

Already a professional musician, Taylor worked his way through Virginia State University. When he contracted tuberculosis in 1942, it took him a year to recover, but it kept him out of World War II. He continued to practice while he recuperated and by 1943, had moved to New York, where he began playing in Harlem and on 52nd Street. More than most musicians of his generation, Taylor was equally fascinated by both the past and the future of jazz. A protégé of the amazing Tatum, Taylor was an early supporter of the bebop movement ("I knew Charlie Parker before he was Charlie Parker," he told Mr. Myers) and was also eager to soak up everything he could from legendary masters, such as Willie "The Lion" Smith. "That's where I first met Thelonious Monk," Taylor told me about 10 years ago. "He was just another young pianist hanging around the Lion then."

By the mid-1940s, Taylor was well established on the jazz scene, first with the legendary violinist Eddie South and as part of a famous 1945 all-star concert at Town Hall. He worked with virtually every veteran jazz giant of the golden age (including, famously, Ben Webster) as well as those of his own generation. He was well known enough to become the house pianist at Birdland after it opened in 1949 and by the 1950s, had branched into broadcasting as a studio musician (he was at the center of *The Subject Is Jazz,* the first and most famous television program dedicated to the music) and as a host and DJ. In the mid- to late 1950s, he was already making some of the most famous albums of his career, such as *Taylor Made Jazz,* taped with most of Duke Ellington's horn section; *My Fair Lady Loves Jazz,* with orchestra conducted by a young Quincy Jones—both in 1957—and *Billy Taylor with Four Flutes,* two years later.

From 1969 to 1972, Taylor served as the first African American conductor on a major network series (*The David Frost Show*). He received his doctorate from the University of Massachusetts in 1975. He later said that he had written "I Wish I Knew How It Would Feel to Be Free" as a dedication to his daughter, Kim, as early as 1954, although it was not recorded (most famously by Nina Simone) until a decade later. In the late 1960s, the song was sung in schools all over the country—that's where I first heard it and sang it—especially in Black neighborhoods.

Taylor became best known as the voice of jazz on both radio and television, hosting *Jazz Alive* for NPR and managing the even more difficult task of keeping the music visible on television—his reports on *CBS Sunday Morning* exposed millions of viewers to the art form. He was a tireless promoter for the jazz cause, one of the first such advocates to serve on many government councils, including the committee that first formed the National Endowment of the Arts Jazz Masters Award (which he himself justly received in 1988). He was appointed the artistic director of Jazz at the Kennedy Center in 1994, the same year he began hosting its NPR radio series *Jazz from the Kennedy Center.* He was still performing both roles up until the time of his death.

What's amazing is that although Taylor was a full-time jazz spokesman a major presence in all the acronym organizations (the NEA, the National Association of Jazz Educators, and the Jazz Foundation of America), he never stopped being a full-time musician, bandleader, and recording artist. When Marian McPartland launched her long-running NPR series *Piano Jazz* in 1978, the first guest she had on was Billy Taylor. It was impossible to do any better.

(*The Wall Street Journal,* 2010)

MCCOY TYNER (1938–2020)

Back in the day, long before the improvisations of John Coltrane and his pianist, McCoy Tyner, were memorized by several generations of music students, it was tough to come up with the right words to describe Tyner's style of playing: distinctly postmodern but no less obviously steeped in the entire history of jazz piano. He was the leading pianist in what was commonly thought of as the "modal" idiom, but he also had a working knowledge of traditional harmonies that was surpassed by none. Tyner was a key participant in some of Coltrane's furthest-reaching music, such as "Chasin' the Trane" and "Ascension," but he also excelled at rapturously romantic readings of pop standards. While Coltrane's own approach was described, famously by Ira Gitler, as "sheets of sound," we have yet to come up with a comparable term for Tyner's own playing—although by now we can simply agree to call it McCoy Tyner style.

Tyner's playing on "Greensleeves" on his 2007 album, *Guitars*, is dark and mysterious, full of deep power grooves that seem to go all the way back to Africa. Yet because the source material is an English folk song, it moves in two directions at once, and that's just geographically. Yet a third dimension is added with the realization that "Greensleeves" is a song from the pianist's own past, which he played famously with Coltrane. Tyner has good reason to celebrate his own legacy: around the time the album was released, he turned 70 and was anticipating the 50th anniversary of his entry into the jazz big times—when he arrived in New York; made his first recording session; joined fellow Philadelphian Benny Golson's The Jazztet;

McCoy Tyner; JVC Newport Jazz Festival; August 14, 1999

and soon enough, attained immortality in the classic Coltrane Quartet. (He further commemorated the occasion with a celebratory concert at the New Jersey Performing Arts Center in Newark.)

The new album (the second release on his new label, McCoy Tyner Music) is also cause for celebration; no one has quite done an album like this in which a legendary jazz pianist matches wits with five leading guitarists. Yet even here, it's not entirely unprecedented in his career: in 1964, Tyner played on two albums with the brilliant guitarist Grant Green, of which the first, *Matador*, is as inspired a meeting of strings and keys as has ever been captured on vinyl. When Tyner plays "My Favorite Things" with Bela Fleck on *Guitars*, it's not only an obvious reference to Tyner's best-known solo with Coltrane; it's also a nod to the treatment of the same arrangement that he recorded with Green.

As McCoy Tyner has said in many interviews, the piano is an orchestra, an entire ensemble, complete unto itself. Pianos and guitars most often shared the stage in the swing era, when the latter was usually relegated to purely rhythmic responsibilities. In modern jazz, they are often perceived as competing for the same space, both harmonically and melodically. Tyner approached this challenge, he told me, by "letting them do what's natural for the instrument. I listened to some recordings of these guys, so I had a general idea of just what they were all about. Then we established some ground rules. But what they played was up to them—I didn't want to give them any restrictions."

Interestingly, not one of the five guitarists is an obvious choice—a player of Tyner's own generation, such as Kenny Burrell or Pat Martino (yet another Philadelphian), and not one is a completely straight-ahead bop-based player. They all were likely to have been inspired by *Looking Out*, Tyner's 1982 collaboration with guitar star Carlos Santana. If Mr. Tyner is simultaneously a classicist and a postmodernist, the guitar stars here are all distinctly post-postmodern: blues rock headliner Derek Trucks; 1970s fusionista John Scofield; jazz experimentalists Bill Frisell and Marc Ribot; and banjo virtuoso Bela Fleck, who phrases the melody to "My Favorite Things" with the exact nuances of both Coltrane and Grant Green.

On the album, Ribot prods Tyner into some atypically free-form playing on the two spontaneously composed tracks titled only "Improvisation 1" and "2." Commemorating the release of the *Guitars* album, Ribot joined Tyner's long-standing trio, with bassist Gerald Cannon and drummer Eric Gravatt, at the Blue Note, and in this context, the guitarist's playing was much more inside, utilizing an octave-based approach that made me think Wes Montgomery was on the bandstand.

The birthday week celebrations were also graced by the presence of two other long-standing collaborators of Tyner, the brilliant alto saxophonist Gary Bartz and dancer Savion Glover. If Glover is not the only tap dancer in the world sporting shoulder-length dreadlocks, he is surely the only one performing in a McCoy Tyner T-shirt. Glover closely communed with the pianist–leader, an extremely percussive player, and alongside Gravatt, making the quintet sound like it had gained a second percussionist and helping to reanimate such Tyner classics as "African Village" and

"Sama Layuca." One of Tyner's most widely widely-heard originals, "Passion Dance," seems to have been written expressly for Glover—the title even describes him in action—in spite of how the dancer wasn't born until six years after the tune was introduced on Tyner's 1967 *The Real McCoy*.

With Glover, Bartz, and Ribot all adding to the trio, this was a louder and more extroverted set than Tyner customarily plays. But there were intimate moments as well: he played a lovely unaccompanied solo version of "I Should Care" by Sammy Cahn (with whom he later teamed up for his own most famous song with lyrics, "You Taught My Heart to Sing"). Later, there was also an outstanding treatment of the Oscar Hammerstein waltz "I'll Take Romance" ("I like that song!" he announces), which like the best of Tyner's music, was at once rhythmic and romantic.

"I grew up playing standards," he told me. "I used to play for singers, they would call me for gigs when I was a teenager. It was very healthy for me, because [collectively] they had a heck of a repertoire, so I learned to play everything. I mix standards with my own originals and I hope it makes for an interesting experience for the listener." Tyner's next album, recorded in San Francisco last year for a 2009 album, will be his first solo album in a decade and will doubtless contain many classic tunes. He adds, "I also like to be able to play 'free,' with no restrictions of any kind, as well as standards, it helps one to keep the ears open." He concludes, "As a kid, I studied Chopin, Beethoven, Bach, Tchaikovsky, all that stuff, and I'm glad I did. It's not that I'm trying to be a classical pianist, but I think that when you're a teenager and you're trying to find out about music and the piano, whatever you do, it all adds up."

(*The Wall Street Journal*, 2008)

***

Most people spell "African-American" with a hyphen, but Larry Wilmore, known as the "Senior Black Correspondent," on Comedy Central's *The Daily Show*, feels the term more rightfully deserves a pair of question marks. "African? American? Make up your mind!"

The music made by the 67-year-old pianist McCoy Tyner between 1968 and 1970 steadfastly refuses to make up its mind: it is hardcore American jazz with a decidedly African spin. Captured on a new three-CD boxed set, *Mosaic Select: McCoy Tyner* (mosaicrecords.com) is incredibly little-known music by one of the most famous contemporary jazz keyboardists; had I not known to whom I was listening, I might have assumed it was Dollar Brand or another jazz composer–pianist who was born and raised in Africa.

This is the same McCoy Tyner who collaborated with John Coltrane on his famous exploration of modes from that continent, *Africa Brass*, yet it sounds nothing like that 1961 classic. During his half-decade as Coltrane's pianist, Tyner also recorded as a leader on Coltrane's label, Impulse Records. In 1967, the year of the tenor giant's death, Tyner switched to Blue Note, where he made three well-received albums in 13 months: 1967's *The Real McCoy* and *Tender Moments* and 1968's *Time for Tyner*. All, more or less, were in a modal hard bop tradition—a logical outgrowth of the music he had been playing with Coltrane.

Tyner was one of the last signings of Blue Note label founder, Alfred Lion, who had sold the company to Liberty Records two years earlier and retired in 1967. Beginning the following year, Tyner's music for Blue Note started to reflect a distinctly post-Lion sensibility; *Tender Moments* and *Time for Tyner* included one or two compositions with African elements, but this would increasingly become the dominant element of in Tyner's music in the late 1960s. He did seven sessions for Blue Note in these three years, resulting in two albums that were issued at the same time—the compatibly named *Extensions* and *Expansions*—and two more that were not released until considerably later—1974's *Asante* and 1976's *Cosmos*—the latter being a double LP catchall of everything Tyner had recorded for the label but that had not yet been released.

In the years when Lion ran Blue Note, the music had a very clear identity, whether it was the avant-garde stylings of Andrew Hill or the soul jazz it pioneered with its many organ stars. Without Lion's guiding force, the label essentially housed a cadre of inspired individuals more or less in business for themselves. Tyner assembled an outstanding quartet with the trumpeter Woody Shaw, the alto saxophonist Gary Bartz, the bassist Herbie Lewis, and the drummer Freddie Waits. But remarkably, Blue Note failed to sell many records for him, and opportunities for the band were sparse. According to reissue producer, Michael Cuscuna, Tyner resorted to driving a taxicab during dry spells to feed his family.

Even as his music grew more African inspired, Tyner was increasingly asserting himself as a composer—nearly all of the 21 tracks on the three CDs break the 10-minute mark, but they're not just bouts of extended solos. Not that the solos are short either. In fact, they generally pivot around an involved theme in addition to lengthy improvisations; there's a lot going on here.

The most African element of Tyner's music is his percussive touch at the keyboard, which is something he has in common with such predecessors as Thelonious Monk, Bud Powell, and even Cecil Taylor. It's widely said that Taylor plays the piano "like 88 tuned drums." But the expression applies equally to all four pianists, and Tyner's playing in this period is especially drumlike. "Vibration Blues," a trio title with Lewis and Waits, is essentially a four-measure phrase that Tyner plays up and then down, repeating it until he has played a whole chorus worth of it, then improvises on this motif. The repetition of that short, catchy phrase is an example of a pop-style element without any resorting to things like electronics or fusion techniques. By the end of the piece, Tyner works himself into a swirl of notes that taken alone, might suggest a devotee of Taylor, but it's how he builds up to that frenzied passage, gets into it, and then resolves it that sets Tyner apart.

Tyner's African inspiration was rarely taken literally (in fact, on the cover of *Extensions*, which parodies an issue of *National Geographic* magazine, it's taken somewhat comically). Most sessions utilized no African instruments or any percussion beyond the standard American trap kit. Some of the instrumentation on the recordings is surprisingly Eurocentric: The first date has Ron Carter on cello, playing a remarkable arco solo on "Vision" and pizzicato on "Smitty." Both Carter and Alice Coltrane (John's widow), who begins "Message from the Nile" on harp, use these European instruments in an urgently rhythmic way, meant to suggest an African approach, combining the harp, for instance, with the saxes of Wayne Shorter and Gary Bartz. Tyner even gets a distinctly African effect from the string quartet that is heard on three pieces as well as from the waltz time signature employed on "Song for My Lady," which is known today as perhaps Tyner's most famous composition.

Finally, on the last date, the *Asante* session, Tyner drops the other shoe and gives himself entirely over to the African groove: He adds a conga player (Mtume, the son of the veteran saxist Jimmy Heath and at the time, a regular member of Miles Davis's working band). Plus, Tyner has his drummer (Billy Hart) playing additional percussion instruments and uses a guitarist (Grant Green's successor, Ted Dunbar) to emphasize the rhythm. Lastly, the leader–pianist brings in a vocalist, one Songai Sandra Smith, whom the liner notes inform us was a New York schoolteacher making her only appearance on records, chanting wordlessly.

Tyner also supplements the alto of his saxophonist, Andrew White, with a wooden flute, which he plays himself. This is dense, multitextural (not to mention, multicultural), polyrhythmic music that combines jazz based on scales, chords, modes, and even completely free playing for a rich sonic vista that sounds like it could be the score to a film or a play set in the Ivory Coast. The only difference is that it's better than any film music I've ever heard.

After these recording sessions, Tyner stayed out of the studio for two years before launching a new relationship with Milestone Records and steadily establishing himself as one of the most durable pianist–bandleaders on the postmodern scene. He has made all kinds of wonderful music since and even led his own big band, but these 21 tracks represent a special period when a pianist from Philadelphia took us back to his roots in Africa.

(*The New York Sun*, 2007)

POSTMODERN POSTER CHILDREN

SUN RA (1914–1993)

St. Louis Blues: Solo Piano

To see Sun Ra in performance was to realize that planet earth could not contain him—hence, he sent his spirit soaring across the galaxy. Likewise, his music could not be contained to any single genre or music, especially not any subgenre of jazz. He was at once a survivor of the big-band movement and a pioneer of what we came to call the avant-garde and was proficient in bebop and every other phase of modern jazz along the way. In the last decades of his life—the years in which I got to see him—he was more eclectic than ever. Within the course of a single year, in New York alone, you would typically see him performing the original works and outer space jazz that he was known for or alternatively, a program of vintage 1920s hot jazz by Fletcher Henderson, a selection of Disney songs, or even a Valentine's Day presentation of love songs by Cole Porter and Jerome Kern. (I'd love to find out if there's a tape somewhere of that one in particular.)

Sun Ra, who was born Herman Blount in Birmingham, Alabama, in 1914, was originally a pianist and composer, long before he became the most celebrated orchestra leader of the free-jazz era and made solo and keyboard-centric albums throughout his career. The 1977 *St. Louis Blues* is often cited as his best unaccompanied performance. It was recorded on the day before Independence Day in 1977 at a jazz loft called The Axis or sometimes, "The Axis in Soho."

The concert itself was officially produced by Andy Plesser, and the proceedings were recorded under the aegis of Paul Bley, a leading postmodern jazz pianist. The resultant album would be one of about two dozen releases of cutting-edge jazz released on Bley's label—what we would today call a "boutique" label—Improvising

Sun Ra; Prospect Park Bandshell; June 22, 1985

Artists, or simply IA. In addition to the LP, released in 1978, and then the CD, Carol Goss, the photographer who was then also Bley's wife and partner in IA, filmed the performance, and it was briefly available as a VHS tape. (I've never seen it.)

The concert recording consists of three jazz standards and four originals, although Sun Ra's treatment of the standards is every bit as original as the originals. We come to the title song, "St. Louis Blues" with the second track. The three standards are grouped together in sequence.

That second track opens with an off-center introduction, which actually leads us to think that we're about to hear an original. Sun Ra plays one introductory phrase and then another, and next thing we know, we are recognizing the opening notes of one of the most played jazz standards and American songs of all time, W. C. Handy's immortal "St. Louis Blues." He plays along with the A strain for a while but instead of moving on to the next part of the tune, repeats it. Moving forward, instead of going through the song as written, he plays variations on the opening section and pushes it into different directions, and it gradually becomes a set of original improvisations on the basic blues. Near the end, he returns to the opening strain ("I hate to see the evening sun go down"), but just when we think he might go to the rest of the song as written, he plays a few more varying phrases and reaches the coda. Overall, Handy would recognize it, but it's as much Sun Ra as it is the Father of the Blues.

"Three Little Words" opens with Sun Ra playing the recognizable melody in a series of fast, zingy staccato phrases and a cadenza-style left-hand intro that sets up great contrast for the ensuing right-hand figures. Overall, it's in the tradition of the way that a piano wizard such as Earl Hines or Oscar Peterson might set up a set of variations. It leads us to expect that following this intro, he's going to pour on the speed and give us a set of superfast runs. Instead, Sun Ra lays down a sequence of disjointed melodic bits, which eventually lead back to the tune, or sort of. Actually, it sounds like three little words are struggling to break out of a cluster of notes like roses popping out of a bush of thorns. He brings back the tune in different guises, never completely abandoning it—at times light and delicate, like a will-o'-the-wisp of a song, and at other points, dark and heavy when he phrases the tune in a sequence of highly staccato bursts. He dances all over the song, forward and backward. He ends on a dark note, a big heavy chord, followed by a tinkly, diminutive "Three little words."

Sun Ra begins "Honeysuckle Rose" by tinkling out the first five notes of the basic tune ("ev'ry honey bee"), but rather than play the rest of the line, he improvises a different ending to each line. He reaches the bridge after a minute or so, then plays the last A closer to how it's written—as we know it. At the end of the first chorus, there's a big rolling *tremolo* as he goes into the next section, which sounds like a set of variations on top of other variations. Eventually, he comes back to a slow-ish and stylish, rather jaunty rendition, of Fats Waller's tune and ends by playing that main five-note phrase a few times as a conclusion.

"Sky and Sun," which sounds like a prewritten original, transpires mostly in the upper half of the keyboard, which the pianist apparently views as the sunnier portion of the instrument. There's a sequence of tinkling notes in the treble supported by darker chords from around the middle C area. Near the end, it gets darker, then lighter again—you keep thinking some famous tune is about to break out, such as "I'll Remember April," but it never quite does. It resembles a day at the beach when clouds keep passing overhead, first sunshine and then shade.

"I Am We Are I" seems like a direct continuation of "Sky and Sun"; it plods along a similar trajectory—upscale (literally) notes in the right hand and darker chords in the left—but overall is much bleaker. He creates a low key mood and instills an ill-defined sense of space by tonally filling with direct finger strumming of the bass area strings (springs), using sustain pedal to extend and blend a further sense of impending dread. Unlike the previous piece, his trills in the treble pick up more and more notes, and he lays them out in a spinning pattern or series of patterns. It proceeds to a point where it just seems to unexpectedly come to an end, like a hike through the woods where you just run out of trail.

The title of "Thoughts on Thoth" refers to the Egyptian god of writing, wisdom, and magic. Sun Ra pounds out a steady pattern that seems to be getting higher and higher and more intense. I keep seeing a distinct image of some trepidatious soul slowly climbing up a ladder to the top of a circus tent, with the tension building all the way, as if he's going to jump off—either to do a high dive, or walk a high wire, or do a trapeze act—either way, it's pretty tense. The suspense finally breaks, but the second part is still very dissonant and even dire; this is the most that Sun Ra sounds like what we would think of as avant-garde piano, like Cecil Taylor. There are a bunch of swirling patterns, then some heavy thuds, lots of skittering up and down the keyboard à la Cecil. It's like he's been building to his heaviest note with the final piece in the program. He pounds down on the keyboard with a conclusive band, the applause sounds, and we're out of here.

Ostensibly, the album features four original compositions. However, the very first track, "Ohosnisixaeht," doesn't necessarily sound like a composition unless it's in the sense of a spontaneously created work—which is, in this case, another way of saying it's a pure improvisation. This matches the title, which seems like a random sequence of letters. (It took several readers to point out to me that "Ohosnisixaeht" was actually "The Axis in Soho" spelled backward.)

"Ohosnisixaeht" starts slowly, with just one note, then a pause, then another note, then a kind of squiggle of notes that forms itself into something better described as a phrase rather than a melody. Soon, a melody makes itself known, one that feels more like a stream of consciousness—or a stream of something. Sun Ra's extensive use of the sustain pedal in his work, in general, allows chords and figures to blend into one another, weaving in and out of dissonances. Here, there's one long phrase that goes on for a while, keeps building. The piece becomes different things at different times; he keeps a steady tempo—doesn't speed up or slow down—until the end, when he gradually grinds to a halt. Throughout, it's never really clear where he's going, but it's a fun trip just the same.

(*Slouching Towards Birdland*, Substack, 2024)

CECIL TAYLOR (1929–2018)

Now, about that red piano: Charles Bourgeois, the longtime integral member of George Wein's Festival Productions, which produces the ongoing JVC Jazz Festival, told *The New York Sun* that the company simply requested a standard nine-foot concert grand but was as surprised as anyone when the instrument that was delivered turned out to be encased in bright red enamel, with a bright red bench to match. Little did anyone suspect that this was actually a magical piano with the power to transform itself into an entirely new instrument each time a different master touches it.

On Friday and Saturday, the piano was played by three separate colossi of the keyboard, each from a different generation and subgenre of jazz: the bebop-styled George Cables (born 1944); the uncompromising titan of free-jazz piano, Cecil Taylor, who is pushing 80; and the swing-to-bop keyboard legend Hank Jones, who turns 90 in a few weeks.

Mr. Cables was regarded as a young master of the modern jazz idiom—a neo-bopper—even when he earned his reputation in the 1970s and 1980s in the bands of Freddie Hubbard, Dexter Gordon, and Art Pepper. Health issues have kept him out of action for the last few years, but though he is still awaiting a kidney transplant, Mr. Cables is working again with a vengeance and has just released a two-CD set of solo piano, *You Don't Know Me* (Kind of Blue Records).

Cecil Taylor; Merkin Hall; October 12, 1995

One has to assume that the title song, which served as the centerpiece of his solo recital on Friday, was not only an homage to the late Eddy Arnold but also an indication that Mr. Cables, who is known primarily as a sideman to iconic horn players, means to establish himself as a bandleader and soloist in his own right. His concert was notable for its extremely personal interpretations of standards, including romantic yet modernistic renditions of "My Foolish Heart" and "You Don't Know What Love Is," set in a haunting minor, as well as spirituals, such as "Going Home." The latter started simply, with a lot of space between each note, and even as it grew more elaborate, Mr. Cables did not lose the thread of the tune's inspirational message.

The pianist also sought to identify himself as a composer with several originals inspired by people in his life, such as the unsentimental waltz "EVC" (for his mother) and "Helen's Song." It wasn't necessary for him to explain to whom the latter was dedicated—after a chorus or two, I felt like I knew her myself.

Normally, when Cecil Taylor performs, I try not to sit too close; he attacks the keyboard with such ferocity that I'm afraid an F-sharp key might come loose and hit me in the face. After a lifetime of listening to Mr. Taylor (whose first major concert was at the Newport Jazz Festival in 1957), I didn't think he could possibly surprise me: Did he come out in shiny black pajamas and heavy woolen socks? Check. Recite surrealistic poetry in a thespian speaking voice? Check. Pound away relentlessly to create almost shockingly original music that owes nothing to any conventional concept of melody or harmony? Check.

But wait just a darn minute here! This was a much more lyrical and listenable Cecil Taylor than I have ever heard in concert, resembling the more measured steps into the enveloping avant-garde of his albums from the 1950s and early 1960s. Playing from some kind of prewritten score, he utilized an approach that seemed inspired by Ornette Coleman's definition of free jazz: a fragment of a tune is stated, then varied between bass and treble, then flowing logically into a series of well-developed phrases. Mr. Taylor made brilliant use of dynamics and other kinds of contrast, adroitly juxtaposing soft with loud, busy with tranquil, jarring with soothing. Normally, one hears volcanoes and earthquakes in his playing, but on Friday, we also heard waterfalls, verdant valleys, and blue jays. It was by far the most accessible performance I have ever heard Mr. Taylor give—for once, his playing seemed to obey the laws of physics and even music—yet accessibility seemed beside the point.

The concert pairing Messrs. Taylor and Cables, produced by Jill Newman, was a miracle of economy—two masters at their peaks playing the red Steinway without unnecessary amplification. (In fact, he played with characteristic magnificence on Wednesday in a short set at the Jazz Journalist's Association Awards, both with and without Joe Lovano.) I wish Saturday's show had followed the same format, with the great Hank Jones playing a simple solo or trio set. Instead, the producers opted to present Mr. Jones as the center of a jam-session-style evening in which nearly all the playing was brilliant but the man of the hour himself was barely heard from.

The show began with three trio numbers in which the outstanding bass and drum team of George Mraz and Willie Jones III, respectively, were miked much louder than the piano and seemed to solo for much longer on every tune. Mr. Jones was absent for a long section in which Roberta Gambarini sang (a strange decision considering that Mr. Jones and Ms. Gambarini have just released a duet album), accompanied by the pianist Gerald Clayton and tenor saxophone giant Frank Wess. There were features for the trombonist Steve Davis and his beautiful tone ("We'll Be Together Again"), guitarist Russell Malone ("Ain't Misbehavin'"), and trumpeter Roy Hargrove ("My Foolish Heart," which was introduced as "These Foolish Things," a "foolish" mistake—and the second time the Victor Young song was heard in the Music Hall of the New York Society for Ethical Culture in two days).

Sadly, Mr. Jones hardly soloed at all, acting instead like a sideman at his own concert. Perhaps his many years as an accompanist and studio player left him reluctant to seize the spotlight the way the exceptional Mr. Clayton (a dreadlocked, 24-year-old whippersnapper) did without a qualm on his solo feature, Cole Porter's "I Love You." Finally, in the last segment, a septet sequence with all the rhythm and horns, Mr. Jones at last left us with a memorable 32 bars on "I'll Remember April." The group also played Ellington's "What Am I Here For" with an intriguing tenor-trombone lead and concluded with a solid reading of "Midgets," Mr. Wess's famous fast blues for flute and muted trumpet.

Much marvelous music was heard, but overall, this was a concert that did everything except what it was supposed to, namely, leave us with a sense of the iconic greatness of Mr. Jones, one of jazz's major living masters. A week after his 90th birthday on July 31, Mr. Jones will begin a four-night stint at Birdland, and with any luck, he will not be joined by any guest stars or other distractions. In the meantime, thank you, Steinway & Sons.

(*The New York Sun*, 2008)

***

Dick Katz, the late pianist and veteran of the bebop era, could remember the exact moment when he heard the innovations of Charlie Parker incorporated into elevator music. It may be true that any successful artistic uprising eventually has to be absorbed into the cultural mainstream, yet Cecil Taylor is the one revolutionary whose music will never be co-opted by the establishment: he still sounds just as radical and explosive as when he first "blew a hole in the side of jazz" (as pianist Craig Taborn put it on Tuesday night) nearly 60 years ago. The remaining four nights of this celebration consist of an instrumental homage by pianist Thollem McDonas, bass clarinetist Arrington de Dionyso, and percussionist–bandleader William Hooker (May 16); a film screening at Anthology (May 22); and the main event, two solo nights of the man himself in Harlem (May 17) and Brooklyn (May 19). This music can never lose its power to astonish.

Built in 1890, the Gatehouse is a curiously appropriate structure to house the music of Cecil Taylor: with its buttresses and turrets, it looks for all the world like the Harlem Campus of Hogwarts. I assumed it had to have once been either a fortress or a lighthouse (although it wasn't clear what either would be doing in the middle of 135th Street); it's somewhat anticlimactic to learn that it was tasked with the more mundane function of controlling the Croton Aqueduct system.

On Tuesday and Wednesday, the Cecil Celebration began with two nights of three pianists . . . and a poet: Vijay Iyer, Craig Taborn, and Amina Claudine Myers, each of whom played for about 15–20 minutes in solo. Ms. Myers's music was affirmatively spiritual, quickly bringing to mind Mary Lou Williams and her relationship with Mr. Taylor. Mr. Taborn and Mr. Iver both played with that combination of utmost primitivism and sophistication that marks Taylor's work: at times, it seems like somebody's kid brother pounding randomly on the keys, and others, it's a musical language so dense that even Stephen Hawking couldn't do the math. There are moments when all the avant-gardes run together, when the jazz avant-garde sounds indistinguishable from the classical avant-garde, but this isn't one of them. The Taylor-esque allusions to the blues and African roots make this music undeniably jazz.

The two hours of rather extreme piano were interrupted only by the recitation of Mr. Baraka, the critic, poet, philosopher, and longtime advocate of free jazz; he was accompanied by Ms. Myers, who gradually joined in by chanting from the sidelines. The content of his verse wasn't easy to follow, but it was in a jazzlike meter, punctuated by cries of "play that," which hung in the air like a Monk chromaticism.

The most creative playing arrived with the duets in the second half, wherein all three players joined in four-handed fun on two huge concert grands. When Mr. Taborn and

Mr. Iyer worked together, the sonic landscape was so thick that it could have been a tape of Oscar Peterson overlaid with Art Tatum and then played backward. Ms. Myers's melodic approach offered more of a contrast. At points, both Mr. Taborn and Mr. Iyer used a Taylor-ian device of repeating a specific phrase over and over with very slight variations, making it only slightly different with each repetition. It was as if they were standing at the Gates of Heaven, trying every possibility of a password that might allow them entrance. Maybe that's why the builders named the place "The Gatehouse."

We were told at the beginning of the evening that Mr. Taylor himself was in the house; clearly, the participants found his presence more inspiring than intimidating. At the conclusion, he came down and joined with the four artists in a group hug and bow as if to convey his approval—like a father giving away the bride. It was a magnanimous if somewhat unnecessary gesture; this music is no longer exclusively his. He gave it to the world a long time ago, and now it belongs to us all.

(*The Wall Street Journal*, 2012)

PAUL BLEY (1932–2016) AND CARLA BLEY (1936–2023)

"Play ball!" Whenever I hear someone shout that phrase, as when baseball season opened last week, I can't help but think they're exclaiming an anagram for the outstanding Canadian pianist Paul Bley (aka "Bley, Paul"). In turn, that puts me in mind of Mr. Bley's famous ex-wife, the marvelous composer, bandleader, and pianist, Carla Bley, who is appearing this week at Birdland with her trio, the Lost Chords.

The idea of anagrams—taking the components of something and reworking them into something else—is at the heart of Ms. Bley's music, and so, too, surprisingly, is baseball. She began on Wednesday with an extended work titled "National Anthem," which just as easily could have been named "National Pastime." Ms. Bley's longtime collaborator, the bassist Steve Swallow, introduced the work by warning us to be prepared for a long, uninterrupted piece, but it was laid out in five shorter chunks and was easy to digest.

It immediately became clear that "National Anthem" is a musical anagram of "The Star-Spangled Banner." At one point, it was a bebop-style harmonic variation, with tenor saxophonist Andy Sheppard laying down fast flurries of notes over the cycle of chords, while Francis Scott Key's melody was shunted to the sidelines; at another, it was a soulful, R&B-style rendition as if "The Star-Spangled Banner" had been written by Curtis Mayfield. At other times, it became a funk number with a heavy backbeat, a funeral dirge, and even a 12-bar blues.

At various periods in Ms. Bley's career—as with her big band and even more so, on her highly acclaimed and ambitious *Escalator over the Hill* (1971)—her work has been musically complex and additionally saddled with theoretical and political baggage. The music of the Lost Chords trio, however, is admirably simple and direct:

everything is exactly what it seems to be, and yet the three group members create all the musical elements—harmony, melody, and rhythm—at once. Even though any one of them may come forward at any time, you never feel as though you're listening to a bunch of musicians merely taking turns.

That was one factor that reminded me of Ornette Coleman; another was that Mr. Swallow played a five-string electric bass, which like Al MacDowell's in Mr. Coleman's group, became a guitar when he played with Mr. Sheppard's tenor saxophone and remained a bass when he played with Ms. Bley's piano.

Ms. Bley showed more of her talent for musical anagrams with "Awful Coffee," which, if my decoding skills are working properly, was a variant on "Tea for Two" in which the "T" could have stood for "Thelonious." Monk was further referenced in "Mister Misterioso," which uses the legendary pianist–composer's classic as a jumping-off point. When jazz composers use an existing tune as a basis for a composition, it's often said that they "elaborate" on the original, yet Ms. Bley seemed to be doing just the opposite: her take on "Misterioso" was as much a simplification as an elaboration, reducing the song to its most fundamental elements (the basic blues) while adding to it at the same time.

Two ballads, "Permanent Wave" and "Valse Sinestro," featured a bittersweet, Fellini-like quality, especially the latter, which was played in 3/4 time and in minor keys, with Mr. Sheppard switching to soprano saxophone. But the most striking amalgam was "Sidewinders in Paradise," a mix of the most famous melodies of the late trumpeter Lee Morgan and the even more late Russian composer Alexander Borodin, on top of a Pan-American beat: a hard bop-opera amalgam played on coconut shells. Ms. Bley uses a similarly Morgan-esque beat on "Hip Hop" on her group's marvelous debut album, *The Lost Chords*, from 2004.

This combination of piano, sax, and whatever it is Mr. Swallow is playing doesn't sound like any other trio. Likewise, the five-piece edition, heard on the group's new album, *The Lost Chords Find Paolo Fresu*, doesn't sound like any other quintet, even though it features the standard rhythm-section instrumentation, namely, tenor and trumpet (in the form of the titular Sardinian brass man Paolo Fresu, whom they recorded with in Rome last spring). Ms. Bley's compositions are as whimsical as ever, as indicated by such titles as "Liver of Life" and the comic strip–like packaging of the new album. Even her website (carlabley.com) is laid out in the form of a map of a penitentiary.

I'm not sure what's supposed to be funny about prison, but it's altogether likely that Ms. Bley (who, at 72, still has the distinctive blond bangs that make her look like Cameron Diaz's mother) is making a further statement about the nature of freedom. This brings us back to "The Star-Spangled Banner" and in turn, to the famous line about the song's composer, Francis Scott Key, in *Angels in America*: "He set the word 'free' on a note so high no one could reach it." Ms. Bley makes both the note and the concept of freedom itself imminently attainable.

(*The New York Sun*, 2023)

VIJAY IYER (BORN 1971)

Vijay Iyer Trio, *Uneasy* (ECM Records)

People talk about improvisation as if it were the most important thing in jazz, but I would make the case that interpretation is at least as significant. To clarify, improvisation, essentially, is making up an entire new melody (usually based on existing harmonies), and interpretation is taking a tune and personalizing it, rendering it in a distinctly individual and personal way such as—hopefully—no one has ever done before. The lines between the two approaches are often blurred, but the greatest musicians are invariably masters of both.

Pianist Vijay Iyer, who is appearing as part of his outstanding trio with bassist Harish Raghavan and drummer Tyshawn Sorey at Dizzy's this weekend, reminds me that jazz is also the major music where it's possible to have an interpretation of an interpretation. There's a famous arrangement of "Honeysuckle Rose" with a classic "shout chorus," as musicians call it, that's sometimes attributed to Benny Carter but may go back even earlier. Likewise, Ahmad Jamal's 1958 recording of the 1936 song "Poinciana" has become so iconic that it's hard to imagine the melody being played any other way.

In 1964, tenor saxophonist Joe Henderson included Cole Porter's "Night and Day" on *Inner Urge*, a classic Blue Note album costarring pianist McCoy Tyner, bassist Bob Cranshaw, and drummer Elvin Jones. The 1932 song was already one of the most performed in all of jazz, but Henderson's version proved to be, as they say, a game changer.

Henderson interprets the melody mostly straight and, certainly, recognizably. After a delightfully florid intro, the saxophonist dances into the tune with a grace suggesting Fred Astaire, for whom the song was written (in the Broadway musical *Gay Divorce*), and treats the tune respectfully, goosing it with a minor flourish here and there. He improvises energetically in his second chorus, and Tyner's piano solo is equally impressive.

Younger musicians have come to regard Henderson's version as the essential template for "Night and Day." Pianist Renee Rosnes, who played in one of the late saxophonist's final bands, included it in her 2009 album *Black Narcissus (A Tribute to Joe Henderson).* Mr. Iyer, too, uses it as the jumping off point for his treatment of the song, which served as the centerpiece of his opening set at Dizzy's on Thursday as well as on his current album, *Uneasy* (ECM Records).

In fact, in Mr. Iyer's version, there's just as much Henderson and Tyner as there is Porter; he, too, opens with a brief, understated flourish, similar to the one from 1964, which gracefully introduces the familiar melody. He gives us just enough of the tune for us to get our bearings and then goes off on his own.

There are eight bars we can recognize, then eight bars of variations, a pattern that is then repeated and allows him to render the bridge for us more or less as Porter composed it. In his own improv, he seems to be Henderson and Tyner at the same

Vijay Iyer; Jazz Standard; January 23, 2013

time, spinning elaborate lines in his right hand and painting supportive splashes of color in his left.

The bassist (Linda May Han Oh on the album) takes the spotlight for a chorus, as does Mr. Sorey on drums, and when Mr. Iyer frames the drum solo with piano interjections, it again has the feeling of choreography, as if Mr. Iyer were taking a great big balletic leap into the middle of the drum solo.

At Dizzy's, "Night and Day" arrived right in the middle of the set, following what, from a distance, seemed to be two longish numbers but were actually sequences of songs that flowed uninterrupted, one into the other. The first such block began with a few short bursts of notes interspersed with longer pauses as the melody of the album's title track, "Uneasy," comes into focus. The piece isn't entirely accurately named: there are aspects of it, like a rumbling bass and drum part underneath, that do suggest a kind of unease, but the melody itself is soft and warm and even easy on the ear.

The second tune at Dizzy's—which came directly out of the first without a break—was a standard of a different stripe, Stevie Wonder's "Overjoyed." As far as I can see, Mr. Iyer and company have not yet recorded this, but his approach to the tune was angular in a way that again put me in mind of McCoy Tyner.

The rest of the set was mostly Mr. Iyer's originals as well as a piece by the late Geri Allen. Perhaps Mr. Wonder knows Mr. Iyer better than he knows himself; his music gives us many more reasons to be joyful than it does to be uneasy.

(*The New York Sun*, 2023)

GERI ALLEN (1956–2016)

For more than 20 years, Geri Allen has been an archetype of the new breed of contemporary jazz musician who is equally versed in the most modern, cutting-edge music as well as the most traditional. When she works with more experimental player–composer iconoclasts, such as Ornette Coleman or Steve Coleman (no relation), she may break a few rules, but when she plays jazz standards and the American songbook, it becomes clear that she knows how to follow those rules and to be creative within them.

Ms. Allen and her trio—with the drummer Jimmy Cobb and the bassist Darryl Hall—are appearing this week, through Sunday, at the Village Vanguard in support of her new album, *Timeless Portraits and Dreams.* As with her previous release, *The Life of a Song* (from 2004), she is again leaning more toward the traditional side. The new album—and the music she played at the Vanguard on Tuesday night—draw heavy inspiration from two cultural institutions that are obviously major influences in Ms. Allen's life and music: the Black church and the living legacy of her musical forefathers and foremothers.

She began the opening set with a two-part spiritual statement, the traditional "Oh Freedom," which she refashioned into a brief, rubato introduction to a new work in a similar vein, "Melchezedik," by her brother-in-law, the saxophonist Antoine Roney. This opening segment was the slowest part of the evening: the extra-long composition is more satisfying on the CD, where it is sweetened considerably by the subtle, background singing of the Atlanta Jazz Chorus; in person it seemed rather long and repetitious.

Geri Allen; Charlie Parker Jazz Festival; Tompkins Square Park; August 27, 1995

From there, things picked up considerably, as Ms. Allen launched into two interconnected subsets of compositions by George Gershwin and by Charlie Parker. Coincidentally, Ms. Allen did not play the familiar melodies of either Gershwin song, both of which were inspired by earlier jazz interpretations. "Embraceable You," used as its point of departure, Herbie Hancock's 1998 performance from his classic album *Gershwin's World*, though where Mr. Hancock played the melody in an abstract, stretched-out fashion, Ms. Allen avoided it entirely but sounded warm and embraceable just the same.

"Ah-Leu-Cha" was essentially a variation on a variation of a variation: she used the 1955 arrangement by Miles Davis (which also featured Jimmy Cobb) of one of Parker's many transfigurations of the "I Got Rhythm" chord changes, this one from 1948 and in the key of F. She followed this with "Another Hair-Do," a seldom-played Parker blues in B-flat from 1947. This was anything but abstract but rather, was an exceedingly lucid statement of the bebop blues—there was no mistaking it for anything else.

There are several additional spiritual pieces on the album, which were directly inspired by *Mary Lou's Mass*, by Mary Lou Williams. The CD, somewhat confusingly, includes a piece called "Portraits and Dreams," which is actually heard twice, and another called "Timeless Portraits and Dreams."

At the Vanguard, Ms. Allen used the first "Portraits" as an intro into the overtly spiritual "Well Done," whose lyric directly addresses the Creator. As on the record, this was sung by Carmen Lundy, an outstanding singer whose crystalline voice is a good match for Ms. Allen's touch at the keyboard. On the album, Ms. Lundy also sings the other "Portraits" (the "Timeless" one), and she would have been welcome joining Ms. Allen for more songs at the Vanguard.

Ms. Allen closed the set with "In Appreciation," which was essentially a blues with a down-home churchy feel. She is a bop-based pianist who rarely overwhelms you with run after run of as many notes as the ear can process; rather, every note she plays means something. She is no less eloquent or elegant whether she's playing the blues or Gershwin or for that matter, the Italian film composer Nino Rota, whose "La Strada" served as the prettiest part of the Vanguard set, as well as the new album.

I wouldn't be surprised if Ms. Allen heard it for the first time in the same place I did, as played by the late, wonderful pianist Jaki Byard on the 1980 *Amarcord Nino Rota* album. Like Byard, she plays it unaccompanied and with extreme sensitivity, playing up the contrast between the tender theme and the rather brutal story of the film it accompanies. It's something of a surprise that the most moving piece of the evening comes neither from the Church nor the jazz tradition, but then this music is about surprises.

(*The New York Sun*, 2006)

***

Geri Allen Trio, *The Printmakers*

Consider the basic structure of your typical jazz performance: customarily, we start with the theme and then hear the usually improvised variations, and in many cases, the improvisation gets further and further away from the melody the musicians began with. This general outline often also applies to the large-scale evolution of the music itself. In 1917, jazz musicians generally stayed fairly close to the melody; however, by 1967, there was an entire faction of musicians who made a point to completely avoid any conventional definition of melody.

Sometimes we expect jazz in the postmodern era—everything since the arrival of Coltrane, Ornette, and Cecil Taylor—to follow that format: to start in one place and then consistently get further and further "out."

Geri Allen's *The Printmakers* reverses the equation—at least at first. It starts with what might be called abstract sound; in fact, we're not quite sure what it is—a ball bouncing? Popcorn popping? The popping doesn't quite have a regular beat, but it meanders, until it encounters, and then steps aside, for a drum interlude by Andrew Cyrille. This is, as you'd expect, pure rhythm—in the extreme. After a minute or so of drums, we go into the full trio, including bassist Anthony Cox, playing an unbelievably catchy melody. Allen's tonal and rhythmic strokes evoke an Afro-Caribbean diaspora sound, reminiscent of Dollar Brand or Monty Alexander.

The Printmakers, recorded in Germany in 1984, was the first album as a leader by Geri Allen. By that point, she had already graduated—as had her colleague Cassandra Wilson—from the loose collective of players associated with alto saxophonist–bandleader Steve Coleman, which he called M-Base. Apart from the music of Mr. Coleman and some of the individual members, it was hard to get a bead on exactly what that term was supposed to mean. M-Base was never as clearly defined a movement, say, as what was referred to, and not necessarily metaphorically, the "Lennie Tristano school" of a few decades earlier. But maybe that was part of the point too: all the major players of M-Base were excellent musicians who made excellent music in their own way.

The second tune on *The Printmakers*, "Eric" (subtitled "For Eric Dolphy") starts slowly, with a few chords that serve as an introduction. Allen plays something that might be better described as a pattern of notes rather than a distinctive tune, and she starts running laps around it even as she's laying it out for the first time. She slows down into a statelier, ballad-like line, which gradually opens up into a lovely, shimmering melody, one that makes me think of rippling water. When she drifts into tempo, we then hear Anthony Cox's bass (electric, from what I can tell) playing behind her. When it moves into something more like a jazzy beat, we notice the subtle presence of Mr. Cyrille, with his beautiful brushstrokes on Geri's lyrical canvas.

If "Eric" is mostly piano and you barely notice the bass and drums, by contrast "Running As Fast As You Can . . . TGTH" is all about the trio. It starts off with a drum passage, and then Mr. Cyrille is joined by Mr. Cox, and finally, about 90 seconds in, Allen enters. This is one of several pieces we might describe as free jazz. In Allen's case especially, the term refers to a means of creation, not necessarily the way of a piece of music as received by the listener. On "Running," like most so-called free piano, the music is rambling and at times almost chaotic, but there's always, if not a melody, at least something that the listener can follow. There's always something more than just total randomness.

Alas, "Running As Fast As You Can . . . TGTH" doesn't have a subtitle that might communicate the intentions of the composer. "M's Heart," which concludes the first side of the original LP, is subtitled "In Memory of Mrs. Barbara Jean Allen," referring to the pianist–composer's mother. This, too, sounds like a free-jazz piece—and it's completely solo—but in a very different way. Here, there is a distinct melody, played in a way that's easy to follow, yet it does sound completely improvised, as if she hadn't worked out anything at all before she sat down at the keyboard to play it.

This chaotic messaging conjures visually a running *away*, out of fear from something rather than toward a destination or goal. It could also be that the busy-ness of the piece and what seems to be an entirely spontaneous creation speak to the "complexity" of the relationship and the emotional turbulences between a daughter and her mother, which in the end melts and resolves into a beautiful brief phrase about their deeply shared love.

"Printmakers (altosaxophonistic poetic type printmakers)" starts side two, with the full trio; it opens with a thorny but distinct melody that gets more twisty and gnarly as it progresses. But then, about three minutes in, she resolves in to a funky, followable tune that sounds like Horace Silver or Vince Guaraldi. This is the showcase, namesake piece that is a summary statement for the album *The Printmakers* and where Allen was at this point in her journey. It features driving, recurrent left-hand rhythms, supported in this instance by Cyrille's rimshots, which create the feel of the 3 measure of a 3/2 clave. Allen injects oodles of right-hand frenetic dissonances, splashes of color, and brief explorations into new thematic turf, with an occasional return to the home base. With these signature techniques and tools, she weaves her tapestry, at once a committed, complex, and conflicted piece of musical art.

The piece continues, getting darker and more discordant; then it resolves into another tune. "Printmakers" could be at least five different pieces in one, all of which seem to exist in stark contrast to each other. When Cyrille plays a solo in the middle, it sounds like a direct extension, albeit played on drums, of the twisty melody line that Allen has been developing thus far. When Allen returns, it does sound like the expected "tutti" at the end of a solo and the return of the full ensemble, in this case the trio, and that's the closest thing to a conventional moment on the track. Might "altosaxophonistic" also refer to Dolphy?

"Andrew" is subtitled "(For Andrew Cyrille)" but is not the kind of loud, percussive piece of the sort we might expect to find dedicated to a drummer, rather a deeply introspective, even lyrical ballad. In fact, we notice Cyrille less than the other players here. Allen sets up a highly rhythmic, often percussive left-hand repeating pattern, weaving through the piece several different themes to which Cyrille's drum figures are closely, almost adhesively attached. Cox's bass figures are not quite as closely committed but beautifully complementary, and then Cyrille is rewarded with some untethered solo time in the latter half.

Another solo piece, "When Kayuba Dances" starts fast, gets faster, and ends faster still—I pity the dancer who tries to keep up with it. At least that's the impression Allen wants to create, that it's speeding up, but actually, the left-hand figures remain well anchored in a steady tempo. It is the right hand where all the frenetic mischief plays out and repeatedly chomps at the bit as it creates rhythmic and tempo tensions against the steady-as-you-go left hand. Tonally, there are a lot of suspensions as open 4th (11th) chordal progressions (almost, but not quite à la Cecil Taylor), which alternately are speared by harsh dissonances or lightened by bright major hues . . . in the end, the dancing never stops, just simply fades. It's essentially the same melody throughout, which grows denser and then occasionally lightens up as it proceeds. It also seems completely improvised; for one thing, it doesn't really have an ending—it just seems to stop.

Cox takes out his bow to play arco on the final piece, "D and V (For Daddy and Vernie)," an obvious dedication to her father, Mount Allen Jr. (and possibly also to Vernon Reid). It's a lovely and, yes, lyrical duo that provides a satisfying ending to what has been a very busy album, full of new ideas and new intentions. At a mere two minutes, "D and V" is an intensely emotional, all too brief piece that leaves us wanting more.

Fortunately, Geri Allen, who was 28 at the time of the recording, left us a lot more. By the time of her death, at age 60 in 2016, she had completed another 20 albums as a leader, with fruitful collaborations with, among many others, the legendary Ornette Coleman and her husband, trumpeter Wallace Roney, along the way. Quite possibly, my single favorite recorded performance by Allen is her amazing interpretation of Nino Rota's "La Strada" on her 2006 album, *Timeless Portraits and Dreams*. Still, it's generally agreed that *The Printmakers*, her first album as a leader, was the recording that best captured what she had in mind, her compositions and the limitless scope of her imagination.

(*The New York Sun*, 2024)

JASON MORAN (BORN 1975)

From the Dancehall to the Battlefield **(Yes Records)**

One of the very first serious discussions of jazz was published in a 1924 book by Gilbert Seldes, *The Seven Lively Arts*. In discussing the music in racial terms—as people were wont to do back then—Seldes observes that the very best of the Caucasian bandleaders "by a little joke, is called Whiteman." If that's humor, then this, by the same standard, is irony: even before Paul Whiteman, the maestro who did the most to lay the groundwork for the coming of jazz and indeed, much of subsequent American music, was named Europe.

James Reese Europe (1880–1919) was a pioneering Black bandleader, who was easily the dominant figure in all of American music in the 1910s. It's not a stretch to identify him as the link between such earlier avatars of American music as march king John Philip Sousa and ragtime king Scott Joplin and the first superstar jazz ensembles, such as those of Fletcher Henderson and Duke Ellington.

Further, as is made clear by the title of pianist Jason Moran's new celebration of Europe's music, *From the Dancehall to the Battlefield*, Lieutenant Europe and his men distinguished themselves both musically and militarily as the 369th Infantry Regiment (the "Harlem Hellfighters") band during what was then known as "The Great War" or "The European War."

Mr. Moran's project takes two forms, an album (also available as a two-LP set) and a live concert presentation, which he performed last Friday under the auspices of Jazzmobile at the uptown park named after another African American thought leader of the same era, Marcus Garvey.

Now 48, Mr. Moran is well known as a purveyor of what we think of as the most far-out jazz being played today, a direct extension of the free jazz of the 1960s. At the same time, he has the deepest respect for and knowledge of the entire history—or even, in this latest project, the prehistory—of jazz.

Previous projects have found Mr. Moran reimagining the music of such piano predecessors as Fats Waller and Thelonious Monk, and he has also done a spectacular job in curating an exhibit of Louis Armstrong's effects and personal memorabilia, currently on display at the newly opened Louis Armstrong House Museum at Corona.

Mr. Moran has taken a dozen or so themes of the era, including popular songs ("The Darktown Strutters Ball"), dances ("Ballin' the Jack"), blues (three by W. C. Handy, "St. Louis Blues," "Memphis Blues," and "Hesitating Blues"), numerous rags, and a folk tune ("Make Me a Pallet on the Floor"). He and his 10-piece ensemble, which includes both an electric string bass and a tuba, will often start with a highly faithful re-creation of a historic Europe performance (as preserved and documented on acoustic recordings) and then will gradually work it into something else.

In some cases, as with "Darktown Strutters," he'll update the piece into something more modern, from a raggy 2/4 into a swinging 4. "Russian Rag" travels from the dancehall to the battlefield and even beyond, into a downtown jazz loft of the kind we frequented in the early 1970s.

"That Moaning Trombone" is a ragtime virtuoso piece that spotlights both of the sliphorn players here, Reginald Cyntje and Chris Bates, and also emphasizes Jose Davila on tuba. "All of No Man's Land Is Ours" is co-credited to Europe and Noble Sissle, then a violinist with the 369th, who also sings on the original 1919 recording. Mr. Moran recasts it as a lovely ragtime piano ballad in the style of Europe and Sissle's great associate, Eubie Blake.

While the album is terrific, the concert incarnation is an even more memorable experience. Mr. Moran and his men take the stage dressed in vintage World War I military uniforms, and he frames the work with narration he delivers himself, discussing Europe and his impact on American music in agreeably poetic terms. Then, the 10-piece ensemble performs in front of a slide show of mostly historic images and even some newsreel footage—the Harlem Hellfighters famous march up Fifth Avenue, perhaps the first time a crowd of mostly white people cheered an all-Black organization of any kind.

One of the work's centerpieces is "Flee as a Bird," in which the ensemble starts with a spiritual and dirge traditionally played at New Orleans funerals. They literally deconstruct it in front of our ears, carrying it to the furthest extremes of what jazz is, incorporating "Ghosts," a 1960s avant-garde dirge by postmodern saxophonist Albert Ayler.

Perhaps we shouldn't read too much into Mr. Moran's treatment of a piece that is clearly about death and the afterlife. It was Eubie Blake who described Europe as the "Martin Luther King of music," and unfortunately, they both were murdered at roughly the same age. Mr. Moran closes the work with a wholly original piece titled "For James." This project is one of the very few that would satisfy lovers of both the earliest traditional jazz and the most modern "outside" music. Somehow, it's Black history and Afro-futurism both at the same time.

(*The New York Sun*, 2023)

ROBERT GLASPER (BORN 1978)

School's out for the summer, which means the late sets at the Village Vanguard are no longer crammed with youngsters from NYU, New School, and SUNY taking advantage of the student discount. (Since when did I get to be the oldest guy in the room?) But for the 27-year-old pianist Robert Glasper, this week's run at the Vanguard represents a graduation of sorts.

Throughout his early 20s, Mr. Glasper built his reputation as a sideman with Roy Hargrove, Terence Blanchard, and Wallace Roney. In 2004, he recorded his first album as a leader for the Spanish label Fresh Sounds, and last fall he released the excellent *Canvas* (Blue Note), his first CD on an American label. His Vanguard runs last November and this week mark Mr. Glasper's emergence as a star in his own right.

Mr. Glasper's first-rate trio, which includes bassist Vicente Archer and drummer Damion Reid, keeps finding new things to do with the piano–bass–drums format. At one point during Wednesday's late set, Mr. Archer soloed on the bass while Mr. Reid accompanied him with his bass drum, matching the tone to make it sound even deeper. Mr. Glasper also has a unique way of alternating phrases with the other two musicians; other bands will sometimes trade fours in the last chorus, but the Glasper trio makes these exchanges part of the central melody.

On *Canvas*, Mr. Glasper plays with a lyricism reminiscent of Bill Evans and a percussive, Afrocentric feel influenced by Randy Weston and other Thelonious Monk disciples. On Wednesday, however, he reminded me of Bud Powell in that he played the heaviest, most baroque bebop phrases imaginable, dispensing knotty, modernistic, European chords over equally thick African rhythm patterns.

His first tune, "G and B," combined two familiar phrases, one reminiscent of Chick Corea's "Spain" and the other suggesting "The Kerry Dancers," the traditional Irish song famously quoted by Charlie Parker. It seemed that Mr. Glasper was commenting on the African roots of both Iberian and Gaelic music. Both "G and B" and the second tune, "Of Dreams to Come" were laid out in similar patterns: the trio alternated dense phrases, four or so bars each, with wide-open spaces in which the bass and drums would go it alone. It wasn't that Mr. Glasper needed to rest—he has the chops to keep going indefinitely—but the pauses gave audience members a welcome chance to breathe.

The bulk of the set, however, was a 20-minute collage that combined Herbie Hancock's "Maiden Voyage" and a tune by the rock band Radiohead. At least that's what Mr. Glasper said afterward. I wouldn't expect to recognize the Radiohead. But I know "Maiden Voyage" by heart, and still I couldn't recognize it.

In any case, the combined piece was both meditative and folkish. It traveled from very quiet to very loud, tumultuous to contemplative, wide open to thick, with chords on top of chords on top of chords. This was the only part of the set that could be called conventionally "pretty."

Mr. Glasper is the first young, bop-oriented instrumentalist to be signed to a major label for many a season. He's found an appropriate home at Blue Note Records, which already works with Bill Charlap and Jason Moran, the two most imposing young piano stylists on the contemporary scene. Mr. Glasper is not as cutting edge as Mr. Moran nor as brilliantly old school as Mr. Charlap, but his gigs at the Vanguard made clear that he's well on his way to developing a sound and style of his own.

(*The New York Sun*, 2005)

WORLD JAZZ AND ETHNO-PIANO

MARTIAL SOLAL (BORN 1927)

"Solal" is a French noun and adjective meaning brilliant, ceaselessly inventive, daring, and provocative; guaranteed to keep an audience on the edge of its collective seat; the ability to take the most familiar jazz standards and ingeniously reconstruct them into something wholly original; a propensity for taking the most abstract fragments and shards of melody and making them seem, by turns, either foot-pattingly swinging or heart-movingly lyrical.

The definition above comes from my jazz fan's Francais–Anglais *dictionaire*, which also mentions that the term is taken from the name of one of the great living pianists, the Algerian-born French jazzman Martial Solal, who is celebrating his 80th birthday this week with six nights of solo recitals at the Village Vanguard.

It was appropriate that Monsieur Solal chose "Here's That Rainy Day" as his third number: As 9:00 p.m. approached during his opening set on Tuesday, the Vanguard was packed to the walls with soggy clods like me, who in our unrestrained zeal to catch M. Solal in a rare New York appearance (his previous such appearance at the Vanguard occurred during the week of September 11, 2001), neglected to bring our Umbrellas of Cherbourg. The room was so full that no one apart from Mr. Solal himself and a few slim waitresses could even move.

No, it wasn't the most physically comfortable 75 minutes I've ever spent at the Vanguard, but it was one of the most musically rewarding. Mr. Solal treated us to a dozen ur-jazz standards, all of which he made seem completely brand new. His playing references every piano style ever invented in jazz (and a few that weren't), from the stride of Fats Waller to the Harlem sophistication of Duke Ellington to the reckless adventure of Art Tatum to the impish humor of Erroll Garner—sometimes all at once.

Martial Solal; Iridium; June 2, 2003

Like Garner, he'll often start a tune way out in left field before letting us in on the melody, and then, just when we think that we've found our bearings, he'll veer off in another direction. Yet he never stops driving or pushing forward; even when he relinquishes the tune and plays down the rhythm, there's no mistaking that he's still taking us someplace, even if most of the familiar guideposts aren't there.

Mr. Solal also alternates between transparent lines, where there's nothing visible but the most essential notes of the tune, and dense harmonic clusters laid atop the melodic skeleton. When he lets you recognize the tune, it reminds me of a Disney cartoon of a little train chugging along on a track. Pow! There's an upset, and now the train has been broken down into a dozen individual cars, each proceeding along a track of its own. Frantic as it sounds, somehow the eye and ear have no problem following all of the cars by themselves, even before they all link together once more to make the train whole again.

On "Rainy Day," Monsieur Solal danced around the tune as though he were darting between the raindrops falling outside on Seventh Avenue and concluded with a tag from "Lohengrin," which he said was dedicated to Madame Solal. He then apologized for not being fully warmed up, and taking him at his word, his playing did grow even sharper and more dynamic as the set continued. In "Prelude to a Kiss," he threw in what at first seemed like an irreverent quote from "Satin Doll" but then quickly began alternating between the two tunes, not so much in a medley in which A relinquishes the stage to B, but as if he had spontaneously collaged them into yet a third tune. Even when he gives you more of the familiar melody, he doesn't let you take anything for granted.

Mr. Solal rendered "Tea for Two" with a pumping bass line à la Thelonious Monk and then sailed into the most optimistic major key treatment of Monk's "'Round Midnight" I've ever heard, throwing in a snatch of "Misterioso" at the coda. He treated "I Can't Get Started" with abstract elegance and surprised us all with the slowest, most romantic arrangement of "Cherokee" that I've ever heard. He delivered "Body and Soul" with thick, spikey rhythms and conversely, boiled "Lover Man" to the absolute minimum number of notes necessary to get the idea across.

A great quality of some of the best musicians is that you can hear the whole history of the music in their playing. And while that's certainly true of Martial Solal, what's even more remarkable is that you also get a sense of the future of the jazz piano as well, and it's hard to imagine a brighter one.

(*The New York Sun*, 2007)

TOSHIKO AKIYOSHI (BORN 1929)

In jazz, the roles of virtuoso pianist and successful big-bandleader are surprisingly exclusive: Duke Ellington and Count Basie were brilliant players but not virtuosos like Fats Waller or Art Tatum. Many important modern jazz pianists—Oscar Peterson,

McCoy Tyner, Ahmad Jamal, Randy Weston, John Lewis, and others fronted large ensembles on occasion—but of the regularly working pianist–leaders, such as Gil Evans, it's hard to think of one you would want to hear extensively as a soloist.

In other words, there's no one quite like Toshiko Akiyoshi, the inspired pianist and bandleader who this week is making a rare New York appearance with her trio at Birdland (it's billed as the first such appearance in 30 years). Ms. Akiyoshi is a diminutive woman, barely bigger than her husband's tenor saxophone, and despite all the time she has spent outside of her native country, she still speaks with a thick accent. Yet to hear her music, you would think she was raised in Memphis, Philadelphia, or Chicago.

She was, in fact, born in Manchuria during the Japanese occupation in 1929 and moved to Tokyo immediately after the war. Somehow, she caught the bebop bug and organized one of the first modern jazz groups in Asia. By the time Oscar Peterson heard her, she had amassed piano chops to compare—as much as any mortal could—with Bud Powell, Tatum, or Peterson.

Ms. Akiyoshi was separated from most of her fellow jazz players by every possible influence: distance, culture, religion, race, and even gender. Experiencing World War II from the other side must have given her an outlook on American culture that no native-born jazzman can imagine. Yet she came up with both a piano and an orchestral style forged solidly in the thick of the jazz mainstream.

Ms. Akiyoshi has always played the cultural card very carefully. At one of her earliest important American concert appearances, at Newport in 1957, she wore a traditional Japanese kimono. Four years later, on a return to Tokyo and a reunion with her former bandmates (including alto saxophonist Sadao Watanabe, later famous for playing both Charlie Parker–style bebop and smooth jazz), she was photographed in solidly Western, Jackie Kennedy–esque togs.

There have been occasions when Ms. Akiyoshi incorporates elements of Asian culture into her music, but even then, she does not approach jazz from an Eastern perspective. Rather, she approaches the East from a jazz perspective, one as distinctly personal as Duke Ellington's "Far East Suite," Horace Silver's "Tokyo Blues," or John Coltrane's Hindu meditations.

Ms. Akiyoshi first encountered American jazzmen and vice versa during the 1953 Jazz at the Philharmonic tour, which is when impresario Norman Granz recorded her with Oscar Peterson's rhythm section. By the time she came to Boston to study at Berklee, in 1956, she was already a world-class bop pianist whose work suggested Bud Powell's high-speed dissonances rather than Mr. Peterson's digital tours de force. George Wein was an early supporter, recording her in both trio and quintet settings for his Storyville label and featuring her both at that club and Newport.

Ms. Akiyoshi played piano for Charles Mingus on several important occasions, such as his famous 1962 Town Hall concert. But for all the brilliance of Mingus's music, he probably gave Ms. Akiyoshi an object lesson in how not to lead a band and organize a concert. And it wasn't until 1974 that Ms. Akiyoshi organized her first big band, with herself as musical director, composer, and pianist, and Lew Tabackin as principal horn soloist.

Her partnership with Mr. Tabackin began in the late 1960s, when the two of them made one of their most valuable recordings, *Toshiko at Top of the Gate*. That album costarred bassist Ron Carter, who took "Willow Weep for Me" as a solo feature (much as he did at the Blue Note a month ago), and trumpeter Kenny Dorham, who shines on "Manha De Carnival."

Ms. Akiyoshi here convincingly asserted herself as a composer. She had already introduced her theme *Long Yellow Road* in 1960, and the album's opener, "Opus No. Zero," sounds like an expansion of the same material. Mr. Tabackin is a strong, virile player with a big tone reminiscent of Sonny Rollins; his most notable feature on the album is the aggressively Rollins-esque "Night Song."

Too often Mr. Tabackin has been discounted as a mere journeyman. The fact is he has worked in the saxophone section of just about every important jazz big band since the 1960s, and his contributions to Ms. Akiyoshi's music, both on tenor and flute, are immeasurable. Their series of albums for RCA would be well worth collating into a Mosaic-type collection. (A few years later, there was indeed a *Mosaic Select* set of these recordings.) Unfortunately, the bulk of Ms. Akiyoshi's best work, done on both sides of the Pacific, isn't easily available over here. (A new compilation, however, *New York Sketch Book*, has been released this year on the Japanese Crown label.)

The big band's most recent release is an extended suite, *Hiroshima—Rising From the Abyss* (True Life Jazz TLE-1000082), recorded live in Japan a few weeks before September 11. It's a potentially grim work, incorporating recitations from "Mother's Diaries" kept at the Hiroshima Memorial Museum. Yet though part of *Hiroshima* deals with the tragedy, mostly it concerns hope.

In the notes to *Hiroshima*, Ms. Akiyoshi quotes the Dalai Lama, "We human beings cannot live without hope." The work portrays in musical terms how the world managed to survive the events of 1945. Its longest portion is a circular theme on which such contemporary leading lights of the New York scene, such as trumpeter Jim Rotondi and saxophonists Dave Pietro and Scott Robinson, join Mr. Tabackin in a roughly simultaneous improvisation. Mr. Tabackin's tenor ends the piece on a highly positive note with "Hope."

This December, Ms. Akiyoshi turns 75—her orchestra has already turned 30. Here's hoping there's many more birthdays to come.

(*The New York Sun*, 2004)

MONTY ALEXANDER (BORN 1944)

You can learn a lot by watching television: in one episode of *The Odd Couple*, Felix Unger informed us that calypso music originated not with Harry Belafonte but in Ancient Greece with a sea nymph in Homer's *Odyssey* named "Calypso." Actually, well before Mr. Belafonte, the first North American to champion the irresistible rhythms of Jamaica and Trinidad was R&B star Louis Jordan in such numbers as

Monty Alexander, piano; Hassan Shakur, bass; Blue Note; February 21, 2012

"Run Joe" and "Stone Cold Dead in the Market." Jordan took the music a step further in his 1949 "Push-Ka-Pee She Pie (The Saga of Saga Boy)," in which Jordan proclaimed to the world that he had invented a music he called "The New Calypso Bebop." Not to be outdone, shortly thereafter, the Trinidadian star Lord Kitchener, then living in England, recorded an homage to Dizzy Gillespie and Charlie Parker titled "Kitch's Bebop Calypso."

If anyone is perfectly equipped to perfect the new calypso bebop, it's pianist Monty Alexander, who immigrated to the United States from his native Kingston as a 17-year-old veteran of the Jamaican music scene in 1961. He was already equally versed in island music and North American jazz and over the next few decades, became one of the most in-demand pianists in the contemporary jazz scene, becoming the keyboardist of choice for bop pioneers Milt Jackson and Ray Brown. He was also a protégé of sorts of Frank Sinatra, serving as the house pianist at Jilly's, the Chairman's favorite hangout (certainly a baptism of fire for a musician wanting to master the Great American Songbook).

But Mr. Alexander has always remained consistently true to his West Indian roots; in the last decade or so, nearly all of his albums have focused on combining various elements of jazz with West Indian music, most impressively two exceptional CDs interpreting the Bob Marley songbook.

On Friday and Saturday at the Allen Room, Mr. Alexander played four sets of his ambitious program, "Lords of the West Indies," employing a wide cast of Jamaican, Trinidadian, and North American musicians. Over a very tight 90-minute set, Mr. Alexander spanned the islands as well as the different approaches he's used in the

West Indian jazz fusions he's experimented with in the course of his career: from a bop piano trio (with Herman Shakur, bass, and Herlin Riley, drums, who mastered many a Caribbean beat in his New Orleans upbringing) with nods to Caribbean rhythms to full-scale calypsos mixed with jazz harmony and improvisation.

With a minimum of patter, Mr. Alexander presented a program that was equally enlightening and entertaining. He showed us, rather than merely told us, how mento (the original Jamaican folk music form), calypso, ska, and reggae are as different from each other as bossa nova, salsa, and tango are in other parts of the Pan-American world. He used different ensembles to illustrate the various forms; the calypso segment presented the contemporary vocalist Designer evoking Lord Kitchener and The Mighty Sparrow on "Calypso of Bebop" and "Love in the Cemetery," while bassist Happy Williams sang a topical calypso seemingly inspired by the 2008 primaries and the Iraq War.

Mr. Alexander then introduced three veteran mento instrumentalist–vocalists, "Calypso John" Morgan (rhumba box), "Blackie" James (banjo), and "Powda" Bennett (shakers). The mento ensemble's big number was "Nobody's Business," the mento incarnation of a folk tune that is all over the map of early jazz and blues, showing up in fascinatingly different interpretations by Mississippi John Hurt and Bessie Smith, not to mention Louis Jordan and Ella Fitzgerald. Particularly impressive were two Jamaican saxophonists, Dean Fraser (alto) and Cedric IM Brooks (tenor), the latter of whom had a big, compelling sound drawn from the same wellspring of inspiration that launched Sonny Rollins's ongoing calypso numbers.

The show reached its peak with a surprisingly intimate moment, when Mr. Alexander and the saxophones played reverential, prayerlike treatment of two canonical Bob Marley ballads, "Redemption Song" and "No Woman, No Cry." Even at a slow tempo, Mr. Alexander brought out the essential kernel of island rhythm, showing that this music has its own equivalent of the Cuban clave. Then, it was time to close with a carnival climax, including such familiar tunes as "Sly Mongoose" (a calypso favored by Charlie Parker) and the Belafonte hit "Banana Boat Song"; the crowd roared as "Powda" Bennett spontaneously launched into an eccentric rubber-legged dance.

It was a brilliant presentation that inspired me to do further research, in the course of which, I discovered that the originator of this music may not have been Homer but Socrates. According to no less of an eminent ethnomusicologist than Steve Martin, the great Greek philosopher's dying words were, "Come Mister Tally-man, tally me bananas. Daylight come, and me wanna go home!"

Monty Alexander's show not only inspired me to go home and listen to all my calypso and reggae records; it put me in the mood to hear more great pianists. Therefore, I was in the right place at the 92nd Street Y to sample five keyboard masters who gathered around the Y's long-standing piano master Dick Hyman for the latest in his Jazz Piano series. It was a varied presentation in which everything came in pairs, and consistently, every other number worked beautifully. For instance, Mr. Hyman opened with Ray Kennedy in a rather tepid and tinkly two-piano treatment of "Yes Sir, That's My Baby," followed by an ingeniously boppish four-handed attack on "Idaho." Ted Rosenthal swung harder than I've ever heard him on "Let's Call the Whole Thing Off," using the Gershwin's either/eye-ther verbal scheme as the basis for call and response with bassist Jay Leonhart. Turkish pianist Meral Guneyman explored Duke Ellington's classical side with the amazing "Clothed Woman" and "Come Sunday." Norman Simmons challenged drummer Eddie Locke with a vigorous "Speak Low" that actually spoke rather loudly. Whenever things seemed on the verge of getting dull, Houston Person, the only horn player on the bill, took out his tenor sax and woke us all up, with two additional slices of Ellingtonia. For a finale, Mr. Person played "Mack the Knife" with all five pianists slicing and dicing the familiar Kurt Weill melody like the knife-bearing sharks of Bertolt Brecht's equally famous lyric.

(*The New York Sun*, 2008)

***

It's small wonder that jazz, an American music that draws on a wide range of multicultural influences, should have chosen New York, the most polyglot city on the planet, as its home base for most of its history. And it's equally appropriate that the Jamaican pianist Monty Alexander, who opens tonight for a week at Birdland (and whose new album, *Uplift*, is just being released), should have also made his home in New York for most of the last 50 years.

"My music is the product of having experienced different cultures and different vibrations," Mr. Alexander said yesterday in a phone conversation from his Midtown apartment. Most of us first heard Mr. Alexander, 66, in the early 1970s, when he represented the new generation of beboppers. Some Manhattanites even then remembered his earlier career, when he was first brought to the city by Frank Sinatra's right-hand man, Jilly Rizzo, to serve as house pianist at the famous Jilly's; the experience motivated him to become one of the major interpreters of the songs of Sinatra and the Great American Songbook overall (he has also collaborated memorably with Tony Bennett). Yet even prior to that, growing up in Kingston, he had yet a previous incarnation as a session pianist on embryonic reggae and ska recordings.

In recent years, Mr. Alexander has both returned to his roots and brought together several of the various facets of his music, most famously on two breakthrough jazz albums of the music of Bob Marley, *Stir It Up* (1999) and *Concrete Jungle* (2006). Mr. Alexander may be the first—and is certainly the most successful—musician to combine Jamaican music with North American jazz, but he downplays the achievement as "just being myself." He says, "Growing up in Jamaica, there were two things that happened that I remember distinctly: the first were all the groovy songs and sounds coming from the USA, and the other were all the rhythms and the beats that were happening locally with the folks in Jamaica."

The Birdland show is his "Harlem-Kingston Express" presentation, which features a full contingent of multiple bassists and percussionists, a second keyboardist, and the Israeli guitarist Yotam Silberstein, "to get everybody moving below the waist," as he puts it, in his unmistakable Kingston accent.

Uplift opens with "Come Fly with Me," in which Mr. Alexander evokes Sinatra and Oscar Peterson in the same breath, while "I Just Can't See for Lookin'" shows deference to the piano innovations of Nat King Cole. The album includes his distinctive treatments of a parade of iconic standards, among them "Sweet Georgia Brown" (with echoes of both Bizet's and Monk's "Bright Mississippi"). He ends by bringing it all together with Blue Mitchell's "Fungii Mama," a melody that combines hard bop and calypso, throwing out humorous nods to Monk and *The Flintstones*, without departing from an "I Got Rhythm" foundation.

Uplift also contains several island-flavored originals, which are brilliant examples of how to swing, Jamaican style. "No matter what I'm playing, I like to spice it up," he says, indicating his unique grooves and harmonies, "whether it's Cole Porter or Bob Marley."

(*The Wall Street Journal*, 2011)

***

This weekend caps a 14-night celebration of Jamaica's greatest export to the international jazz scene: the amazingly versatile pianist Montgomery Bernard Alexander. Rather than waiting for Mr. Alexander's 70th birthday in 2014, the Blue Note is using the anniversary of his debut as a professional musician (in Kingston at the age of 17) as the premise for a career retrospective. That he's released two outstanding new albums in the last year, one of which received a Grammy nomination, doesn't hurt either. (The nomination, not surprisingly, was in the reggae category rather than jazz.)

Mr. Alexander is bringing the run to an exciting conclusion by celebrating his West Indian roots: on Friday he teams with Jamaican super duo Sly and Robbie (his collaborators on a classic album from 2000), and Saturday and Sunday, it's the remarkably rhythmic Harlem Kingston Express.

It takes two weeks to cover all the many aspects of Mr. Alexander's music, mainly because it's impossible to say what he's best known as: bebopper, standard bearer of the Great American Songbook, or the creator of the most successful fusion of North American Jazz with the traditional and popular music of the Caribbean. In that final guise, he may have been the first to establish that Jamaica and Trinidad are sources of Pan-American "crossover" jazz no less than Cuba and Brazil.

Is there another pianist who can lay down reggae beats with Sly Dunbar, Robbie Shakespeare, and Ernest Ranglin; then play Cole Porter for Frank Sinatra (who first brought him to New York); then swing Christmas songs with Tony Bennett and the Count Basie Orchestra; and then turn around and play the bebop blues with one of the major living masters of the form, guitarist Pat Martino?

Last Friday, Mr. Alexander began his set with his regular working trio, costarring Herlin Riley, the exceptionally polyrhythmic drummer from New Orleans, and Hassan Shakur, who as the son of the formidable Los Angeles pianist Gerald Wiggins, knows a thing or two about working with piano players. The trio-only set started with "Look Up," a bright, optimistic riff that Mr. Alexander has recorded both with his island-style band, Ivory and Steel, and with his straight-ahead jazz trio.

Mr. Martino joined the trio for the second half of the set, and it was possibly the best I've ever heard him sound. He's normally a hyperintense player, a truly virtuosic improviser whose sets generally consist of one high-energy, up-tempo modern blues after another—exciting, but with little contrast. With Mr. Alexander, there was considerably more variety: the set focused on two homages to iconic guitar gods—Charlie Christian on "Air Mail Special" and Wes Montgomery on "Road Song"—and also featured one of Mr. Martino's best standards, "Alone Together."

Did I say every aspect of Mr. Alexander's music is being covered at the Blue Note series? Wrong! His great love of and skill at playing country-and-western music and cowboy songs is unaccounted for. (It is, however, documented on guitarist Bucky Pizzarelli's 2010 *Back in the Saddle Again*.) Maybe an addendum to the series is necessary, possibly at the Rodeo Bar.

(*The Wall Street Journal*, 2012)

***

Monty Alexander has long been a one-man Kingston Trio. That's a wise-guy way of saying that the pianist, who was born in 1944 at Kingston, Jamaica, has always had three major strings to his bow, three big feathers in his cap: a modern jazz virtuoso who apprenticed with the originators of the form, a stalwart champion of the Great American Songbook, and the world's foremost avatar of Jamaican jazz who combines the "riddims" (as he puts it) of his Caribbean homeland—calypso, mento, and reggae—with North American harmonies and forms.

A typical set by Mr. Alexander, such as the one he performed at Birdland last week, will combine all three and introduce a great many more strings and feathers as well.

Mr. Alexander has long been a December regular at Birdland, and he was in town the week before Christmas to, among other things, launch his new album, *Love Notes*. This latest project is the first full album to feature Mr. Alexander as a vocalist. He has occasionally sung before; in fact, sometimes as an encore, he will surprise a crowd by launching into Nat King Cole's 1947 trio arrangement of "Too Marvelous for Words," complete with a carefully enunciated vocal in the King Cole style.

Here, he sings on every track. In the notes, he recounts how Carmen McRae heard him singing during one of these encores in the 1970s and encouraged him to keep at it. Clearly, this album is something he's been working toward for a long time.

There are several songs from the King Cole songbook that have resided in the vault for a while, including a performance of "Too Marvelous" taped at Barcelona in 1982; a "Straighten Up and Fly Right" from Frankfurt in 2004; and a lovely, understated treatment of "Faith Can Move Mountains" featuring trumpeter Roy Hargrove, who died in 2018. Likewise, his original "These Love Notes" costars keyboardist Joe Sample, who has been gone since 2014.

Mr. Alexander combines all of his strengths here; we get the same eloquent, inspired piano solos that we're accustomed to hearing from him, great songs such as "Day In, Day Out," "The Nearness of You," and "For Sentimental Reasons" as well as a steady island beat that continues consistently through nearly every track.

"As Time Goes By" starts rather rhapsodically, à la Max Steiner and "Casablanca," but then shifts into calypso time. Mr. Alexander's phrasing as a vocalist is no less steady and consistent, staying on the beat and singing with as much sincerity as he can muster. He sings like a man who has loved words and music for 70 years and now wants to give himself the gift of at last being able to work with both.

The set at Birdland last Thursday, with bassist Jason Brown and drummer Luke Sellick, was no less exemplary. He started with the "C-Jam Blues," then gifted us with a few Christmas songs, notably a Count Basie–influenced "Silver Bells" from an album he cut with Tony Bennett and the Basie Orchestra. He also favored us with a few jazz standards, among them an exceptional "Body and Soul" out of the Nat Cole lineage, which referenced several of Cole's classically styled signature quotes, "Humoresque" and "In the Hall of the Mountain King."

Mr. Alexander also delivered a few Bob Marley classics that seemed seasonally appropriate: "Redemption Song" has the right message for the end of the year and a time of new beginnings, while "Exodus" is precisely the song you want to hear during Chanukah.

He surprised us with a piano trio interpretation of one of the major works of relatively modern symphonic music, the *Concierto de Aranjuez*, that seamlessly transitioned between the work as composed by Joaquín Rodrigo in 1939 and Mr. Alexander's own improvisations; even as someone who's heard this *Concierto* a thousand times, it was impossible to tell where Rodrigo ended and Mr. Alexander began.

He further included "Brilliant Corners" from his 2019 album *Wareika Hill*, a set of what he describes as "Rasta" variations on the music of Thelonious Monk, thus, a further bebop–reggae mashup.

Monty Alexander is that rare virtuoso who knows how to understate, and his singing chops—admittedly considerably less opulent than his piano chops—allows him to do that, to concentrate on the essential melody and lyrics with a highly focused intensity. His title song, "These Love Notes," the track with Joe Sample on Fender Rhodes, shows how the British West Indies has its own equivalent of the Central and South American bolero, a slow, sensual rhythm for dancing or even just romantic contemplation.

Likewise, "Island in the Sun" is a marvel of profound simplicity, featuring Mr. Alexander by himself, just his own piano accompaniment, singing the Harry Belafonte favorite with the warmth that befits a song of home.

Mr. Alexander ended the set at Birdland with "Blue Monk," not only extending the Monk theme, but ending, as he began, with the basic blues and thus, tying up the whole package with a big red Christmas bow.

(*The New York Sun*, 2022)

DANILO PÉREZ (BORN 1965)

If you were to ask me to tell you one thing about Danilo Pérez, until recently, I would have said that he was a prodigiously gifted pianist, composer, and bandleader from Panama who works in the idiom generally known as Afro-Latin jazz.

That's still largely true, but it's become increasingly clear over the course of his career that he isn't driven by the idea of working in any one specific area of jazz but rather, in bringing different aspects of the music together. In other words, he strives to transcend borders and walls. One of his first significant albums was the 1995 *Panamonk*, which, as the title suggests, was a fresh interpretation of the music of Thelonious Monk as heard through Pan-American ears. In 1999, he played on another favorite tribute to an iconic pianist–composer–iconoclast in "Mr. Jelly Lord," Wynton Marsalis's homage to Jelly Roll Morton.

This notion of musical and geological transcendence was driven home to me both in Mr. Pérez's latest release, *Crisalida*, and his performance of that music last weekend at Birdland. The album features nine musicians working with Mr. Pérez on two extended works he describes as suites. Larger ensembles and concert-style forms are nothing new to him—he's done several orchestral albums, among them *Motherland* (2000); *Panama Suite* (2006); *Panama 500* (2014); and my favorite, *Across the Crystal Sea*, a 2008 collaboration with the now late, brilliant German composer–arranger Claus Ogerman.

Still *Crisalida* isn't quite like anything else in terms of either form or content. The album consists of eight tracks, which make up two works in four movements each. It's highly melodic and rhythmic music that nonetheless requires several hearings to take in, and I'm grateful to have heard roughly 90 minutes of it at Birdland, albeit in a smaller ensemble.

The group combines strings, wind instruments (including the human voice), and international rhythm in a way that sounds like nothing I've ever heard. In a way, the smaller five-piece ensemble he employed at Birdland, with Naseem Alatrash, cello; Vasilis Kostas, laouto; Tareq Rantisi, percussion; and vocalist Farayi Malek, sounded more tightly focused and easier to follow.

On the album, it's easier to see the big picture—like a view from an airplane. Mr. Pérez explores the idea of crossing boundaries—both stylistic and geopolitical—in the two primary works here, "La Muralla (Glass Walls) Suite," and "Fronteras (Borders) Suite." Mr. Pérez clearly is not a fan of walls or borders and doesn't intend to honor them but to transcend them.

Mr. Pérez uses the human voice in many different ways: there's wordless singing from a female vocalist named Erini on many of the tracks as well as spoken word passages (most not in English). The first movement of the first suite, "Rise from Love," also utilizes a children's choir, Kalesma Children's Choir of The Ark of the World (Kivotos tou Kosmou). The second movement, "Monopatia (Pathways)" also includes two voices singing in harmony.

Portions of "Monopatia (Pathways)" sound like a waltz, although at spots, the surroundings are so disorienting that I don't feel like I can trust my own ability to count. The longest track on the package, the 12-minute "Al-Musifir Blues," is a genuine blues but so thoroughly expressed in exotic effects that I'm not sure if I would have realized that if not for the title. The main melody is played on the laouto, a Mediterranean instrument that looks like the love child of an oud and a bouzouki.

At Birdland, it was easier to appreciate the music on a granular level, bit by bit, passage by passage. Mr. Pérez has a way of crossing borders that reminds me of the newish movie *Everything, Everywhere at Once* in the way he seamlessly hops from one musical universe to another. One second we're listening to something that sounds South American. Then all of a sudden, we're in Athens or Istanbul, and next thing you know, he's gone all Asian on us.

Mr. Pérez's intentions for this music are noble and optimistic, and the message is clearly that if musicians from all over the globe—who don't even speak the same language, at least not verbally—can work together in harmony, why not world leaders? Quick, does anybody have Putin's mailing address?

(*The New York Sun*, 2022)

PIANOFORTE AFRICANUS

RANDY WESTON (1926–2018)

The tallest trees in Southern African are shrouded in mystery; a grove is said to exist in Zimbabwe where they sprout to unimaginable heights. But no researcher has visited the site in decades, and these claims remain unverified. There's far less mystery regarding the outstanding pianist and composer Randy Weston, who, for well over 50 years, has towered over the jazz world as both the most imposingly tall and most aggressively Afrocentric performer in the music. Mr. Weston, who was about to turn 81 at the time of this writing, is still at the treetop of his game, playing at a level so high that it takes a fan of the stature of Kareem Abdul-Jabbar to get a bird's-eye view of what he's doing.

Mr. Weston is spending this week at Jazz Standard with two different ensembles, his African Rhythms Trio (with Alex Blake, bass, and Neil Clarke, percussion) and his quartet, which adds the tenor saxophonist Billy Harper to the lineup. Unlike that mysterious patch of forest in Zimbabwe, there's no secrecy regarding where Mr. Weston's music comes from: he came of age musically at the height of the first bebop era and very early on, came under the spell of both Duke Ellington and Thelonious Monk. In the mid-1950s, he cut several fine albums of show tunes (his first LP was the 1954 *Cole Porter in a Modern Mood*) and wrote several tunes that became jazz standards, such as "Hi Fly" and "Little Niles," which were outfitted with words by Jon Hendricks. Yet as early as the 1960 *Uhuru Africa*, a collaboration with the great poet Langston Hughes, Mr. Weston became the first major jazz musician to fully explore the African roots of both music and culture, at least a full generation before the back-to-Africa movement of the 1970s.

The basic complexion of Mr. Weston's music is a distinctly African exterior, enriched by Mr. Clarke's use of an elaborate Pan–African American percussion set

Randy Weston; Prospect Park Bandshell; September 15, 1991

up in place of a traditional American trap drum kit. Yet apart from the "heads," or opening choruses of melody, Mr. Weston's own piano solos still essentially consist of North American–style bebop and blues, albeit with an Afrocentric flavor.

The African Rhythms Trio is one of the most percussive ensembles around. It often seems like a unit of three drummers: a drummer on piano and a drummer on bass as well as Mr. Clarke on hand drums. And, in the tradition known in the West as "talking drums," Mr. Clarke is just as likely to play melody on his congas as Mr. Weston is to play percussion on the keyboard. Mr. Blake is frequently a one-man band unto himself, slapping his strings low down on the fretboard as if they were part of the drum kit, moaning and chanting as if he were caught up in the religious spirit and keeping time further by stamping his feet on the floor. He often plays the dexterously staccato lines we associate with the fender bass but with the greater acoustic resonance of the full-sized wooden instrument.

Mr. Weston began the opening set on Wednesday with two of his own African-style works from the 1998 *Khepera*: "Boran Xam Xam," a word from the Wolof people of Senegal, and "Anu Anu," which alludes to the African origins of Egyptian religion. Mr. Weston spun riffs and melodies over the deep grooves laid down by Mr. Blake and Mr. Clarke. Then came "Caravan," the leadoff track in his excellent 1989 album *Portraits of Ellington*, but played here in a very different treatment, beginning with an elaborate introduction that combined essentially Ellingtonian chromaticisms with an Art Tatum–esque sense of drama. After "Caravan," the trio wound up with an elemental 12-bar blues, obviously informed on some level by "Blue Monk."

Mr. Weston let us all know exactly where he was coming from when he introduced "Caravan" as "the first piece of African music I ever heard." (At this point, he added "back when I was a tot—not a small tot, but a tot." Indeed, he must have been a lot of tone.) The lyrics famously describe a trek across the desert, and the music itself originated with the Puerto Rican trombonist and composer Juan Tizol. But Mr. Weston's "Caravan" sounded more like a pilgrimage across over the Serengeti.

Mr. Weston has taken every measure to make his music as authentically African as possible, as when, on his 1999 album *Spirit! The Power of Music*, he recruited the Gnawa master musicians of Morocco. But for him to refer to "Caravan" as African music indicates that he realizes that the Mother Continent is a state of mind, an idea as much as a place, and an eternal source of inspiration for jazz musicians of all nations, genders, and skin tones.

(*The New York Sun*, 2007)

***

The cover of his new album tells you a lot: Randy Weston is sitting at the piano, but in this particular shot, instead of actually playing it, he's turned toward the audience and is speaking to us, with his index finger poised straight up in the air, as if he's making a point. No wonder the album is titled *The Storyteller*.

Knowing Mr. Weston, the story he's telling is probably about Mother Africa. "It's all Africa, all of it," as he told the *Journal* recently. By that he means literally everything: civilization, culture, spirituality, and especially music. Later in our phone conversation he added, "You see, the whole human race came from Africa, that's the big secret."

Pianist–composer–philosopher Randy Weston is the jazz world's biggest Afrocentrist, and at six feet, seven inches, that statement can be taken rather literally. At 84, he is the elder statesman of musical Afrocentrism, as reflected in the new album, subtitled *Live at Dizzy's*; his first book, *African Rhythms*; and two upcoming appearances: a return to Dizzy's on November 9 (2010) and a new concert performance of his classic 1960 orchestral suite, *Uhuru Afrika*, on November 13.

Mr. Weston was born in Brooklyn in 1926 and has lived most of his 84 years in New York—with the exception of a seven-year stay in Morocco and the many months of his life he's spent disseminating his music and message touring all over the world. Mr. Weston's Africanist stance could be seen as exclusionary since it is entirely focused on culture from that particular continent. Yet when you look more closely, it's incredibly inclusive since Mr. Weston believes that Africa is the source of all human creativity. "It's all the same, whether I'm doing the 'Berkshire Blues,' or the music of the Gnawa Masters of Morocco. This music that came out of Africa is universal, and the foundation is so powerful that we go in any direction. I can play Alban Berg or Schoenberg and put some rhythms to it, it's a bossa nova, it's a calypso, it's a tango, they're all African rhythms."

While some might see African music as a category, Mr. Weston maintains it's just the opposite. "It's a universal concept of music that I learned from Duke Ellington. He said to get rid of the categories, and when you do that you see it opens up a whole world of music. We're all related to each other, that's what Ellington was all about, and so was Dizzy Gillespie, when he said 'We don't play jazz, we play music.' I might do some Bach, or some Mozart, Stravinsky, or [Heitor] Villa Lobos."

The new book was cowritten with veteran journalist and producer Willard Jenkins, who, at six feet, five inches, is one of the few writers around with whom Mr. Weston can see eye to eye. *African Rhythms* is part memoir, part travelogue, part philosophical treatise—even though he goes on for pages in detail about his trips to Morocco and Japan (to name just two of his many global stops), it never stops being interesting. He's especially informative about how he briefly fled New York in his early 20s to escape the drug scene, which was then becoming endemic among young jazzmen, and about the making of classic albums such as *Uhuru Afrika*.

He also illuminates his collaboration process. Mr. Weston is a composer, not an orchestrator, and he enjoys working hand in hand with musical directors and arrangers, such as the late Melba Liston, on his large-form works and the saxophonist T. K. Blue in his current quintet. (And, indeed, Mr. Jenkins on the book project.)

Mr. Weston put his musical theories to good use recently at a solo concert at the Rubin Museum of Art as well as a set at the Jazz Foundation of America's annual loft party. Mr. Weston's group was by far the best-presented act of the evening: his music, which emphasizes community, was ideally suited to the party atmosphere. Hudson Studios was selected for its layout and visuals rather than its acoustics (which are dreadful), but thanks to Mr. Weston's prescience in using longtime percussionist Neil Clarke, rather than a conventional trap drummer, he was the only keyboardist who could actually be heard—and seen—above the crowd all evening. Mr. Weston's trio, with guest saxophonist Billy Harper, was a hard act to follow, particularly when he played his jazz standard, "Hi-Fly," in a vigorous 2/4.

I sometimes wonder what Mr. Weston's music might have been like had his father not helped him discover the Afrocentrist impulse. Would he be one of several post-Ellington, post–Thelonious Monk pianists, like the late and brilliant Mal Waldron? Mr. Weston's music passed something of an acid test two years ago when the young trumpeter Dave Douglas performed an entire concert of his Weston compositions at the Abrons Art Center. Mr. Douglas played Mr. Weston's tunes strictly as modern jazz, without any particular emphasis on their African qualities—and even bereft of the context they were conceived in, they sounded beautiful. (I wish there was an album of that particular program, even though neither Mr. Douglas nor Mr. Weston is remotely underrecorded.)

Mr. Weston sees himself as coming out of the tradition of both Ellington and Monk. "The one thing that all those guys before me had, which was extremely important, was love. That's the key word of this music, going all the way back—it has always been full of life and in love with the beauty of our planet. I try to continue that tradition; when you look in the audience, you see all the colors of the rainbow, you see all the ages, you see all the sexes and the sizes. And when the music is right, everybody's smiling."

(*The Wall Street Journal*, 2010)

MUHAL RICHARD ABRAMS (1930–2017)

One of the forgotten truths of early jazz—all the way up through the big band era, at least—is that in the Black community, the piano was the clearest path to bandleading. This first occurred to me while I was writing the biography of Nat King Cole. If we were to make a list of all the major Black bands, starting with Duke Ellington, Fletcher Henderson, Count Basie, Earl Fatha Hines, and Claude Hopkins, there would be at least as many piano-playing leaders as all the other instruments combined. (Conversely, for whatever reason, there were virtually no major white piano-playing leaders until Claude Thornhill and Stan Kenton, relatively late in the game.)

There are at least two kinds of piano-playing bandleaders, those who have to occasionally remind you that they were also great pianists, such as Ellington and Basie, and those who never let you forget it, such as Hines. There were also those from whom you may not want to hear play long keyboard solos, such as Henderson.

Muhal Richard Abrams; Vision Festival; Abrons Arts Center; June 24, 2010

Muhal Richard Abrams probably belongs to the first category; like Ellington, especially, he was a major composer of works for a wide range of mostly jazz ensembles, and like the rest of these men, he was at the center of a group of remarkable individual soloists, including many of the greatest in all of American music. More than the others, however, Abrams was also an educator, a musical theorist, and a performing artist who was always coming up with new ways to think about music. Even more than a teacher, Abrams was a veritable pied piper and played a central role in the thriving postmodern music scene of Chicago and later New York.

Most comments about *Afrisong*, Abrams's 1975 solo piano album, were all about how important it was that Abrams remind us that he was first and foremost a pianist in addition to everything else. Nearly 50 years after it was first recorded, it remains a stunning if underappreciated achievement.

Afrisong places the Memphis-born, Chicago-raised Abrams in the category of Afrocentric pianists, like the slightly older Randy Weston, from Brooklyn, and the slightly younger Dollar Brand (Abdullah Ibrahim) from Cape Town. Unlike Weston, however, *Afrisong* is a unique project for Abrams—he wouldn't devote his entire career to pursuing the Afrocentric ideal.

The presence of African elements in *Afrisong* may be somewhat random: Abrams later told Alan Nahigian that an African girl happened to be at the session and when she told him that she thought the first tune reminded her of Africa, that's when he came up with the title.

It's open to interpretation how much of the rest of the album, if any, Abrams intended to sound African. I personally hear a lot of the album as Abrams's intention to capture the Afrocentric spirit at the keyboard, and while there are similarities with the *pianoforte Africanus* of Weston and Ibrahim, Abrams's instrumental voice is always much stronger than that of his influences.

The opening track, "Afrisong," is perhaps the only one where Abrams telegraphs his intentions, but even under any other title, this would sound distinctly African. He opens with a somewhat out-of-tempo intro that actually sounds like we're traveling somewhere; in my mind's eye, it's through a thicket of bushes and trees and then into an open field. All of a sudden, we are there; there's a sprightly melody, apparently based on a traditional African air. (One listener referred to it as "a two-chord folk song.") Abrams spins variations and keeps the tune as a framework; even when he departs from it, he's never gone long and returns to this tune, recognizable, even danceable at several points, leading up to the end, where he slows and spirals down to a satisfying conclusion.

If "Afrisong" feels like traveling across a field, "The Infinite Flow" suggests a river. The constant melodic motion gives a feeling of floating downstream, while the pianist's phrasing, dynamics, and use of rests and pauses suggest bobbing up and down slowly on the waves. The journey gets more intense as it goes on. The flow continues as we navigate around rocks and Abrams interrupts the infinite flow with heavily pounded, percussive chords. After six minutes, we reach the end of the river, and the stream becomes a trickle.

"Peace on You" is slow and contemplative and still African sounding, at least to my ears; he plays a heavier chord in his left hand, then spins out notes around it in his left. The melody occasionally reminds me of the show tune and jazz standard, "Lazy Afternoon." Unlike the first two pieces, the melody occasionally slows down and speeds back up, giving it less of a traveling feel; the metaphor would be more like an internal journey, like the thought process, rather than an external one.

"Hymn to the East" makes me think about how the piano, more than most Western instruments, can create instrumental sounds meant to evoke different ethnicities and cultures. Think about silent movies; if you're watching a western, the pianist would play a specific phrase that would let the audience know there are Native Americans approaching; in Buster Keaton's *The Cameraman*, there's a scene when the hero enters a den of Chinese gangsters; both of those ethnic groups would be represented with a specific sound, a set of specifically voiced chords and harmonies. True, they were not even remotely authentic to the actual groups they purport to represent, and those sounds are a kind of stereotyping in and of themselves; I cite this mainly to underscore the power of the piano. "Hymn to the East" uses some of that distinctly Asian phrasing, but unlike most times when you hear that particular sonic effect, it doesn't sound like a cliche.

"Roots" has a steady beat and is a kind of series of phrases that is meandering and yet urgent, going somewhere but perhaps not by the most direct route. Each phrase sounds somewhat incomplete, like it's not exactly there yet but rather, leading somewhere else.

The two final pieces, "Blues for M." and "The New People," seem to be the least explicitly African, except in the vaguest sense, as in the philosophy of Randy Weston and others that all jazz and blues essentially come from Africa. "Blues for M." is the piece where Abrams shows that he can not only play the very old-fashioned blues but stride as well. Abrams was a dominant figure in what we loosely call the jazz avant-garde, but this piece shows that to move into the future, you don't have to discard the past. Abrams probably never had the intention of including this piece merely to show off what he could in terms of stride and the blues but rather, deemed that those forms were the best suited to the melody he heard in his head and the story that he wanted to tell. For me, at least, this is the most easily enjoyable track—the one most firmly in my own personal comfort zone—and regrettably it's also the shortest on the album.

At 10 minutes, the final track, "The New People," is by far the most overtly avant-garde or free-form of the seven compositions here. First, there's a brief flurry of notes, then a plink, followed by a surprisingly long rest. The pattern repeats and varies; there's a flurry, a silence, then a cascade of a few notes, then another silence. It kind of goes on like that: a burst of what seems like random adjacent notes, then a silence. There are alternating patterns of sound and silence, and sometimes one goes on longer; six minutes in, there's a two-note, one–two phrase that gets repeated up and down the keyboard. This expands and evolves into another ongoing melodic line of sorts and calms down almost to a complete halt near the end, about 9:30.

I confess that as I play and replay the album, I tend to linger more on "Blues for M." and pay less attention to "The New People," but just the same, it's a glorious ride from start to finish. It's become somewhat trite, in the 21st century, to characterize a musical performance as a "journey," but I can't think of any other word to describe a work like *Afrisong*, which starts with you in one place, transports you to some other place, and then leaves you at someplace else entirely.

(*Slouching Towards Birdland*, Substack, 2023)

ABDULLAH IBRAHIM (BORN 1934)

African music is usually depicted in American pop culture as extremely percussive, loud, and noisy. While it's unfair to generalize the music of an entire continent with any brief description, most of the authentic African sounds I have personally encountered have been just the opposite—tranquil and sonorous.

The music of the Cape Town pianist and composer, formerly known as Dollar Brand, (who, since his conversion to Islam in 1968, has gone under the name of Abdullah Ibrahim) is above all understated, meditative, and hymnlike. His opening set of a weeklong stand at the Blue Note was as extraordinary an event as anything I have ever encountered at that club: for the first time at that most boisterous of bistros, the crowd sat intently listening with a concentration not even often found

Abdullah Ibrahim; JVC Jazz Festival; Bryant Park; June 27, 1996

at concert halls. The place was so quiet that I was afraid to even rip open a packet of sugar, much less touch my metal spoon to my ceramic coffee cup.

There's a school of jazz piano generally regarded as originating with Duke Ellington, who was, among many other things, one of the first major jazzmen to contemplate Africa as an ancestral homeland for his music. Ellington's use of a slow, deliberate rhythm, wide-open voiced chords, and lightly dissonant intervals were perceived as the African characteristic of his playing. This sound was extended in the modern era, echoed and reinterpreted in the basic approaches of Thelonious Monk; Randy Weston; Mal Waldron; and others, such as Stan Tracy and the contemporary Rodney Kendrick.

Mr. Ibrahim's essential approach derives from both his South African upbringing and admiration of Ellington (who brought him to the West, produced his breakthrough album, and generally facilitated his entry into the international jazz fraternity) and Monk. Like both of these men, Mr. Ibrahim is fond of using secondary intervals for coloration, which can sometimes sound romantic, as they do in Duke's piano playing, or jarring, as they do in Monk's. His interest in long-form works is obviously inspired by Ellington, although even the maestro himself never composed a full-length work for small band or trio. This is what Mr. Ibrahim has now done with *African Magic*, an album-sized suite for piano, bass (Beldon Bullock), and drums (George Gray), which he is presenting both at the Blue Note this week and on his new release of that title (Justin Time/Enja), recorded at Berlin's Jazz Across the Border Festival in 2001.

Mr. Ibrahim plays *African Magic* more or less as it's heard on the album, and as on the disc, rather than pausing between sections (he never so much as announced a title or a band member or told us that CDs were for sale in the gift shop), he connected the individual parts of the suite with a transitional melody titled "Blue Bolero." Mr. Ibrahim is a master of melody, rhythm, and emotion; he can sound progressively more intense without playing either louder or faster, and he can also sound languid and tranquil while playing at an up-tempo clip.

Most of the time, though, Mr. Ibrahim played very slowly and unaccompanied. Mr. Gray would occasionally sneak in with a funky backbeat—the drummer also kept us distracted with entertaining tricks, such as keeping his brushes twirling in between beats and creating an Afro-Latin percussion effect by clattering two drumsticks together.

Although "African Magic" never stopped being beautiful, at times it seemed to go on for too long, and the interconnecting melody was occasionally overused; one yearned for the trio to play Ellington's "In a Sentimental Mood" and "Solitude," as they do on the album. The crowd (which, as always at the Blue Note, is largely foreign tourists) was surprisingly patient, especially since Mr. Ibrahim had never enlightened them as to what they were hearing.

The Journey, just reissued by Chiaroscuro, showcases the more aggressive side of Mr. Ibrahim. This 1977 album, whose cover imagery suggests a live concert recording, although the date was actually recorded in a studio, used a nine-piece band, including trumpeter Don Cherry, four saxes (one of which is Mr. Ibrahim doubling on soprano), two trap drummers, and a Latin percussionist. The three tracks offer a successful mixture of the form known to Westerners as "Africa highlife" and free jazz.

Track one, "Sister Rosie," is a jaunty, Caribbean-style melody, stated by the reed ensemble, which is how track two, "Jabulani (Joy)," starts, before baritone saxophonist Hamiet Bluiett enters and wrestles the tune to the ground, jumping on with a squealing solo that makes his deepest of saxes sound higher than a sopranino.

Yet at the Blue Note and on "African Magic," Mr. Ibrahim played with a serenity that makes it hard to believe that he's considered part of the avant-garde jazz experience. Of all the subcategories of jazz—swing, bop, whatever—only postmodernism is a wide enough umbrella to accommodate all the possibilities of these enlightened sounds from the so-called dark continent. From screams to grunts, serenity to cacophony, all things are possible in Mr. Ibrahim's enlightened music.

(*The New York Sun*, 2003)

***

Seated at the piano, Abdullah Ibrahim explains his ideas on how spirituality and music relate to each other. "The key of F activates the physical body," he says. As he plays a brief melody with three essential chords, he continues, "When you analyze the actual music on the instrument, you relate it to your life and to the universe. You discover that I (the first chord) is Heaven and The Father, V (five) is the dominant and represents the elements, and IV (the subdominant) is the child." He then goes on to explain that the chords that emphasize that fourth note—the child—can be described as "pregnant."

The remarkable South African musician, formerly known as Dollar Brand, turned 70 last year, at which time Enja Records (his label since 1979) assembled a retrospective of his work, *Abdullah Ibrahim: A Celebration.* This single-CD collection has more recently been released in North America by Enja's partner label, the Montreal-based Justin Time. At the same time, Music Video Distributors has also released, for the first time on DVD, the 1986 documentary profile *Abdullah Ibrahim: A Brother with Perfect Timing.*

This film is not a conventional biography; in fact, the only concession it makes to that tradition is a brief timeline at the very beginning offering some of the barest outlines of Mr. Ibrahim's career. Rather, *Abdullah Ibrahim: A Brother with Perfect Timing* is essentially an exploration of the composer's spiritual and musical philosophies. Director Chris Austin intercuts between Mr. Ibrahim speaking and demonstrating his ideas at the piano in his apartment at the Chelsea Hotel, his band Ekaya in performance at the old Sweet Basil, and footage filmed in South Africa illustrating his folktales.

There are only a few points in Mr. Ibrahim's discussion when he detours into autobiography, and then it's usually to illustrate a larger point. In talking about the relationship of music and religion, he relates how he first became attracted to music in the Christian church where both his mother and grandmother played keyboards—and then explains, shades of Jelly Roll Morton, that he had to "physically fight" for the opportunity to take piano lessons, "'Why do you want to play the piano?', they told me, 'Only girls play piano!'" Yet he never takes himself the least bit seriously or makes a bid for sympathy, then laughs heartily even as he admits "It was hard." He also does not go for the melodramatic, even when he bitterly describes South Africa's transition from a comparatively open society in the 1940s and 1950s to the oppressive regime of apartheid, which he describes as like "living in a concentration camp."

This year, 2004, also marked the 50th anniversary of Mr. Ibrahim's first recording session, which occurred shortly before his 20th birthday, with a Cape Town–based swing band called the Tuxedo Slickers. Even then, Mr. Ibrahim, who had been born Adolphe Johannes Brand and was by then working under the professional name Dollar Brand, was attracted to the modern jazz sounds coming out of America. By 1960, he had formed the Jazz Epistles with future Afro-pop crossover star Hugh Masekela playing trumpet. Despite the similarity of the name to Art Blakey's (American) Jazz Messengers and the British Jazz Couriers, this was the first modern jazz group with a distinctively African sensibility.

After the Sharpeville Massacre of 1960 (in which as many as 300 people were murdered), it was clear that there was no place in the new regime for a free-thinking creative musician and political thinker such as Mr. Ibrahim—no more than there were for "modern" artists in Stalinist Russia. In 1962, he escaped to Europe with his trio and his wife, the "coloured" jazz singer Sathima Bea Benjamin. In Zurich, they were heard by both John Coltrane and Duke Ellington, and it was Ellington who arranged for the group to be heard in the West.

Recording in Switzerland, the Maestro produced *Duke Ellington Presents the Dollar Brand Trio* as well as an album of Ms. Benjamin's singing, accompanied by Mr. Ibrahim as well as Ellington and Billy Strayhorn, which was released 35 years later. Dollar Brand was the only musician from outside of his orchestra that Ellington so enthusiastically sponsored: he eventually helped the couple to immigrate to the United States. He even employed the pianist–composer as a pinch-hitter leader for the Ellington orchestra: "In 1966, I did five dates substituting for him," said Mr. Ibrahim. "It was exciting but very scary! I could hardly play."

Surprisingly, Mr. Ibrahim barely mentions Ellington in the 1986 film. Yet on a blindfold test, a listener could easily mistake Mr. Ibrahim's 1979 solo piece, "The Perfumed Forest Wet with Rain" for later Ellington, as on "Single Petal of a Rose" or "Meditations." Like Ellington, Mr. Ibrahim is equally fond of both chromaticisms and romanticisms here. He does discuss Thelonious Monk, who was an equally huge influence. He relates how he came up with a tune that was heard by the former Ellington bassist Jimmy Woode, who said it reminded him of Monk: "He was right—subconsciously I had been thinking of Monk." Since then, Mr. Ibrahim has devoted a whole suite to Monk and remembers (in the film) that even in the 1950s in South Africa, "People were listening to Monk and assuming that he was crazy, but when I heard Monk for the first time, I thought 'Oh yes!'"

In 1968, Mr. Brand converted to Islam and became Abdullah Ibrahim. Just as he is known by both names, his music is equal parts African and American jazz—and there's much of it that could just as easily be filed in the classical section as well. In the film, he speaks of how "African jazz," as it were, relies upon the "oral tradition of traditional South African music being translated to the instrument." On his own work on the soprano saxophone, such as on "Ishmael" (on *A Celebration*), Mr. Ibrahim shows what he means, evidencing a distinctly African timbre—similar to the saxophonists playing in earlier Afro-pop groups, such as the Bulawayo Sweet Rhythms Band.

What's especially impressive is the way that Mr. Ibrahim was able to find American saxophonists who were able to create their own version of this sound, most notably Ricky Ford (tenor) and Carlos Ward (alto, flute). Mr. Ford and Mr. Ward were the two principal players in Mr. Ibrahim's best-remembered band, his septet Epaka, which is heavily featured both in the film and on *A Celebration.*

Mr. Ibrahim spent three decades as an exile from his native land, and in the interview, from near the end of that period, he speaks with hope and not bitterness, as he imagines his native land in a more enlightened future. In his speech as well as in his music, he embodies that hope, much the same way that the hymns he learned in childhood look forward to the Second Coming of Jesus and the arrival of Heaven on earth.

That feeling was most perfectly captured by the Ekaya ensemble, shown in performance at Sweet Basil (and in rehearsal) and heard on Mr. Ibrahim's most celebrated album, the 1985 *Water from an Ancient Well*, two tracks of which are on the *Celebration* retrospective. On "The Mountain" and "Mannenberg Revisited," simple folklike riffs and harmonic textures that could be considered Far Eastern as much as African, slowly gather momentum and build into moments of high intensity—even though Mr. Ibrahim maintains an even pianissimo dynamic and never stoops to shouting. Mr. Ibrahim is perhaps the only composer in jazz whose music is equally suited to both meditation and dancing.

Writing in Mr. Ibrahim's native land, a local journalist named Janet Smith proclaimed that the composer's music contains "all the influences that have made our young country so desperately alive" and that it "makes me proud to be a South African." Mr. Ibrahim's countrymen are obviously entitled to feel a special attachment to their native son and hometown hero, who has since returned to his roots in the post–Mandela age. But still, to paraphrase an American political–cultural leader, in listening to his music, we are all South Africans.

(*The New York Sun*, 2005)

***

The jazz of pianist and composer Abdullah Ibrahim is unlike any other the world has ever heard. Throughout his 70-minute performance at the Jazz Standard on Tuesday night, Mr. Ibrahim seemed to be telling us to rid ourselves of the archaic, Western notion that music, or any kind of an artistic statement that exists in time, has to have a beginning, a middle, and an end, much less in that order. Mr. Ibrahim played a single uninterrupted piece with no obvious starting point or finishing line, just a lot of middle, and yet there were middles within middles and interior monologues galore.

Mr. Ibrahim, who was formerly known as Dollar Brand and turns 73 this fall, has long been the most celebrated of all African jazz musicians. He is in town this week at the Jazz Standard, playing solo piano Tuesday (when I heard him) through last night and then with his trio (with bassist Beldon Bullock and drummer George Gray) from tonight to Sunday.

There are composers in the classical and jazz avant-garde who work without any traditional linear form—such as Karlheinz Stockhausen and Cecil Taylor. Mr. Ibrahim did go through a phase where his music was more chaotic and discordant and had more of an element of free jazz to it. But what's remarkable about what he's currently playing is that it is so traditionally melodic, harmonic, highly rhythmic, and completely accessible. The only aspect of his current music that might be considered avant-garde is this rather unique approach to form.

The traditional narrative shape of music preconditions the listener to certain expectations—in a sense, as soon as a piece begins, you're waiting for it to get to the next step to see how it transitions through these agreed-upon points, and you try to follow the "plot" of the music as if it were a movie. Mr. Ibrahim's set-length piece was very much like a long and very scenic journey in which you're not sure where you're heading or where you began. You're not necessarily sure of where you happen to be at any particular moment, but wherever it is, it's someplace mighty attractive. You may not be in any hurry, yet there's still an unmistakable feeling of going somewhere. You're not thinking about making your way toward the ending; you're just sort of enjoying where you happen to be right at the present time. (It's all rather Zen, hey.)

A lot of music starts quietly and gets noisier and more exciting as it progresses. Mr. Ibrahim's piece starts quiet and gets quieter still at select points, so quiet that you can hear a knuckle crack. There were a few passages where everything was so motionless that even my glass of club soda had more activity. At these moments, the music is truly minimalist; there's so little going on that when anything actually does happen, you can't possibly miss it. So much contemporary jazz is about young players exhibiting their chops and their ability to reel off barrages of notes over complex chord patterns at lightning speed—jazz's equivalent of a car chase in a summer movie that would be advertised as a "thrill-packed roller-coaster ride." Mr. Ibrahim's music, on the other hand, is pure tranquility, eerily hypnotic and completely compelling, jazz that's based on ideas as much as technique.

At various points, the tempo picks up and gathers momentum, like a rock rolling down a hill. For the most part, the melody and harmonies are completely transparent, but there are other sequences where the tune gets more intricate and the chords more complex. In certain spots, he seems to be playing a long vamp; at others, it's a set of rhythmically charged riffs that play off each other. Here, there's a sequence of Ellington-like romantic chromaticisms; there, it's a bunch of Monk-ish dissonances. Eventually, we travel past something that sounds vaguely like the blues, and then in the distance, we sight an object that could be a waltz; at certain times, you could swear that you're listening to a love song or a ballad, and at many times, it all becomes more spiritual, like a hymn. There's not much in this particular piece that makes me jump to my feet and dance, but there is a lot to make me get on my knees and pray.

Mr. Ibrahim continues to play with our expectations to the very end: at one point, an hour or so in, he starts to hit the keyboard with greater force and fury, producing dark rumblings from the bass end. He sounds like he's building toward a conventional conclusion, but no. The piece goes on for another few minutes, and when it ends, it just stops, with no forewarning or fanfare. Abdullah Ibrahim rises from the piano bench, places his hands together, and bows slightly in deference to the crowd.

Mr. Ibrahim and his wife, singer Sathima Bea Benjamin, left Cape Town in 1960 to escape apartheid. While Mr. Ibrahim returned to his native land at the end of that oppressive regime, Ms. Benjamin continues to reside in New York at the Chelsea Hotel, her home for 30 years. Ms. Benjamin, who turned 70 last fall, at that time released *Song Spirit* (Ekapa), a CD anthology of her favorite tracks from her eight previous albums. Ms. Benjamin sings mostly American jazz standards—including a lot of Ellington—with a distinctively African timbre, a cool, even, hypnotic tone and beguiling pitch that often seems just slightly under the note, not to mention a catch in her throat and a way of bending notes that makes show tunes seem like an incantation. For a singer who has been indirectly allied to a movement of liberation, she also sings quite a few standards that are tied to old "imperialist" European operetta, such as Franz Lehar and Noel Coward. The highlight of the current collection is a previously unissued reading of "It Never Entered My Mind," done as a piano–voice duo between husband and wife, in which they show that even Rodgers & Hart can benefit from their cool Cape Town sonorities. Whatever Ms. Benjamin sings, she is a vocalist of daring and imagination and should be heard.

(*The New York Sun*, 2007)

***

When jazz was in its infancy, people thought of it as music—if they regarded it as music at all—that was invariably loud, fast, and rambunctious. From the beginning, "to jazz something up" meant to make it more exciting. Yet for nearly 100 years, the music has consistently also attracted more thoughtful and introspective players and composers, such as Bix Beiderbecke (in his piano compositions especially), Billy Strayhorn, and Bill Evans. It might seem ironic, then, that one of the most lyrical of contemporary jazzmen comes from the very continent often cited as the inspiration for the aggressive energy that jazz on the whole was originally known for.

The pianist, composer, and bandleader Abdullah Ibrahim was born in Cape Town, South Africa, in 1934 and in the earlier part of his career, worked under the name Dollar Brand. He has been a major presence on the international jazz scene since 1963, when he was discovered and subsequently recorded by Duke Ellington. On July 15 of last year, a few months before his 89th birthday, Mr. Ibrahim recorded two remarkable sets in London's Barbican Hall. On both, he was joined by Cleave Guyton Jr., on flute and piccolo, and Noah Jackson, on bass and cello. Mr. Ibrahim's new album, *3* (Gearbox, out January 26), comprises both of these performances.

The first set, which totals 17 minutes, was taped without an audience in the afternoon and consists of six original compositions. The opening track, "Barakat," starts with a few slow piano notes, first as an intro but quickly as a background, before Mr. Ibrahim is joined by Mr. Guyton on flute and briefly, Mr. Jackson bowing his bass, arco style. The second piece, "Tsakwe," is much faster and more urgent, with the flute soaring over frantic, pizzicato bass playing; just 82 seconds long, this work features only a few chordal colorings from the pianist at the very end.

"Krotoa - Crystal Clear" is the slowest track, a piano solo in which Mr. Ibrahim creates a musical picture of, in my mind's eye at least, a tropical pool, with staccato individual notes resonating like ripples in the water. It's more of a painting than a story, and he accomplishes these swirls with left-hand 1/2-step dissonances and right-hand octaves; half-diminished tonal centers, which then open into Lydian and altered chords; and finally, evanescent modal changes (major–minor), providing a rich tonal panoply. There's also no smooth ending here—rather, it's as if a stream of running water just suddenly stopped flowing.

The second set, which was performed in the evening in front of an audience, includes works by composer–musicians in the jazz pantheon. "Giant Steps" is the John Coltrane standard; and while "In a Sentimental Mood" is by Duke Ellington, the Ellington–Coltrane version clearly served as Mr. Ibrahim's inspiration, so this may be considered a dedication to Coltrane as well.

"In a Sentimental Mood" finds Mr. Guyton stretching out expansively in a Coltrane-like manner, while "Giant Steps" has Mr. Jackson playing unaccompanied, plucking out Coltrane's melody and then rapidly running variations. Thelonious Monk's "Skippy," a variation on "Tea for Two," is the most playful piece here; it opens with Mr. Ibrahim playing a cascading sequence of notes that take the shape of another Monk standard, "Misterioso." Then the piece changes tempo and mood quickly, as piccolo and bass go through a lighthearted romp on the main tune.

Both sets feature new versions of several vintage works by Mr. Ibrahim, among them "Water from an Ancient Well." First recorded on the pianist's 1986 album of that title, it is a lovely and blissfully tranquil piece that sounds especially so here as a feature for Mr. Guyton's flute. "Mindif" was most famously heard on *African Suite*, a celebrated 1998 album that paired the pianist with a string orchestra. He plays it on both sets here, and both times, it's nothing less than mesmerizing, climaxing with a majestically cinematic flourish, and the live version concludes with two full minutes of audience applause.

Other tracks contain surprises: Mr. Guyton seems to be playing clarinet on another Ibrahim classic, "The Wedding." As the title implies, the melody is more romantic than many of the other pieces, but it's also rendered in a placid fashion, with arco bass, that speaks to the role of weddings as an engine of communal continuity. The final track, "Trance-Mission," finds Mr. Ibrahim chanting in several different languages.

The six tracks in the afternoon sequence constitute a complete, albeit brief, album unto themselves. The 13 live tracks from the evening performance have a very different feel. There's an audience here, but the atmosphere is more like a classical concert than a jazz event; throughout, the house keeps incredibly still, like it is hanging on every note and doesn't want to miss a single one of them.

(*The Wall Street Journal*, 2024)

BOKANI DYER (BORN 1986)

Is Bokani Dyer a good representative of contemporary African jazz? Of course he is, but at the same time, his music is so special and so unique to him that I would have a hard time describing it as being "typical" of anything other than Mr. Dyer himself—certainly I can't imagine anyone else creating music like this.

Mr. Dyer is a pianist, bandleader, composer, and frequent vocalist regarded as South African, though he was born in Botswana in 1986 at a time when his father, the prominent saxophonist Steve Dyer, was exiled there during the last years of apartheid.

His music is, in fact, more than one thing: he has a new album, *Radio Sechaba*, and did a gig at Dizzy's in the last weekend of April, ostensibly to promote the May release. Most artists, when plugging their latest albums, will play mostly that content; some will vary it but essentially give you music cut from the same cloth. Mr. Dyer, though, has given us two very different kinds of music with two very different bands, neither of which fits into conventional categories.

The music on the CD is ostensibly jazz with heavy elements of pop and soul, though I don't think I'd describe it as "fusion." *Radio Sechaba* starts with Mr. Dyer delivering a message in multitracked harmony, using his voice in something that's halfway between singing and speaking. Under the vocals, there's an electronically manipulated guitar background. The words tell us: "Don't fight with the moment / just be where you are." Those last four words are the song title.

Throughout the album, Mr. Dyer combines a wide range of textures, vocal and instrumental, electronic and acoustic, and those vocals themselves incorporate virtually every form of musical expression that the human voice is capable of, beyond singing and chanting to narrating (i.e., speaking) and rapping—and in multiple languages, English as well as African tongues. Most tracks use electric rhythm instruments, including Mr. Dyer on keyboards but with traditional trumpets and saxophones. The beat is consistently danceable, much more so than most modern jazz, but I don't know that I would automatically identify it as being distinctly African; it just seems to uniquely belong to Mr. Dyer.

The lyrics are philosophical, upbeat, and affirmative, often repeating a single idea many times, as on "Move On," wherein Mr. Dyer chants over and over as the track fades out, "Just move on—and be strong." "State of the Nation" features Damani Nkosi delivering what is essentially a set of instructions for social and political involvement, ranging from the general ("strengthen the family") to the specific ("grow your own food"). "Tiya Mowa" features the very attractive sounds of what seems to be a female vocal group mixed in with the ensemble, behind Mr. Dyer's voice and the other soloists. It turns out to be a single singer, Sibusisiwe Dyer. Keeping it in the family, Steve Dyer also plays on three tracks, including "Amogelang."

At Dizzy's, Mr. Dyer performed with bassist Zwelakhe-Duma Bell le Pere and drummer Kush Abadey and as a special guest, a celebrated young tenor saxophonist from Chile, Melissa Aldana. The quartet, which became a quintet when Mr. Dyer senior joined the four younger players for several tunes, played completely acoustically, but whether the tunes were fast or slow, they all had that distinctive loping beat that must be a signature among South African players.

Mr. Dyer dedicated several pieces to iconic African musicians—Abdullah Ibrahim was the one name that everyone in the crowd recognized—and there was a touch of Thelonious Monk in his rhythms as well, or at least those aspects of Monk that sound most directly African.

Even though Mr. Dyer described the two rhythm players as "homeboys," the rapport between the pianist and the saxophonist was even more remarkable; clearly, she knows and understands his music very well. She fits with the group even to the point of adjusting her intonation to match the mood of the piece; on several tunes, she changed the sound of her instrument to that of what we might hear if a tenor saxophone and a soprano had a baby, a kind of B-flat hybrid. Still, on other pieces, she sounded perfectly in tune, at least according to the conventional notions of Western ears and North American jazz.

The high point of the all-too-brief Dizzy's set was the moment when Steve Dyer, who earlier had led his own group with Bokani on keyboards, joined his son's quartet. At this point, Ms. Aldana unveiled yet another saxophone sound when she and Mr. Dyer Sr. played long, slow-ish ensemble passages together—as on "Medu"—producing a sound that was both haunting and otherworldly. They were playing so closely together that I wasn't sure if it might actually be unison rather than harmony.

Mr. Dyer demonstrated another sound one doesn't hear very often when he "prepared" his piano—the term is from John Cage—by placing sheets of paper on the strings to deaden the resonance and make it sound like an African percussion instrument.

Jazz at Lincoln Center's Seton Hawkins, who facilitated the booking and introduced the show, reminded us that the Dyers last played Dizzy's in 2019 and that the club has been trying to get them back ever since. The Dyers are used to borders and boundaries holding them back and dictating where they can play, but lately they, as everyone else, have had their professional fortunes determined by the pandemic as well. Still, it would take considerably more than politics and even a pandemic to stifle this music and the message of hope that it brings.

(*The New York Sun*, 2023)

CLASS OF 1970

ERIC REED (BORN 1970)

Is there an expression that means the opposite of wearing out one's welcome? Some musicians seem to grow so much each time you hear them that you start to wonder whether it's they or you who's doing the changing. Long known as a valuable sideman and accompanist, pianist Eric Reed—who is leading his New York Seven at the Village Vanguard until Sunday—is rapidly establishing himself as one of the most valuable bandleaders around.

More than any of the similar figures on the scene today—Cyrus Chestnut, Jason Moran, and Brad Mehldau—Mr. Reed makes entertaining an audience his primary ambition. Some leaders act like they're in a classroom; Mr. Reed creates a party atmosphere, gathering together players who are no less extroverted than himself. While nearly all the tunes on his new album, *The Quintet* (Savant 2051), are his own originals, at the late show on Wednesday he included tunes by other members of the band, lesser known but worthy pieces by other musicians and one completely reimagined jazz classic.

Mr. Reed is one of the few contemporary bandleaders—particularly among the younger generation (he is 32)—to appreciate the value of shorter tunes. Even when ensembles entirely comprise living legends, it becomes tiring to hear each player solo at elaborate length on every number. But a time-honored string-of-solos format can still sound fresh and lively when you have musicians as exuberant as trumpeter Jeremy Pelt, trombonist Wycliffe Gordon, and saxophonists Brad Leali (alto) and Marcus Strickland (tenor and soprano).

While Mr. Reed stays true to the hard-bop style associated with Horace Silver and the late Art Blakey (his first album, *Soldier's Hymn*, released in 1990, was dedicated to Blakey), he knows the value of variety. Some tunes, such as Mr. Leali's "Special

Eric Reed at Clark Terry recording session; Chesky Records;
St. Peters Episcopal Church, NYC; December 1999

K," employ blues grooves. "E-Bop" conveys the baroque nature of early bop, while "Ornate" is a witty reference to Ornette Coleman's "harmolodic," or free, jazz.

Mr. Reed shifted to the rhythm trio for the set's one slow ballad, "'Round Midnight"—which is also when he played it. He at first suggested some of composer Thelonious Monk's wide-open spaces (the album concludes with a solo medley of Monk's "Evidence" and "Think of One") but gradually filled them in, shifting to a harmonic opulence reminiscent of Bill Evans.

For a climax, the group brought out a new arrangement by Mr. Gordon of the venerable "St. Louis Blues," which comes out of a long tradition of Latin interpretations of W. C. Handy's classic. Mr. Reed and Mr. Gordon competed for solo honors here, the pianist using Cuban-style voicings and referencing "My Heart Belongs to Daddy" in the minor strain. Mr. Gordon, to the accompaniment of Mr. Green's cowbell, growled out animal noises of his own.

Between the young musicians and the largely collegiate crowd, I was practically the oldest person at the Vanguard on Wednesday night. They came to make merry, and Mr. Reed left everyone thoroughly entertained.

(*The New York Sun*, 2003)

***

Normally, I resent it when a bandleader begins a show by milking the house for applause, letting us know that he's not going to play unless he hears evidence of real enthusiasm from the crowd. To heck with that! Cheers and whistles of approval are supposed to be a reward for a good performance, not to encourage one that hasn't happened yet. That said, the pianist Eric Reed is one of the major exceptions to this rule. I've heard him play so brilliantly on so many occasions that by now I'm more than willing to extend him a little kudos on credit.

Mr. Reed's current ensemble, performing this week at Dizzy's Club Coca-Cola, is a quintet he calls Tenor Madness, and it features a front line of Seamus Blake and Stacy Dillard doubling on tenor and soprano saxophones; Dezron Douglas on bass; and especially important, Willie Jones III on drums. Mr. Jones is probably the best drummer I've heard with Mr. Reed: the two have a way of locking down the rhythm in an especially propulsive way, which works terrifically with Tenor Madness's hard-bop–centric program. Mr. Jones helps solidify Mr. Reed's reputation as possibly the most joyful pianist in jazz since Erroll Garner: everything he plays is unfailingly upbeat; he can even make a minor blues ballad sound happy.

The quintet opened the set with a declaration of allegiance to the classic Blue Note bebop of the mid-1960s by jumping into Lee Morgan's "Stop Start" (from *The Procrastinator*)—which, despite the title, is more the latter than the former—and "Devilette" (from Dexter Gordon's *Club House*), which featured Mr. Douglas's best solo of the night. Mr. Reed then interrupted the jubilant mood with a contemplative, low-key original called "Prayer," which he dedicated to two leading jazz figures currently on the sick list: pianist George Cables and bassist Dennis Irwin.

Three more pieces followed, each of which illustrated Mr. Reed's knack for unearthing worthy, lesser-known "heads" from the modern jazz songbook. Joe Chambers's soulful "Third Street Jump" rested on a backbeat that was so strong, I expected the setting sun to come out again; Wynton Marsalis's tricky and intricate "Delfeayo's Dilemma" followed, and Donald Brown's "Theme for Malcolm" featured a ska–reggae rhythm that whetted my appetite for the Jamaican pianist Monty Alexander's show this weekend.

One thing the band didn't do was build to a big tenor-bashing gladiatorial match of the kind that Sonny Rollins and John Coltrane whipped up in the original 1956 "Tenor Madness." But I'll wager that nobody missed it. I certainly won't be asking Mr. Reed to refund me any of the applause I advanced him at the beginning.

(*The New York Sun*, 2008)

***

Eric Reed, *Black, Brown, and Blue* (Smoke Sessions)

Usually, when an artist celebrates a new album with a "launch" performance, we expect there to be a correlation, at least, between the show and the record. Pianist

Eric Reed's new release, *Black, Brown, and Blue*, had almost nothing in common with his recent opening set at Smoke—except that both were excellent in their own way.

The set was the sort that Smoke is known for, a rather aggressive, muscular hard bop with an all-star New York–centric quartet featuring tenor saxophonist Chris Lewis, bassist Dezron Douglas, and drummer Kendrick Scott. The new album, conversely, is almost all slower and more contemplative pieces, played by a trio with bassist Luca Alemanno and drummer Reggie Quinerly and taped in Los Angeles.

Another thing they have in common is Mr. Reed's ambition to celebrate Black composers. That's the way he put it both in his spoken introduction at Smoke and on the notes to *Black, Brown, and Blue*. All the music in both projects is entirely the work of African American writers; however, it also is true that nearly everything here is written by jazz musicians—there are no vintage pop standards or show tunes.

When I say the music at Smoke sounded like quintessential hard bop, I mean that very literally. The combination of the players and the remarkable sonics of the room make you feel like you just time traveled into a Blue Note recording session circa 1960, with Horace Silver or Bobby Timmons at the piano and Wayne Shorter or Joe Henderson on tenor.

The set was framed by "Yes or No" and "Twelve More Bars to Go," Shorter compositions from the classic 1964 album *Juju*. In between, they essayed "ICHN," a Reed original dedicated to Herbie Nichols, and Thelonious Monk's eponymous "Thelonious." On the latter, Mr. Reed and company stayed true to the spirit of Monk by sticking mainly to the melody but playing with the tempo, stylizing the tune by playing it faster and faster.

On the album, Mr. Reed begins with the only original, the title number, "Black, Brown, and Blue," played as a relatively jaunty, unaccompanied keyboard piece. The mood slows down considerably, and the piano is highly predominant the rest of the way; at times Messrs. Alemanno and Quinerly offer support that's so subtle and restrained, you're barely aware they're even present. They also contribute an original each, Mr. Reggie Quinerly's thoughtful ballad "Variation Twenty-Four" and Mr. Alemanno's insightful "One for E."

While all the songs are by Black and jazz composers, they're divided between traditional romantic numbers, Duke Ellington's "I Got It Bad" being the major love song, and somewhat spiritually driven melodies, along the lines of Horace Silver's "Peace" and McCoy Tyner's "Search for Peace."

There are two stunning interpretations of Black singer–songwriters of the 1970s, each with worthwhile guest vocalists: Calvin B. Rhone on Bill Withers's "Lean on Me" and David Daughtry on Stevie Wonder's "Pastime Paradise." In both cases, Mr. Reed supplies the foundation for the singers to transmute pop songs into something more like gospel hymns.

Shorter and Monk are also represented on the album but on different songs: "Infant Eyes," another widely popular 1964 work, is in the same vein as John Coltrane's "Naimi," a highly tranquil, meditative tune that seems both romantic and spiritual at the same time. Monk's famous waltz, "Ugly Beauty," ends the album in a way that stresses the beauty rather than the ugly.

The only tune that the live set and the album had in common was Benny Golson's "Along Came Betty," and fittingly, it seemed more militant at Smoke and more liltingly lyrical—not to mention lovely—on the album. Mr. Reed has always been an intensely soulful player, and that aspect of his music has been increasing and improving in his recent series of albums for Smoke Sessions (following *Everybody Gets the Blues* and *For Such a Time as This*, from 2019 and 2020, respectively).

This is Mr. Reed's most personal statement yet. Although we've been talking about musical creators classified by both race and genre, it's ultimately really about none of those things—it's about a message of common humanity and hope for all God's children, whether we happen to be Black, Brown, or even Blue.

(*The New York Sun*, 2023)

GEOFFREY KEEZER (BORN 1970)

***Playdate* (Markeez Records)**

Most of us first noticed Geoffrey Keezer in the last edition of Art Blakey and the Jazz Messengers. But even before he played piano on the final three albums by that legendary band, Mr. Keezer had already recorded several CDs of his own—starting when he was all of 17. Now, at 51, he is among the youngest of contemporary jazzmen to have apprenticed with such giants of the bebop era as Blakey and Art Farmer.

Since then, Mr. Keezer has recorded a total of 23 albums as a leader and close to 100 sessions (at least in Tom Lord's *The Jazz Discography*) as a sideman. On Wednesday, he launched his latest release with a one-night, two-show appearance at Dizzy's Club Cola-Cola in Jazz at Lincoln Center.

Mr. Keezer came up in an era when regular working bands were the coin of the realm in this music. But the economics of the last few decades and the pandemic of the last few years have combined to underscore that such full-time, steadily employed ensembles are increasingly rare. Most jazz performances now are more about getting the musicians you want just to do a one-shot album or a gig; perhaps that's why Mr. Keezer has titled the new release *Playdate*.

At Dizzy's, Mr. Keezer remarked about how difficult it was to reconvene the same colleagues from the album sessions even to do the record-launch show. Granted, this is a rather unusual ensemble. Looking at the musicians on the stage, it almost seemed like Mr. Keezer had assembled two distinct bands to somehow perform at the same time. First was a standard piano trio, with himself, bassist Richie Goods, and drummer Kendrick Scott. The other was a 1960s-style organ combo, with tenor saxophonist Ron Blake; guitarist Aayushi Karnik; Shedrick Mitchell playing a Hammond B-3, and again, Mr. Scott on drums.

There are other musicians on the album—no room on the small stage at Dizzy's, alas—including an additional percussionist (Munyungo Jackson) and guitarist (Nir Felder). And oh yes, there's an 18-piece string orchestra on two tracks.

Mr. Keezer obviously intended this ambitious project as a vehicle for his considerable skills as a composer, and yet only half of the six tunes here are new originals, the opener, "Refuge," "I. L. Y. B. D.," and "M's Bedtime Blues." Of the others, "Her Look, Her Touch," and "Bebah," are by Mr. Mitchell, while "Tomorrow" is an optimistic funk tune by the Brothers Johnson from their 1976 debut album, *Look Out for #1*.

Just as the setup on stage looked like it could be two different bands—connected by a common drummer—the music performed moves in multiple directions. Some of these sounds could be described as "third stream," an archaic term meaning a hybrid, of sorts, between improvised jazz and formal classical music, and "fusion," an also increasingly obsolete term describing the mashup of jazz and rock (and or soul or funk).

As *Playdate* shows, these terms are anachronistic because the genre boundaries between jazz, classical, and pop are considerably more fluid these days. Mr. Keezer opened the set at Dizzy's with a dramatic solo on "Refuge"—as if to assert that despite all the instruments on stage, this is still predominantly a piano project.

On the album, he gets straightaway into the strings. The use of the violins, here and on "Bebah," also suggests yet another genre: movie music. Still, it's the rare film score that includes full-on jazz improvisation—as on "Refuge," where the most salient feature is the big-toned tenor of Mr. Blake wailing over the string background. When Mr. Mitchell and then Ms. Karnik take the center stage immediately after, it feels like a moment in a movie when the director has crosscut to a different scene in the same story.

Mr. Mitchell's two tunes, particularly "I. L. Y. B. D." (which, the composer explained, is a quote from his wife, "I love you, but damn!"), have more of a soul–jazz feel, but essentially, no one tune on the album is just one thing. They all begin in one spot, end up in another, and travel off into all sorts of unforeseen stops along the way. Mr. Keezer also plays Latinate clave patterns on several tunes, while "Bebah" has a flamenco-style opening that puts me in mind of "Concierto de Aranjuez."

Mr. Mitchell's other contribution, "Her Look, Her Touch," is a romantic ballad. At Dizzy's, he opened it with an extended organ intro that I described in my notes as "amazing." Still, both live and on the album, the primary voice is Mr. Blake's soft, crooning voice on soprano saxophone. "Tomorrow (A Better You, Better Me)," which Mr. Keezer explained he actually learned from Quincy Jones's celebrated album *Back on the Block*, adding, as he said, "a thousand more modulations," featured an extended solo by Richie Goods on a six-string electric bass.

"Bebah" makes the most of the two keyboards. Normally, the last thing a Hammond player needs is another keyboard instrument—they don't even require a bass player—but Mr. Keezer and Mr. Mitchell used the two big instruments as the foundation to support a formidable wall of sound. The opening set at Dizzy's wasn't long enough to include "M's Bedtime Blues," but on the album, this final selection combines multiple keyboards and diverse genres from stride piano to soul–jazz to a little Monk-ishness. The conjoined force of those two keyboards can not only support a lot of weight; between the two of them, they cover a lot of territory.

(*The New York Sun*, 2022)

BRAD MEHLDAU (BORN 1970)

Meanwhile, down in the Village, the line stretching down Seventh Avenue, all the way past the Psychic Reader and up to the front of Fantasy Lingerie, can only mean one thing: Brad Mehldau is at the Vanguard. Early in his career, Mr. Mehldau was often characterized as an Evans successor, but he rarely plays in such a way as to invite a direct comparison. If I had been hearing him for the first time on Wednesday, I would have been much less likely to notice any resemblance, with the exception of the one ballad on the set, "Baby Plays Around," an Elvis Costello melody that Mr. Mehldau recast with jazzy chords and a sensitive touch, an overall approach reminiscent of Evans playing Paul Simon.

Mr. Mehldau is amazingly popular with listeners his age (37) and younger, who are not generally part of the jazz audience. I can only surmise this is partly because he's far from a typical neo-bopper, burying an audience in an avalanche of notes and chords usually derived from old standards. Mr. Mehldau opened on Wednesday with four originals (one inspired by the guitarist Kurt Rosenwinkel and another, by the movie *Easy Rider*), all of which began with very simple short tunes. Each piece started with the pianist determined to confine his playing to a narrow rhythm and dynamic range, with drummer Jeff Ballard given the freedom to dart all around him.

As each piece progressed, the groove widened, with Mr. Mehldau beginning to lay down phrases with increasing expression, and the overall mood became more freewheeling and openly swinging. Mr. Mehldau also played one classic bop number, Clifford Brown's "Brownie Speaks," for contrast and possibly, to show that he can handle the characteristic note-heavy, superfast bebop style.

It's unlikely that Mr. Mehldau will ever do a full-length tribute to Bill Evans, although during the course of his career, he has played a couple of the late master's signatures, such as "Nobody Else But Me" and "Solar," also from the Miles Davis band book "How High the Moon." Evans and Mr. Mehldau both recorded it live at the Vanguard, and it's on Ms. Elias's album as well.

As far as I know, Mr. Mehldau has never played "My Foolish Heart" (although he has done "Young and Foolish"), but it's the highlight of Elaine Elias's Bill Evans project. At Dizzy's, clearly inspired by the knowledge that her husband is playing a bass owned by Scott LaFaro—the bassist in Evans's first legendary trio—she turned in her most sensitive and moving performance, recapturing Evans's subtle, exquisite touch and the torrent of emotion that it unleashed. It's further evidence of how Evans and his spirit continue to venerate the foolishness in all of our hearts.

(*The New York Sun*, 2008)

***

Brad Mehldau, *Your Mother Should Know: Brad Mehldau Plays The Beatles* (Nonesuch Records)

An outstanding contemporary songwriter, Jimmy Webb once told me about a trick he used whenever he was trying to sell a song to one of the heavyweight star singers—especially Sinatra. Rather than work hard to make the song sound as good as possible, he would deliberately underperform. Mr. Webb knows that this would touch off a tingle in Sinatra's interpretative skills as well as his competitive nature. The singer would hear that Jimmy wasn't getting everything he could out of the song, and he would start to think of ways he could improve upon the composer's performance.

This is the main reason why nearly all of the so-called covers of the classic songs of the Beatles seem entirely beside the point. Unlike their colleague, Bob Dylan, who possesses what even his fans would describe as an idiosyncratic voice, Lennon, McCartney, Harrison, and even Starr all had remarkable vocal chops, and the original driving force behind the group was the miraculous harmony of Lennon and McCartney, which everyone seemed to recognize even when they were teenagers. The Beatles did more than just write their songs for themselves: for them, the composing, arranging, recording, and performing were all essentially the same process.

There are a million things one could do with "Blue Skies," but "A Day in the Life" is so perfect as it stands as part of the *Sgt. Pepper* album that there's really nothing else to be done with it. The notion of "improving" on it, even as Sinatra did with Jimmy Webb's songs, is not only out of the question, but it's hard to imagine that there could be something new that could be done with any of the great Beatles numbers that would be even a fraction as good as the originals.

Born in 1970, Brad Mehldau is easily the biggest jazz piano headliner of his generation—what Keith Jarrett, Herbie Hancock, and the late Chick Corea were and are to slightly older jazz fans. Still, the odds were against him when he recorded this album, released a few months ago, as a live solo piano concert in September 2020.

This was still the pre-vaccinated height of the pandemic, and he had decided to record the 11 solo piano tracks live in concert at the Philharmonie de Paris. Even though each number ends with the sound of a loud, enthusiastic crowd, the situation still must have been somewhat dicey, performing this music before a house of cautious, masked Frenchmen.

Regardless, *Your Mother Should Know: Brad Mehldau Plays The Beatles* is an unqualified success. Mr. Mehldau begins in an unusual place, with one of John Lennon's strangest, most psychedelic texts, "I Am the Walrus"; in 1967, the random, abstract imagery of the lyrics must have seemed especially baffling to anyone over age 30.

Mr. Mehldau surprises us by dwelling on what might have seemed the most conventional part of the song: Lennon deliberately emphasized his weirder moments by contrasting them with the conventional picturesque thought of a proper "English garden." Mr. Mehldau dwells on those parts of the melody and as a result, makes me think more about sitting in that old-fashioned garden than it does about comparing oneself to a walrus or an "eggman."

"Your Mother Should Know," conversely, was Mr. McCartney's hymn to intergenerational respect and understanding, and as such, was embraced at the time by the very popular old-guard "trad jazz" trumpeter–singer, Kenny Ball. Mr. Mehldau sets in a solid two-beat and phrases it with a nod to older piano styles; in fact, at different points, it sounds like it could have been written by Scott Joplin. Likewise, "I Saw Her Standing There" reflects upon the Beatles' fondness for early rock superstar pianist–singers, such as Jerry Lee Lewis and especially, Little Richard, and on their own influences, such as boogie-woogie keyboard superstars Maurice Rocco and even Meade Lux Lewis.

Reviewing the album, my colleague Martin Johnson observed that Mr. Mehldau "aims for smaller changes rather than full-blown reinvention." Indeed, that's the whole idea: Why reduce the songs down to their essential chord changes, the way the early beboppers did with Gershwin? What's the point of playing Beatles songs if you're not going to play the melodies? "He Said, She Said" and "For No One" are more or less the same tunes as heard on *Revolver* (1966). Both are rather delicate and full of melancholy, the first describing a rather fragile relationship that sounds like it's just about to fall apart and the second sounding like that has already happened.

One might expect Mr. Mehldau to recast the 1964 "Baby's in Black" as a jazz waltz, but he surprised me by slowing it down and treating it more like a gospel number, reminding me of the halting, soulful fashion in which Ray Charles reinterprets the French song "The Three Bells." "If I Needed Someone" is tentative and ambiguous, alert to the possibility of love. Likewise, "Here, There and Everywhere" is more optimistic still, though Mr. Mehldau plays it so slowly, he gives it a deliberately tentative quality, essentially joyous but somewhat guarded.

"Maxwell's Silver Hammer," the happiest song ever about a murderous rampage, begins rubato and stretches out the melody to the point where it briefly becomes a dead ringer for the 1966 popular song "For Once in My Life." When he gets to the familiar refrain, which carries the words of the title, the number becomes rather like a slow vaudeville dance. Somehow, I picture Bert Williams or more recently, Ben Vereen strutting to it with measured, deliberate steps, like "Nobody" or "Mr. Cellophane" in the musical *Chicago*.

The two final tracks are exceptional. "Golden Slumbers" has always been one of my personal favorite Beatles items—both on its own and in its familiar place as part of the amazing medley on the 1969 album *Abbey Road*. The original version is barely

90 seconds, which is far too short, and thus, Mr. Mehldau's interpretation, which is more than eight minutes long, is highly welcome.

"Golden Slumbers" is both a song of nostalgia and one warning us to be wary of pure nostalgia; it's about going back home and at the same time, not going home. Although famously inspired by an Elizabethan playwright, Thomas Dekker, I first heard it around the same time I was reading *Alice in Wonderland*—more archaic English lit—and somehow it remains linked in my mind to Lewis Carroll's "All in the golden afternoon." Mr. Mehldau's extended, elegiac reading is entirely golden and not at all slumber inducing.

He winds up, with a slight perverseness that Lennon would have appreciated, with a non-Beatles song, David Bowie's "Life on Mars?" Is Mr. Mehldau making it a point to show us that there are other British rock songwriters whose work is worthy of this level of scrutiny and attention? If so, he succeeds.

(*The New York Sun*, 2023)

THREE OF A KIND

CHICK COREA (1941–2021)

He's a wily man, that Chick Corea, and he knows the value of contrast and surprise. The 65-year-old pianist, composer, and bandleader, who is celebrating his 65th birthday week at the Blue Note, is the rare jazz musician with the following of a rock star. In the 1970s, he established himself as an industry leader in the music we were then calling jazz–rock fusion, as a member of Miles Davis's first electric band and as the leader of his own fusion supergroup, Return to Forever.

Yet his first influence was Bud Powell, and he is as fine a bebop pianist as he allows himself to be. He made some of the most valuable music of his career with the free-jazz quartet Circle, and he has also composed and performed classical music, including a symphonic setting of his most famous tune, "Spain."

Yet not every album can be a career highlight. His most recent release, the 2004 *To the Stars*, was credited to Mr. Corea's so-called Elektric Band, and it's always a bad sign when rap-style bad spelling is employed. Inspired by the science fiction novels of L. Ron Hubbard, *To the Stars* was trite, electronic bubblegum music that sounded like a cheesy video-game soundtrack.

But Mr. Corea's latest effort, *The Ultimate Adventure*, also inspired by Hubbard's stories, is what he does best: accessible jazz with engaging rhythms and catchy melodies that don't insult anyone's intelligence. Here, he combines acoustics with electronics and infuses straight-ahead modern jazz grooves with a Latin tinge. Because Hubbard drew on the *Arabian Nights* in his writing, Mr. Corea has also thrown some Middle Eastern rhythms and tonalities into the mix.

The new album and the shows at the Blue Note mark Mr. Corea's reunion with percussionist Airto Moreira, his costar in both Return to Forever and the Miles Davis Quintet of 1970. Bassist Eddie Gomez worked extensively with Mr. Corea in the late

1970s, but this is the first time the three have has worked together as a trio, which the leader calls Forever Returns. (This is, in fact, a better title than "Return to Return to Forever" or "Return to Forever Returns.")

Considering that Mr. Moreira is Brazilian and Mr. Gomez is Puerto Rican, it seemed only natural that Forever Returns should open their late set on Tuesday night within an Iberian vein. It began with what seemed like random noises: Mr. Moreira chanted doggerel in various vocal registers and played odd percussion instruments in irregular rhythms while Mr. Corea, on his synthesizers, hit a variety of musical colors not found in nature. Then, Mr. Corea's acute sense of contrast came into play. He gradually transitioned from this amorphous mass of unrelated sounds to a very clear melody, with sharp, almost exaggerated Spanish accents. At times, this reminded me of the lounge-music maestro Juan Garcia Esquivel, who was sort of the Mexican Spike Jones, incorporating sound effects and abstract noise.

Mr. Corea moved over to the Blue Note's acoustic Bösendorfer piano for two standards, Richard Rodgers's "With a Song in My Heart" and Jimmy Van Heusen's "But Beautiful." The latter began with an extended intro solo from Mr. Gomez, then transitioned from one section to the next in a subtle, organic manner. Mr. Moreira left aside his battery of Latin percussion devices in favor of plain old North American trap drums, on which he played all sorts of unexpected patterns that complemented the piano's melody lines. Mr. Corea kept these melodies front and center, spinning variations on the tunes themselves rather than just running the chord changes.

The last tune of the set commenced with another wild, abstract intro. At first, it seemed confusing and redundant, as if they were opening the set all over again. But they knew what they were doing: the abstraction gradually took the shape of a highly original reading of the Antonio Carlos Jobim standard "Desafinado." The song is usually done in a gently undulating Brazilian style, but the trio subjected it to the sharper Hispanic rhythms of Spanish, Cuban, or Argentinian music. For an encore, Mr. Corea treated the crowd to one of Return to Forever's most famous tunes, "500 Miles High," which I found myself humming late into the night.

(*The New York Sun*, 2006)

***

Apparently, Carnegie Hall believes that anybody who likes Chick Corea couldn't possibly also like Michael Feinstein. It was on a Wednesday in April 2008 that Carnegie scheduled them both at the same time; Mr. Feinstein was downstairs in Carnegie Zankel Hall, offering the latest installment of his long-running "Standard Time" series, and Corea was upstairs in the main (Isaac Stern) hall, performing as part of a unique trio with vocalist Bobby McFerrin and drummer Jack DeJohnette. My salvation was that the Feinstein show, a songbook program celebrating the great lyricist Leo Robin, started at 7:00 and would only be a one-act set to end at 8:30 p.m.

When Mr. Feinstein's concert ended, I didn't wait for the encore, but rather, I raced upstairs and around the corner. I reached Isaac Stern Auditorium at about 8:40 p.m. and encountered a surprising sight: patrons who had arrived shortly after the 8:00 p.m. starting time were still standing in the back. Carnegie has a practice of not seating latecomers in the middle of a number, and at 8:40, the ushers were waiting for the first number to end before seating them. Finally, as the clock approached 9:00 p.m., we were at last led to our respective seats.

The performance, it turned out, was a 100-minute free-form improvisation for a trio consisting of Mr. Corea on piano, Jack DeJohnette on drums, and Mr. Bobby McFerrin doing whatever it is that he does—vocals, sound effects, and spontaneous inventions of every kind that can be created using the human instrument.

As the title of his 2002 album, *Beyond Words*, indicates, Mr. McFerrin has spent a great deal of his career demonstrating that lyrics are not a necessary part of singing. This evening, he seemed to be taking it a step further, saying that creative musicians need not be dependent on prewritten melodies of any kind either.

At times, this was pure free jazz of the kind Mr. Corea used to play in his avant-garde days (particularly with the valuable quartet Circle). At other points, the threesome settled into randomly discovered but mutually agreed-upon familiar patterns of chord changes—there was at least one section based on the blues for instance. Mr. McFerrin likes to spend a lot of time interacting with the audience, leading it as an ad-lib choir; the effect is playful and charming but is most effective in very short doses. (Had I wanted to hear myself sing, I would have stayed home.)

The most entertaining moments occurred when the trio went out of its way to be entertaining: at one point, Mr. DeJohnette began poking at an electronic sampling device that made a boingy sound, like a jew harp, which Mr. McFerrin took as a cue to start mumbling improvised country-and-western lyrics, rather like a hillbilly Clark Terry.

Later, Mr. McFerrin joined Mr. Corea at the concert grand, and they improvised a four-handed piano duet. Mr. Corea even whipped out a set of drumsticks at several instances and began using found objects, including the piano and the monitors, as percussion instruments. During one of these interludes, Messrs. Corea and McFerrin huddled behind Mr. DeJohnette's enormous trap kit and began mimicking clockwork automatons, a move reminiscent of a classic sketch by Sid Caesar on *Your Show of Shows*.

After the main event was finished, the crowd called the three musicians back, and they encored with "Blue Monk." I would have preferred it the other way around—if they had built most of the concert around music that had utilized some kind of agreed-upon melodic starting point and followed that with a free-form piece as an encore.

The hall was packed, but in the second hour—this was a one-act concert—I have never seen such a continual migration toward the exit. Still, those who remained were more than enthusiastic enough to compensate for the departed, cheering and whistling at every motion. This was a performance that necessitated, even demanded audience participation, even when Mr. McFerrin wasn't specifically choreographing it.

(*The New York Sun*, 2008)

***

It wasn't an anniversary of any kind, but there were two major celebrations of Bill Evans during the same week in May 2010. At Jazz at Lincoln Center, Bill Charlap led Wynton Marsalis and the JALC orchestra plus guitarist Jim Hall in an intriguing program of an orchestral interpretation of Evans music—something that's only rarely been attempted before—with newly commissioned arrangements by Ted Nash. And the other was an equally -inspired trio program masterminded by Chick Corea, titled Further Explorations of Bill Evans. *It seemed more logical to include the write-up of Corea's tribute to Evans in this section rather than the one on Evans.*

One Tuesday night at the Blue Note, Chick Corea made it clear why "Alice in Wonderland" (by Sammy Fain and Bob Hilliard) was a song that Bill Evans wanted to play at the Village Vanguard. The song derives from Walt Disney's not-fondly-remembered animated film of the Lewis Carroll classic—I say that because this was always a movie that Disney himself was supposedly disappointed in. That 1951 film and the story, in general, were much in the cultural zeitgeist in 2010; that year Disney had released a new movie adaptation of *Alice in Wonderland*, this one directed by Tim Burton, which was well on its way to becoming a blockbuster by the time of this Vanguard set in May.

"Alice," as everybody knows, is about a young girl exploring a magical realm where things make sense in a topsy-turvy way, a land of possibilities, challenges, dreams, and nightmares. In that sense, it directly parallels where Evans was when he played it on his most famous album, the 1961 *Sunday at the Village Vanguard.* He had indeed fallen through the rabbit hole and was continually discovering new ways to play: ways to interact with his bassist and drummer (the self-same Paul Motian, who is working with Mr. Corea during this two-week celebration at the Blue Note), to expand the harmonies, to interpret the melodies, and to express himself. Even the time signature was a breakthrough: composer Sammy Fain had written this main title theme as a waltz, and Evans would play a key role in establishing 3/4 time as a viable option for modern jazzmen. Small wonder that Evans played "Alice" twice in two different sets on that legendary Sunday.

Mr. Corea, Mr. Motian, and bassist Eddie Gomez have titled their project *Further Explorations of Bill Evans*; in collaborating with two of the most celebrated members of various Evans trios, Mr. Corea seems to be suggesting that this is the group that Evans might be leading had he not died at 51 in 1980. One of the all-time master interpreters of what we call the Great American Songbook, Evans had a brilliant and original way of interspersing the written melodies into his improvisations—as far out as he could get, he would sprinkle hints of the tune here and there, like bread crumbs for listeners to find their way back to a familiar place. Mr. Corea does the same thing here—not only with the tune but with the Evans style—he'll throw in an Evans-style chord voicing here or an Evans-esque phrase there (he had a particular passage that he used frequently for transitions in and out of different choruses), not to imitate Evans but to lay sign posts.

The late set on opening night included an imaginative treatment of Thelonious Monk's "Reflections" in which Mr. Corea made it seem like he wanted to embellish that basically simple line in an elaborate arrangement, but the tune itself refused to cooperate and kept fighting him off, as if it wouldn't go along peacefully. One of Evans's own most thoughtful ballads, "Turn Out the Stars," was essayed in an arco solo by Mr. Gomez that contrasted the composer's ballad soul with a hint of distortion, while Mr. Corea also brought a fair amount of dissonance to an unnamed blues. The trio finished with "Star Eyes," in which the blend of aggression, energy, and lyricism continued to honor Evans's memory.

Inspired, no doubt by Evans, Corea would record the Fain–Hilliard Disney song "Alice in Wonderland," at least twice, in Japan and Poland. More importantly, in 1977, Corea recorded the most elaborate jazz homage to Lewis Carroll yet. This was *The Mad Hatter*, a full-length work—equal parts what Duke Ellington would call a jazz suite or what rock bands call a concept album. It consisted of nine tracks inspired by the Alice books, with titles such as "Falling Alice," "Tweedle Dee," and "The Mad Hatter Rhapsody."

This is surely one of Corea's most ambitious works, not least because of the wide range of instrumental textures: there's his acoustic quartet, with Joe Farrell switching between tenor saxophone and flute, bassist Eddie Gómez, and drummer Steve Gadd. Various tracks also use electronic instruments, keyboards and synthesizers, essentially the sound of Corea's Elektric Band of the period, as well as a classical string quartet and a brass quartet. Other "movements" ("Falling Alice") employ a human voice, Gayle Moran, and even lyrics.

The Mad Hatter, which shows Corea on the cover in full-on hatter drag, is quite possibly my single favorite Corea project—one of the jazz repertory organizations should consider performing it with a cast of musicians in Carroll costumes.

But hearing Corea play "Alice in Wonderland" at the Vanguard underscores one interesting point: Bill Evans was known to play the song twice, at least as documented on recordings, once at the classic 1961 Vanguard recording and then again on a 1968 Vanguard set that was later released as part of the package *Secret Recordings*. Why did Bill Evans and then Chick Corea want to play "Alice in Wonderland" at the Village Vanguard? The answer is obvious: because the place is a literal rabbit hole.

In any case, no less than Tim Burton, Chick Corea has brought us back to Wonderland.

(*The Wall Street Journal*, 2010)

FRED HERSCH (BORN 1955)

Strange, dear. The pianist Fred Hersch, who is appearing this week with his trio at the Village Vanguard, has a unique way of playing introductions so that they seem like ships on the far horizon. You can see them way off in the distance, at the very edge of the water, and as they sail closer and closer, their outlines gradually become clearer and more familiar. By the time the first ship reached port on Tuesday night, it was at last recognizable as "So in Love." Hersch knows well how to make the melody announce itself with a mere two notes, only an ascending half-step apart. He goes on to play the rest of the tune, but those two notes are all that's needed to identify Cole Porter's classic. Hersch can play these two notes in almost any sort of context—fast, slow, high, or low—but his grasp of the melody is so firm that no matter how or where he puts them, we hear the opening words of the melody, "Strange, dear . . ." in our heads. He makes these notes sound far more dear than strange.

"So in Love" launched both Fred Hersch's opening set and his new album, *Night and the Music* (Palmetto). The show marks his first appearance at the Vanguard since a year ago, when he became the first pianist to play a completely solo engagement at jazz's longest-running venue, and this album is his first studio-recorded trio set since 1994. This particular lineup of the trio, with bassist Drew Gress and drummer Nasheet Waits, has been playing together at least since 2002, when they recorded a live album at the Vanguard.

Hersch gives listeners a lot of bang for their buck, not merely in that he played a long and very full set (80 minutes) on Tuesday, but that each piece was crammed with a lot of ideas into a very small space. In other trios, bass and drum solos sometimes seem like mere filler in a set, but Hersch deploys these not just as a token gesture but only when they actually help the music—many of his best pieces are just him all the way through, with nary a rhythm section interruption.

That's the way he plays Irving Berlin's "Change Partners," although it opens with a short bass intro and relies heavily on Gress's support. Still, no partners are actually changed. Such a performance, too, was "So in Love," which, without making a point of it or grandstanding, he proceeded, after the intro and then the opening melody, to play it every which way: hard driving like a boppish blues, Latinate and danceable, abstract and almost free form, and highly melodic, using what is sometimes called the "locked hands" (or block chords) technique but sounding nothing like George Shearing.

Ten years ago, Hersch recorded *Thelonious*, an album of solo interpretations of 12 songs by Monk. He continues to find new approaches to Monk's compositions, two of which ("Boo Boo's Birthday" and "Misterioso") are on *Night and the Music*, while another was heard on Tuesday. "San Francisco Holiday" (aka "Worry Later") came from a period in the pianist–composer's career when he was working regularly in that city, recording several albums there, one of which, *Thelonious Alone in San Francisco*, sported the iconic cover that depicted the longtime New Yorker clinging trepidatiously to a Bay City cable car. The tune "San Francisco Holiday" is one of Monk's

Fred Hersch, piano; Jazz Standard; May 22, 2012, photograph ©Alan Nahigian

most memorable locomotives, choo-choo-ing along with a disarmingly rhythmic, train-like beat. Hersch, who announced that the trio was playing "San Francisco Holiday" for the first time, kept it steadily on track, at times slowing down like a steam engine trying to make it over the hill and at other times, deliberately derailing the melody to deconstruct it in a postmodern fashion. This is a percussive tune in which one wants to hear a drum solo, and Waits obliged, while Hersch sprinkled notes around him.

Elsewhere on the early set, the trio played several originals, including the new "A Lark" and "Gravity's Pull," a gentle piece without unnecessary heaviness (also heard on the album). There was also a collage of two Wayne Shorter tunes from the composer's classic Blue Note period, both of which evoke exotic, far-flung lands. It started with the introspective "Miyako" (1967) in which Hersch made time elastic, stretching it out and elongating the tune. Then, Hersch used a bass solo as a transition into the more boppish "Black Nile" (1964), on which the pianist revealed more of a Bud Powell influence, which in this case, means *God almighty* fast, with Latin accents à la "Un Poco Loco."

There was one other standout standard, "How Deep Is the Ocean." Another Berlin ballad, this 1932 song is one of the most profound tunes in his canon, and Hersch's treatment was suitably deep. Despite the interaction of two other musicians and Hersch's incredible keyboard chops, here, both the pianist and the piano seem to be made of glass, not in the sense of being delicate or breakable, although he is an extraordinarily sensitive player, but in terms of being completely transparent. You don't see the instrument; you don't see the player. But you can see the music clear as day in front of you, even in a dimly lit cellar like the Vanguard. By the time that this ship pulls into port, there's no mistaking that the ocean is very deep indeed. Strange, dear, but true, dear.

(*The New York Sun*, 2007)

***

For the fourth of Hersch's annual weeklong invitationals at Jazz Standard (2007), he again introduced something new: a whole week of four-handed two-piano duets. Anyone with any familiarity with the modus operandi of the series would hardly expect Hersch to do the usual thing in such a situation, which would be a "dueling pianos" style competition in which the two pianists are more like combatants and the whole thing is more like a competition, where the first player will shoot a few bars at his opponent and then duck. Rather than the expected give-and-take, the Hersch–Mehldau duos were a case of give-and-give, with one participant leading and the other keeping up with him: they stayed together, even when taking off for parts unknown.

The duo had a different approach for each of the three most familiar melodies. On the opener, "Think of One," they kept Thelonious Monk's tune in mind but tinkered continually with the time. On "I Fall in Love Too Easily," they scattered the melody to the hinterlands but retained the ballad mood. On the official closer, "You and the Night and the Music," they threw both the tune and the time to the four winds and headed straight for the twilight zone, yet they never lost each other or the crowd.

In between, they duetted on Mehldau's pretty "The Secret Beach" and on Jane Ira Bloom's "Janeology," which Hersch aptly described as a contrafact taken from the harmonies to Charlie Parker's "Confirmation"; this latter piece was the most abstract, with the two pianists skittering about their keyboards like two mice in tennis shoes. They each played a solo, Hersch's being Jobim's "Insensatez"—itself allegedly inspired by Chopin's Fourth Prelude—in which the Brazilian rhythm was deemphasized. The set ended with huggies between the two pianists and even though it was almost 11:00 p.m., a spur-of-the-moment encore on "Blue Monk." Here, they stayed true to tune and the tempo and the spirit of the basic blues. The set that began with Monk, now, appropriately ended with Monk, and the evening as a whole had progressed from funk to Monk.

Perhaps the most memorable of Hirsch's duets took place at the Blue Note in the 10th anniversary year of the series and resulted in one of the most exciting of the prodigious pianist's many albums. *Free Flying*, a set of duets with guitarist Julian Lage, further illustrated how it's a false notion that jazz is strictly *about* solos; most of the absolute greatest playing in all of the music is driven by the concept of interplay rather than the individual statements. In 2013, Hersch, who was then 58, made this point most strongly in conjunction with the prodigious 25-year-old guitarist. On *Free Flying*, each of the two instruments become as wings to a bird; it takes the two of them, both wings that is, to keep the tune aloft. This is as symbiotic a duo as you'll ever hear: the guitar and piano generally occupy the same harmonic and even philosophical space, and yet rather than each staking a claim for their own territory, Hersh and Lage seamlessly blend together so that you literally can't tell where one begins and the other ends. Hersch composed seven of the nine songs on *Free Flying*, but the two standards were also standouts: the album closer was another Monk tune, "Monk's Dream," which solidified Hersch's tradition of framing his sets and albums with Monk's music. Sam Rivers's "Beatrice" was taken somewhat faster than the composer did on his most famous album, *Fuchsia Swing Song*, but no less purposefully, with the twosome deftly exploring the spaces in and around each other.

(*The New York Sun*, 2006, 2007; *The Wall Street Journal*, 2011, 2013)

***

The saga of piano at the Village Vanguard isn't only about Bill Evans, Thelonious Monk, Tommy Flanagan, and other departed icons; it's also about Fred Hersch, Barry Harris, Bill Charlap, Renee Rosnes, Martial Solal, Sam Yahel, Jason Moran, Uri Caine, and Evan Iverson. In fact, there are possibly more exceptional pianists appearing there regularly now than at any previous point in the storied club's 75-year history. Born in 1955, Fred Hersch is precisely in the midpoint of the contemporary keyboard canon, both generationally and musically: he's as cutting edge as any of the younger lions yet is as true to the melody and the bop tradition as any of the elder statesmen. His current trio, with bassist John Hébert and drummer Eric McPherson, who help him create an exceptional ensemble in which all three players are equal partners yet don't eat up all the playing time with a lot of unnecessary bass and drum solos, provides a persuasive argument that the golden age of Vanguard piano is right now.

Considering that the Vanguard itself is essentially a very big Steinway in a comparatively small, underground space, obviously designed for its acoustics rather than its view (trust me, you won't be distracted by any panoramic windows or a gorgeous view of Columbus Circle), this may be the best venue in the city to hear jazz piano. I haven't done the math, but I would wager that a disproportionate share of the club's most regular performers—those who appear multiple times a year—are keyboardists.

The late show on opening night reminded me of a really classic Broadway score in which every number is a gem, completely free of filler. Coincidentally, the set was bookended by show tunes, beginning with a densely polyrhythmic "From This Moment On," in which it's to Cole Porter's credit that one of his most basic (not to mention "hoop-de-do") songs showed that it could withstand an extremely heavy-duty harmonic bombardment.

The pianist's first original was "Stuttering," a piece driven by an idea as much as a melody—multiple repeated notes suggesting a speech impediment—but in which the tune was memorable beyond the call of duty. He solidly stated said melody, for the most part, using just his right hand, which displayed such autonomy that when the left hand entered the picture, it seemed like two distinct individuals conversing, both stuttering all the while. (In other areas of modern jazz, the main improvisor who has shown us how attractive a "stuttering" approach can be is the great Sonny Rollins.)

"Whirl" is the title track from Hersch's trio album released last year, which he described as a dedication to ballet living legend Suzanne Farrell. Though it started modestly with a simple melody line suggesting a single dancer, by the time it reached its busiest point, the trio was conjuring up mental pictures of an entire corps de ballet. From the same album, "Sad Poet" was inspired by Antonio Carlos Jobim and is cut from the same high-quality cloth as Hersch's excellent 2009 solo piano album of Jobim's music.

Hersch's treatment of "Boo Boo's Birthday" is a unique de facto collaboration with the late Thelonious Monk; Hersch's arrangement was almost epically large, especially in comparison to the simple treatment given by the composer himself on his 1967 album *Underground*. If Monk were to have ever followed the example of Bill Evans and done an album of conversations with himself via multitracking, this is what it would have sounded like.

By now, the late set was reaching the pinnacle of its arc. The pianist treated us to a surprisingly tender "If Ever I Would Leave You," surprising because the song is more usually the province of bravura baritones like Robert Goulet and extrovert tenors like Sonny Rollins. Wanting to leave us with something zippier, he played an "against type" version of "You Don't Know What Love Is"—big and upbeat rather than slow and melancholy. It's understandable why he wanted to close with a bang, but he had really said it all with "If Ever I Would Leave You." In all the hundreds of times I've listened to that *Camelot* ballad, this was the first occasion when I felt like somebody was actually leaving something.

(*The Wall Street Journal*, 2011)

***

In jazz, live and recorded music are forever engaged in an intricate *pas de deux*. The improvisations in front of flesh-and-blood audiences are where the magic happens. Yet without the technology of audio reproduction, all would be lost the instant after each note was created and heard.

This is the standard "creation model" of nearly all jazz: performances for a live audience are the main event, and recordings—whether made then or in the studio—are necessary yet secondary. But pianist Fred Hersch has devised a new approach in which the music is both created and listened to in social isolation. His new solo album, *Songs From Home*, shows that musicians of Mr. Hersch's high caliber not only refuse to be stopped by the pandemic but in this case at least, can be inspired by it.

If "Pandemic Jazz" is a new musical genre, it is one defined not only by the circumstances of its creation but also by that of its intended audience. *Songs From Home*—Mr. Hersch's 11th album of solo piano—consists of 11 songs he recorded in his living room in August. This is music about solitude not only created in social isolation but meant to be listened to in the same way.

In his liner notes, Mr. Hersch states that the eight well-known songs here all have "meaningful lyrics." And even though he's playing the songs and not singing them, it's those lyrics (and the song titles) that he's interested in. There is also "Consolation (A Folk Song)," by the trumpeter Kenny Wheeler, and two of Mr. Hersch's own originals, "Sarabande" and "West Virginia Rose." The latter is inspired by his mother and serves as an intro to the traditional "The Water Is Wide."

The album begins with a few reverent notes, almost like a hymn, before leading into "Wouldn't It Be Loverly," the opening number of the classic Broadway musical *My Fair Lady*. In Act 1, Scene 1, the heroine, flower girl Eliza Doolittle, is surrounded by her fellow street vendors and expresses a deep inner longing to have a warm "room somewhere" of her own, shared with someone who loves her. But unlike Eliza, Mr. Hersch is performing the song from the point of view of someone who already has what Eliza wants—a room to be alone in or to share with someone who loves him. His interpretation expresses deep, heartfelt contentment and serenity rather than Eliza's yearning for something that requires the full power of her imagination just to describe.

The 10th of the 11 songs here is Duke Ellington's "Solitude." And in between, Mr. Hersch gives us other songs of solitude—ballads, as it were—for this contemplative and melancholy moment. Cole Porter's "Get Out of Town" could here describe the exodus of many New Yorkers who had that option (including the pianist himself, sequestered in rural Pennsylvania). The slightly jauntier "After You've Gone" observes solitude from another angle, this time as a cautionary tale and an admonishment. Jimmy Webb's "Wichita Lineman" is an aria of existential loneliness; Mr. Hersch makes it even more so by eliminating one of the song's best-known melodic features, that famous rhythmic burst that approximates a message in Morse code. The pianist is signifying that in this telling of the tale, there's no one on the line. The lineman is entirely—and eerily—on his own.

Throughout the album, the music sounds very little like anything I ever heard Mr. Hersch—or anyone else—play in, say, the Village Vanguard, even when he performed as a solo pianist there. Rather, it sounds like it was made in one person's house and meant to be enjoyed in another—not just *Songs From Home* but songs *for* home.

The last track, however, may be an exception. "When I'm Sixty-Four" is an exuberant, optimistic note to end on, recorded just shy of the pianist's then-impending 65th birthday (on October 21). In looking toward what was the near future, Mr. Hersch reminds us that all things, including the terror and confusion of the current moment, must pass.

(*The Wall Street Journal*, 2020)

***

Fred Hersch Trio with the Crosby Street String Quartet, *Breath by Breath* (Palmetto Records)

"Monkey Mind" opens with a few bars of a bass playing a single-line solo; these are echoed by a violin playing pizzicato. This pattern is repeated about three times overall, first a few notes of bass, followed by the violin. Then, the idea is repeated and varied, with the same notes but different instruments.

The piano and the drums get into the act: first a few piano notes, then a few drum beats in the same pattern. Next, the exchange is between the piano and the pizzicato violin. Then, it's the drums and the bass. The piano next plays a slightly longer phrase, with the drums in the background, which gradually expands into something more like an improvised solo. Taking its cue from the title, the piece does sound like a playful exercise in repetition and variation that might find a parallel in the notion of one monkey seeing and another doing.

This is one of eight movements that comprise Fred Hersch's "Sati Suite," a work for jazz trio, with bassist Drew Gress and drummer Jochen Rueckert, played with the Crosby Street String Quartet. The suite forms the central portion of Mr. Hersch's new album, *Breath by Breath*, and it also was performed live by this combination in a brilliant concert at 92Y on Saturday evening.

Mr. Hersch explained that the term *sati* does not refer to the French composer Erik Satie but rather to a word in the Pali language, spoken on the Indian subcontinent and employed in Buddhist meditation practices there. It refers to "mindfulness" or "awareness." Confession: I don't claim to understand even the first thing about Buddhism, yoga, or meditation, but I am proof positive that one doesn't need to have any sort of familiarity with these concepts to enjoy this music. To me, it fulfills all the requirements of both American jazz and European classical music while at least partly inventing a new musical vocabulary all its own.

The first movement of the "Sati Suite" is titled "Begin Again," and yes, I can imagine that the idea of beginning something more than once is part of Eastern spirituality. Yet let it be said that there's no appreciable Eastern music here; if anything, the piece is inspired by the baroque counterpoint of Bach or Vivaldi. At times, the strings form a background to the jazz trio; at other points, they play opposite each other, like two complimentary ensembles in something like a concerto grosso format.

The second and third pieces, "Awakened Heart" and "Breath by Breath," both have titles that apparently refer to meditative practices. We don't think of breath as being particularly relevant to nonwind instruments, but pianos and violins rely on breath—at least as a rhythmic imperative—even as much as horns do. "Breath by Breath" is one of several pieces in which the quartet backs up Mr. Gress in solo, giving us the unique sound of arco strings backing up a bigger, deeper string-playing pizzicato.

"Mara," conversely, employs a lot of pizzicato in the background while a solo string up front plays arco. In his program notes, Mr. Hersch says it was inspired by the story of the deity called Mara who "tempted Buddha with wine, women and riches as he was trying to attain enlightenment under the bodhi tree." If I hadn't been aware of that, I would have guessed it was a musical essay on the nature of time since the click of the plucked strings suggests, to my ears, the tick-tock of a clock, or several, in a polyrhythmic pattern. Some pieces are mostly the piano trio; this one is primarily the strings, with keyboard notes essentially at the end.

Likewise, by listening to the fifth movement, I would have assumed it was a love song and never guessed the title was actually "Rising, Falling," which apparently refers to another part of the breathing and meditation process. Indeed, the entire "Sati Suite" might be described as a meditation on the act of meditation itself. Mr. Hersch plays a lovely, deliberately rambling piano solo in a way that suggests a journey inward. It's beautiful enough with just the bass and drums but even more so as the strings gradually enter behind him. He hits a few notes that momentarily suggest Johnny Mandel's "A Time for Love," and indeed, it is.

The album concludes with a ninth piece, titled "Pastoral," inspired by Robert Schumann. The 92Y concert featured more encores, among them two more originals, "Heartsong" and "Valentine." The latter is possibly Mr. Hersch's best-known song, with lyrics written and sung by the British jazz vocalist Norma Winstone. Also known as "A Wish," it's a perfect candidate for the trio plus string quartet treatment.

Mr. Hersch ended symmetrically with two standards, one from Hollywood, "This Is Always," eternally associated with Charlie Parker, and one by a jazz composer, Thelonious Monk's "Pannonica."

There followed a standing ovation and a genuine encore—Mr. Hersch didn't deliberately end the set early for the purpose of milking the audience, like Keith Jarrett, great musician that he is, always seemed to do. Mr. Hersch concluded the all-too-short concert with Billy Joel's "And So It Goes," a contemporary song that to me at least, is a much more exquisitely moving blend of a hymn and a love song than Leonard Cohen's overdone "Hallelujah." Mr. Hersch played it unaccompanied, as he did on his 2017 album *Open Book*, in a manner reminiscent of the spiritual "Balm in Gilead" as well as William Blake's "Jerusalem."

Mr. Hersch's astute combination of his own arrangements and mostly original compositions for jazz trio and string quartet (Joyce Hammann and Laura Seaton, violins; Lois Martin, viola; and Jody Redhage Ferber, cello) is precisely the kind of music that the late critic Gunther Schuller famously described as "third stream," equal parts jazz and classical. Does this open a debate as to whether something can be two things at once without actually being a whole new third thing? I'll ponder the philosophical implications later. Right now, I'm too busy loving the music.

(*The New York Sun*, 2023)

KEITH JARRETT (BORN 1945)

After a lifetime of listening to Keith Jarrett on records, my first full-on experience of him in concert was truly a baptism of fire. The occasion was the 20th anniversary of Mr. Jarrett's celebrated trio, with bassist Gary Peacock and drummer Jack DeJohnette, being commemorated in one of his series of concerts at Carnegie Hall. I happened to be sitting next to my friend Ben Ratliff, then the regular jazz critic for *The New York Times*. Ben had written a glowing preview of the concert, describing Mr. Jarrett's ensemble as a "high-flying trio" and letting *Times* readers know that this concert was going to be one of the must-catch jazz events of the fall. It clearly was a major compliment, and a great many of the audience were there because Ben had given the concert such an enthusiastic recommendation.

Mr. Jarrett began the evening by storming on stage, and he then read Ben's preview—in a mocking, sarcastic tone of voice, as if Ben had written something negative. I don't remember his exact words, but they were something like "Can you believe this jerk had the nerve to call this a 'high-flying trio?'" What was really surprising was that the crowd went along with it, joining in with him as he dissed poor Ben, in direct contrast to their own ears. I watched as Ben sunk deeper and deeper into his seat, hoping that nobody would realize he was the guy who had the nerve to write something so enthusiastic about Keith Jarrett.

Clearly, Mr. Jarrett was looking to pick a fight. I'm hardly the first to describe him as the John McEnroe of jazz, both for the excellence of his playing and his infamously volatile temper. I theorized then that his strategy, apparently, was to act obnoxious and then play twice as hard to make both the press and the crowd love him.

It succeeded: the amazingly empathetic threesome, which comes out of the lineage of the Ahmad Jamal and Bill Evans trios—the first in which the bass and drums were treated as equal partners and not merely in support of the star pianist—held us riveted through two full hours of mostly highly lyrical standard ballads (most notably "You Won't Forget Me" and "I'm Gonna Laugh You Out of My Life," associated with pianist–singers Shirley Horn and Nat Cole) and funky, soulful blues–folk originals.

At times Mr. Jarrett, as is his wont, grew a little too self-indulgent in terms of great, even epic, climactic cadenzas that went on so long they took on lives of their own, although the more I heard Mr. Jarrett in live performance, the more I grew to love them. Temper or no temper, his performances were invariably brilliant, and also always capped by at least 30 minutes of standing ovations and encores—which I eventually realized was also a familiar device of Mr. Jarrett—among them a remarkable, gospel-styled interpretation of "God Bless the Child."

(*The New York Sun*, 2003)

***

The edition of the 2005 JVC Jazz Festival was highly piano-centric; in fact, I referred to it more than once in my write-ups as "the year of the piano." Among other events, there was an all-star salute to the brilliant Barbara Carroll on her 80th birthday; an evening of piano duets by John Hicks and Cyrus Chestnut; and the main event, the latest concert at Carnegie by the Keith Jarrett Trio.

By then, I had realized that certain aspects of a Keith Jarrett performance were entirely predictable. He does not announce tunes or even mention the names of his two collaborators, Mr. Peacock and Mr. DeJohnette. Then, there was his tradition of formally ending the concert surprisingly early, which inevitably resulted in the house applauding and calling him back, which he always did.

When Mr. Jarrett plays, he rises up from the keyboard in a series of astoundingly ungraceful contortions, leaning into the instrument like a downhill skier, twisting sideways as if he were trying to scratch his back with his nose, hunching forward as if someone had just punched him in the gut (which wouldn't be entirely surprising).

And one thing you always can count on is his inevitable opening tantrum. In fact, a Keith Jarrett concert is inevitably described less like a musical performance than a boxing match. The first thing everybody wants to know is who got bashed. When

Mr. Jarrett starts swinging, the term refers to verbal punches rather than what he does at the keyboard.

This time he started by promising us he was not going to launch into his usual tirade—because he said, the reelection of President Bush made him feel "mellow" (meaning "complacent"). Once we were primed to expect a round of Bush bashing, though, he instead launched into another attack on *The New York Times*. This time, he castigated the paper because its (very positive) review of his new solo album, *Radiance* (2005), wasn't long enough to suit him. It's always something!

Mr. Jarrett, however, was swinging at the keyboard soon enough, especially on two fast numbers, a boppish barn burner by Bud Powell and an upbeat original blues. He usually finds great and unusual tunes to play, but no one could have anticipated that he would have given us spectacular renditions of the two major hits by Nashville songwriter Pee Wee King, "The Tennessee Waltz" and "You Belong to Me." The latter was especially moving, though not in the usual way. It's normally done as a song about travel ("see the pyramids along the Nile"); Mr. Jarrett, however, cut to its core as a song of romantic possession.

Another predictable aspect of the Carnegie show was that the sound was particularly bad (a far cry from the crystal-clear piano shows at Rose Hall, Merkin Hall, and the Kaye Playhouse), even worse than the pianist's temper. During the fast numbers in the first set, Mr. DeJohnette's drumming tended to overwhelm the keyboard. Perhaps to compensate, Mr. Jarrett called only slower numbers after the intermission.

His very rhythmic (but not over-fast) "Green Dolphin Street" began with a long Pan-American vamp. Then, he gave us two killer ballads associated with Sinatra, "Only the Lonely" and "Last Night When We Were Young." Both were extremely touching and tender, and the second veered off briefly into "The Glory of Love," then reprised the Latin-style vamp from "Green Dolphin" 20 minutes earlier.

The bad boy of jazz ended with three "encores," as the sold-out crowd clambered to its feet over and over again: Leonard Bernstein's "Somewhere"; Monk's "Straight No Chaser"; and from the Nat King Cole songbook, "When I Fall in Love." Fortunately, his playing is as marvelous as the man himself is obnoxious. Keith Jarrett is the original sore winner.

(*The New York Sun*, 2005)

***

One of the many remarkable things about the pianist Keith Jarrett is that for a musician who has done as much as anyone to promote the cause of spontaneous, improvised music, much of what he does is obviously calculated beforehand. Not only that; he seems to be hell-bent on causing as much tension as the human psyche can absorb.

Think of Mr. Jarrett as a juggler who keeps spectators on the edge of their seats by throwing three knives in the air and keeping them there for as long as possible.

No juggler, however, could sustain the tension like Mr. Jarrett does, piling on the suspense throughout numbers that go on individually for at least 10 minutes. His concert at Carnegie Hall on Thursday night, as part of the 2007 JVC Jazz Festival, featured a full two and a half hours of just piano, bass, and drums. (Mr. Jarrett is also a long-distance runner in the sense that this trio, with the bassist Gary Peacock and the drummer Jack DeJohnette, is nearing its 25th anniversary.)

That nervous energy was palpable, even as Mr. Jarrett walked out on the stage. Perhaps the key lesson he learned from his experience with Miles Davis, with whom he played for about a year and a half in 1970 and 1971, was the concept of "reverse showmanship," or playing hard to get—to ignore the crowd and present himself as downright hostile. This year, Mr. Jarrett had shifted the target of his now-expected diatribe from *The New York Times* to "stupid people" who insist on taking his picture with camera phones (this was a new concept in 2007).

Although Mr. Jarrett has absorbed a lot from such piano predecessors as Bud Powell and Bill Evans, sometimes it seems as though his greatest influence is Alfred Hitchcock. His first tune started unaccompanied, a wash of impressionistic harmonies rendered ad-lib. But even after he kicked it into tempo, he refused to give us a hint as to the identity of the melody. Rather, Mr. Jarrett dangled hints of it here and there, leading us ever forward like horses following a carrot on a stick. He played faster and faster, without ever dropping the other shoe and letting us in on the tune.

As it happened, I was prepared: I had just watched the DVD of the Jarrett Trio live in Japan in 1986, so I was quick to recognize the piece as his arrangement of Cole Porter's "All of You." But I could sense the craze building in the crowd as he pushed onward, finally to resolution.

Mr. Jarrett's fast, boppish numbers are dazzling and even thrilling; his blues originals, "One for Majid" and "Is It Really the Same?" are funky and moving (in the physical as well as emotional sense), and his rearrangements of standards, such as an Afro-Cuban "I'm a Fool to Want You," are smart and engaging.

The blues gives him the best opportunity to showcase his infamous body contortions, which become a sort of interpretative dance. Thelonious Monk used to dance when others in his quartet soloed, but Mr. Jarrett does Monk one better by dancing in the middle of his own solos, even while still seated on the bench. The pianist also displayed a propensity for time in contrasting tempos, beginning the second half of the show with Dave Brubeck's "It's a Raggy Waltz" followed by Snow White's somewhat less raggy waltz, "Someday My Prince Will Come."

But it's Mr. Jarrett's slow ballads—such as "Yesterdays" and "God Bless the Child," both performed on Thursday—that are something else entirely. His harmonies are lavish, ornate, and beautiful without being fussy. He stretches everything out as long as it can be stretched before resolving it, giving us chorus after chorus of tense chords that cry out for resolution, like so many sinners in search of salvation.

As is his custom, Mr. Jarrett ended early, leaving time for three encores (another calculated move). The ballad highlight was the official closer, Cy Coleman's seldom-heard "I'm Gonna Laugh You Right Out of My Life," which surged into one of Mr.

Jarrett's mega-extended, never-ending codas—not that you'd ever want them to end. This particular coda went on so long that it could have met a nice girl, settled down, and had kids before it was finished.

Even in those cases when Mr. Jarrett gives us the melody straight away—as on "Stars Fell on Alabama"—he prolongs it in the most suspenseful way, extending it and revealing the tiniest bits at a time, a striptease artist slowly removing his gloves. On this tune, Mr. Jarrett made us cling to every note like drops of water in the Sahara. Had I ever realized previously that Alabama could be so beautiful, I would have never left there.

(*The New York Sun*, 2007)

***

I attended many more Keith Jarrett concerts than I was able to write about—including several of his allegedly, completely improvised solo recitals at Carnegie. Sadly, it was announced in 2018 that following two debilitating strokes, Mr. Jarrett was retiring from playing. His departure from the world of jazz is a loss to all of us. I find that I even miss his tantrums.

CONTEMPORARY MASTERS

HERBIE HANCOCK (BORN 1940)

Early in 2004, it was announced that Herbie Hancock and Wayne Shorter were reuniting for a special Carnegie concert at that year's JVC Jazz Festival. If it had been anything less than magnificent, a lot of people would be very disappointed. These two veterans of one of Miles Davis's greatest bands have since become monumental forces in their own right as instrumentalist–composer–bandleaders. JVC presented them in one of their all-too-rare reunions in a quartet format, with Dave Holland, bass, and Brian Blade, drums. The group had so much star power—Mr. Holland and Mr. Blade were also already famous as leaders and name attractions in their own right—that the big hall would be packed no matter what they chose to play. And at Carnegie that night, it could have been just about anything.

Individually, as a team and as sidemen with Miles Davis, Shorter and Mr. Hancock have made many different kinds of music. As composer–soloists in the celebrated Davis quintet of the mid- to late 1960s, they produced a highly aggressive blend of postmodern jazz. Then, both men, like Davis, spent most of the 1970s and 1980s making commercially oriented sounds with electric jazz–rock fusion bands. But the music they played at Carnegie Friday night was probably the least accessible, most purely abstract that they've ever made.

Mr. Hancock was playing exceptionally well; in fact, this was the best I've ever heard him live. Mr. Holland (also a Miles Davis alum) and the very propulsive Mr. Blade are also highly animated players. But Mr. Shorter was the central figure at Friday's 90-minute set.

Mr. Shorter, who once played with a Coltrane-like intensity, has become increasingly introverted in his return to acoustic, straight-ahead jazz. He sounds more withdrawn now than even the late Joe Henderson did, with a pristine tone reminiscent of

Danilo Perez and Herbie Hancock; Newport Jazz Festival; Fort Stage; August 3, 2013

Stan Getz at his most intimate. He refused to speak above a whisper or to assert himself in any way. His tenor sax playing was even less forceful than that of his soprano. But his was the dominant voice nonetheless, and he forced us all to listen hard.

This was not a standard saxophone plus rhythm foursome, of the kind that Getz and Lester Young typically used. Rather, it was something more like a classical ensemble or the Modern Jazz Quartet, in which all four members had an equal footing and individual solos mattered less than the group interplay. I only recognized two songs—Mr. Shorter's "Footprints" (most of the crowd figured out what was coming as soon as they counted six beats to a measure) and Mr. Hancock's "Cantaloupe Island," which served as a crowd-pleasing encore. This was by far the most extroverted number of the night, and the house responded in kind.

(*The New York Sun*, 2004)

***

Some musical auteurs keep each of their feet in different aesthetic worlds; Herbie Hancock achieves this with his hands instead. At this week's JVC Jazz Festival concert at Carnegie Hall, he had a smaller electronic keyboard mounted on top of his Fazioli F278 concert grand (as well as a fuller-sized electric piano), and he often played the electric in the treble clef with his right hand while keeping his left on the acoustic instrument in the bass clef.

Mr. Hancock is a man in two worlds at once, and at 68, he is only getting better at it. Two years ago at JVC, he gave a major concert at Carnegie in which he performed with expected brilliance in several different acoustic settings—trios, duos, and quartets. But he sabotaged his own concert by performing with, at one point, a mediocre all-electric band of young, pop-styled players half his age. Yet with his 2007 album *River: The Joni Letters*, Mr. Hancock found a way to bring both halves of his musical career onto the stage at the same time, making pop music and jazz that satisfied both strata of fans.

Currently in the midst of what he calls his "River of Possibilities Tour" (referring also to his previous album, *Possibilities*), Mr. Hancock continues to intermingle the elements of electronically driven pop and adventurous, hard-edged jazz, with the two elements complementing rather than distracting each other. He reinterprets widely known songs by Joni Mitchell in such a way that her fans will recognize them without feeling as though he is merely paying lip service to them. But at the same time, he reinvests these songs with brilliant new chords as well as astute improvisations.

River was so prized by the pop music industry that it was awarded the Grammy for Album of the Year. When I was half-watching the telecast in February (while reading the latest issue of *The Simpsons* comics) and I saw Mr. Hancock stroll onstage to collect his statuette, I assumed he had merely won the jazz award. I didn't realize until the next morning that he had snatched the top prize of the evening, a rare victory for jazz in general.

At Carnegie this week, nearly every performance featured elements of jazz and pop, electric and acoustic playing, and improvising and rocking out: The first number, "Actual Proof," used the electric rhythm section in the opening but shifted to an acoustic improvisation in the center, courtesy of Mr. Hancock and the monstrously talented tenor saxophonist Chris Potter. The two numbers that followed spotlighted a pair of female vocalists. Sonya Kitchell, who sounds like a folk-tinged singer–songwriter and is sonically compatible with Norah Jones and Joni Mitchell herself, sang "River." Then, Amy Keys, who is more of a straight-ahead soul singer, took the lead on "When Love Comes to Town" (written by U2), although both ladies performed on both tunes in a way that reminded me momentarily of Sergio Mendes.

The highlight for the hard-core jazz fans in the house was the middle section of the set, which began with Mr. Hancock introducing the bassist Dave Holland and then leaving the stage. Mr. Holland, who was playing a smaller-than-usual upright acoustic instrument (which he identified as a "Czech-Ease road bass"), launched into an understated, unaccompanied solo, which turned out to be an introduction for Mr. Hancock, who returned to the Fazioli and delivered the evening's nicest moment: a long and rewarding, completely unaccompanied and abstract meditation on his own most famous composition, "Maiden Voyage." For the rest of the evening, when other instruments were playing, the Fazioli was somehow miked to sound completely lifeless and free of resonance, like a toy Casio keyboard. But when heard only by itself, the instrument sounded glorious.

There were other highlights, but the high point had been reached: Mr. Hancock played "All I Want," a Joni Mitchell song not on the album; Leon Russell's 1970s standard "A Song for You" (vocal by Ms. Keys); and two of his own most famous works in different fields, the modal jazz "Cantaloupe Island" and the funk "Chameleon." He played the latter as an encore, with a big drum solo by Vinnie Colaiuta. It's been said that you can't please everybody. Herbie Hancock may just be the first.

(*The New York Sun*, 2007)

BILLY CHILDS (BORN 1957)

Billy Childs Quartet, *The Winds of Change* (Mack Avenue Jazz)

It's kind of an unwritten policy in jazz clubs that the crowd mostly applauds for individual improvised solos. Generally speaking, the prewritten ensemble parts of the performance rarely elicit that much attention from the house. On Friday at Dizzy's, though, those in attendance were not only standing up for the solos; they were cheering Billy Childs's compositions themselves. (This was underscored to me, incidentally, by the guy sitting to my left at the bar at Dizzy's, who turned out to be the highly respected jazz pianist and composer Aaron Goldberg.)

Billy Childs, who turned 66 on Wednesday, is a musical auteur who enriches jazz with techniques and ideas from classical music. In his case, that often means his pieces take the overall outlines of classical forms but are very much pure jazz in terms of the content. It's jazz content presented in what can seem like classical shapes.

Mr. Childs has a new album out on March 17, *The Winds of Change*, which he unveiled at Dizzy's. In both the album and the show, the music is for a quartet, including a trumpet and a rhythm section of bass and drums in addition to Mr. Childs on piano. On the album, those roles are filled by, respectively, Ambrose Akinmusire, Scott Colley, and Brian Blade. At Dizzy's, they were Sean Jones, Hans Glawischnig, and Ari Hoenig.

The centerpiece of both the album and the show is the title track, "The Winds of Change." In his spoken introduction, Mr. Childs informed us that the piece was inspired by music from the neo-noir films of the 1970s, specifically Jerry Goldsmith's in *Chinatown* and Bernard Herrman's in *Taxi Driver*. On the CD, this is an 11-minute work that almost seems like a movie unto itself.

There is a slow introduction, sort of like the main titles are flashing before us, and then we shift into a faster piece in 6/8, which feels like the plot is starting to get under way. Most of the story—the solos, for instance—takes place here. Eventually, the whole work starts to slow back down into rubato again. Just when you think you've got it all figured out, though, Mr. Childs starts to throw in surprises, and the plot twists and turns many more times before we finally reach the end titles.

Mr. Childs introduced "Master of the Game" as having been roughly inspired by the Modern Jazz Quartet—to this day a viable model of how jazz and symphonic ideals might interact. In the same way one hears echoes of Bach throughout much of the MJQ oeuvre, likewise one detects the faint footsteps of John Lewis throughout this piece. In Mr. Childs's piano parts in particular, I kept being reminded of "La Ronde" and in particular, "The Queen's Fancy." "Master of the Game" also ends effectively, with a tag that goes for baroque.

Both the album and the Dizzy's show include Mr. Childs's fascinating take on Chick Corea's 1972 "Crystal Silence." This has become perhaps the late pianist's best-known song, and it's been arranged and rearranged by ensembles of many sizes. In a sense, Mr. Childs is taking it back to its roots: "Crystal Silence" was originally a duet between Corea and vibraphonist Gary Burton, and the most salient part of Mr. Childs's interpretation was an extended duet between piano and trumpet.

As the bass and drums dropped out, Messrs. Childs and Akinmusire proceeded into a very effective duet in which the trumpet and piano threw very short phrases back and forth. At Dizzy's, it seemed especially intimate and Mr. Jones remarkably expressive, followed by the first extended bass solo of the set by Mr. Glawischnig.

Mr. Childs concluded the set with "Dance of Shiva," from his 2015 album *Rebirth*, which, he said, grew out of his fascination with Indian Carnatic music. It actually sounded like it was inspired by everything, a fast and lively piece that frequently switches moods and in which Mr. Childs briefly turned his piano into a percussion instrument by reaching inside the case and holding down the appropriate strings so that all we got was the sound of the keyboard itself rather than the usual notes.

The 2015 version featured the excellent Steve Wilson soloing on alto saxophone, but here, Mr. Jones essayed this rather breathless, tricky melody, with its many stop-and-start rhythmic shifts, as if he'd played it a zillion times before.

Before introducing the last tune, Mr. Childs described his music and what it takes to play it as being "chops intensive." That's very accurate, but it also should be said that this music is heart and emotionally intensive as well.

(*The New York Sun*, 2023)

MULGREW MILLER (1955–2013)

The Village Vanguard is perhaps the world's most celebrated venue for great jazz piano trios, from canonic legends, such as Bill Evans and Tommy Flanagan, to contemporary masters Cyrus Chestnut, Fred Hersch, Uri Caine, Bill Charlap, and Cedar Walton (who is coming to the Vanguard in August). Do the photos of keyboard giants Thelonious Monk and McCoy Tyner, looking down from the wall, encourage or intimidate the pianists who bring their trios into the Vanguard, I wonder?

Mulgrew Miller, the Mississippi-born pianist, whom I caught late Tuesday night, is there all week with Brandon Owens, bass, and Karriem Riggins, drums. But it isn't a piano predecessor that's his inspiration but a trumpeter: Miles Davis. Both at the Vanguard and on his new album, *Live at Yoshi's* (Max Jazz MXJ-208), Mr. Miller began with a nod to Davis. The CD starts with the chime-like opening of Davis's iconic treatment of Frank Loesser's "If I Were a Bell," whereas on the late set on Tuesday night, Mr. Miller started with Victor Feldman's "Joshua."

Sony is just about to release a seven-CD set of all of Davis's recordings (studio and live) from 1963 to 1964. It begins with a previously unissued version of "Joshua," which is somewhat mellower and more relaxed than we're used to hearing it. Mr. Miller's version, though, was extremely fast and steadfastly boppish—even more intense than the well-known reading on "Seven Steps to Heaven."

Mr. Miller's new album includes Donald Brown's "Waltz for Monk," a dedication to another Vanguard predecessor, but on Tuesday, Mr. Miller played the late pianist's own "Monk's Dream." Monk is, after Ellington, the most played of jazz composers, but for pianists, Monk's music is perhaps even more of a challenge: you have to walk a fine line between being faithful to the composer's idiom and finding your own approach. Mr. Miller maintained his own voice within Monk's spacey dissonances and jagged rhythms.

Mr. Miller's third piece was the set's only original composition, "Waltz for Darnelle." Three-quarter time is always good for spare melodies with what could be called Monk-like open spaces; the lack of a fourth beat in a bar almost always makes listeners subconsciously think that something is missing. As he tore into the tune, though, it became considerably less waltzy. Even more fervent was an extended improvisation on "What Is This Thing Called Love?," which held the melody under wraps until the end. This was bop piano at its most extreme, with phrases so long and dense that they would have suffocated a wind player.

Mr. Miller's shirt was, by now, wringing wet with perspiration, even though the air-conditioning in the basement club was working just fine for the rest of us. It was clearly time to cool down. He did so with a stately solo reading of "A Child Is Born," by cornetist Thad Jones (still another major composer associated with the Vanguard). Mr. Miller's left-hand bass register accompaniment was so thorough—and so detached from the right-hand melody—I could have believed I was hearing two instruments. He grew a little ornamental in subsequent choruses, but the tune never slid into sentimentality.

The only number I heard late on Tuesday that is also on the *Yoshi's* album is Antonio Carlos Jobim's "O Grande Amor." Rather than playing it romantically, à la Stan Getz, Mr. Miller employed the same power and severity hard boppers, such as Hank Mobley and Kenny Dorham, did in their approach to the bossa nova: more New York than Rio and hardly exactly easy listening for the beach.

Then it was for a blues, "Now's the Time"—Charlie Parker's reworking of a traditional theme—that got the nod. It was unquestionably a climactic performance, with the pianist getting everything out of it that could be gotten, including a drum solo—usually a sign of conclusion. Mr. Miller surprised us all, however (including the tech guy, who had already turned up the lights), by playing a full-length and thoroughly satisfying treatment of "The Theme." Clearly, he wanted to go out with another nod to Miles.

(*The Wall Street Journal*, 2004)

BILL O'DONNELL (BORN 1953) AND TED ROSENTHAL (BORN 1959)

At the Zinc

Can it be that Manhattan's West Third Street is the jazz capital of the world? First, a few feet down from Sixth Avenue, there's the Blue Note, which celebrated its 40th anniversary two years ago. Heading east about a hundred yards, you come to the Zinc Bar, situated between Sullivan and Thompson streets. For about a dozen years at the end of the 20th century, there was also Visiones, on the corner of MacDougal Street.

The Zinc Bar at 82 West Third was once Club Cinderella, which opened in 1939 and where, according to Greenwich Village lore, Thelonious Monk served as house pianist and Billie Holiday sang while Frank Sinatra listened enraptured in the front row.

For 16 years, the original, smaller Zinc was two blocks south, at 90 West Houston Street. Then, around 2008, the sibling partners, Alex Kay and Kristina Kossi, moved and expanded into the West Third Street space. I'll admit that until recently, I always considered the Zinc a bit of a dive; whenever the lights came up, the furniture looked rather ragged and shopworn. As Stephen Wright says in the 1985 movie *Desperately Seeking Susan*: "I don't think we'll ever see Tony Bennett in a place like this."

Having not been there at least since the start of the pandemic, I was delighted to see that the furnishings have been thoroughly upgraded and the place looks much more presentable—now, you shouldn't be ashamed to bring your wife or even your mother.

Certainly, from the beginning, there's been excellent music at the Zinc, where the producer and the promoter is Charles Carlini, who has inaugurated two long-running series themed around specific instruments. Mondays are for "Guitar

Masters" and Tuesdays mean "Piano Jazz." Both series are commendable for featuring impressive lineups of musicians well beyond the usual suspects and headliners.

Bill O'Connell held forth at the Tuesday piano spot this week. I'd heard him as a sideman and on his many excellent albums but never in person leading his own trio. The Zinc show underscored what I already knew from the CDs: that he is a fantastic player and a gifted composer and leads a terrific trio with two celebrated sidemen, bassist Santi Debriano and drummer Billy Hart.

Mr. O'Connell's current album, *A Change Is Gonna Come*, is mostly a quartet project with saxophonist Craig Handy, bassist Lincoln Goines, and drummer Steve Jordan. The set is divided between familiar tunes and new originals, including a lovely treatment of the titular anthem by Sam Cooke, a melody too much overlooked by jazz instrumentalists.

One can appreciate Mr. O'Connell's dilemma here; the tenor saxophone is a natural choice to state this soulful melody, but I can readily understand his desire to play it himself. Thus, he splits the difference; he has Mr. Handy play an intro on tenor before he plays half a chorus on keyboard and lets Mr. Handy return for the second half. On the whole, it's an intensely passionate performance, a powerful prayer for tenor saxophone and piano.

"A Change Is Gonna Come" is followed by an adorable original titled "Sun for Sunny," which, despite the spelling, seems to be a dedication to Sonny Rollins and his flair for jazz calypsos—a format also neglected by virtually everyone else in jazz except native Caribbeans such as Monty Alexander and more recently, Etienne Charles and Russell Hall. "Sun for Sunny" features Mr. Handy on soprano and starts with a few quotes from Mr. Rollins's most famous calypso, "St. Thomas," which is another tip-off.

I was hoping to hear both these pieces at the Zinc, but Mr. O'Connell launched the set with the announcement that he and the current trio were trying out a whole new program of music prior to recording a few days hence. With this particular trio, Mr. O'Connell made me think about the major pianists of the 1960s, such as McCoy Tyner—particularly on the first piece, "Spa Glass," a minor-key waltz with a particular kind of clipped rhythmic accent—as well as Herbie Hancock and Chick Corea.

The trio also gave us "War No More," which shifted to 4/4 from 3/4 after the first chorus, and "Blues for Billy," an effective showcase for the drummer in the most basic 12-bar blues form in C major. The trio ended the all-too-brief set with its only standard, Mr. Hancock's "Maiden Voyage," played mostly *en clave* and very fast, building to an exciting trade of fours between the three of them.

Mr. Debriani, who was born in Panama in 1955, also has a new album out, *Ashanti*, and it's an ambitious set of originals for a nine-piece ensemble known as Arkestra Bembe, consisting of five horns and four rhythm. I was expecting a Latin-leaning set, but *Ashanti* covers a wide range of contemporary styles.

Even having said that, the track I'm going to play the most often is "Arkestra Boogaloo," a funky tune with Latin underpinnings boasting excellent solos from flutist Andrea Brachfeld, who has a bright, clean sound reminiscent of the late Dave Valentin; trumpeter Emile Turner; pianist Mamiko Watanabe; and TK Blue, whom I remember fondly from the bands of both Randy Weston and Little Jimmy Scott, on alto.

I'm looking forward to further Tuesdays at the Zinc—January 17 it's going to be the formidable David Hazeltine—and I plan to check out the guitars on Monday as well as other groups on other nights. It's not my last night on West Third Street, not by a long shot.

***

Between the Zinc Bar on West Third Street and Mezzrow, about a 10-minute walk to the west, Greenwich Village now has two low-key and highly intimate rooms that are perfect spaces in which to enjoy jazz piano. The Zinc's Tuesday evening "Piano Jazz" series boasts an admirably diverse lineup of contemporary keyboard masters, including names both new and familiar to me.

In the case of Ted Rosenthal, both are true. I first heard him playing in the cavernous space of a Midtown hotel lobby in the early 1990s, and since then, I have encountered him in every conceivable context. Most recently, he served as accompanist for Marilyn Maye's spectacular New Year's Eve show at Birdland, and he has played for all kinds of singers and artists. His playing piano for Ann Hampton Callaway, an accomplished keyboardist herself, is a bit like playing bass for Ron Carter—both an honor and a challenge.

Mr. Rosenthal has played virtually everything with virtually everybody, and not just in the field of jazz. In 2019, his full-length opera inspired by his family history during the Holocaust, *Dear Erich*, had its very successful premiere at the Museum of Jewish Heritage. For decades, he's also served as a guest star in 92NY's "Jazz in July" series.

In short, I feel like I've heard Ted Rosenthal in every context except leading his own trio in a New York club; thus, this past Tuesday at the Zinc was the perfect time to catch up. For the occasion, he essentially borrowed Bill Charlap's rhythm section, bassist Peter Washington and drummer Kenny Washington, and delivered a tasty set of standards as well as surprises.

You could say it was a "happening" show: He started with "It Could Happen to You" and followed with "Everything Happens to Me." Both opened with Mr. Rosenthal stating the melodies deliberately vaguely in rubato before bringing them sharply into focus and into tempo, and he concluded both with elaborate, imaginative codas. There were two classics by jazz composers, Tom McIntosh's lively, bop-pish "The Cupbearers" and "San Francisco Holiday," a relatively lesser-known work of Thelonious Monk, in which Mr. Rosenthal retained the essential Monkish-ness even while inserting a Latin vibe, particularly behind Peter Washington's bass solo.

In February 2014, conductor Maurice Peress and bandleader Vince Giordano re-created one of the milestone events in all of American culture, Paul Whiteman's

An Experiment in Modern Music concert of 1924. Mr. Rosenthal played the all-important piano solo on *Rhapsody in Blue*, the part originally performed by George Gershwin himself.

A few months later, he went into the studio and recorded a set of eight jazz arrangements of classic Gershwin works, all popular songs except for the opening, an ambitious interpretation for jazz trio of the *Rhapsody* itself. (The work is so iconic, that whenever you use the word *rhapsody*, people will generally know which one you mean, and it isn't Liszt or even Queen.)

Mr. Rosenthal's trio arrangement of *Rhapsody* is a monumental extended work unto itself, one that includes most of the major themes as Gershwin wrote them plus a lot else besides, including a section in Cuban clave à la Chucho Valdés, and other passages that amp up the blues and swing that Gershwin alluded to in 1924. This one gets a high placement among the short list of first-rate unconventional adaptations of the work, like those of Duke Ellington and Glenn Miller. The whole album is worth hearing, and Mr. Rosenthal is due for a new one since that 2015 release is, alas, his latest. Most recently, for the Rhapsody's Centennial in 2024, he performed an even more adventurous interpretation with the Park Avenue Chamber Symphony.

At the Zinc on Tuesday, Mr. Rosenthal found time for an attractive original, "Forever Young," and then also caught us off guard with two well-known melodies not often heard via jazz trio. There was a stunning, modernist reading of a theme from Tchaikovsky's Fifth Symphony—the same one we know from its pop adaptation, "Moon Love"—but the standout was a hard-swinging romp through Rodgers and Hammerstein's "People Will Say We're in Love."

This was an inspired follow-up to my favorite of Mr. Rosenthal's albums thus far, his 2006 jazz adaptation of the score to *The King and I*; if he happens to do a full jazz version of *Oklahoma!* as his next project, then he will find in me that I'm just a bald guy who can't say no.

(*The New York Sun*, 2023)

RENEE ROSNES (BORN 1962)

A saxophone and a piano are playing at the same time: which of the two are you going to listen to? Me too. The saxophone or a horn, in general, is always going to draw your attention first. In your basic jazz quartet—a sax plus piano, bass, and drums—the saxist is usually the leader and takes the lion's share of the melody choruses and the solo improvisations.

That's why I always admire pianists like Renee Rosnes who are not afraid to put a horn player in front of their quartets: it means they welcome the potential competition and don't worry that audiences might regard the player who is standing up as the "front man" and the guy or gal sitting at the keyboard as a mere sideman.

Renee Rosnes; Sweet Basil; December 10, 1997

It's been a few years since I've heard Ms. Rosnes, who is constantly working in other people's bands, leading her own group in a New York club. But that's just what she's doing this week at the Village Vanguard. Pianists frequently expand from piano trios to quartets with sax because using a horn gives them a larger canvas for their compositional ambitions. But it was clear during Ms. Rosnes's opening set Tuesday night that she was not trying out a series of new originals to go on a future album—she just wanted to play some flat-out bebop in the hardest, fastest, and most exciting possible way. Woe unto the sax player (Steve Wilson), bassist (Peter Washington), or drummer (Bill Stewart) who failed to keep up with her breathtaking pace.

Mr. Wilson is one of the contemporary masters of the alto saxophone and is not resigned, as are some, to the idea that most of the saxophonic glory in jazz is reserved for tenor titans; he knows there's a lot of experimentation and individuality up for grabs on the smaller E-flat alto. Mr. Wilson has a distinctive sound, landing on my ears slightly on the sharp side of the tonal palette; when I first heard him he struck me as a worthy successor to the late Jackie McLean. Mr. Wilson also plays soprano sax, and his alto playing has something of a soprano tinge to it (as on the most recent recording I've heard of his, which is a new album by drummer Carl Allen and bassist Rodney Whittaker, *Get Ready*). On Tuesday, Mr. Wilson seemed content in his role as a sideman not trying to pull focus from the leader but just the same, making the most of his spots with his commanding style.

Ms. Rosnes began with "Summer Night," a Harry Warren song from the 1936 B-movie musical called *Sing Me a Love Song*. It was introduced by James Melton, an operatic tenor who had a brief film career. "Summer Night" surely would have been forgotten had Miles Davis not introduced it into the modern jazz repertory in 1963. Ms. Rosnes played it as a fast jazz waltz, phrasing the melody at first delicately, in lightly clipped staccato phrases. But as her improv continued, she grew louder and hotter and more agitated. You know Ms. Rosnes wants to get your attention when she has her drummer play a solo during the first number of the evening—a custom generally reserved for the climax of a set.

From there, Ms. Rosnes dished out a compatible series of standards and somewhat lesser-known works by jazz and like-minded composers. Next was "Love for Sale," on which Mr. Wilson played both of his saxes and Ms. Rosnes broke down the melody into its scalar components—it could have been titled "Love for Scale." The other show tune was, coincidentally, the one other Cole Porter song associated with Miles Davis, "All of You," on which Ms. Rosnes and Mr. Wilson phrased the melody in pointillistic unison.

The most ambitious work of the evening was Antonio Carlos Jobim's "Modinha." This is not one of the bossa baron's pop songs, but rather, Ms. Rosnes interpreted it as an intricate and complex chamber work with several distinct sections marked by tempo, each with a carefully controlled balance of form and improv, in-tempo and out-of-tempo passages. With little Brazilian rhythmic underpinning, it sounded more like something by John Lewis and the Modern Jazz Quartet.

Ms. Rosnes also included two lesser-known works by two of her piano inspirations: "You Know I Care" by Duke Pearson (introduced by Joe Henderson on *Inner Urge*) and "Hogtown Blues," an earthy and fundamental effort by fellow Canadian keyboardist Oscar Peterson. The Pearson tune was a lovely ballad that underscored the compatibility of the quartet: Ms. Rosnes began unaccompanied, and the others just slid in and out, almost imperceptibly. (At the time, I expressed the desire that some contemporary group should do a whole album of Duke Pearson tunes, and this was, in fact, done a few years later by the band Swingadelic.)

The blues—about the only thing she hadn't played up to that point—was right in the pocket, as musicians say. Ms. Rosnes and company latched on to a groove and rode it for all it was worth, with the leader getting funkier, louder, and more exciting as the choruses flew by. If you looked closely, you would have sworn you saw steam rising from the piano at the Vanguard.

(*The New York Sun*, 2007)

***

It was a very warm day in late November, 70 degrees in Midtown Manhattan on Saturday, and New Yorkers were out in full force, carrying our coats rather than wearing them—and this barely a week away from Thanksgiving. Renee Rosnes and her quartet captured perfectly the heated spirit of the moment at the end of her late set at Dizzy's Club.

Out of nowhere, she floated Harry Warren's "Summer Night," a longtime Rosnes favorite, which I had her play at the Vanguard 15 years earlier. It was an unusual vintage standard in the middle of a set of mostly originals from her excellent new album, *Kinds of Love*, and perfectly captured the feeling of a Summer night in November.

Most pianists these days can be safely described as triple-threat artists—they play, arrange, and compose—yet Ms. Rosnes wears all three hats better than most. She's a formidable pianist, with technique and sheer chops galore. She can rearrange an existing melody and turn it into something even more special (as she frequently does for her husband Bill Charlap's programs in the Jazz in July series at the 92Y), and her originals, unlike many, are the kind you don't mind listening to for an entire evening.

On the album, her ensemble is saxophonist Chris Potter; bassist Christian McBride; and two percussionists, Carl Allen and Rogério Boccato; at Dizzy's, the group was saxophonist Steve Wilson, bassist Peter Washington, and Mr. Allen. The bulk of the late set consisted of four originals, all but one from the new release.

"Kinds of Love"—the title track from her new album—led directly into "Swoop" in a way that suggested the two were an interconnected, multipart composition. "Kinds of Love" functioned as a question, with Mr. Wilson playing his soprano saxophone with a probing, inquisitive sound, and "Swoop" might be the answer, for which Mr. Wilson switched to his customary alto sax. "Swoop" is a righteous, ever ferocious, up-tempo bebop number that climaxes in a trade of fours in which

Mr. Wilson, Ms. Rosnes, and Mr. Washington all seemed to have ganged up on Mr. Allen, but the drummer was more than equal to the challenge.

At Dizzy's, Ms. Rosnes also contrasted two of her more classically informed compositions against each other: "Evermore," inspired by a Bach sarabande (from the German master's English suites), and "Mirror Image," from her 2018 album *Beloved of the Sky*. She flowed from one into the other, without a pause, in a way that made them seem a conjoined work that started very baroque but grew progressively boppish.

Both the ensembles are considerable, yet even with these virtuosos around her—especially the two saxmen, Messrs. Potter and Wilson—the chief asset is Ms. Rosnes's own playing. After listening to her for 30 years, I still can't decide if she's primarily a lyrical pianist who is also highly rhythmic, like Bill Evans, or a hard-driving bopster who is also lyrical, like McCoy Tyner. Maybe a little bit—or a lot—of both.

In either case, the late set on Saturday was the sixth out of a four-night, eight-show run, and they were amazingly tight and together, not to mention well beyond thoroughly warmed up. They generated even more heat than was felt outside.

There were two other tunes by heavyweight jazz composers: a blues, Thelonious Monk's "Ba-Lue Bolivar Ba-Lues-Are," and a waltz, which began the set. This latter was a lovely and wistful yet irresistibly swinging piece that in Ms. Rosnes's interpretation, reminded me of both "Someday My Prince Will Come" (from *Snow White and the Seven Dwarfs*) and "Alice in Wonderland" (from the Disney version). While it was playing, I kept thinking that an appropriate title might be "Waltz in Search of a Princess."

It turned out to be "Everybody's Song But My Own" by the Canadian-born, British-based trumpeter Kenny Wheeler. After listening more than once to Mr. Wheeler's original 1988 recording, fine as it is, I must admit that I prefer Ms. Rosnes's arrangement. Not only that: I like my own title better too.

(*The New York Sun*, 2022)

CYRUS CHESTNUT (BORN 1963)

There's a concert recording of Elvis Presley playing in Las Vegas in 1973 in which he does something totally unexpected: he launches into "Hound Dog," one of his earliest hits, but instead of giving it the familiar 1956 rhythm and blues–style treatment, he sings it completely differently, back-phrasing it over a funk vamp inspired by Motown and Southern swamp rock. The point isn't that the new treatment is necessarily better but that it shows that Elvis, at this late stage in his career (though he was only 38), had the capacity to experiment and grow as an artist. He had the restless nature not to leave well enough alone and was motivated to retool his signature works, the way Frank Sinatra did with "All or Nothing at All" and Joe Williams did with "Every Day I Have the Blues."

The great barrier between rock and jazz is not just one of rhythm, harmony, and instrumentation but the concept of interpretation. That's the meat of the matter that separates rock-oriented pop from jazz and pop that's based on the Great American Songbook. In rock music, the basic idea that there is only one definitive version of any given song, usually by the guy who wrote it. All other performances of the song are not interpretations, as they are in the world of Sinatra and Williams, but mere covers, a disparaging term to be sure.

Interestingly, 2007 may be remembered as the year in which more jazz musicians than ever made efforts to break down these boundaries. In only the past few months, we've discussed in these pages albums by jazz musicians addressing the music of Bob Dylan; The Beatles; and most recently, Herbie Hancock's magnum Joni Mitchell opus. Now, you can add Elvis Presley and Elton John to the list of rock icons whose work has been retooled for jazz purposes.

There have been jazz tributes to everyone from President Kennedy to Burt Bacharach. But until now, no jazz project has gone directly into the heart of rock and roll and addressed the canon of the music's single most dynamic and central figure, the King himself (and I don't mean Joe Oliver, Nat Cole, or Benny Goodman). Pianist Cyrus Chestnut's new album, *Cyrus Plays Elvis*, is the first full-length homage (that I know of) by a major jazz artist to the man who almost single-handedly effected the greatest sea change in all of American pop.

As a Southern musician whose playing is immersed in gospel, blues, and soul, Mr. Chestnut is a likely candidate to reinterpret Presley's catalog, from early breakthroughs, such as "Don't Be Cruel," to such mature statements as "Suspicious Minds" and "In the Ghetto." What's commendable is that Mr. Chestnut doesn't feel the need to get all downtown and weird on us—he puts his personal stamp on the material while staying true to the spirit of the originals. "Minds" is still a dance-driven vamp with a minor undercurrent that mirrors the message of the text; "Ghetto" is a slow, somber ballad with a spiritual message—even the way the title phrase repeats itself suggests a church choir.

The only track I find myself skipping on replays is "Can't Help Falling in Love," on which Mark Gross's soprano saxophone makes the whole thing sound like smooth jazz. Conversely, on "Don't" (a comparatively lesser-known Leiber–Stoller–Presley hit from 1957), Mr. Gross perfectly captures the cadences of Presley's voice on his alto. The most abstract treatment is "Heartbreak Hotel," which has a grandly Asian opening, almost like John Coltrane's "A Love Supreme," leading into Presley's darkest and scariest blues, an altogether fitting visit to an establishment that the lyrics describe as a sort of roach motel of the soul.

Overall, what makes *Cyrus Plays Elvis* so successful is that it's an instrumental jazz album produced by a mindset very much in tune with Presley's own, rooted in blues and dance rhythms. At times, I couldn't help but be reminded of Phineas Newborn Jr., the Memphis-based pianist who was close to Elvis and played modern jazz with a Presleyan sensibility.

Cyrus Plays Elvis opens with an elemental treatment of "Hound Dog," which although it sounds nothing like Presley's 1973 revision, also returns the Leiber–Stoller song to its deep blues roots. Contrastingly, the album ends with a moving solo treatment of "How Great Thou Art," which shows that these songs and the great gospel hymns in particular, mean as much to Mr. Chestnut as they did to the late Elvis.

(*The New York Sun*, 2007)

ENSEMBLES

NAT KING COLE (1919–1965) AND THE KING COLE TRIO

I hope the reader doesn't mind that Nat King Cole is in two sections in this book. Cole surely belongs in the category of jazz keyboard royalty, along with the Duke, the Count, and the Earl, as well as in this section, which talks about unique piano-centric ensembles, which is to say, groups outside of the basic piano-trio format of the last 75 years or so (i.e., piano, bass, and drums). (That is the format that The Bad Plus employs, but I don't think that anyone will disagree that they are a unique ensemble.) The following essay has been liberally rewritten and adapted from my 2020 biography of Cole, Straighten Up and Fly Right.

***

"It's Only a Paper Moon" was the breakout hit from Nat King Cole's first album, 1944's *The King Cole Trio* (which retroactively has been known as *The King Cole Trio Volume One*), and Cole classic that he returned to thousands of times over the next 20 years. It shows that even at the start of his career—he was only 24 when he recorded it—he not only already knew how to effectively create musical moods but also how to mix them. The tune was originally performed as a melancholy, reflective love song during the Great Depression and opens with the poignant lines, "Say, it's only a paper moon / Sailing over a cardboard sea / But it wouldn't be make-believe / If you believed in me." Cole, however, radically retooled "Paper Moon" into an up-tempo swinger for the war years. The act of combining these opposite moods served to bring out the best qualities of each, transforming "Paper Moon" into a tantalizing hybrid, simultaneously brash and bittersweet.

The King Cole Trio, with guitarist Oscar Moore and bassist Johnny Miller, first recorded "Paper Moon" at their second session for Capitol Records on December 15, 1943. Eleven years earlier, the song had also represented a beginning for the new songwriting team of composer Harold Arlen and lyricist E. Y. Harburg, who in this instance, shared credit with Broadway producer Billy Rose. Commissioned for a 1932 Broadway play, titled *The Great Magoo*, that bombed and then featured in the 1933 film *Take a Chance*, the song, with its poignant imagery of paper moons and cardboard seas, was intended to highlight the discrepancy between reality and illusion.

The original 1933 recordings of the song, including those of entertainer Cliff Edwards and Paul Whiteman's Orchestra, are more than a little blue and pensive, emphasizing its minor-key aspects. By contrast the trio's treatment is upbeat and optimistic.

Its salient feature is the harmonic interweaving of Cole's keyboard and Moore's guitar, a combination that utilizes elements of block chords as well as octave playing, creating a remarkable sound in which the piano and guitar are so close together that you literally can't tell where one ends and the other begins. It's as if Arlen's melody were being played by a two-headed, four-armed giant, a fabulous creature playing a mythical instrument, all of which fully suits a song about blurring the boundaries between fantasy and reality.

Cole updated "Paper Moon" into an ebullient, bouncy jingle for the wartime era. It was an age when most men were thousands of miles away in foxholes, women were wearing overalls and working on assembly lines, and nothing seemed quite real—especially the news arriving constantly from Europe, about entire populations being decimated. With reality seemingly up for grabs, the moon might just as well have been made of paper.

Cole starts his vocal by expanding the contraction of the first word from "it's" to "it is," which gives the line an extra beat, making it much more syncopated and rhythmically arresting. He radiates a euphoria that both supports and undercuts the lyric "But it wouldn't be make-believe, if you believed in me." In the end, the final message is that the craziness outside doesn't matter if you have your lover's support. That love is the thing, he is telling us—the only thing that matters, even in a world where the nature of reality itself can't be taken for granted.

Cole's "Paper Moon" was somehow a genuine hit when first issued, even though it wasn't officially released as a single but as one of eight songs on *The King Cole Trio*. Yet it reached the number five spot on the Billboard R&B chart and became one of his career perennials. At least 14 different versions exist, including rerecordings on two classic albums, *After Midnight* (1957) and *The Nat King Cole Story* (1961).

In taking a happy–sad ballad and reworking it into a joyful and optimistic—not to mention, thoroughly irresistible—swinger, Cole was directly anticipating what Frank Sinatra would achieve with reenergized ballads such as "I've Got You Under My Skin" and "Night and Day" a decade later. Effectively, Cole reinvented "Paper

Moon" as a song for the early postwar era, overflowing with peacetime optimism, and for all time.

(*The Wall Street Journal*, 2020)

JOHN LEWIS (1920–2001) AND THE MODERN JAZZ QUARTET

"Show up at the studio at noon" the voice on the phone said. "They'll be able to talk to you after they've finished rehearsing." The Modern Jazz Quartet rehearsing? Surely, if there's one group in jazz that doesn't need to rehearse, it's the Modern Jazz Quartet. It's been 30 years since they've even had a personnel change! They've been playing together so long that not only can they anticipate each other's every move, but one also suspects that they all get hungry at the same time and wake up at the exact same time every morning. ("And more importantly," emphasizes bassist Percy Heath, "we all play cards at the same time!")

But the more they rehearse, the better they get. It's the only way they'll add to their ever-growing list in the mythical Guinness Book of Jazz Accomplishments. The list already includes one of the most successful mixtures of composition and improvisation in all of music, the longest-lived and most consistently excellent small group in jazz, and the most satisfying fusion of jazz and European classical music ever achieved. The new addition to this list is a worthy one: the most important comeback in jazz history.

John Lewis, piano; Milt Jackson Tribute at Merkin Hall; January 29, 1996

As even the newest *Down Beat* reader must know by now, the MJQ is back. After seven years of heading in separate directions, they temporarily re-formed for a tour of Japan in 1981. This led to the decision to stay together a few months a year, and from there, they moved to full-time activity. Last summer, the group's first record since their 1974 farewell concert was released to almost unanimously positive reviews, and their second disc since the reunion, a 1982 concert at Montreux, is due this month (February 1985) from Pablo Records.

In photos, the group resembles Mount Rushmore, not only for the stately majesty of their faces, but also for the way in which any one of the four would somehow seem incorrect without the other three beside him. In conversation, they are anything but statuesque and instead, resemble and oppose their stage personae in revealing ways. As he sounds on wax, vibraphonist Milt Jackson is the most aggressive and animated member of the group, while bassist Heath and drummer Connie Kay, who never were content or even expected to be mere timekeepers, always have something to add. On the other hand, John Lewis, the group's pianist and musical director, is reticent to the point of embarrassing shyness. "But not when I'm performing," he conceded recently to Gary Giddins. "I love to perform."

The origin of the Modern Jazz Quartet has been told so often that it hardly bears repeating here, but a few points require clarification. Although it is well known that the MJQ came into the world as the combination rhythm section and band within a band of the 1947 Dizzy Gillespie Orchestra, Lewis is too often portrayed as a sort of counterrevolutionary who sought to harness the free-blowing style of the first generation of beboppers with European formal techniques. Actually, Lewis was doing nothing more than building on an idea that Gillespie had initiated. With the big band, Gillespie sought to reconcile his new music with the conventions of both premodern jazz and the mainstream of popular music. Lewis took this notion of reunification a vital step further, beyond jazz and pop and into a shadowy domain that up to that point, had only marginally explored by jazz men: Western classical music.

By 1956, when Connie Kay had replaced the group's first drummer, Kenny Clarke, and helped relocate them to Atlantic Records ("I put Atlantic in business," says Kay, who was the label's house drummer before joining the MJQ), Lewis's search for a linking point between jazz and classical music had borne fruit. He built his bridge at the same place where engineers always build bridges: the narrowest point between the two musics. Baroque music stands in relation to the later Classical and Romantic styles at about the same point where ragtime prefaces jazz, and it suited Lewis's purposes for any number of reasons. For one, Baroque composers rarely used the extramusical, programmatic associations that later became part of the Romantic period (Berlioz and Beethoven are good examples); in its place was a concern for form that drew attention to itself, much the same way Lewis wanted his forms to compete with the individual statements of his soloists. For another, Baroque style was built on repeated rhythmic patterns with filled-in chords, much the same way bebop was, and even left the choice of these chords open to the player, making Baroque the only genre of European concert music that provided space for improvisation. Lastly, Lewis proved that the Baroque fugue form—which emphasized the repetition and variation of a given musical motive (riff)—could be as valid a vehicle for jazz performance as the blues or the popular song.

Only a group that worked with such dedication and stayed together as long as the MJQ could have pulled it off. They were on the road for 22 years, not even taking time for a summer vacation until 1962, building up "years of prestige" (as Heath put it) and a considerable following along the way. They also found time to become jazz's ultimate high-class act, performing in concert halls instead of cabarets, starting and ending sets on time rather than showing up late and then endlessly jamming, and avoiding drugs and any other of the million hobgoblins that have stereotypically bedeviled jazz musicians. As Lewis told Nat Hentoff, "We don't want to look like a bunch of tramps." This provoked a much-quoted and characteristically generous reaction from Miles Davis, who compared the MJQ's dignified approach to "Ray Robinson bringing dignity to boxing by fighting in a tuxedo" (which didn't stop Davis from joining the ever-increasing list of jazzmen, from Stan Kenton to Wynton Marsalis, who have recorded Lewis's best-known composition, "Django"). But Davis's wisecrack might have been made out of jealousy for a group that achieves the highest possible level of audience rapport every time out. "It's just a middling night for them," one young fan was overheard saying between sets at a recent gig at New York's Blue Note, "meaning they're only terrific."

Fans like these wanted the MJQ to go on forever, but in jazz, 22 years is forever. In 1969, Milt Jackson said, "The quartet will never break up." But 15 years later, the same Milt Jackson, with an obvious chip on his shoulder after a decade of being asked the same question, pleaded mea *maximus culpa* for the group's disintegration: "I decided to leave, and when I left, they decided to disband." Lewis, quoted in *The New York Times*, accused Jackson of shortsightedness, and Kay not long ago said aloud what they all had been thinking, that "the break-up was a pretty foolish thing to do." Though the split was inevitable, the reunion turned out to be equally so. There's no doubt in anyone's mind—including the MJQ themselves—that they would have re-formed, even without the lucrative impetus of the Japanese tour. When Kay, who was the only one not to organize his own band during the years of silence, was asked what the re-formation meant to him, he said, "Money."

That the MJQ, one of the highest-paid acts in the bebop business, was never able to make money on a level comparable with its enormous pool of collective talent has always been a sore point to its members. Jackson feels that the critical fraternity has done much harm in segregating jazz from the large popular audience. "They used to write in magazines," charges Jackson, "that jazz was too sophisticated and that you couldn't dance to it. Now that's a restriction; that's a block right there. People who wanted to go out dancing would say, 'We don't want to go to a jazz concert because we can't dance.' The critics told them that beforehand, and now they come to us with a closed mind, and that's wrong."

"Dancing has changed," adds Heath. "Music means nothing; they're dancing to rhythm with fake instruments and fake everything else—their so-called dancing is just shaking their behinds. If you expect us to accommodate that, no!" "It's just an attitude," Jackson continues. "Take [Bobby Timmons's] 'Moanin" played by Art Blakey and [Lee Morgan's] *The Sidewinder* over to Dick Clark. If they can't dance to those, send 'em home and don't let 'em come back!"

Still, within the narrower parameters of the jazz world, the Modern Jazz Quartet is the original supergroup. Lewis's star, too, is rising again, now that a new generation of jazz avant-gardists are turning to classical music for ideas. Young players, such as David Murray, have learned Lewis's lesson of paying as much attention to the form a solo appears in as to the solo itself. As the late classical conductor Ernest Ansermet once prophesized for Sidney Bechet and for all of jazz, "His 'own way' is the highway the whole world will swing along tomorrow."

The re-formed MJQ travels Lewis's highway as far as they can go. Today, it is more of a quartet than ever before. Instead of the leader, star soloist, and sidemen setup, which they began with in the very early 1950s, the group has long since accomplished its goal of equal partnership between all four creative allies. When this observation was raised to Heath, he disagreed, but Lewis countered, saying that "It's intentional." Heath, Kay, and Jackson are also doing more writing for the band than ever before, although "John Lewis is still the musical director as far as my compositions are concerned," says Heath, "and I wouldn't try to infringe on that."

In addition to writing for the group, Heath and especially Jackson, who says he "has been writing as long as I've been playing music," will continue to work with their own units during the MJQ's off-seasons: Jackson with his continuing series of Pablo albums and Heath (and brother Jimmy) with the Heath Brothers Band. Kay, the least individually active, will lay off when he can, while Lewis is currently hard at work on his version of Bach's *Well-Tempered Clavier*. His intention, he says, is "to play the pieces straight, with some feeling and then with improvisation." He continues, "It's mostly for solo piano, but there are some other voices."

But for most of the year from now on, they'll be touring as the Modern Jazz Quartet, under the personal management of the great bassist Ray Brown. ("Ray showed me how to hold the bass properly," Heath told Whitney Balliett. "I always considered Ray the great rhythm man.") Through Brown, who previously managed Quincy Jones, they've signed with a new agency, the Association of Performing Artists, which is preparing for Lewis and the MJQ to work with symphony orchestras again, a reminder that in the 1950s and 1960s, the four worked with no less than 36 such ensembles. However, Lewis has no plans for any permanent additions to the group because, he says, "This quartet is way too big for any guests right now."

It's a tricky thing to begin with a theoretical concept and then try to make music that sounds good in practice and performance. It's something that took generations of European opera composers hundreds of years to perfect, and it's something that countless others in all types of music are still working on. But that is precisely what John Lewis, Connie Kay, Percy Heath, and Milt Jackson have accomplished, even if one chastises them for having what Lewis Carroll called the "poor sort of memory that only works backwards." Thus, they'll continue to swing down Lewis's highway as four souls with a single voice. A voice that speaks to history.

(*DownBeat*, 1985)

***

For nearly 50 years, the most generically named group in American music was also the most ambitious. The Modern Jazz Quartet is often described as the most successful and enduring of the handful of ensembles that tried to combine jazz and classical music, but their actual achievement was that they played hard-swinging jazz—thoroughly steeped in the blues—with the clean articulation and impeccable virtuoso musicianship of the great chamber groups. No other unit set the bar so high for intensely creative music that combined the best of both worlds. The young pianist Aaron Diehl, who studied the MJQ as part of his training at Juilliard, was recently asked why the MJQ is rarely re-created, and his answer was direct: "Because it's so incredibly hard to play!" If anyone is up to the challenge, it's the brilliant pianist Kenny Barron, leading vibraphonist Steve Nelson, bassist Peter Washington, and drummer Lewis Nash.

When Dizzy Gillespie was asked to describe the playing of vibraphonist Milt Jackson, the trumpeter exclaimed, "Why man, he's sanctified!" The playing of pianist and composer John Lewis also had an unmistakably religious relevance to it, except rather than sounding like a sanctified church, Lewis's spirituality was more closely related to the *Mass in B Minor* of Johann Sebastian Bach. The success of the Modern Jazz Quartet drew from these two poles—the freewheeling, unrestricted, hard "blowing" of the one contrasted with the more carefully controlled formality of the other. At times, the two approaches complemented each other perfectly; at other points, there was something of a musical clash between the two, but that only added to the overall excitement of the music, which was always clean but never dry.

In retrospect, it might have been more logical that the MJQ would have been conceived in a musical laboratory by a group of Berkeley professors looking to bring their classical training to bear on the jazz tradition. It seems surprising that Lewis and Jackson were both baptized by fire as key players in the first generation of bebop as members of Gillespie's pioneering modern jazz big band, where they first played together in 1946. The pianist and the vibraphonist were initially part of an intermission act: Gillespie's rhythm section would perform as a quartet while the rest of the band grabbed a smoke, and it was there that they gradually realized that they were an essential team whose collaboration would be solidified by their differences as much as their similarities.

In 1955, they recorded their first full-length album, *Concorde*, which was also the first session by the group in its familiar form, with bassist Percy Heath and drummer Connie Kay. Lewis did indeed tend to lean toward concepts that were prevalent in classical music that had rarely been translated into jazz terms, such as fugal form and baroque counterpoint, and he also made his music seem more formal by titling so many of his most famous compositions after European cities—"Milano," "Afternoon in Venice," and even "A Day in Dubrovnik." Famously, even when he dedicated what became his single most widely performed work to a legendary jazz musician, he picked the greatest of all non-American players as his inspiration, "Django" (as in Reinhardt).

But Lewis's structures were always primarily vehicles for solos, and in himself and Jackson, the group had two of the greatest. When you listen to the MJQ's masterpieces, such as "The Golden Striker" and "Three Windows," you're not primarily drawn to the delicate balance and classical ambience but rather, to the deep, hard grooves that Jackson and Lewis create. Kay, before joining the MJQ, was best known as an R&B drummer, and the MJQ played many more blues than fugues. Jackson and Lewis were both highly percussive players, no less than Kay, and at its most intense, the MJQ sometimes seems like the hardest-swinging percussion ensemble that ever existed. With so much drumming going on, Kay was free to create a wide range of tonal colors with an arsenal of implements. I heard the MJQ live once about 25 years ago, and no other Jazz at Lincoln Center event this spring fills me with as much anticipation.

(*The Wall Street Journal*, 2011)

***

In the spring of 2011, there were, for the first time in memory, not one but two tributes to the Modern Jazz Quartet, one presented by Kenny Barron at Jazz at Lincoln Center and the other at the Village Vanguard by drummer Paul Motian. The only thing pedestrian about the Vanguard show was its title: "A Tribute to the MJQ" brings to mind one of those ghost band–style re-creations of some heavy metal act you can hear in Atlantic City or Vegas. Then again, I guess "A Brilliant Drummer–Bandleader Reinterprets the Music of one of Jazz's Most Venerated Ensembles in a Highly Personal Way" somehow doesn't make for a snappy title to put on the marquee either. Mr. Motian uses the same instrumental lineup as the MJQ, with vibraphonist Steve Nelson, pianist Craig Taborn, and bassist Thomas Morgan, and for the most part, plays the compositions of John Lewis and Milt Jackson. Yet from that point on, he goes his own way—this is anything but a re-creation. Instead, it is a tribute in the truest sense of the word, one that the MJQ themselves would have felt honored to hear.

For years, it seemed as if the music of the Modern Jazz Quartet, John Lewis, Milt Jackson, Percy Heath, and Connie Kay, could no longer be heard live in performance after the passing of Mr. Jackson and Mr. Lewis in 1999 and 2001, respectively. There was little precedent for keeping the music of a bebop-era small group alive, no tradition of Glenn Miller–style posthumous bands, even for groups that sported immediately recognizable signature sounds, such as George Shearing's. In the last few seasons, the music of the MJQ has been stealthily creeping back into New York clubs and concert stages. Last September, a pair of very young, but already-well-seasoned players, pianist Aaron Diehl and vibraphonist Warren Wolf offered an exceptional evening of the MJQ at Dizzy's. (There's a bunch of excellent video clips on YouTube to back up that statement.) Last month, in the Allen Room, veterans Lewis Nash and Kenny Barron also staged a first-rate presentation of MJQ classics.

With so much "Q" in the queue, there was no need for Mr. Motian's foursome to attempt an out-and-out "repertory"-style re-creation—this wasn't Wynton Marsalis playing Duke Ellington or the Fab Faux doing the complete *Sgt. Pepper* album. In fact, at the late show on Tuesday, he began with three originals offered in the spirit of Lewis and Jackson, "Sunflower" (which is apparently no connection to Jackson's 1972 composition of the same title), "Wednesday," and "Olivia's Dream." Like much of the MJQ's music, all three pieces are tranquil and ruminative yet at the same time, filled with direction and purpose; one can well imagine John Lewis and company playing their own versions of these melodies.

The next three tunes, however, were all MJQ classics: "Django," "Afternoon in Paris," and "Delaunay's Dilemma." Just to show how different the two approaches were, both shows actually featured the same vibraphonist, Steve Nelson: at the Allen Room, he played like he was fitting into the arrangement and serving the memory of Milt Jackson; at the Vanguard, he played more like himself and didn't do Bags's memory any less of a service.

Generally, the so-called classical elements were much less apparent in Mr. Motian's presentation, and the rhythm was much looser overall. The MJQ's charts were always tight, even on the more freely improvised pieces, while Mr. Motian prefers a more ambiguous, flowing beat. "Afternoon" was a particularly astute choice: Lewis wrote it in 1949 before the quartet coalesced, and it became a bouncy, bop standard and favorite of hard-driving tenors named Sonny (i.e., Stitt and Rollins). More than most of Lewis's tunes, "Afternoon in Paris" is a vehicle for improvisation, and Mr. Motian's 10-minute version featured long, meaty solos from both Mr. Taborn and Mr. Nelson. All the individual statements were highly idiosyncratic—no one was emulating anyone. Perhaps that's the best tribute of all, to show that John Lewis's tunes can withstand different interpretations and approaches, no less than those of Ellington or Monk.

(*The Wall Street Journal*, 2011)

JOE ZAWINAL (1932–2007) AND WEATHER REPORT

Funny enough, the thing that seemed most important to me about Weather Report during the years when the band was together, from 1971 to 1985, is the very thing that seems least interesting about the band today: that they used electronic instruments. Today, I say "big deal," but at the time, that was more than a lot of us old hard-liners could take (all right, so I was a very young old hard-liner). We were prepared to listen to Count Basie and his orchestra playing second-rate Tin Pan Alley or to great horn soloists, such as Bobby Hackett, trying to capture the commercial market by playing "romantic jazz" with big string sections or the quasi pop–jazz of "crossover" musicians, such as George Shearing and Wes Montgomery. (And at the same time, we even steeled ourselves to listen to the occasionally unlistenable screams and shrieks of the extreme 1960s' avant-garde.) But the idea of overtly fusing jazz with rock elements was the one place we could not bring ourselves to go.

It's only now, in fact, that I realized how much I missed by avoiding Weather Report 20 years ago. As a new boxed set from Sony Legacy makes clear, and as WR cofounder Joe Zawinal will doubtless show in his concert this Friday and Saturday at Jazz at Lincoln Center's Rose Hall, perhaps the least significant aspect of the band was its use of electricity. Actually, only half the band was electrified: Mr. Zawinal played a battery of electric keyboards and synthesizers, and the bassist (most famously, Jaco Pastorious) always used something out of the guitar-style Fender family. But co-leader Wayne Shorter always played standard acoustic saxophones, soprano and tenor, and the drummer (most famously, Peter Erskine) used his own variation on the traditional trap kit.

The use of those instruments, which seemed so heinous way back then, was a perfectly natural development. Both founders, Wayne Shorter (1933–2023) and Joe Zawinal (1932–2007), had been working with Miles Davis's early semi-electrified band at the time of their decision to form their own group. There had always been strong elements of blues and pop in their music as individuals—Mr. Shorter with Art Blakey and then Miles Davis (and in his own classic series of albums for Blue Note Records) and Mr. Zawinal with Ben Webster, Dinah Washington, and most extensively, Cannonball Adderley—and these elements were no less present whether they were working in acoustic or electric contexts.

Clearly, Davis was the focal point of what we were calling "fusion" in the 1970s: the movement was essentially led not just by the trumpeter himself but by five of his most storied sidemen—Chick Corea (Return to Forever), Tony Williams (Lifetime), and Herbie Hancock (Headhunters) in addition to Mr. Shorter and Mr. Zawinal of Weather Report—and all were leading headlining electro-jazz groups. Yet the term "fusion" seems less useful now than it did then. It was intended to a describe a music comprising both jazz and rock components. Yet though there can be jazz with rock elements and rock with jazz elements (most famously, Steely Dan), it seems to me that something either is or isn't jazz—and the music of Weather Report surely was—and is—pure jazz.

Other than the electricity (and let's face it, jazz guitarists had gone electric 15 years before rock ever rolled), there was little about WR that could be considered a rock element: the compositions of Mr. Zawinal and Mr. Shorter relied on the rich harmonic palette of jazz and not the three-chord headbanging style of blues and rock. They played driving, accessible rhythms, to be sure—although it would be hard to describe these as any more driving than those that Mr. Zawinal and Mr. Shorter played with Cannonball Adderley ("Mercy, Mercy, Mercy") and Art Blakey ("Lester Left Town"). Rock was essentially a dance music, whereas WR was strictly a concert band—it's hard to imagine any of their tunes other than the pop hit "Birdland" and the proto–hip-hop "125th Street Congress" (heard here both in the original version and a new mix by D. J. Logic) being heard in a dance club.

At the time, rock fans viewed WR as a "supergroup," the jazz equivalent of Crosby, Stills & Nash, but for sidemen to regroup in their own units was long a common practice in the jazz world—by those standards, the Clark Terry–Bob Brookmeyer Quintet of the mid-1960s was similarly a supergroup.

One point that comes through in the accompanying DVD of a live concert in Germany from 1978 (if not their official releases) is that the band even played jazz standards: there's a lovely medley of Mr. Zawinal playing "I Got It Bad" leading into a piano–sax duet on "Midnight Sun." A real highlight—and a mega-surprise—is Mr. Shorter, an avid movie and pop culture buff, doing an unaccompanied reading of Bob Hope's theme, "Thanks for the Memory," Sonny Rollins–style, which leads into Pastorious playing Mr. Shorter's "Dolores," as if in a reference to Mrs. Dolores Hope.

As longtime WR associate Hal Miller and producer Bob Belden both suggest in their notes, the band started more firmly in the more spontaneous, largely improvised tradition of jazz, but the longer they worked together, the more ambitious Mr. Shorter and especially, Mr. Zawinal became as composers. Yet the most successful of their largely through-composed pieces was Mr. Zawinal's 1971 "Unknown Soldier." Whatever it is, it's not rock: it seems more like the soundtrack of a postmodern silent film depicting the composer's memories of growing up in Austria during World War II. He juxtaposes the sounds of an expanded musical ensemble, including flute and piccolo trumpet, and wordless vocals from three singers, along with martial drumming and other sound effects. It's a highly vivid and extremely personal musical *tableaux vivant* that's ultimately unclassifiable stylistically.

The included DVD is especially valuable, as drummer Peter Erskine says in his own essay, as the best visual record of what most people regard as the essential edition of the group, with himself and the revolutionary electric bass virtuoso Jaco Pastorious. By 1978, the latter was being given as much melodic responsibility as either leader, and he is something to see, particularly on dedications to two ladies, "Dolores" and his own "Portrait of Tracy." He is in the rhythm section and the front line simultaneously, while doing choreography, partially disrobing (it was apparently killer-hot in Offenbach in September: the two leaders are drenched in perspiration, and the other two are shirtless), and engaging in all sorts of showboating stunts while continuing to play astonishing music on the electric bass. He builds to an unexpected quote from the title song from *The Sound of Music*, which refers, I am guessing, to Mr. Zawinal's Alpine origins.

It probably doesn't matter to Mr. Zawinal that this concert is being produced by Jazz at Lincoln Center, the organization whose artistic director, Wynton Marsalis, once positioned himself as the spiritual leader of all of us anti-fusion young old hard-liners. It was only a matter of time before both Mr. Marsalis and I came to the realization that here was the band that put Benjamin Franklin's and Thomas Edison's discoveries to better use than anybody.

(*The New York Sun*, 2006)

ETHAN IVERSON (1973) AND THE BAD PLUS

A 20-something friend who accompanied me to the opening set of The Bad Plus at the Village Vanguard on Tuesday night asked me if the group was controversial in the jazz world. Not exactly, I replied—there are plenty of jazz fans who love the group and maybe one or two (not more than that) who don't, but I have yet to meet anybody who resents the success this trio has enjoyed.

The Bad Plus, in a nutshell, is a jazz trio with a rock-and-roll sensibility—other than that, it's easier to say what Ethan Iverson, Reid Anderson, and David King are not. They are not, for instance, a 1970s-style "fusion" band like Weather Report, nor are they what has come to be known as a "jam" band like Medeski, Martin & Wood. As far as I can tell, The Bad Plus is a tradition and a genre unto itself.

Messrs. Iverson, Anderson, and King play piano, bass, and drums, but that's about all that they have in common with earlier piano trios, like that of Bill Evans or Bud Powell. Ultimately, they eschew as many jazz traditions as they embrace: their music is not based on the ideal of theme and variations nor upon the contrast between prewritten ensemble playing and improvised solos. And though they leave carefully chosen spaces for improvisation and depend heavily on interaction and interplay—earmarks of the best jazz tradition—their pieces are often composed works from beginning to end, a creative model that dominates in classical music and rock but is rarely utilized in jazz. They almost never play lyrical jazz ballads, and their use of extreme dynamics, again, suggests a link between rock and classical, with hard, pounding beats that could suggest either Wagner or heavy metal.

Their opening piece at the Vanguard, for instance, was Mr. Iverson's "Let Our Garden Grow," which is from the group's new album, *Suspicious Activity* (Columbia 94740). It began with one of the most distinctively jazzy—and conventionally "pretty"—moments of the evening, a bass solo by Mr. Anderson that vaguely suggested the jazz standard "My One and Only Love."

After this long intro, Mr. King entered in a rather dramatic fashion, scraping his cymbals with the bottom of his sticks. Rather than keeping time, the function normally expected of a drummer in a jazz piano trio, he then took up an intricate part that verged on soloing; as he played, he seemed to be continually taking apart and reconstructing his entire trap kit. (In fact, all three instrumentalists kept wiggling and writhing like Keith Jarrett times three throughout the set.) Mr. Iverson played a steady classical-style line throughout, but remarkably, the piano melody seemed to be accompanying the bass, drums, and other shenanigans rather than the other way around. This was jazz upside down in that the song slowly built up to the head rather than starting there.

At times, The Bad Plus seems intent on proving Duke Ellington wrong: swing isn't everything. Indeed, many of their rhythms have more rock-ish "drive" than the syncopation and "swing" of big bands and bebop—though some of their rhythms are so syncopated and catchy, they almost literally make your head spin.

Other influences seem to be from beyond music. A piece called "Physical Cities" switched moods so often, it had the feeling of radical jump cuts from some kind of experimental cinematic collage. At one point, Mr. Iverson was playing boogie-woogie patterns with his left hand while pounding out random tonal clusters with his right elbow, creating two very different moods with the same instrument at the same time.

Early on, The Bad Plus attracted notoriety for their unique jazz trio–style adaptations of rock anthems—among others, Kurt Cobain's "Smells Like Teen Spirit" on their 2003 album, *These Are the Vistas*, and Black Sabbath's "Iron Man" from 2004's *Give*. In some cases, these seemed to be done primarily to startle and, therefore, attract the attention of listeners on both halves of the equation. But some of their more recent "covers" (a term from the rock lexicon that is anathema to jazz listeners) reinterpret genuinely worthy material (i.e., they're not just there for shock value). Their jazzed-up version of Bjork's "Human Behavior," in fact, sounded more like traditional jazz than most of the original compositions the band played Tuesday night.

The new album has only one such cover, the 1980s' soundtrack classical–pop crossover hit "Chariots of Fire," which in characteristic Bad Plus fashion, is both a joke and serious at the same time. Above all else, their musical ability allows them to put forth a jazzy sense—I couldn't help but think that Thelonious Monk would find their music and their antics rather droll indeed.

At the climax of "Human Behavior," Mr. King switched from his drums to play a solo of sorts in which he held up two vintage 1980s' E.T. dolls and squeaked them back and forth at each other, as if in extraterrestrial conversation. "That's got to be a first for the Vanguard," my friend said. I was momentarily tempted to be a wise guy and answer, "No, Bill Evans did that in 1961," but no, for once, I kept my big mouth shut.

(*The New York Sun*, 2005)

***

Although The Bad Plus is sometimes known for their treatments of contemporary pop tunes, the group played only a couple of these in their 90-minute Zankel Hall concert on Wednesday night—"Everybody Wants to Rule the World" by Tears for Fears and "Life on Mars" by David Bowie, both of which are included on the trio's current album, *Prog*, released earlier this year by Heads Up. The Bad Plus (bassist Reid Anderson, drummer David King, and pianist Ethan Iverson) is certainly part of the recent movement of jazz groups tackling rock classics (done most brilliantly on Herbie Hancock's new full-length take on the music of Joni Mitchell), but more important, even when they are performing originals, they play acoustic jazz (perhaps symbolized on the cover of *PROG* by an old-fashioned manual typewriter) with a rock attitude. This is jazz that rocks rather than swings.

In the same way that a heavy-metal love song, such as it is, is called a "power ballad," we might describe The Bad Plus's style, a genre unto itself, as power jazz. It certainly isn't like any previous form of acid jazz, smooth jazz, or fusion. It's all achieved rhythmically, not by use of electronic instruments or necessarily the rock repertoire. The rhythmic distinction is established by Mr. King, who plays almost everything completely staccato, right on top of the beat. There are some numbers with more of a familiar jazz feel, such as the bluesy "1979 Semi-Finalist" (part of the cycle that includes "1972 Bronze Medalist" and "1980 World Champion"), in which Mr. King plays with more shading and behind-the-beat phrasing—even swing.

On the one hand, every element of the band's music is inspired by the jazz ideal of melody and solos, theme and variation, but on the other, even when one member plays apart from the other two, it never seems quite like a bebop-style, chordal, or even melodic improvisation. One jazz ideal that The Bad Plus does utilize is a friendly competition between Messrs. Anderson and Iverson, the two dudes with Scandinavian-sounding names. The two often seem to be trying to top each other for audience approval, and Mr. Anderson has an advantage in that the crowd can actually see his face as he plays—not possible when you're operating a nine-foot Steinway.

At times, I was reminded of the somewhat vaudevillian style of the Gene Krupa–Charlie Ventura trio (i.e., "Dark Eyes"), with its tight unison and distinctive staccato phrasing, particularly in what seems to be their signature "Physical Cities," which closed the Zankel concert. The piece, also heard on the new album, winds up with a long segment in which the threesome pounds down hard on the beat in perfect unison and in a manner that's somewhat syncopated but more impressively, perfectly synchronized. The three included this segment (diverse as it may be) in both the opening ("Let Our Garden Grow") and the finale. It's like an instrumental equivalent of trapeze acrobatics.

The Bad Plus's only other "cover" was Ornette Coleman's "Song X," which culminated in a section in which all three employed a different technique derived from the so-called avant-garde: Mr. Anderson played under the bridge of his instrument, Mr. King scraped his cymbals with the tops of his drumsticks, and Mr. Iverson played inside the piano. Their arrangement also uses silences in a telling way that seems much more inherently Bad Plus than Ornette, although the response of the audience was anything but silent. The group not only takes pop and turns it into art with an Andy Warhol–like sense of irony but takes spinach and feeds it to the crowds as if it were ice cream. This was truly the Plus at their Baddest.

(*The New York Sun*, 2007)

PAN-GENERATIONAL, PAN-STYLISTICS

DICK HYMAN (BORN 1927)

In 1983, Dick Hyman supplied the music for *Zelig*, Woody Allen's classic comedy about the "chameleon man" who could change his identity at will to conform to his surroundings. Certain similarities between Leonard Zelig and Mr. Hyman are hard to miss. In his various roles as a pianist, arranger, composer, and producer of concerts and recordings, Mr. Hyman can re-create any musical style imaginable, from Scott Joplin to Lennie Tristano. As a studio musician in the late 1950s, he played keyboards on many early rock-and-roll hits, including the original version of "At the Hop." And he can also knock out some mean Bach, both on piano and pipe organ.

It was in 1985, two years after *Zelig* that Mr. Hyman first put together a series of July concerts at the 92nd Street Y. He had become friendly with the Y's producer, Hadassah Markson, when he played ragtime piano for a concert in the Y's long-running "Lyrics and Lyricists" series. When she initially proposed a series of concerts at the end of July, he had his doubts. "I thought, 'But there's no one in New York then,'" he said. "But her idea was to have them on Tuesdays, Wednesdays, and Thursdays, before everybody leaves town for the weekend." That first season served as a test, and 20 years later, the concerts continue to sell out almost every night.

In 2004, 92NY announced that the year's "Jazz in July" season would be Mr. Hyman's last. The series has not only provided hours of great entertainment but over the course of its existence, become an essential part of the jazz repertory movement and, like Mr. Hyman himself, a New York institution. I sat down with Mr. Hyman on the Friday before the start of that final season to talk about Jazz in July, his long career, and what the future held for him at age 77.

Mr. Hyman started, like nearly all pianists of the era, with the European classics—and was fortunate enough to win a radio contest that awarded him 12 lessons with the great Teddy Wilson. A child of the swing era, he went in 1937—he was 10—to the Paramount to hear Benny Goodman and his orchestra. "Then my older brother started coming home with these new things called jazz albums, and that was the first time I heard the music of the Jazz Age. I fell in love with Jelly Roll's 'Red Peppers,' Louis Armstrong's 'Hot Fives,' and Bix Beiderbecke."

Already a professional pianist, Mr. Hyman served in the U.S. Navy during the final months of World War II. When he left the service, in 1946, he was just in time to catch the final glory years of the 52nd Street scene. Swing Street, as it had been known, had already begun its descent into a series of, in Arnold Shaw's memorable phrase, "strip-and-clip joints." "I had only one major gig on the street," Mr. Hyman says, "and it was accompanying 'Zorita and her Serpent.'"

In the current era, student jazz musicians—a concept that was unknown when Mr. Hyman was coming up—are taught to appreciate and improvise in different jazz genres, such as Dixieland and bebop. Things were completely different in the period when Mr. Hyman first began playing piano professionally.

In the 1940s in New York, there were supporters of Eddie Condon on one side and Charlie Parker on the other; a third contingent insisted that the only pure jazz was made by New Orleanians who, at 40 or 50 years old, now seemed like ancients. Rather than working together, the various factions could at best agree to disagree with each other, and much of the critical writing of the period consisted less of appreciation than what amounted to arm wrestling.

At this time, Mr. Hyman was, he says, "A die-hard Condon-ite," but when he first heard Charlie Parker and Dizzy Gillespie, "I saw no reason why I couldn't incorporate Bebop into what I was already playing." Mr. Hyman was on the bill alongside Parker, Lennie Tristano, and a pre-calypso Harry Belafonte when Birdland opened its doors on December 15, 1949 (he was a member of Dixielander Max Kaminsky's band). He later served as that club's house pianist, working with Lester Young, Hot Lips Page, and others. In 1952, he played with Parker himself in a television clip that has been shown thousands of times in any number of documentaries.

By the early 1950s, Mr. Hyman had established himself as a studio player of rare versatility. "It may sound like I'm being over-modest, but that really wasn't a big deal then." He points out, "You can't imagine it today, but there were hundreds and hundreds of studio sessions then, not only record dates, but soundtracks, jingles, television and radio broadcasts—you name it. All you had to do was read well and be willing to play anything, and you started getting calls."

Mr. Hyman spent most of his working career in the recording studios, doing more sessions than even a team of discographers could keep track of as well as several Broadway shows (most notably, *Sugar Babies*) and contributing to more than 40 films in capacities ranging from orchestrator to composer to pianist to conductor. But though he made his first solo session in 1950 (for a 78-rpm label called Relax Records) and recorded prolifically as a leader in the 1950s, Mr. Hyman didn't really assert himself as a star of the jazz world until the 1970s.

In 2004, he estimated that he had released approximately 150 albums under his own name, with five coming out that year alone. The most notable are *If Bix Had Played Gershwin* (Arbors Jazz) and a set of duets with trumpeter Randy Sandke; Mr. Hyman is one of the great advocates of the piano–horn duo format.

In 1973, Mr. Hyman worked with George Wein in the New York Jazz Repertory Concert, an organization that became the forerunner of the jazz repertory movement. Its spiritual offspring include such institutions as Gary Giddins's American Jazz Orchestra; the Smithsonian Jazz Orchestra in Washington, DC; and Jazz at Lincoln Center. "Bach and Mozart are still alive and well in the classical world," says Mr. Hyman. "They're long dead themselves and we don't write like that anymore, but we still can perform that music and enjoy it. The same can be said for Duke Ellington, Louis Armstrong, and Bix."

Even though Mr. Hyman frequently presents newly written music, such as this year's "The Longest Blues in the World," the focus is on jazz history, with the emphasis on the hot jazz of the 1920s and 1930s and the swing era of the 1930s and 1940s. But the programming sometimes extends even earlier (to New Orleans and ragtime) and later (to bebop and occasionally, even free improvisation). "After 20 years, I've built up a lot of trust with the audiences there," he says. "They know me and my taste well enough to pretty much go with whatever I want to give them."

So why step down now? "This is the most fulfilling and pleasant project I've ever been involved with," Mr. Hyman says, "but 20 years is an appropriate time. I've been around on a wonderful carousel ride 20 times now." He says he will continue to do the Y's three-concert spring piano series as well as other events around the country (such as the Oregon Festival of American Music). (Postscript: In 2005, the Jazz in July series was taken over by Bill Charlap, who ran it until 2023, and in 2024 Aaron Diehl started his run as producer and musical director.)

Whatever the case, Mr. Hyman promises that Jazz in July will continue to represent the diversity of American jazz. "I disapprove of segregation in any form," says Dick Hyman, "and to me the face of jazz mirrors the face of the American people."

(*The New York Sun*, 2004)

***

The pianist Dick Hyman began his 80th birthday party Saturday night with "Young at Heart," though he played this sometimes sentimental song anything but reverentially. Rather, Mr. Hyman charged through it, part stride and all syncopation, incorporating descending, spiraling lines that paraphrased "Jitterbug Waltz" and a few quotes from "Symphony Sid." Then, turning to the crowd at the 92nd Street Y, he said, "It was either ['Young at Heart'] or 'Old Man River.'"

The Y stage was decked out more like a party than a concert, with balloons everywhere and Mr. Hyman's family scattered about, but this opener was a clear sign that the pianist didn't want to celebrate his 80th by receiving a gold watch or resting on his considerable laurels. In fact, the first of his pianist guests to solo, Bill Charlap (who entered with a mouthful of potato chips), seemed to be playing harder and more brilliantly than ever; rather than taking it easy on his longtime mentor, it was as if he wanted to give Mr. Hyman a royal butt kicking for his birthday.

Wiping the crumbs and grease from his hands, Mr. Charlap dove into a stunning reading of "Where or When" that left one to worry whether the rest of the concert would be able to live up to it. He opened with the bridge and played the first chorus ad lib, drifting into tempo like a ship without a sail, then, joined by bassist Jay Leonhart, essayed the second chorus as a ballad but with absolutely perfect rhythmic assurance. The duo built to a piano–bass exchange that really was all that and a bag of chips.

Yet Mr. Charlap was not so tacky as to steal the show from the man of the hour. He knew Mr. Hyman was not to be shown up on this or any other occasion. The two flew into a dual-piano, harmonic vivisection of "I'll Remember April," in which even the slow introduction was brutally fast. Tearing the melody and chords asunder, the pair took it through a Latin passage (aided by drummer Eddie Locke), a pair of dark and menacing solo sequences by Mr. Charlap, and an unaccompanied four-handed cadenza. Mr. Hyman was not about to have said butt kicked by a whippersnapper half his age.

Mr. Hyman announced early on that the concert was part of the long-running "Jazz Piano at the Y" series, so the pianists were the focal points and everyone else—including two horns, a rhythm section, and two singers—were merely added attractions. So when Mr. Charlap played behind the vocalist Annette Sanders on "A Sleepin' Bee," I found myself more drawn to the accompanist than the spotlighted star, although he was hardly trying to pull focus. Likewise, when Mr. Hyman played behind the clarinetist Evan Christopher, it was hard not to pay more attention to the pianist, even though Mr. Christopher steered through a tricky arrangement of the 1930 waltz "In a Little Spanish Town," which started in 6/4 funk before shifting to a swinging four.

Along the way, trumpeter Joe Wilder ("I Cover the Waterfront") and guitarist Bucky Pizzarelli ("Honeysuckle Rose") both had chances to shine. Mr. Pizzarelli got the biggest hand of the evening with his party-piece feature on the Fats Waller favorite (which built to a back-and-forth routine on "Ebony Rhapsody" with Mr. Leonhart), and he followed with an exquisite Oscar Moore–influenced solo on "Embraceable You," which was much more like classic Pizzarelli to my ears.

Still, it was the pianists' evening, and the major set piece of the show was the opener of the second half, in which all four offered a take on George Gershwin's "Liza." Derek Smith, whose trademark is to play faster than Art Tatum on Red Bull, substituted harmonic density for his usual speed; Mr. Charlap chewed up the changes in a somewhat lighter but no less breathless vein; and Mr. Hyman played it more classically at first, gradually introducing a pumping stride left-handed.

It turned out that Mr. Hyman was setting it up for the fourth pianist to knock it out of the park, and that she did. Meral Guneyman, a Turkish-born player who recently recorded an album of four-handed duos with Mr. Hyman, rhapsodized the Gershwin melody in cascading waves of impressionistic chords and shortly after, did the same for "Embraceable You." Ms. Guneyman then showed she could play in other ways too, joining Mr. Hyman in a duet on an original called "Rap #3," in which the two played in a percussive, highly syncopated style reminiscent of Billy Strayhorn's "Tonk."

The singers in these shows are rarely (with some major exceptions) up to the level of the instrumentalists, and on Saturday, both singers had their best moments in the second half. Ms. Sanders shone with Mr. Charlap on Sondheim's "Not While I'm Around," and Carol Woods, who had previously sung a swinger ("Them There Eyes") and a ballad ("Lover Man"), showed that her real strength is belting the blues in an extroverted, theatrical style. Ms. Woods climaxed the show with a couple of dynamic 12-bar choruses on "I'd Rather Drink Muddy Water"; unfortunately, because this was the finale, Eddie Miller's classic blues was divided up and shared by the entire company, when it was clear that everyone wanted to hear Ms. Woods sing at least a few more choruses on her own.

Throughout, Mr. Hyman showed that though he has joined the octogenarian club (Messrs. Pizzarelli and Wilder are 81 and 85, respectively) and relinquished control of the Y's Jazz in July series to Mr. Charlap, he does not intend to go gently into that good night. A swell party it was.

(*The New York Sun*, 2007)

PETER MINTUN (BORN 1950)

When you first go to hear Peter Mintun play, you can't help but notice a distinct resemblance to "Mr. Nostalgia," one of the more durable creations of the great underground cartoonist R. Crumb. Other people may collect music or memorabilia, but Mr. Nostalgia physically embodies another era. Mr. Mintun's music and lifestyle are like that—when you step into a room where he's playing or into his Washington Heights townhouse, you feel like you've passed through a portal from one era to another. Like Mr. Nostalgia, Mr. Mintun more than looks the part—even in the most contemporary setting, he would look like he ought to exist only in sepia, with his hooked nose and dapper mustache. Yet if his visual image is monochrome, his music itself is vivid and vibrant, not black and white but full-on three-strip technicolor, exploding in harmony and melody.

One problem with musicians who work in the styles of earlier eras, as some have complained, is that they are compelled to ignore influences from later periods. Mr. Mintun doesn't face that problem: he has so completely immersed himself in the music of the great piano wizards of the 1920s and 1930s that he probably thinks a flatted fifth is a cocktail. Mr. Mintun is more of a jazz-age musician than simply a jazz musician. He comes out of an era when the piano was the instrument of choice for vaudeville-style entertainers who were half-jazz and half-classical but ultimately 100 percent traveling prestidigitators. Rightfully called "keyboard wizards," they could make melodies appear and disappear via musical sleight of hand. Now you hear it; now you don't.

Yet Mintun doesn't merely play from memory; he is a brilliant improviser who effortlessly spins ad-lib variations of the most melodious sort—yet he is not likely to get bogged down in chorus after chorus of blues changes. "I hate it when musicians get up there and just spill their guts out like that," he says. "That's why I'd rather go to a comedy club than to a concert these days—most music now is so depressing." Appropriately, his own improvisations are terse and to the point but no less brilliant for that—he can spontaneously craft a medley inspired by any subject, from W. C. Handy to Shirley Temple.

Mr. Mintun became a New York institution in a comparatively short time. He first worked here at the New York Palace and then spent seven years at Bemelmans Bar at the Hotel Carlyle.

A fourth-generation Californian, Mr. Mintun was born in 1950 to a medical couple (an "old-fashioned family doctor" and a nurse) in Berkeley. He was the third of four children, which aided him in his musical training in that when it came his turn for piano lessons, he'd already heard his two older siblings stumble through all the basic exercises. He was able to play them from memory, but he didn't fool the nice little old lady who gave piano lessons for very long. "She realized I wasn't turning the page. She said, 'You're just mimicking, like a parrot!' To this day, I'm much more of an ear player than a reader."

He first started getting a feel for the music of the interwar period by listening to 78s handed down to him from his grandparents and their friends. His father also was a jazz fan, a longtime member of the local branch of the United Hot Clubs of America, who constantly played Fats Waller records in the Mintun household. "That was the basic music we grew up with—we had no idea that it was 20 or 30 years old then." He began to seek out the sounds and the artifacts of the era that produced it by haunting San Francisco's secondhand shops. "That opened a door to something that was gone but fascinating to me," he says. "I would go through old magazines and imagine myself sitting in one of those old cars; just think about sitting in the back seat of a sedan and being able to stretch your legs!"

As a youngster, Mintun was already accumulating massive amounts of sheet music and 78s by the carload. His first steady job as a musician was playing piano for another little old lady, this one who gave dancing lessons. "She taught what used to be called a 'social dancing' class. This was 1962, I was 12, and she was in her 60s. I loved working for her because she had been a little girl in the ragtime era and grew up with all the music that's come since. She taught me all the different dance tempos, foxtrots, waltzes, and rhumbas. To this day, I still love playing for dancers more than anything. We'd hold dances, and all the mothers of the kids would come up to me and start humming songs—I could see how much this music meant to people."

His first big job in San Francisco was also the longest-lasting of his career, at L'Etoile, in the Huntington Hotel on classy Nob Hill. That lasted from 1973 to 1989, and it was followed by a five-year stint around the corner at the Fairmont, the city's most famous hotel. "I always wanted to try New York, and I got my chance thanks to my friend [singer–pianist] Steve Ross, who recommended me to the Helmsley people."

He played the Madison Room for more than a year until a fire closed the room temporarily. (I first heard him there in the early 1990s, at the recommendation of Leonard Maltin.) He then switched to Bemelmans, where he alternated with the equally elegant but more modern jazz–oriented pianist Barbara Carroll for seven years. "That's the way I like to work," he says, "five nights a week, at least four or five hours a night. If you don't know your craft when you start, you certainly will after 30 years of that. You have to be there; you have to know all the tunes and get them right—and not be drunk!"

Early in 2001, he realized that there was more going on for him in New York than in San Francisco, so he sold the house he'd been living in for 25 years and bought a townhouse in the West 160s. It had been owned by the same family from when it was built in 1897 until 1981, then by a couple who maintained it and put in a pool and eventually sold it to Mr. Mintun and his partner, Eric Bernhoft. The toughest part of the ordeal was transporting their combined collections from coast to coast. "We had an enormous 16-wheel moving truck, and the movers said that they had never filled one of those with any two people's stuff before—it was so packed, we could hardly close the doors." The statistics were 39,000 pounds of stuff, including furniture, pianos, 970 boxes of records, music, and other assorted bric-a-brac.

Mr. Mintun's and Ms. Carroll's contracts with the Carlyle were terminated abruptly in 2002—which was probably a major career break for reasons I'll get into elsewhere. But he was already a steadfast converted New Yorker. His steadiest job since then has been at the Greenbrier, a 200-year-old resort in West Virginia, which he calls "the best-managed hotel I've ever seen."

He works mostly out of town but continues to call New York his home. He often performs unofficially at the Film Forum, on occasions when friend Bruce Goldstein mounts a program of silent film or early musical shorts, or at the Times Square Grill, where Vince Giordano and his Nighthawks hold forth twice weekly with their take on the jazz and pop of the same era of Mr. Mintun's specialization.

By 2004, he had also recorded four CDs—which isn't much considering the extent of his career and the depth of his repertoire. Of these, the easiest to come by is *Grand Piano* (MM 1875), while *Yours for a Song—Here's to the Ladies* (Premier 1065) reflects his interest in female composers, such as his late friend Dana Suesse. That last album was also the first (and so far last) to feature his singing—"I only did that because people requested it," he says. "Now they've got to listen to it!"

Mr. Mintun and Mr. Bernhoft's home could easily feel like a library or an archive; there's a concert grand piano, which he acquired from the late Ms. Suesse; a player piano, which Mr. Bernhoft tinkers with; and a very rare reproducing piano from the

1920s. The walls still have push-button igniters for the gas-jet lamps (pre-electricity illumination), call buttons (for servants), speaking tube system (an early intercom), and a working dumbwaiter. It's a time warp, yet the house doesn't feel like a museum but rather, a place where real live people live and make music and from time to time, enjoy it on such newfangled conveniences as CD and DVD players.

"I said to Vince Giordano recently, 'You know, we've been playing this music longer than the '20s and '30s actually existed.'" He adds, "When people used to ask me why I love this music so much, I never used to have a good answer, other than that it's exciting, it's danceable, it has so much personality, and the songs are so good. Now when I get asked that question, I always ask a question in return. I say, 'This music is so great—how could anybody not love it?'"

(*The New York Sun*, 2004)

BILL CHARLAP (BORN 1966)

At the Vanguard and on the Beach

The first time I wrote about Bill Charlap at the Vanguard, he was 36 and was about to record *Somewhere: The Songs of Leonard Bernstein*, his third album for Blue Note. Born in 1966, Charlap was technically a member of the "Young Lions" generation. Most musicians who came of age in the 1970s wore psychedelic outfits and played psychedelic music, such as fusion and the avant-garde, the mode of the 1980s. However, Charlap represented a simultaneous return to the bebop and hard bop of several generations earlier as well as the more conservative fashions that went with it.

The so-called Young Lions, or at least the publicists who promoted them, were the first generation to capitalize on their youth, to make it into both a selling point and a marketing hook. Yet when Charlap first began making regular appearances at the Village Vanguard, he seemed to be making every attempt to look as formal and old school as possible, always in a suit and tie that made him look like a banker or a businessman. Even the rest of his trio was never quite so formal: bassist Peter Washington usually wore a jacket but not a tie, and drummer Kenny Washington wore a tie but not a jacket; only Charlap wore both. This was the Vanguard, which meant a basement full of college kids mostly in jeans. Yet all formality ended the instant his fingers touched the piano. It's only a slight exaggeration to say that he then transforms into a thunderous juggernaut of energy, suddenly reanimated with enough vitality and enthusiasm to light up not only the keyboard but the entire room.

Charlap had established his bona fides as an interpreter of standards with his first album for Blue Note, *Written in the Stars* (2000), titled after a lesser-known but beautiful Harold Arlen song. It also contained "Where Have You Been?," a beautiful but lesser-known Cole Porter number so obscure—by Cole Porter standards at least—that when Charlap played it at the Vanguard, the legendary Barbara Carroll, who was sitting next to me, asked me what it was. (I was amazed that both Charlap

Bill Charlap; South Orange Performing Arts Center, New Jersey; November 16, 2019

and I knew a song that she didn't.) The next album, *Stardust*, was even better musically and also a stronger seller, thanks not least to several guest stars, including Frank Wess, Jim Hall, Shirley Horn, and Tony Bennett, who waxed one his most vulnerable ballads ever in "I Get Along Without You Very Well." *Stardust* (2001) was the first of Charlap's songbook albums, devoted to the music of Hoagy Carmichael, and not surprisingly contained some beautiful but obscure Hoagiana, including "I Walk with Music." By the time he played the Vanguard in March 2003, he had announced that the third album would focus on the songs of Leonard Bernstein.

At this point, Charlap's career was in a particularly multigenerational state. Even then, he was a regular at the 92nd Street Y's "Jazz in July" series, in which the average age was always somewhere, as the late Mel Tormé would say, between 70 and deceased, but when he played the Vanguard, he had the distinction of playing the exact same music and the same songs for an audience of mostly NYU undergrads who were very likely the grandchildren of the *alter cockers* at 92Y. In every context, he never fails to surprise; you would think the Y crowd, ensconced in the formality of a concert hall, would demand a more reverential treatment of the familiar melodies, but no, he was particularly rhythmically charged at the Y, taking the tunes and then splintering and fragmenting them six ways from Sunday.

Conversely, you would think the loose and funky afterhours vibe of the Vanguard at midnight, just when the roomful of younger patrons with fake IDs were swilling their first-ever adult beverages, would demand plenty of strong, driving rhythm and energy. Instead, Charlap responded with the most lyrical playing I've ever heard him do. He favored big, lush chords with plenty of wide-open spaces and as always, plenty of interplay between himself and the two Washingtons.

The opener, Chick Corea's "Tones for Joan's Bones," set the mood. Charlap's playing was minimal yet intense, swinging but spare, not laying down zillions of notes at once but starting small and building up to a much fuller, denser finish and gradually filling in more and more of the empty spaces. Another tune by a pianist–composer, "Monk's Mood," was the major instrumental ballad of the evening, delivered with a romanticism reminiscent of "April in Paris," another Thelonious Monk favorite.

Charlap reserved some of his best ideas for three standard songs. "Out of This World" began and ended with Harold Arlen's melody first emerging from and then retreating into a Latin polyrhythm. "Aren't You Glad You're You" and "Put on a Happy Face" both climaxed in glorious exchanges with Kenny Washington. In both cases, the drumming Washington demonstrated that loudness is not a prerequisite for swinging—at least, not all the way through. He started quietly on the second, but by the end of his episode on the *Bye Bye Birdie* bromide, Washington had built up to a peak of volume and excitement, and by this point, Charlap was flying all over the keyboard, spinning gorgeous harmonies all over Washington's two-bar bursts.

The best was yet to come. The veteran jazz singer Carol Sloane was in the house and was invited to take the stage. She rendered "Stardust" every bit as movingly as Shirley Horn does on Charlap's album. Ms. Sloane was, as always, melodic and soulful, with a Tormé-like concentration. She brought the proceedings to an even higher level (Charlap's closing instrumental, the rousing "Half Step," was the hardest-swinging item yet) and reminded us all that there are still very good reasons why people still play and sing the old songs and why other people are willing to go to the Village Vanguard at midnight on a school night to hear them do it.

(*The New York Sun*, 2003)

***

Recently I had the chance to hit the beach with Bill Charlap. We were in Clearwater, Florida, at the March of Jazz, the annual weekend-long jazz party thrown by Arbors Records, and Charlap was leading his four-year-old daughter, Vivian, across the strand. It was the sight of Bill Charlap standing barefoot, however, that gave me pause: it was hard to believe he had feet like any normal person and that they could serve any purpose other than operating the sustaining pedal of a piano—except for, possibly, walking up to the piano.

At 37, Charlap may be younger than many of his contemporaries on the jazz-and-standards circuit, but this child of a songwriter and a singer has been playing piano nearly all his life. He and his trio, costarring bassist Peter Washington and drummer Kenny Washington, were about to open for their latest two-week run at the Village Vanguard, a gig in which the main order of business was to promote their new album, their third for Blue Note, *Somewhere: The Songs of Leonard Bernstein*. When I caught up with Charlap, we talked about Bernstein, the resilience of the Great American Songbook, and how it is that—in the hands of a master like Charlap—music from the 1950s and earlier continues to inspire musicians and attract young listeners.

"Shows and show tunes were more popular then than reality TV shows are now [2004]," Charlap said. "The songs are in their time and of their time, but they're so well constructed that we could keep playing them forever and not run out of things to do with them." I'd put it this way: Jazz and standards have the content and depth of classical music but the flexibility and energy of pop. They stimulate improvisation and encourage an active response from both performer and listener.

Charlap mentioned to me, in this context, the veteran songwriter Jule Styne, who told him that "a song must be melodically simple and harmonically attractive." By this he meant, according to Charlap, that they must be written "with harmonies that automatically make you hear other melodies." Getting technical, he observed that songs from Broadway make a better basis for jazz improvisation because their harmonies "go to the seventh note of the chord. Pop, rock, and country songs may be lovely, but because their harmony rarely goes beyond the fifth, there's not much we can do with them."

> As jazz musicians, we have three things to cover. The blues, the songbook—songs that are primarily from the theater—and original jazz composers, such as Kenny Dorham, Gigi Gryce, Thelonious Monk. Songwriters like Gershwin, Berlin, Porter represent the absolute top drawer, the best that America had to offer. Their music conforms to certain rules: They were continually looking for a new melody, a tune that hadn't been heard before, and the harmony had to go somewhere. The same way that classical composers used forms like the minuet and the trio, songwriters used specific forms like AABA and ABAB.

Born in 1966, Charlap is the son of the Broadway composer Mark "Moose" Charlap, whose most successful work was the hit Broadway show *Peter Pan*. Charlap's mother is the well-respected singer Sandy Stewart, known to the public primarily for the hit song "My Coloring Book," which she introduced on *The Perry Como Show*, but well known to songwriters, such as Styne, as their number one choice as a demo singer. If you were trying to raise money for a show in 1960, you got Ms. Stewart to sing the score.

Charlap Sr. died when his son was seven, but the youngster's piano talent was encouraged both by his mother and a distant relative—pianist and producer Dick Hyman. Hyman, one of the first major figures in jazz to become famous for his proficiency in all styles, from ragtime to bebop, also developed a reputation for being generous to young talents. He was one of several jazz giants (a few of the others being Phil Woods, Gerry Mulligan, and Tony Bennett) who encouraged Charlap, giving him both advice and work.

Charlap told me that he chose Leonard Bernstein as the subject of his new album for several reasons. He felt that *West Side Story*, which inspired 4 of the 12 selections here, was not part of the long-dead past. "That was a show and a movie which my generation grew up with. People my age and younger know those songs." The *West Side Story* songs, Charlap noted, presented a special challenge.

"Unlike [Bernstein's two earlier Broadway shows] *On the Town* and *Wonderful Town*, and most traditional Broadway shows, the score and songs were more thoroughly through-composed, like an opera," he said. At the piano in the hotel bar, he demonstrated for me Bernstein's famous use of a tritone phrase. By putting the different notes of the tritone in different places, the composer devised three interrelated numbers in different moods: "Prologue," "Cool," and "Maria." "The trick is to retain what's special about these songs without completely changing them but putting our own stamp on them at the same time. I can make them mine, but they've still got to be his."

On the album, Charlap achieves this largely by accentuating the rhythmic strengths of the music. Bernstein's major achievement on Broadway was the complete integration of ballet into musical comedy, and all his scores are distinguished by their dance music. "Cool," the album's opener, begins with Bernstein's famous introductory riff. But the meat of the piece is all rhythmic, angular jabs of melody. "Jump"—a dance section from the gym sequence, which is not usually isolated on the cast recordings of *West Side*—Charlap renders in fast, boppish rhythms.

Charlap's ballads are equally noteworthy. "A Quiet Girl" is a waltz from *Wonderful Town* with echoes of both Richard Rodgers and Tchaikovsky, but Charlap makes it memorable on its own as a jazz instrumental. He recasts "Glitter and Be Gay," originally Barbara Cook's showcase in *Candide*, in a 32-bar song form with a distinctly minor mood. "Big Stuff" has traditionally been heard at the start of the ballet *Fancy Free* coming out of a jukebox in the voice of Billie Holiday, and Charlap admitted to me that in this one case, he didn't begin with Bernstein's melody from the published music but with the slightly different interpretation Lady Day laid down.

But "Lonely Town" is the album in microcosm. It is one of Bernstein's most haunting minor-key torch songs, and Charlap's treatment of it is strong and emotionally direct. Where "Cool" is all introduction, "Lonely Town" has no intro at all—he just dives right in. Though his improvisation is particularly abstract, with no reference to the melody, there's never a doubt where you are in the song—or who's playing it. Charlap described this as "letting the chords resolve before you hit the bass note. It works as long as you develop it in a natural way—it has to be organic. And as long as you don't lose the drama—it's all about drama."

Because for Charlap, as for Bernstein, the show's the thing. "With Bernstein, everything was theatrical," Charlap said. "He wrote a symphony before he wrote a show tune, but whether he was conducting Mahler or 'The St. Louis Blues,' it was all a form of theater." This album was important to him, Charlap told me, because he believes Bernstein stood at the nexus of 20th-century music: he was a star in the classical world, established himself as a leading composer of show music, and was well known for his love and support for the jazz world. "To me, Leonard Bernstein is not only culture, he's not only theater, he's distinctly American, distinctly New York." The same thing, of course, could be said about Bill Charlap.

(*The New York Sun*, 2004)

***

Halfway through Bill Charlap's early set at Birdland on Friday night, the great pianist played "You're All the World to Me." He then picked up the mic, turned around to face the crowd, and marveled at the way Fred Astaire introduced the song in the 1951 movie musical *Royal Wedding*. This is the classic number in which the legendary song and dance man literally defies gravity by strutting, whirling, tapping, and pirouetting all over the walls and ceiling of a room. Astaire, Mr. Charlap explained, used a devilishly clever bit of "practical effects" to achieve this feat of movie magic. But after hearing this pianist and his amazing trio for 25 years now, I still can't figure how he does it—how he makes his own magic happen.

"You're All the World to Me," which composer Burton Lane had repurposed from an earlier song of his by virtue of a new lyric by Alan Jay Lerner, is also a highpoint of Mr. Charlap's latest album, *Street of Dreams*. Mr. Charlap starts slowly, tentatively, with the verse, rendering it in a hesitating, probing fashion as if he were looking for an answer or seeking a pathway. His confidence increases when he arrives at the melody; it's like he's now found his musical compass, and by the time he completes a full chorus of the tune, he is ready to improvise and fully tear down the highway with gusto. Or more literally, he starts defying gravity in his own way, even as Astaire did, teleporting across the globe. He's playing the tune but is driven by the lyric, which moves from "Paris in April and May" to "New York on a silvery day" in just two lines, and next, just as swiftly, transports us to the Swiss Alps and Loch Lomond before we're even 16 bars into it.

Could it be that this mixing of moods—using tempo as an indicator—is a key part of Mr. Charlap's magical musical tool kit? He faked us out several times at Birdland—as in the opener, which began with the bouncy intro to "Squeeze Me (But Don't Tease Me)," with rumbling bass notes, but then followed with an understated reading of "What Is This Thing Called Love?"—swinging but spare, with lots of open spaces along the way. Conversely, there was an "All the Things You Are" that started as a ballad but unexpectedly broke into a double-time bop number—just when we least expected it—and then proceeded to get faster still.

Along the way, we stopped at Leonard Bernstein, Dizzy Gillespie, Duke Ellington, and George Gershwin. "Glitter and Be Gay" is almost predestined for a schizophrenic treatment, varying as it does between dirge and jubilant aria of joy. "Woody 'n' You" is the bop standard, which, among other things, showcases Kenny Washington's drumming. "Mood Indigo" served as a lead into a haunting "Sophisticated Lady" followed by a lightning-fast "Who Cares?"

Yet both live and in the studio, Mr. Charlap's strongest point is increasingly his slow love songs—slow isn't the word, it's something more like "glacial"—showing tempo is an especially pertinent factor, even when there is virtually none. At Birdland, he gave us "Here's That Rainy Day"—which matched the weather, although it was a rainy night by that point—played like he was stirring a slowly simmering bowl of soup. The title song, "Street of Dreams," rates a similar treatment on the album.

Mr. Charlap delivers his biggest impact on the CD with "What Are You Doing the Rest of Your Life?" and "I'll Know." Both songs are supposed to be delivered by guys who are completely sure of themselves: I'll know when my love comes along, and I am so confident that I am willing to commit to you forever—I'll love you till the end of time, and then ask for an extension. That's the message of the words, but the performance tells us otherwise. Mr. Charlap interprets the songs more like he's questioning himself; he may say, "I'll Know," but he doesn't. He conveys an element of doubt and trepidation that somehow makes the love song seem even more profound: "No one knows anything, but I'm willing to take a chance." It makes him sound more like an actual human being and not merely a character in a song or a show.

It's one thing to be able to sing—even more remarkably to play—the lyrics like they mean something and quite another to deliver the song as if it means something else entirely, as if the lyrics were not the whole story but just one of many clues as to what's really transpiring. He's communicating the subtext, or enacting the deeper meaning of the songs, without even resorting to the words. Like I say, 25 years after the Charlap–Washington–Washington Trio made its first recording, I still don't know how he does it—there's nothing in the way of practical effects that can explain it. His theme song should be "It's Magic."

(*The New York Sun*, 2022)

MORE THAN ACCOMPANISTS

BILL MILLER (1915–2006)

In the end, Bill Miller outlived "the old man" by eight years. As everyone reading this hopefully knows, Miller was a pianist and conductor who served as Frank Sinatra's primary accompanist for more than 40 years. He died at the age of 91 in 2006 in Montreal General Hospital, following a heart attack.

Sinatra once introduced Miller at a concert as "my partner at the piano." Through the most essential part of Sinatra's career—the glory years of the 1950s and 1960s, his comeback in the 1970s, and his frequent touring of the late 1980s and 1990s—Miller was celebrated as an essential part of the Sinatra experience. The singer's son and later, conductor, Frank Sinatra Jr., recently described Miller as "the greatest singer's pianist there ever was."

On key records, most famously "One for My Baby," Miller is more than an accompanist—he is a de facto collaborator. Miller's contribution to the mood and message on the record rivals Sinatra's. Though best known for his saloon-style piano on Sinatra's songs of heartbreak and loss, Miller was equally skilled at the swinging piano interludes on "The Lady Is a Tramp" and "The Lonesome Road." His contribution is perhaps easiest to appreciate in those few Sinatra concerts where Miller is not present and Sinatra didn't swing as convincingly or communicate nearly as effectively.

Miller, born in Brooklyn on February 3, 1915, was almost one year older than Sinatra, although in later years, he referred to the singer as "the old man." Like Sinatra, he first came up through the big bands: he started, at the age of 18, with Larry Funk and his Band of a Thousand Melodies and then went on to play with arranger Joe Haymes and his orchestra.

Miller played with his first great band and first great singer when he joined the band led by vibraphonist Red Norvo and jazz vocalist Mildred Bailey. One of his favorite stories, recounted many times over the years, was how he initially ignored Norvo's offer because he couldn't believe the vibraphonist could actually get his act together enough to form his own band. When he actually heard Norvo and Bailey over the radio, he was so impressed that he fibbed and told Norvo that he had never received the telegram.

The Norvo–Bailey band was one of Sinatra's all-time favorite musical groups, and that was how the singer heard Miller for the first time. Miller first heard Sinatra's voice at that time too, when he and Bailey heard Sinatra singing with Harry James's band over the radio. After his stint with Norvo ended, Norvo broke up his band. Miller was heavily featured in saxist Charlie Barnet's great band of the prewar period, and after a stint in the service, played with a variety of bands—Tommy Dorsey, Benny Goodman, and Barnet again—and singers, including Martha Raye.

Miller was recommended to Sinatra by the songwriter and Sinatra pallie, Jimmy Van Heusen. Miller began working with him in Las Vegas in 1952. He climbed aboard the singer's bandwagon at the low point of his career and was an essential part of his return to glory. Miller played a prominent role in virtually every Sinatra album and single. "Bill is the best," Sinatra's longtime guitarist, Al Viola, said. "If you listen to the few records they did without any orchestra, like 'Where or When,' you can hear the strong structure of his harmonies backing Sinatra—it's perfect!"

From working with Sinatra at Capitol, Miller became the pianist of choice for Sinatra's arrangers, Nelson Riddle and Billy May, and became a very busy studio musician. He took great pleasure in accompanying one of his all-time inspirations, a jazz pianist turned pop singer, Nat King Cole. "Whenever I played for Nat, I always asked myself, 'How would Nat play this?'"

Sinatra and Miller had their differences over the decades—it sometimes seemed a little cruel when the singer would address the pianist as "Sunshine Charlie" onstage, an ironic reference to the way that Miller, like Sinatra himself, was a creature of the night and almost never awake during the daytime. Yet when Miller lost both his wife and his house in a mudslide in the Los Angeles hills, it was Sinatra who paid his hospital bills and bought him a new apartment. The two had a serious falling out in 1979. "He took me for granted and I took him for granted," the pianist told me in an interview in 1992. But Miller was back at the piano bench in 1985 in time for the final phase of Sinatra's career.

Miller continued to work with Frank Sinatra Jr. after Sinatra's retirement in 1995 and his death three years later. He played on "That Face!," a new album released last month by Frank Sinatra Jr., and was on tour with him last week in Montreal. On July 1, he suffered from a broken hip and then from a heart attack following surgery. "He was sharp as a tack until the moment he died," as Sinatra Jr. told *Variety*'s Army Archerd, "When he was being wheeled into the operating room he said, 'Fly me to the moon.' This is a very dark hour for us all. We cried together."

(*The New York Sun*, 2006)

ROGER KELLAWAY (BORN 1939)

Roger Kellaway opened a recent late show at Mezzrow with "Don't Get Around Much Anymore." To a certain degree, this was an accurate instance of truth in advertising: his two-night stand was the first in-person appearance of the veteran pianist since 2019.

Yet in other aspects, it wasn't quite true. Mr. Kellaway was actively playing around the city and the world right up to the start of the pandemic and in the last 10 years, has continued to work prolifically as a musical director for singers. In that decade, he released three new albums as a leader—more than a majority of players of his generation—the most recent of which, *The Many Open Minds of Roger Kellaway*, came out in 2019, the year he turned 80.

Mr. Kellaway's appearance at the diminutive West Village club was enough of a big deal that both Thursday shows were completely jammed. The later show had 20-, 30-, and 40-something listeners, but the crowd for the 7:30 p.m. show were mostly older peeps who, like Mr. Kellaway himself, were veterans of the jazz piano scene of the 1970s and 1980s. Mr. Kellaway may be the last survivor of an era when legendary keyboardists were playing practically every night in the Village, long-departed colossi, such as Tommy Flanagan, Jimmie Rowles, Dave McKenna, Sir Roland Hanna, Hod O'Brien, and Harold Mabern. All were larger-than-life masters who split the difference between swing and bebop, could use modern harmonies and rhythms to enhance jazz standards, knew the whys and wherefores of personalizing a tune without distorting it.

At Mezzrow, Mr. Kellaway worked in a trio with bassist Jay Leonhart and drummer Dennis Mackrel, and explored different themes and sources throughout both sets. There were three themes by Duke Ellington, including a fast, quick-like-a-bunny rabbit-y romp through "Cottontail" (Ellington's most famous variation of "I Got Rhythm") and the second set opener, a lush, laid-back treatment of "Don't Get Around Much Anymore," rendered much more slowly and thoughtfully than usual. "Take the 'A' Train" was also rendered opulently, with exquisite descending phrases and a big, dramatic rolling tremolo. Somehow, I thought not of the current rat-ridden NYC subway but the plush, luxurious pullman car that transported the Ellington band from town to town in the 1930s.

There were also a pair of show tunes: The first set commenced with a brief but haunting "Try to Remember," performed unaccompanied, in which the central tune was revealed somewhat cryptically among classical flourishes—almost as if a pair of curtains were opening up to reveal the melody hidden underneath—or like someone literally trying to remember. Then, in the second set, he used a sequence of clarion-like notes to lead into a highly swinging reading of "If I Were a Bell" while Mr. Mackrel extracted bell-like tones from his cymbals.

But "If I Were a Bell" also ties into Miles Davis, who was heavily represented on Thursday with three numbers from the epic masterpiece *Kind of Blue*: "So What," in which he and Mr. Leonhart divided up the melody, with Mr. Kellaway playing the notes that connect to the title phrase; "Blue in Green" became a brilliant showpiece that actually presents the tune in a more clearly delineated fashion than the actual album; and "All Blues," which is somehow is a modal number, a waltz, and a blues all at once. The trio also gave us "Doxy," the jazz standard composed by Sonny Rollins (a variation on the Dixieland warhorse "Ja-Da") but introduced by Mr. Rollins with Davis's quintet and here, serving as a feature for Mr. Leonhart.

The first set ended with two beautiful, exotic tunes by the late Italian composer and conductor Ettore Stratta, "Pages of Life" and "Good Morning Bahia," the latter of which featured an eloquent, octave-driven solo by guest guitarist Roni Ben-Hur. Pat Philips, who put the evening together, is also producing an album of this music by this trio for the SmallsLIVE Living Master Series. (The album, *Roger Kellaway Live at Mezzrow*, was released in May 2024, just as this book was being edited.) Other musicians were in the house, including the veteran bassist Rufus Reid and piano guru Bill Charlap; clearly they were there to study Mr. Kellaway's musical lessons and fully fathom his very vivid demonstration that one never has to choose between exalting a melody and swinging it.

(*Slouching Towards Birdland*, Substack, 2023)

BILLY STRITCH (BORN 1962)

A line attributed to Artie Shaw about Lester Young, "You know, Lester played better clarinet than a lot of other guys who played better clarinet," comes to mind as I watch Billy Stritch, who has been playing this weekend at Birdland with his trio. To paraphrase, "Billy Stritch plays more jazz piano than a lot of other guys who play more jazz piano."

What I mean is that Mr. Stritch is known for a lot of things. He is primarily the musical director for virtually all the top divas, from Liza Minnelli to Marilyn Maye, and in Stephen Holden's memorable phrase is "the accompanist *du jour*," though that "*jour*" has lasted many decades. He's also an excellent pianist–singer and occasional songwriter in the tradition of Matt Dennis and Bobby Troup.

He has led his own vocal group, the late and much-missed Montgomery, Plant and Stritch, which followed the lead of The Manhattan Transfer and Lambert, Hendricks & Ross. In all these guises, he is also the primary torchbearer of the legacy of Mel Tormé. In fact, at least half the songs on his opening set on Friday evening had some connection to the late and legendary Mel.

Everything else aside, Mr. Stritch is a fabulous jazz piano player on a purely instrumental level or any other level. This year alone, I've heard him play for numerous singers; he shepherded an excellent Judy Garland centennial concert (which also honored Tormé's contribution to her legacy) and did a terrific tandem show with the inspired Gabrielle Stravelli. I can't remember the last time I heard Mr. Stritch just playing for himself, with his own group.

Mr. Stritch has the technique to play almost anything he wants, and more than most musicians who have worked so extensively in cabaret and musical theater, he is at heart—and on the surface—a jazz musician. At the start of every show, I find myself wanting him to do more of what we think jazz pianists are supposed to do: play a lot of superfast up-tempos and improvisations. Yet I invariably quickly settle into the groove with him. Mr. Stritch goes his own way, to use a line employed by the late Freddy Cole, and his show is an "invitation to relaxation" rather than a display of chops for its own sake.

Working with bassist Tom Hubbard and drummer Anthony Pinciotti, Mr. Stritch began the first set on Friday with two songs from the Tormé band book, Kenny Rankin's archetypical jazz waltz "Haven't We Met?" and "No Moon at All," which Tormé learned from the King Cole Trio (for whom it was written).

Apart from the Melvin connection, Mr. Stritch has also undertaken to advance the cause of two singer–songwriters of the 1970s; somehow, it's hip for jazz musicians to play Joni Mitchell or Tom Waits—as it should be—but not Barry Manilow or Peter Allen. Mr. Stritch makes an eloquent case for both. Mr. Manilow's *2:00 AM Paradise Cafe* served as half of a moody noir medley with Cy Coleman's "With Ev'ry Breath I Take." Later, he concocted a very moving mashup of two Allen songs that use the symbol of flight as a metaphor, "Fly Away" and "Planes."

Still another Stritch specialty is bossa nova, as heard on his excellent 1997 release, *Waters of March—The Brazilian Album*. Friday's set included "This Happy Madness," "If You Went Away," and a collage of "One Note Samba" with "Night and Day," Brazilian style. Along the way, he also delights in lesser-known songs by iconic songwriters, such as two comparatively obscure Gershwin Brothers gems, "I Was Doing All Right" and "Changing My Tune," and a sweet spot from a Jule Styne flop, "I Said It and I'm Glad."

Tune detective—that's another of the many hats that Billy Stritch wears. Throughout the first show at Birdland, he performed with even more warmth, ease, and charm than he did during his pandemic-era internet sessions, titled *Billy's Place*—also reflected in his latest solo album.

He encored on a cheerful note with "Life Is Good," a relatively recent song by Mr. Manilow, notably recorded by Dianne Schuur. Marty Panzer's lyrics include the memorable phrase "It's taken me so long to learn / That stories change, and pages turn." It ends with "The hurts don't last too long / Life is good, like a song." It was a beautiful note—and thought—to end on.

(*The New York Sun*, 2023)

TEDD FIRTH (BORN 1976)

During a Tedd Firth show at Birdland this week, I spotted the veteran singer Jane Scheckter in the house. Mr. Firth usually plays Birdland many times a month, almost always as the accompanist to some lucky singer. Yet this show was a rare opportunity for Mr. Firth to perform with his own trio as a featured attraction.

The presence of Ms. Scheckter reminded me that she was the first to pull my coattails to Mr. Firth; about 20 years ago, she called me—on a landline, no less—fairly bursting with enthusiasm over a pianist she claimed to have discovered. In fact, she described Mr. Firth as "the new Bill Charlap."

Notwithstanding that Mr. Charlap was then only about 35 and hardly finished with being the original Bill Charlap, she had a point: Mr. Firth was clearly a remarkable young pianist with formidable virtuosity, a deep harmonic sense, and swing for days. Whether he was serving as an accompanist or a soloist, he always played exactly enough, never overwhelming the listener with too many notes or alternatively, providing an overly passive and bland, skeletal background.

Over the past two decades, Mr. Firth has become the accompanist of choice for all the top singers in town. The side benefit of working with master storytellers, such as Marilyn Maye, Melissa Errico, Tom Wopat, and Brian Stokes Mitchell, to name less than a handful, is that the association has doubtlessly helped sharpen Mr. Firth's inherent sense of drama and narrative. Mr. Firth never just plays a song merely for the sake of playing a song: he's always telling a story, with plenty of tension, plot development, and comic relief along the way.

Mr. Firth's general attitude is that he's content to spend most of his time serving as a musical director for someone else and only rarely feels the desire to step into the spotlight. He has, in fact, recorded an album of his own, titled *Starting Now*; it is, as of yet, unreleased, but Mr. Firth offers downloads to anyone who asks. (I asked.)

At Birdland, he was among friends, starting with his bassist David Finck and drummer Mark McLean (for that matter, the whole house might be considered friends of Firth), and I counted at least half a dozen singers who have worked with him, among them Ms. Scheckter, Ms. Maye, Karen Oberlin, and the redoubtable Rex Reed.

The album and the Birdland show started with a rather remarkable harmonic construction that about halfway in—after Mr. Finck played his solo—turned out to be the 1926 jazz standard "Sunday." Few in the house recognized the incredibly catchy piece that followed in which the melody was essentially a line of five notes going up followed by another line of five notes going down. It was actually derived from a 1972 number by Stevie Wonder, "Superwoman (Where Were You When I Needed You)." Mr. Wonder's eight-minute track is effectively two complete songs joined together, and Mr. Firth and his trio soloed on what is more properly the second of them.

The next two songs, Harry Warren's "This Is Always" and the Gershwins' "For You, For Me, Forever More," were introduced in forgettable Hollywood musicals of the mid-1940s, but the former, in particular, became a jazz standard thanks to Charlie Parker.

"This Is Always" opens with a shimmering piano intro that recalls Erroll Garner on the 1947 Parker record, almost like he's setting it up for a singer or a horn to enter, but then, he plays the tune with a touch that, indeed, suggests that a second "voice" has taken over. He plays the first chorus in a haunting romantic style, then gets somewhat friskier in the second before Mr. Finck plays a whole chorus bowing arco (though he plucks pizzicato on the album).

What he did for Stevie Wonder, turning a soul ballad into a bop confection, he did for David Shire and Richard Maltby with "Starting Here, Starting Now," which may be the first time I've heard that title song from a 1977 Off-Broadway revue transformed into a jazz instrumental—albeit a lovely and lyrical one, prefaced by a really stunning, completely solo introduction that sets it up beautifully.

He introduced one piece by Mr. Finck, a lovely arrangement of Burt Bacharach's "Alfie," rendered sensitively as a bass solo. Mr. McLean shared an original composition, titled "Tango Palace," which wasn't an Argentine dance number but a zingy riff inspired by a coffee emporium at Toronto. (Clearly, there's enough new material here for a second CD—assuming that the first one ever gets released.) He also re-created Oscar Peterson's 1953 arrangement of the Burke and Van Heusen Oscar winner, "Swinging on a Star," playing from a transcription.

With Marilyn Maye in the house, we would have been disappointed if she hadn't taken the stage at least once, and she obliged with a brief Johnny Mercer montage of a ballad, "I Remember You," that morphed into a swinger, "That Old Black Magic." The trio wound up with a thunderous romp through "What a Little Moonlight Can Do," a playful tune if ever there was one.

After "This Is Always," Mr. Firth told the house, "They don't write 'em like that anymore." He acknowledged that this is sort of a cliché but in fact, it's true. Furthermore, as young as he still is, they don't make piano players like Tedd Firth anymore either.

(*The New York Sun*, 2023)

THE NEXT GENERATION (*PIANOFORTE MILLENIANUS*)

AARON DIEHL (BORN 1985)

Mary Lou Williams's *Zodiac Suite* may be the most important work of American music that virtually nobody has ever heard. Hopefully, after nearly 80 years, that situation will be corrected with the first complete studio recording (Mack Avenue) of Williams's 1945 masterpiece by the outstanding contemporary pianist Aaron Diehl and a full-on symphonic orchestra, The Knights, conducted by Eric Jacobsen.

On December 31, 1945, *Zodiac Suite* had its world premiere, with Williams leading an all-star jazz orchestra and string section in a Town Hall concert. That debut performance was informally recorded, and the acetates were only briefly issued in 1991 on a small collectors' label. Williams seems to have had neither the resources nor the inclination to produce a proper studio version. Later in life, Williams became a devout Catholic, and the notion of using her talent in the service of astrology might have seemed inappropriate.

It's indicative of Williams's place in American music that she dedicated the third movement of the work, "Gemini," to both Benny Goodman and Miles Davis; she's practically the only human being ever who was equally close to those two very disparate jazz icons. As composer and pianist, Williams looms large in both the swing and bebop eras, revered as an arranger for Goodman and Duke Ellington as well as Dizzy Gillespie, and as a mentor to such emerging modernists as Bud Powell and Thelonious Monk.

Williams first recorded the 12 movements with her trio before she collaborated with veteran arranger Milt Orent to produce a fully orchestral incarnation of the suite. She wasn't necessarily a true believer in the zodiac but realized that the 12 signs could provide the inspiration for a series of original compositions. She would dedicate each of the 12 pieces to important musician friends of hers born under each sign; the suite begins, for instance, with "Aries," for Ben Webster, who also performed at the concert, and Billie Holiday. "Aries" opens with a flute that suggests some sort of astrological or mythological creature skittering about the heavens. A romping, skipping melody is introduced; subsequently disappears; and eventually returns before the piece leads directly into "Taurus."

Mr. Diehl is a perfect choice to preside over this landmark recording; the 37-year-old has made a specialty of exploring the connections between jazz and European classical music, with emphasis on the works of John Lewis and Art Tatum. He launches "Taurus" with a dark and brooding piano solo; while this suite isn't primarily a concerto for keyboard, Williams certainly provided herself with sufficient spots for her own playing.

"Gemini" was inspired, she said, by the duality she perceived in her then husband, the trumpeter Harold "Shorty" Baker, who was "gentle and playful" most of the time but became a "real barrelhouse" when he was drinking. Appropriately, the piece changes moods and tempos from slow to fast and back again, showcasing clarinetist Evan Christopher along the way.

"Cancer" opens with atmospheric strings in a way that sounds noirishly erotic—much more effectively, in fact, than most movie music of the period—featuring Nicole Glover in the Webster role. Although both Webster and Williams were known for their work with Ellington, the suite doesn't sound like the Duke or any other jazz composer but has elements that suggest a knowledge of both Stravinsky and French impressionists, such as Debussy.

"Leo" contains a violin passage that leads into a descending phrase in a manner that's unlike anything else in the jazz tradition. The orchestra, deliberately, is a far cry from a jazz big band. Rather than the usual contingent of brass, reeds, and rhythm, The Knights here are essentially a chamber orchestra, with 11 strings, 7 horns (mostly classical woodwinds), and 3 featured jazz soloists. "Leo" opens with a marchlike fanfare that anticipates the music for *Star Wars* and *Indiana Jones* by John Williams (no relation).

"Scorpio" has a bolero-esque beat using mallets in a way that anticipates Ahmad Jamal's "Poinciana" as well as an exotic, Middle Eastern feel that suggests a jazzier version of the Chinese and Arab dances in Tchaikovsky's *Nutcracker Suite*.

Where "Capricorn" is somber, opening with heavy piano chords, "Aquarius," which was dedicated to Franklin D. Roosevelt and the rising Eartha Kitt—then a dancer in Katherine Dunham's troupe—is light and upbeat, making use of flutes and classical woodwinds. The concluding movement, "Pisces," includes lyrics and a vocal by soprano Mikaela Bennett.

The work as a whole effectively succeeds at transmuting jazz content and concepts into classical forms. Much like the 21st-century music of Maria Schneider, the piece uses the texture of jazz, as well as improvised solos, fitting them into a framework that transcends the dance-band and song-form models that were the dominant contexts for popular music at the time. As musicologist Andrew Homzy and other scholars have noted, the 12 pieces are mainly connected programmatically rather than by musical content, and yet in this excellent new recording, they hold together beautifully.

The strongest piece may be the jazziest: "Virgo," which begins and ends as a concerto for trumpet (Brandon Lee), in the tradition of showcases for, among others, Louis Armstrong, with passages spotlighting Mr. Diehl and bassist David Wong along the way. "Virgo" builds to a thrilling dramatic cadenza that illustrates brilliantly what jazz and classical music had been borrowing from each other for decades, even by 1945.

(*The Wall Street Journal*, 2023)

SULLIVAN FORTNER (BORN 1986)

Just how tall is Sullivan Fortner? It's difficult to tell with most piano players—you almost never see them fully standing up. Even when Mr. Fortner walks out of the green room and onto the bandstand, he's slightly hunched over, with the stance of a man much older than 35. At the same time, he seems to approach the piano, almost as if he's sneaking up to it, with a mischievous glint in his eye; he doesn't look like someone about to go to work but rather, like a kid anticipating playing with a "brand new choo-choo toy," as Nat Cole would have sung.

Sullivan Fortner, who just performed a memorable one-night, two-set stand at Dizzy's Club, has played on about a dozen albums in the recent pandemic era. Only one of them can be considered his own project, *Tea for Two*, an exceptional set of duets with the vibraphonist Kyle Athayde. The twosome set the tone with the album opener, a highly playful treatment of "The Way You Look Tonight," a tune usually taken a bit more seriously. In most of these duets, Mr. Fortner lets Mr. Athayde take the lead as far as the melody goes, but still, they divide up the fun fairly evenly.

"The Way You Look Tonight" starts with Jerome Kern's equally famous countermelody—a series of two-note phrases that rise progressively higher—which Mr. Fortner uses to set up Mr. Athayde's entrance with the central tune. Then they're off and running, first skewering the medley this way and that before getting into a harmonic romp that almost seems as much of a dance—the two players create a sensation of movement in physical space—as a purely sonic experience.

Indeed, those notions of playtime and terpsichore are so prevalent that the third number, "I Won't Dance," also by Jerome Kern, starts to seem ironic, even as they start to play it. Not dance? Ha, too late for that. Two bars into the tune, and they're already metaphorically dancing all over the floor.

In between, there's the album's most satisfying ballad, "I'll Be Seeing You," which starts with Mr. Athayde's poignant rendering of the verse in a way that suggests that he learned the song from Tony Bennett.

The sets at Dizzy's by Mr. Fortner and his trio, with bassist Tyrone Allen and drummer Kayvon Gordon, were also filled with wit and wonder. Among other selections, he played a blues medley of "Davidson County Blues" by DeFord Bailey, the first African American performer in the Grand Ole Opry, and his own "Nine Bar Tune." Somewhere in the mix, there was also Woody Shaw's "Organ Grinder," and he also offered an engaging mid-tempo "Confirmation" in honor of the birthday of modern jazz piano pioneer, Bud Powell.

The centerpiece has a French title—one that I shall not attempt to replicate here—inspired, he said, by his half-French girlfriend. Set in 3/4 time, it had the feeling of a 1950s film theme that could have been written by John Lewis and played by the Modern Jazz Quartet.

The album also includes two less frequently heard slices of Ellingtonia, the upbeat "Jump for Joy" and the tranquil "Warm Valley," and it gets most serious with highly intimate readings of Guy Woods's "My One and Only Love" and Jule Styne's "People." Each begins as a lovely solo—piano on the first, vibes on the second—before the other joins and transforms each into an even more beautiful duo.

At Dizzy's, Mr. Fortner concluded with Arlen's "My Shining Hour" and Monk's "Crepuscule with Nellie" before trailing off into a spontaneous mix of blues, boogie, and stride, which also segued between Ellington's "Things Ain't What They Used to Be" and the Warner Bros. cartoon theme, "Merrily We Roll Along." Such is the power of Sullivan Fortner that he can make us believe both of those opposing ideas at once.

(*The New York Sun*, 2022)

EMMET COHEN (BORN 1990)

You start with an "old French quadrille," which is an archaic dance form of the 19th century. First, you render it on the piano with a jaunty 2/4 beat and sparkling syncopations, and essentially, you have ragtime. If you start to play it in 4/4, still as a keyboard solo, then it becomes stride piano. You can then take the same piece and throw in a few somewhat polyphonic horns, and it's New Orleans jazz. Add more horns, and it's big-band swing. That's roughly the evolution of a folkloric melody into the early jazz standard "Tiger Rag" and then from there, into Duke Ellington's orchestral jazz masterpiece, "Braggin' in Brass."

More recently, the brilliant 32-year-old piano superstar Emmet Cohen has arranged his own piano trio version of that classic 1938 slice of Ellingtonia. In Mr. Cohen's treatment, you can hear every level of the work's evolution all at once; the ragtime, stride, Caribbean, and swing manifestations do not simply pass before your ears sequentially but simultaneously. "Braggin' in Brass" is not only served as a mini textbook of the evolution of American music but also an explosion of rhythm and harmony. Ellington used a technique for phrasing his tune that musicologist Gunther Schuller has identified as "hocketing," and Mr. Cohen translates this approach into purely pianist terms in a way that creates a distinct impression that the piano keys and pedals are somehow airborne and flying all over the room.

Emmet Cohen; Birdland; May 2, 2019

Even in a generation rich with outstanding 30-something piano prodigies, such as Sullivan Fortner, Jonathan Batiste, and Aaron Diehl—as well as the 19-year-old wunderkind Joey Alexander—Mr. Cohen is perhaps the most visible young keyboard headliner of the pandemic era. He has nine albums as a leader, of which the latest is *Future Stride* from last year.

Still, he is best known for his series of live streams, "Live from Emmet's Place," accessible on both his own website and YouTube, which are powered not only by his formidable skills as a musician but also his well-above-average affability as an engaging spieler and host. Mr. Cohen's big event is a twice-a-year "invitational" week at Birdland in which he and his remarkable trio, with bassist Yasushi Nakamura and drummer Kyle Poole, team up with a rotating variety of guest stars, singers, and soloists. (And yes, that's the same format as the "Emmet's Place" live streams.)

Tuesday started with Sheila Jordan, the veteran vocalist whose years of experience easily amount to the equal of all three young members of the trio put together. On Tuesday, there was no shortage of mock-familial banter between both of those extroverted personalities, Mr. Cohen and Ms. Jordan, who continually—but not seriously—addressed the pianist in the tone of a strict but loving grandmother. Three exceptional saxophonists, Miguel Zenón, Ruben Fox, and the storied master Houston Person as well as trumpeter Bruce Harris are all joining Mr. Cohen on various nights this week.

Perhaps it's part of the conjoined legacies of Dick Hyman and Bill Charlap that many younger pianists make a point to address the music's history; Mr. Cohen made a short speech in the late set about how a player has to be aware of where the music came from and how it evolved but also to be flexible with tradition. He illustrates that in a sequence of pieces, some of which are originals, such as the title track of *Future Stride*, some are imaginative recastings of standards and lesser-known works from jazz history, among them "Satin Doll" and "Pitter Patter Panther" from the Ellington band book, and some mix the two approaches. In "Spillin' the Tea," he takes "Tea for Two" and spills out the notes as if they were leaves at the bottom of a teacup, showing the connection between ragtime, stride, and Afro-Caribbean music—not to mention, tea.

The album features some highly original quintet pieces with trumpeter Marquis Hill and tenor sax headliner Melissa Aldana, but it's the trio numbers I came to hear. He starts with "Symphonic Raps," a 1928 piece recorded by Louis Armstrong and Earl "Fatha" Hines in Chicago, which he transforms into a stride tour de force. He makes the piece work for a trio—something that rarely works in stride, which is essentially a solo piano artform; he stays, admirably, in the stride idiom, resisting the urge to bop it up. Conversely, "Dardanella" is exquisitely lovely 1919 exotica, but here he takes us through a more modern passage in the center, achieving a wholly organic, intergenerational mashup.

There are also two songbook standards, an up-tempo "My Heart Stood Still" and a touching, heartfelt "Second Time Around," as well as a swinging treatment of the traditional Hebrew prayer, leavened with quotes from "Oop Bop Sh'Bam" and "Happy Birthday" in a minor key.

The late set ended with Birdland's Gianni Valente announcing that Sheila Jordan is returning to the club in November to celebrate her 94th birthday. I'll be there for that, and I only regret that I won't be for Mr. Cohen's in 2084.

(*The New York Sun*, 2022)

***

At 33, Emmet Cohen has time to play with—so much so that the pianist opened a 5-night, 10-show run at Birdland on Tuesday with the 1930 Vincent Youmans standard "Time on My Hands."

I'll wager that he first heard it from Ahmad Jamal. It's not that he emulated Jamal's two famous versions (in the studio in 1960 and live in 1961); the major tip-off was in the quote from "Rockin' in Rhythm," which Jamal plays right as he's about to go into the coda. Mr. Cohen inserted the same quote in the same spot.

The nod to Ahmad, if you'll forgive the rhyme, was highly appropriate. When Mr. Cohen first attracted my attention a few years ago, he struck me as the first young pianist since Bill Charlap to do something entirely new and notable with the traditional Great American Songbook.

Recently, with his mounting popularity—accelerated by his widely watched Monday-night live streams and his exuberant new trio, with bassist Phillip Norris and drummer Joe Farnsworth—Mr. Cohen is increasingly stepping into the well-shined shoes of the great headlining pianist–entertainers of an earlier era, such as Erroll Garner, George Shearing, and Jamal, who left us in April at the age of 92.

After transforming the Youmans ballad into a vigorous stomper, Mr. Cohen wanted to show that he has even more time at his disposal, so he launched into "Time After Time," which again seemed like truth in advertising, or at least a title to be taken literally. There was time and rhythm to spare, and as if to underscore that point, about a minute in, he tossed in the opening bars of "All God's Chillun Got Rhythm." "Time After Time" was another love song reworked as a powerful uptempo, but then before delivering the climax, he briefly dialed down the intensity and put the July Styne medley into 3/4 for a few lines.

Mr. Cohen's only original of the set, "Spillin' the Tea," which is also heard on his current album, *Uptown in Orbit*, was offered as a tribute to the ragtime and stride traditions, which flourished in Harlem, where Mr. Cohen resides and where he live streams "Emmet's Place." Yet rather than striving for strict authenticity in these early jazz piano idioms, he utilized them in a decidedly modern manner. Among other things, Mr. Cohen made full use of the bass and drums in a way that historical ragtime and stride performances rarely do, and he structured the piece in more of a contemporary context.

Having already given us multiple examples of time, he proceeded with another slice of Styne, "People" from *Funny Girl*, which followed in a relaxed, lightly Latin reading. Although Mr. Cohen mentioned Barbra Streisand in his intro, his treatment reminded me more of Nat King Cole's lesser-known 1964 single version—up to a point, at least.

That point arrived in the middle of a bass solo from Mr. Norris, when all of a sudden, the entire tune shifted into "Dardanella," a sample of World War I–era Tin Pan Alley mock–Middle Eastern mishegoss that Mr. Cohen plays on his 2020 album, *Future Stride*. Even more than "Time on My Hands," this is a nod to Ahmad—"Dardanella" becomes a Turkish twin to "Poinciana," featuring the Cohen Trio's own answer to Jamal's signature vamp.

The trio followed with two tunes by legendary pianists, "Thag's Dance" by Oscar Peterson, from the 1961 London House live sessions, and "I'll Keep Loving You" by Bud Powell. While plenty of pianists do the latter, almost no one after Peterson himself has recorded the former.

He then recast Burton Lane's "If This Isn't Love" into an impossibly fast bopper and concluded with Billy Strayhorn's "Satin Doll" as a romper that constitutes a mini miracle of keyboard choreography, utilizing stops and starts, unexpected pauses, rests, and breaks.

A generation ago, around the time Mr. Cohen was born, "Satin Doll" seemed overdone and was almost heard too often in jazz clubs; as the venerable Dan Morgenstern observed, it became sort of what "My Melancholy Baby" had been a generation or two prior to that. By treating the song with freshness, originality, and boundless imagination, Emmet Cohen shows us that there's a dance in the old doll yet.

(*The New York Sun*, 2023)

ISAIAH J. THOMPSON (BORN 1997)

In 2020, pianist Isaiah J. Thompson, then 23, made his first album as a leader, *The Music of Buddy Montgomery*. A few weeks ago in the spring of 2022, he made his debut as a working member of the John Pizzarelli Trio. In between these two points, he released his second album, *Composed in Colors*.

That first CD was all about soulfulness. Buddy Montgomery, the writer of all 10 tunes, was a brilliant vibraphonist, pianist, composer, and bandleader, who enjoyed the mixed blessing of being the younger brother and frequent collaborator of an all-time jazz icon, the great guitarist Wes Montgomery. Mr. Thompson shows how, in Buddy Montgomery's playing and writing for the Mastersounds and the Montgomery Brothers and under his own billing, he was a pioneer of the genre eventually known as soul jazz, which skillfully incorporated the legacies of rhythm and blues and gospel music.

The music Mr. Thompson hopefully continues to create with Mr. Pizzarelli is all about swing and in the classic Pizzarelli tradition, abundant humor. Mr. Pizzarelli has employed roughly half a dozen of the best keyboardists of our time, but this is the first time I was conscious of a player in the long history of this trio who was as much a collaborator as a sideman. Mr. Thompson gave this long-standing, high-flying contemporary swing-centric threesome, which costars the virtuoso bassist Dr. Michael Karn, an entirely different feel.

Mr. Thompson's new album, *Composed in Colors*, which costars bassist Christian McBride and two drummers alternating, Kenny Washington and Joe Farnsworth, is about something else entirely. At first glance, it seems to be a sampler of the most famous works of the most celebrated pianist–composers in all of jazz, starting with Billy Strayhorn's "Take the 'A' Train," Horace Silver's "Señor Blues," and Randy Weston's "Hi-Fly," then back to Strayhorn for "Chelsea Bridge." The set also includes two less widely played pieces by major jazz composers, Thelonious Monk's "Raise Four" and Cedar Walton's "Ojos de Rojos."

With some exceptions, Mr. Thompson does not radically alter these very familiar piano-centric standards. "Señor Blues" still opens with Silver's distinctive Latin vamp, though he plays the main melody with just the trio rather than a quintet. "Chelsea Bridge" is generally thought of as a rather complex composition, but Mr. Thompson plays it like a straightforward ballad, more romantic than rhapsodic. Usually, the ballad impulse is the last to mature for a young musician—particularly of the male gender—but Mr. Thompson is already a master.

Mr. Thompson has already won several key awards and placed second in the Thelonious Monk Competition in 2018. He's currently one of five finalists for the American Pianists Association Cole Porter Fellowship and as such, performed at Dizzy's on Wednesday evening in what was described as "a sneak preview" of the competition, which will take place in Indianapolis in April 2023. (PS: He won.)

Whereas the current album is mostly jazz standards, Mr. Thompson played two originals at Dizzy's. "Cakewalk Dilemma" was about man's relationship with his fellow man and was full of crashing dissonances and Monk-like chromaticisms. "A

Prayer," conversely, was about man's relationship with God and was played more slowly and spiritually with thoughtful spaces between the notes, so much so that it made me want to shout "Amen" when he was finished.

However, as a young musician, Mr. Thompson's greatest strength is neither romance nor reverence but rather, a sense of playfulness—which also makes him a perfect partner for Mr. Pizzarelli. It comes through all across the new album; "Raise Four," for instance, has Mr. Thompson and Mr. McBride chasing each other around Monk's famously minimal 12-bar blues. It's like two kids wrestling on the floor, and you never know who's going to end up on top.

The album opens with its shortest and most exciting track, and in fact, it's a railroad track for "Take the 'A' Train," which is described on the track listing as "featuring Kenny Washington." Mr. Thompson stresses with the secondary melody and only states the main theme near the end. In a nod to John Coltrane, it could be subtitled, "Chasing the 'A' Train." Mr. Thompson and Mr. Washington, using his snare drum and brushes, dart back and forth, then up and down all over what seems like a very fast-moving locomotive in a cinematic high-speed action thriller—in fact, Brad Pitt would be missing a good bet if he doesn't license it as the main title theme of the sequel to *Bullet Train*. Mr. Thompson and Mr. Washington bring it to a close with Mr. Washington's brushes emulating the sound of a railroad engine slowing down to a halt, reminiscent of another Ellington locomotive, "Daybreak Express."

"Take the 'A' Train"—which Duke Ellington always played at the start of every performance—is a perfect vehicle for a remarkable musician whose journey is just beginning.

(*The New York Sun*, 2022)

***

After a hearty meal, one is entitled to dessert. That's what it felt like on Thursday at Dizzy's when pianist Isaiah J. Thompson launched his latest album, *The Power of the Spirit*. Not that the rest of the meal was at all hard to swallow—it was more like eating cake rather than spinach, albeit more savory than sweet.

The opening tune, "The IT Department," is bright and buoyant, upbeat and optimistic, and goes down very easily, especially as expressed by Mr. Thompson's tenor saxophone partner, Julian Lee. If Mr. Thompson makes one mistake regarding the song, it's in the title—"IT" refers to his initials, yet the tune is so profoundly soulful that it deserves a more spiritual and less technical title; I would have called it "The Department of Salvation" or some such.

The Power of the Spirit was recorded live over three sessions and three years at Dizzy's Club between 2020 and 2022, with Messrs. Thompson and Lee joined by bassist Philip Norris and TJ Reddick alternating on drums with Domo Branch. At Dizzy's, the bassist and drummer were Russell Hall and Miguel Russell, who is still too young to legally imbibe the adult beverages served at Dizzy's.

Messrs. Thompson and Lee are even tighter together live than on the album. This is an outstanding foursome that sounds like a real working quartet, with remarkable cohesion, rather than just four guys coming together for a gig. Mr. Lee, who kept reminding me, visually, of the actor Robin Hughes as "Brian O'Bannion" in the classic 1958 film *Auntie Mame*, is a formidable player, who also made a solid impression as a guest member of Toshiko Akiyoshi and the Jazz at Lincoln Center Orchestra last weekend.

Together, Messrs. Thompson and Lee connect with their elders and predecessors not only musically and intellectually but also spiritually. "For Phineas" is inspired by the larger-than-life Memphis-based pianist Phineas Newborn, and "Soul Messenger" is dedicated to Harold Mabern. The latter opens with a lovely lyrical rubato introduction, in which Mr. Hall bows arco; it lasts for almost two minutes and is practically a whole piece unto itself. Mr. Lee enters playing the main theme, which pivots around a phrase that some of us older folk remember Dizzy Gillespie chanting in "Manteca" as "I'll never go back to Georgia."

This is Mr. Thompson's third album, or fourth if you count *Live from @exuberance*, a two-song EP recorded when he was about 20 in 2018. *Spirit* is also his first album entirely of his own original music. The Dizzy's set included a few newer Thompson works, such as "Spring Flower," which incorporated a contemplative unaccompanied piano solo from the same garden as Ellington's and Strayhorn's extensive series of floral works, especially "The Single Petal of a Rose."

The title song, "Power of the Spirit," climaxed both the album and the Thursday night set. It illustrates how Mr. Thompson's music perfectly combines the three major ingredients of jazz, both philosophical and musical: the church, the dance hall, and the academy. "Power" is also prefaced by a dramatic out-of-tempo intro before we get to the meat of the piece, wherein the angular comping of Mr. Thompson behind Mr. Lee suggests the more religiously inclined playing of McCoy Tyner, even as the saxophonist builds to a high-note epiphany.

After "The Power of the Spirit," the whole house was uplifted and satiated, but this is a very young quartet (Messrs. Russell, Thompson, Lee, and Hall are 20, 25, 27, and 29, respectively) with energy to spare. In what was apparently a genuinely unplanned encore, Mr. Thompson returned to the stage alone and played a haunting interpretation of "These Foolish Things (Remind Me of You)."

This particular foolish thing reminded me of Mr. Thompson's ongoing association with John Pizzarelli, who sings a wonderful version of that 1936 British standard. Mr. Thompson's solo version incorporated aspects of both Thelonious Monk and Art Tatum, two iconic pianists who don't sound even remotely like each other.

We were already on our feet cheering well before the encore even started. It was like walking out of church, feeling all sanctified and holy, and discovering an ice-cream truck parked directly in front.

(*The New York Sun*, 2023)

JOEY ALEXANDER (BORN 2003)

I have no doubt that Joey Alexander is looking forward to his 20th birthday this June because when that happens, it will no longer be proper for the rest of us to think of him as a tween or a teen prodigy.

When he first emerged about eight years ago, he was the easiest kind of musician to listen to. Who doesn't love a 12-year-old jazz or classical virtuoso? Even people who don't know the first thing about jazz or couldn't find Birdland on a map were clamoring to hear Joey Alexander. It was clear that this very young man was something extraordinary, a tiny boy from Indonesia who was playing with the technical skill level of a storied master at least three times his age.

As Mr. Alexander evolved as a player, he went in a wholly opposite direction. If a wunderkind is the easiest musician to appreciate, the hardest is a working jazz pianist who plays mostly his own originals, especially if those originals are truly original, new melodies and harmonies that no one's ever heard before, not just familiar variations on blues and standard changes.

In short, Mr. Alexander went from being a "no-brainer" to, well, a brainer. There was a period when it seemed he was determined to make his listeners really work at understanding him, to make it clear to both us and him that he was determined not to coast on his boy-wonder status.

I've heard Mr. Alexander about 10 times since his 2015 breakthrough, at least three in the last year, and he truly gets better every time. His opening set at Birdland on Tuesday night was so strong that after slipping down below to the theater for 90

Joey Alexander; Webster Hall; Winter Jazz Festival; January 10, 2020

minutes of Vince Giordano and the Nighthawks, I crept back up the stairs to catch as much as I could of Mr. Alexander's late show.

At 19, Mr. Alexander is increasingly emerging as an outstanding voice as a player, a bandleader, and a composer. His Birdland set consisted of music mostly from his two most recent releases, *Warna* (2020) and *Origin* (2022), the latter being his first album entirely of originals.

Working with bassist Kris Funn and drummer John Davis, Mr. Alexander opened with "'Tis a Prayer," a lovely piece that's both evocative and invocative, the mood of which suggests saying grace before a meal or a chant as a kind of a prelude. It's kind of surprising that "Prayer" is the second-to-last tune on *Warna*, as it really sounds like the beginning of something.

He followed with "Mosaic (of Beauty)," in which, like everything else in his current set, the technical ability involved becomes strictly secondary—more important is the feeling of warmth he has learned how to instill in every tune, both as writer and performer. All of both sets were completely wrapped in a rapturous glow, whether the tunes were fast or slow; sad or happy; or as usual, somewhere in between.

"Angel Eyes"—and yes, I wish he'd chosen a title that wasn't already attached to a major jazz standard—boasts a romantic, tranquil melody that is propelled by insistent drumming (Mr. Davis at Birdland and Kendrick Scott on the *Origin* album). "Remembering" started very slowly and quietly on Tuesday, but even as it grew louder, faster, and more intense, it displayed incredible heart. Everything he played was soulful and intellectual in equal parts.

He interrupted the program of originals for a deeply moving reading of "I Can't Make You Love Me," incorporating chords from church music and a halting phrasing. He delineated Bonnie Raitt's melody with an earnestness and simplicity that made it seem very vocal, almost as if it were being sung rather than played. This hasn't been on any of Mr. Alexander's six albums thus far, but I surely hope it's on the seventh.

He wound up the early set with two more originals, "Bali" (from his 2017 *Eclipse*), in which he, the bass, and the drummer seemed to be playing three different sets of rhythmic patterns that coalesced more and more the longer the piece went on. "Warna" (meaning "calm") set up another exotic beat—it kept seeming like it was about to shift into a clave grove.

"Warna" also incorporated a drum solo that was treated organically, like a piece of the actual composition and not like the usual show-stopping, showboating drum solo. In fact, Mr. Alexander brilliantly set up Mr. Davis's star turn here.

The late set included two more exceptionally beautiful standards, "'Round Midnight" and "You Don't Know What Love Is," done as a duo with Mr. Funn. Yet no matter what he's playing or who wrote it, he's successfully avoided the trap that befalls many present and past prodigies in that he never places too much emphasis on sheer chops. There's always plenty of soul and smarts too. This is music that he—and all of us—can grow old with.

(*The New York Sun*, 2023)

INDEX

Page references for figures are italicized.

Abadey, Kush, 165
Abdullah Ibrahim: A Brother with Perfect Timing (documentary film), 159
Abdullah Ibrahim: A Celebration (Ibrahim), 159
Abdul-Malik, Ahmed, 49
Abrams, Muhal Richard, 153–56, *154*
Across the Crystal Sea (Pérez), 146
"Actual Proof," 197
Adderley, Cannonball, 49, 57, 68, 93, 220, 221
"African Magic," 158
African Magic (Ibrahim), 157–58
African Rhythms Trio, 149, 151
African Rhythms (Weston), 152
African Suite (Ibrahim), 164
"African Village," 111
"Afrisong," 155
Afrisong (Abrams), 154–56
"Aftermath, The," 66, 67
After Midnight (Cole), 25, 212
"Afternoon in Paris," 219
"After You've Gone," 188
"Ah-Leu-Cha," 127
"Ain't Misbehavin'," 4, 8, 9, 120
"Air Mail Special," 144
Akinmusire, Ambrose, 198, 199
Akiyoshi, Toshiko, 137–39, 256
Alatrash, Naseem, 146
Aldana, Melissa, 165, 166, 252
Alemanno, Luca, 170
Alexander, Joey, *257,* 257–58
Alexander, Monty, 67, 73, 128, 139–46, *140,* 169, 202
"Alfie," 98, 245
"Alice in Wonderland," 100, 180, 181
"All American Rhythm Section," 19
"All Blues," 101, 106, 242
Allen, Carl, 206, 207, 208
Allen, Geri, 125, *126,* 126–30
Allen, Harry, 86
Allen, Mount, Jr., 130
Allen, Peter, 243
Allen, Tyrone, 249
"All God's Chillun Got Rhythm," 253
"All I Want," 198
"All of No Man's Land Is Ours," 131
"All of You," 68, 100, 193, 206
"All or Nothing at All," 77
"All the Things You Are," 237
"Alone Together," 75d, 144
"Along Came Betty," 171
Amarcord Nino Rota (Byard), 127
Ambrose, Bert, 56
Ammons, Albert, 27
"Amogelang," 165

Anderson, Reid, 222–24
"Andrew," 129–30
"And So It Goes," 190
"Angel Eyes," 258
"Another Hair-Do," 127
Anthony, Michael, 30
"Anu Anu," 151
Apex Club Band, 15
Applebaum, Larry, 48
"April in Paris," 46, 234
Archer, Vicente, 132
"Aren't You Glad You're You," 234
"Aries," 248
Arkestra Bembe, 202
"Arkestra Boogaloo," 202–3
Arlen, Harold, 22, 212, 232, 234, 250
Armstrong, Louis: bandleaders loved by, 67; bands of, 16, 17, 43; collaborations, 15; Hines songs featuring, 14; as influence, 85, 227, 249; personal memorabilia exhibitions, 131; songs of, 2, 226, 252; style comparisons, 2, 9; style descriptions, 25
Asante (Tyner), 113, 114
"Ascension," 110
Ashanti (Debriani), 202
Ashby, Irving, 4, 23, 31, 34
Asherie, Ehud, 86
"As Long as I Live," 22
"As Time Goes By," 145
Athayde, Kyle, 249
"At the Hop," 225
At the Piano (Waller), 3–9
"Aura," 102
Austin, Chris, 159
Autry, Herman, 5, 8–9
"Autumn Leaves," 92
"Autumn Serenade," 77
Avakian, George, 37, 38
Avenel, Jean-Jacques, 50, 51
Avery Fisher Hall, 60
"Awakened Heart," 189
"Awful Coffee," 123
Ayler, Albert, 132

"Baby Plays Around," 173
"Baby's in Black," 175
Back in the Saddle Again (Pizzarelli, B.), 144
Back on the Block (Jones, Q.), 172
"Backward Country Boy Blues," 13
Bad Plus, The, 222–24
Badrena, Manolo, 63, 65
Bailey, DeFord, 250
Bailey, Mildred, 239, 240
Baker, Chet, 48, 62
Baker, Harold "Shorty," 44, 248
"Bali," 258
Ball, Kenny, 175
Ballard, Jeff, 91–92, 173
Balliett, Whitney, 216
"Ballin' the Jack," 131
"Balm in Gilead," 190
"Ba-Lue Bolivar B-Lues-Are," 208
"Banana Boat Song," 141
Band of a Thousand Melodies, 239
"Barbados," 77, 94
Barnet, Charlie, 240
Barron, Bill, 80
Barron, Kenny, 73, 78, 79–81, 217, 218, 219
Bartz, Gary, 111, 113, 114
Basie, William "Count," 6–7, 18–23 , *19*, 24, 145, 153
Bates, Chris, 131
Bauer, Billy, 90
Beatles, 174–76, 209
"Beatrice," 185
"Bebah," 172–73
"Begin Again," 189
"Begin the Beguine," 28
Beiderbecke, Bix, 163
Belafonte, Harry, 24, 90, 141
Bell, Aaron, 13
Bell le Pere, Zwelakhe-Duma, 165
Beloved of the Sky (Rosnes), 208
"Bemsha Swing," 46, 51, 76
Benedetti, Dean, 95
Ben-Hur, Roni, 242
Benjamin, Sathima Bea, 159, 160, 162–63
Bennett, Mikaela, 248
Bennett, "Powda," 141
Bennett, Tony, 28, 100, 142, 145, 233
Berigan, Bunny, 5
Berlin, Irving, 8, 182, 184

Bernhoft, Eric, 231–32
Bernstein, Leonard, 62, 100, 192, 232, 233, 234–36
Bernstein, Peter, 58
"Bess, You Is My Woman Now," 85
Best, Denzil, 38, 57, 59
Betsch, John, 50
Better Git It in Your Soul (Gabbard), 12
Beyond Words (McFerrin), 179
"Big Brass," 65
"Big Foot," 92–93
Bill Evans Album, The, 98
Bill Evans Trio, 95–96, 98, 99, 100–101
"Billie's Bounce," 94
Billy Childs Quartet, 198–99
Billy's Place (Stritch), 243
Billy Taylor with Four Flutes, 109
"Bird Feathers," 79
"Birdland," 221
Black, Brown, and Blue (Reed), 169–71
"Black, Brown, and Blue," 170
"Black Christ of the Andes, The," 44
"Black Coffee," 44
Black Narcissus (A Tribute to Joe Henderson) (Iyer), 124
"Black Nile," 184
Blade, Brian, 195, 198
Blake, Alex, 149, 151
Blake, Eubie, 131, 132
Blake, Ron, 171, 172
Blake, Seamus, 169
Blake, William, 190
Blakey, Art: bands and band members, 104, 105, 159, 171, 220, 221; as influence, 171, 220; recordings dedicated to, 167; songs of, 216; style descriptions, 167;
"Blame It on My Youth," 41
Blanchard, Terence, 132
Blanton, Jimmy, 14
Bley, Carla, 122–23
Bloom, Jane Ira, 185
Blue, T. K., 152, 203
Blue Devils, 20
"Blue in Green," 242
"Blue Monk," 46, 49, 146, 151, 179, 185
"Blue Plate Special," 42
"Blue Rondo a la Turk," 60
"Blues for Big Scotia," 32
"Blues for Billy," 202
"Blues for M," 156
"Blue Skies," 44, 174
Boccato, Rogério, 207
"Body and Soul," 28, 105, 145
"Boo Boo's Birthday," 182, 186
"Boogie Woogie on St. Louis Blues," 16
Bop Redux (Jones, H.), 73
"Boran Xam Xam," 151
"Borderick," 94
Borodin, Alexander, 123
Bossas and Ballads (Barron and Getz), 80
Bourgeois, Charles, xv, 118
"Boy in the Boat, The," 8
Brachfeld, Andrea, 203
"Braggin' in Brass," 250
Brahms, Johannes, 41
Branch, Domo, 255
Brand, Dollar. *See* Ibrahim, Abdullah
"Breath by Breath," 189
Breath by Breath (Hersch), 189–90
Brecker, Michael, 75
"Bright Mississippi," 143
"Brilliant Corners," 145
Brooks, Cedric IM, 141
Brown, Clifford, 173
Brown, Donald, 169, 200
Brown, Jason, 145
Brown, Ray, *29,* 32, 33, 34, 73, 140, 216
"Brownie Speaks," 173
Brubeck, Dave, 7, 30, 60–63, *61,* 89, 96, 193
Brubeck, Howard, 62
Buckner, Milt, 57
Bud Plays Bird (Powell), 92–95
Bullock, Beldon, 157, 161
Burke, Johnny, 245
Burrell, Kenny, 111
Burton, Gary, 199
Bushell, Garvin, 7
Bushkin, Joe, 75
"But Beautiful," 178
But Beautiful (Getz and Evans, B.), 97
"But Not for Me," 85
"Buzzy," 93, 97
Byard, Jaki, 127

"Bye-Ya," 49
"By Strauss," 86

Cables, George, xvi, 118–19, 120, 169
Caesar, Irving, 87
"Cakewalk Dilemma," 254
Calhoun, Eddie, 38
Callaway, Ann Hampton, 203
"Calypso Blues," 24
Cammack, James, 63, 65
Canadiana Suite (Peterson, O.), 32
"Cancer," 248
Cannon, Gerald, 111
"Cantaloupe Island," 196, 198
"Can't Help Falling in Love," 209
Canvas (Glasper), 132
"Capricious," 107
"Capricorn," 248
"Caravan," 13, 40, 151
Carew, Benny, 72
Carlini, Charles, 201
Carrington, Terri Lynn, 14
Carroll, Barbara, 191, 231, 232–33
Carter, Benny, 4, 60, 65, 124
Carter, Regina, 81
Carter, Ron, 81, 92, 114, 139
"Casablanca," 145
Casey, Al, 5, 9
Cedar!, 105, 106
Cedar Chest, 103
Celebration, A (Ibrahim), 160, 161
Chamber Music of the New Jazz (Jamal), 64
Chambers, Joe, 169
"Chameleon," 198
Change Is Gonna Come, A (O'Connell), 202
"Change Partners," 182
"Changing My Tune," 243
"Chariots of Fire," 223
Charlap, Bill: arrangements, 207; band members, 232; on Cole, N. K., 31; on great jazz, 32; as influence, 203; influences on, 58; marriage, 58; performances, 58, 180, 185, 200, 228, 232–34, *233,* 237; on Peterson, O., 30, 31; recording partnerships, 133; recordings, 232, 233, 234–36, 237; on Shearing legacy, 58, 59; style comparisons, 133
Charlap, Mark "Moose," 235
Charles, Etienne, 202
Charles, Ray, 48, 175
"Chasin' the Trane," 110
"Chelsea Bridge," 254
"Cherokee," 94, 137
Cherry, Don, 158
Chestnut, Cyrus, 191, 209–10
"Child Is Born, A," 200
Childs, Billy, 198–99
Christian, Charlie, 45, 144
Christopher, Evan, 228, 248
Cinelu, Mino, 80
Circle, 177, 179
"C-Jam Blues," 145
"Clair de lune," 41
Clarke, Kenny, 45, 214
Clarke, Neil, 149, 151, 153
Classical Jazz Quartet, 80–81
Classic Earl Hines Sessions 1928-1945 (Hines), 17
Classic Quartet, The (Monk), 52–53
Clayton, Gerald, 120
Clayton, John, *19*
"Clockwise," 105, 106
"Clothed Woman," 142
Club House (Gordon, D.), 169
Cobb, Jimmy, 126, 127
Cohen, Emmet, 250–53, *251*
Colaiuta, Vinnie, 198
Cole, Eddie, 24
Cole, Freddy, 33–34, 58, 59
Cole, Nat King: collaborations, 57, 59; as influence, 24, 31, 35, 90, 105, 143; influences on, 8, 15, 18; musicians working for, 240; parody impersonations, 39; songs of, 15, 41, 43, 144, 145, 191, 192; style comparisons, 253; style descriptions, 23–26, 31, 57; trio ensembles, 8, 23–26, 31, 33–35, 90, 211–13, 243
Coleman, Cy, 243
Coleman, Ornette: collaborations, 99, 126, 130; free jazz definitions, 51, 120; as influence, 167; songs of, 224; style

comparisons, 91, 123; venue acoustic issues, 62
Coleman, Steve, 126, 128
Cole Porter in a Modern Mood (Weston), 149
Colley, Scott, 198
Coltrane, John: collaborations, 47–50, 60, 62, 75, 103, 110, 112; as influence, 164; influences on, 64; musicians recording with, 7, 111; performances, 47–50; recordings, 99, 103; songs of, 111, 164, 169, 255; style comparisons, 209; style descriptions, 110
"Come Down to Earth, My Angel," 4
"Come Fly with Me," 143
"Come Sunday," 142
"Come to Baby Do," 24
Comin' on Strong (Moody), 80
Complete Blue Note Recordings (Monk), 51
Complete Capitol Recordings of the King Cole Trio, The, 35
Complete Concert by the Sea (Garner), 38
Complete Village Vanguard Recordings, 1961, The (Evans, B.), 99
Composed in Colors (Thompson, I. J.), 254
"Conception," 56, 59
"Concert by the Sea," 30
Concert by the Sea (Garner), 37–38
Concierto de Aranjuez (Alexander, M.), 145
Concorde (Modern Jazz Quartet), 217–18
Concrete Jungle (Alexander, M.), 142
"Confirmation," 94–95, 185, 250
Consecration (Evans, B.), 98
"Consolation (A Folk Song)," 187
"Cool," 236
Cool World, The (Gillespie), 80
Corea, Chick, 133, 177–81, 199, 202, 220, 234
Cosmos (Tyner), 113
"Cottontail," 241
Countdown: Time in Outer Space (Brubeck, D.), 61
Cox, Anthony, 128, 129–30
Cranshaw, Bob, 124
Crazy Rhythm: Exploring George Gershwin (Zeitlin), 86–87
"Crazy Rhythm," 87
"Crepuscule with Nellie," 49, 250
Cristalida (Pérez), 146–47
Crosby Street String Quartet, 188–90
"Crystal Silence," 199
"Cupbearers, The," 203
Cyntje, Reginald, 131
Cyrille, Andrew, 128, 129–30
Cyrus Plays Elvis (Chestnut), 209–10

Dahlander, Bert, 84, 85, 86
Dallas, Sonny, 90
Dameron, Tadd, 75
Dance, Stanley, 15
"Dance of Shiva," 199
Dance of the Infidels: A Portrait of Bud Powell (Paudras), 96
"Dancers in Love," 13
"D and V," 130
"Danny Boy," 28
"Dardanella," 252, 253
"Darktown Strutters Ball, The," 131
"Darn That Dream," 107
Daughtry, David, 170
"Davidson Country Blues," 250
Davila, Jose, 131
Davis, John, 258
Davis, Miles: band members of, 177, 195, 220; collaborations, 47, 48, 49, 60, 62, 103; Ellington recording criticism, 14; as influence, 102, 200, 220; influences on, 64, 67–68; on MJQ dignity, 215; musicians playing with, 99, 193; as performance theme, 241; quintet ensembles, 47, 97; recordings, 48, 49, 56, 60, 87, 98, 99, 101, 103, 200; songs dedicated to, 247; songs of, 12, 56, 173, 201, 206; style descriptions, 7, 106
Davis, Steve, 120
"Daybreak Express," 255
"Day In and Day Out," 145
"Day in Dubrovnik, A," 218
"Day in the Life, A," 174
"Dead Man Blues," 2
Dear Erich (Rosenthal), 203
"Dear Ruth," 104
De Barros, Paul, 96–97
Debriani, Santi, 202

"Deception," 56
DeFellita, Raymond, 4
DeFranco, Buddy, 31
DeJohnette, Jack, 178–79, 190, 191–92, 193
Dekker, Thomas, 176
"Delaunay's Dilemma," 219
"Delfeayo's Dilemma," 169
"Desafinado," 178
Desmond, Paul, 60, 61, 62
"Detour Ahead," 100
"Devilette," 169
"Devil's in My Den, The," 67
"Dewey Square," 95
Dial, Harry, 5
Dialogues for Jazz Combo and Orchestra (Brubeck, H.), 62
Diehl, Aaron, 217, 219, 248–49
Dillard, Stacy, 169
Dionyso, Arrington de, 121
Dizzy Gillespie Orchestra, 48, 214
Dizzy in Hollywood (Gillespie), 80
"Django," 215, 218, 219
Doggett, Bill, 7
"Dolores," 221
Dolphy, Eric, 128, 129
"Don't," 209
"Don't Be Cruel," 209
"Don't Get Around Much Anymore," 241
"Don't Let It Bother You," 5
Dorham, Kenny, 105, 139, 201
Dorsey, Tommy, 5, 43, 96, 240
Douglas, Dave, 50, 153
Douglas, Dezron, 170
"Doxy," 242
"Drifting on a Reed," 92, 93
Dubin, Al, 6
"Duke, The," 60
Duke Ellington and John Coltrane (Ellington and Coltrane), 12
Duke Ellington Presents the Dollar Brand Trio (Ibrahim), 160
Dunbar, Ted, 114
"Dusk," 90
Duvivier, George, 93, 94
Dyer, Bokani, 164–66
Dyer, Sibusisiwe, 165
Dyer, Steve, 165, 166
Dylan, Bob, 174, 209
Dzurinko, Virg, 89, 91

Earl Hines Collection, The (Hines, E.), 16
Early Wayne (Zeitlin), 87
Eastern Rebellion, 104
"Ebony Rhapsody," 228
"E-Bop," 167
Eckstine, Billy, 15, 17, 18, 57
Eclipse (Alexander, J.), 258
Edwards, Jonathan, 49
Ekaya, 159, 160
Eldridge, Roy, 16, 43
Elektric Band, 177, 181
"Elementals," 61
Elias, Elaine, 173–74
Ellington, Duke: arrangers for, 44, 247; bandleading style, 153; as influence, 22–23, 76, 149, 152, 153, 157, 164; musician sponsorships, 160; piano teacher of, 108; recordings, 11–14; songs of, 38, 40, 78, 120, 142, 151, 164, 170, 188, 241, 250, 252, 255; style descriptions, 60, 157; theme appropriation accusations, 44
Ellis, Herb, *29*, 34
"Embraceable You," 85, 127, 228, 229
Emerald City Nights: Live at the Penthouse 1963-1964 (Jamal), 68
Emerald City Nights: Live at the Penthouse 1965-1966 (Jamal), 68
Emerald City Nights: Live at the Penthouse 1966-1968 (Jamal), 69
"Emily," 96, 98
"Enchanted," 58–59
"Enigma," 56
"Epistrophy," 46, 47, 49–50
"Eric," 128
Erini, 147
"Eronel," 51
Errico, Melissa, 244
Escalator over the Hill (Bley, C.), 122
Europe, James Reese, 130–32
"European Echoes," 91
Evans, Bill: death, 98; as influence, 181, 193; influences on, 58, 89; performances, 180; quintet ensembles,

97; recordings, 95, 180; reinterpretations of, 180–81; signature songs, 173; style comparisons, 132, 168, 208; style descriptions, 92, 163; successors of, 173
Evans, Gil, 1, 60, 65, 67
"EVC," 119
"Evermore," 208
Everybody Digs Bill Evans (Evans, B.), 100
Everybody Gets the Blues (Reed, E.), 171
"Everybody's Song But My Own," 208
"Everybody Wants to Rule the World," 223
"Every Day I Have the Blues," 208
"Everything Happens to Me," 203
"Evidence," 46, 48, 49, 168
"Exodus," 145
Expansions (Tyner), 113
Explorations (Evans, B.), 99
Extensions (Tyner), 113–14

Fain, Sammy, 180
"Faith Can Move Mountains," 145
"Falling Alice," 181
Farlow, Tal, 28
Farmer, Art, 171
Farnon, Robert, 57
Farnsworth, Joe, 105, 252, 254
Farrell, Joe, 181
"Fascinating Rhythm," 87
Fatha's Day: An Earl Hines Songbook (Hines), 14
Fats in Fact (Wright), 5
Fats Waller: Complete Recorded Works, Volumes One through Six (Waller, T.), 3
Fats Waller and his Rhythm: If You Got to Ask, You Ain't Got It (Waller, T.), 9
Feather, Leonard, 56, 58
Fedler, Nir, 172
Feinstein, Michael, 41, 178–79
Feldman, Victor, 200
Feldman, Zev, 68, 102
Ferber, Jody Redhage, 190
Finck, David, 244
"Firm Roots," 106, 107
Firth, Tedd, 243–45
Fisher, Fred, 7
Fishkin, Arnold, 90
Fitzgerald, Ella, 71, 72, 141
"500 Miles High," 178
Flanagan, Tommy, 80, 103
Fleck, Bela, 111
"Flee as a Bird," 132
"Fleurette Africaine (Little African Flower)," 13–14
Fly, 91–92
"Fly Away," 243
"Fly Me to the Moon," 39
"Footprints," 196
For All Time (Brubeck, D.), 60
Ford, Ricky, 160
Forever Returns, 178
"Forever Young," 204
For George, Cole and Duke (Zeitlin), 86
"For James," 132
For My Father (Jones, H.), 73, 76
"For No One," 175
"For Once in My Life," 175
"For Phineas," 256
"For Sentimental Reasons," 145
For Such a Time as This (Reed, E.), 171
"For the Grace of God," 76
Fortner, Sullivan, 249–50
"For You, For Me, Forever," 244
Foster, Al, 105
"Four in One," 50, 75
Fournier, Vernel, 86
Fourth Prelude, 185
Fox, Ruben, 251
Fraser, Dean, 141
Fred Hersch Trio, 188–90
Freefall (Barron, K.), 79, 81
Free Flying (Hersch), 185
Fresu, Paolo, 123
Frisell, Bill, 111
From the Dancehall to the Battlefield (Moran, J.), 131
"From This Moment On," 186
"Fronteras (Borders) Suite," 147
"Fungii Mama," 143
Funk, Larry, 239
Funn, Kris, 258
Further Explorations of Bill Evans (Corea, Motian and Gomez), 180–81
Fuschia Swing Song (Rivers), 185
Future Stride (Cohen), 251, 252, 253

Gabbard, Krin, 12
Gadd, Steve, 181
Gambarini, Roberta, 120
"G and B," 133
Garcia Esquivel, Juan, 178
Garner, Erroll: celebrity, xvi; death, 39; modern accessibility of, xviii; recordings, 37–38, 39–40; style comparisons, 16, 30, 79, 244, 253; style descriptions, 28, 37, 39, 76; tributes to, 30
Garvey, Marcus, 131
"Gemini," 247
George Shearing Quintet, 56, 58
Gershwin, George, 40–41, 83–87, 106, 127, 204, 228, 243, 244
Gershwin, Ira, 85, 86, 243, 244
Gershwin's World (Hancock), 127
"Get Out of Town," 188
Get Ready (Allen and Whittaker), 206
Getting Sentimental: Live at The Village Vanguard (Evans, B.), 95
"Getting Sentimental," 96
Getz, Stan, 60, 76, 80, 97, 98, 196
"Ghosts," 132
"Giant Steps," 103, 164
Giddins, Gary, 214
Gillespie, Dizzy: arrangers for, 247; homage songs to, 140; as influence, 18, 226; influences on, 45; on Jackson, Milt, 217; movement associations, 50; musicians playing with, 73, 80; performances, 48; philosophies, 152; recordings, 73, 80; songs of, 43–44, 97; style comparisons, 46; style descriptions, 18, 45
Giordano, Vince, 203, 231, 232
Gitler, Ira, 50, 110
Give (Bad Plus), 223
Glaser, Martha, 38–39
Glasper, Robert, 132–33
Glawischnig, Hans, 198
Gleason, Ralph, 18, 19–23
Glenn, Tyree, 38
"Glitter and Be Gay," 236, 237
"Gloria's Step," 99
"Glory of Love, The," 192
Glover, Nicole, 248
Glover, Savion, 111
"Go Ahead, Make My Day," 25
"God Bless the Child," 191, 193
Goines, Lincoln, 202
"Going Home," 119
"Goin' to Chicago," 24
Goldberg, Aaron, 198
"Golden Slumbers," 175–76
"Golden Striker, The," 218
Golson, Benny, 104, 110, 171
Goméz, Eddie, 101, 177–78, 180–81
"Gone with the Wind," 62
"Goodby J.D.," 30
Goodman, Benny: arrangers for, 247; cartoon recordings, 84; collaborations, 56; composers supported by, 44; musicians with, 83, 240; pianists for, 73; songs covered by, 21; songs dedicated to, 247
"Good Morning Bahia," 242
Goods, Richie, 171, 172
"Good to the Last Bop," 57
Gordon, Dexter, 96, 169
Gordon, Kayvon, 249
Gordon, Lorraine, 78, 79
Gordon, Max, 95
Gordon, Wycliffe, 167, 168
Goss, Carol, 116
Gould, Morton, 64
Grammy awards, xvii, 32, 143, 197
Grand Piano (Mintun), 231
Grand Reunion (Hines), 16
Grand Terrace, The, 15, 17
Granz, Norman, 31, 34, 35, 72, 138
Grappelli, Stephane, 56
Gravatt, Eric, 111
"Gravity's Pull," 184
Gray, George, 157, 158, 161
Gray, Wardell, 44
Green, Freddie, 19, 21, 22, 23
Green, Grant, 111
"Green Dolphin Street," 192
"Greensleeves," 110
Greer, Sonny, 22
Grenadier, Larry, 91–92
Gress, Drew, 182, 188
Griffin, Johnny, 48
"Groovin' High," 97

Groovin' High (Jones, H.), 73
Gross, Mark, 209
Guaraldi, Vince, 129
Guitars (Tyner), 110, 111
Guneyman, Meral, 142, 229
Guyton, Cleave, Jr., 163, 164

Hackett, Bobby, 220
Haden, Charlie, 73
"Half Step," 234
Hall, Darryl, 126
Hall, Jim, 180
Hall, Russell, 202, 255, 256
Hammann, Joyce, 190
Hammerstein, Oscar, 112, 204
Hancock, Herbie: influences on, 58; Miles band member, 220; performances, *195*, 195–98; recordings, 127; rock music reinterpretations, 197, 198, 209; songs of, 133, 202; style comparisons, 202; style descriptions, 195
"Handful of Keys, A," 4, 20
Handy, Craig, 202
Handy, W. C., 131, 168
Hank & Frank (Jones, H., and Wess), 76
"Happy Birthday," 252
"Happy Days Are Here Again," 59
Harburg, Yip, 8, 212
Hargrove, Roy, 120, 132, 145
Harlem Kingston Express, 143
Harper, Billy, 149, 153
Harris, Barry, 73, 77–79, 80, 251
Harris, "Little" Benny, 94
Harris, Mike, 95
Harris, Stefon, 81
Hart, Billy, 114
Hartman, Johnny, 15
Hasselgård, Stan, 44
"Haven't We Met?," 243
Hawkins, Coleman, 16, 48, 72
Hawkins, Seton, 166
Haymes, Joe, 8, 239
Hazeltine, David, 203
"Heartbreak Hotel," 209
"Heartsong," 189
Heath, Jimmy, 66, 105, 114
Heath, Percy, 213, 214, 215–16, 217–18
Heath Brothers Band, 216
Hebb, Bobby, 40
Hébert, John, 186
"Helen's Song," 119
Henderson, Eddie, 81
Henderson, Fletcher, 1, 115, 153
Henderson, Joe, 124
Hendricks, Jon, 149
Hentoff, Nat, 67, 215
"Here, There and Everywhere," 175
"Here's That Rainy Day," 135, 137, 237
"Her Look, Her Touch," 172
Herring, Vincent, 104, 105, 107
Hersch, Fred, 182–90, *183*
"He Said, She Said," 175
"Hesitating Blues," 131
Hicks, John, 14, 191
"Hi-Fly," 149, 153, 254
Higgins, Billy, 104
"High Wire," 40
Hill, Marquis, 252
Hilliard, Bob, 180
Hillman, Rod, 79
"Hindsight," 105
Hines, Earl "Fatha," 3, 14–18, 23, 153, 252
Hinton, Milt, 73
"Hip Hop," 123
Hiroshima—Rising From the Abyss (Akiyoshi), 139
"His Rhythm," 4
Hodges, Johnny, 16
Hoenig, Ari, 198
"Hogtown Blues," 32, 207
Holiday, Billie, 25, 47, 48, 201, 248
Holland, Dave, 195, 197–98
Holland, Peanuts, 97
Holmes, Johnny, 31
"Holy Land," 106
Homzy, Andrew, 248–49
"Honeysuckle Rose," 5–6, 8, 9, 17, 94, 117, 124, 228
Hooker, William, 121
"Hope," 139
Hopkins, Claude, 8
Horn, Shirley, 191, 233
Hot Fives, 2, 15, 226
"Hound Dog," 208, 210

"How Could You Do a Thing Like That to Me," 38
"How Deep Is the Ocean," 90, 184
"How Great Thou Art," 210
"How High the Moon," 94, 173
Hubbard, Freddy, 104, 105
Hubbard, Tom, 243
"Human Behavior," 223
"Humoresque," 28, 145
Hurt, John, 141
Hyams, Marjorie, 57, 59
Hyman, Dick, 3, 20, 141–42, 225–29, 235
"Hymn to the East," 155

"I. L. Y. B. D.," 172
"I Am the Walrus," 174–75
"I Am We Are I," 117
Ibrahim, Abdullah (*formerly* Dollar Brand): biographical information, 159–60; documentary films on, 159; performances, 156–57, *157;* philosophies, 158–59; recordings, 157–58, 159; songs dedicated to, 165; style comparisons, 128, 154, 155; style descriptions, 112, 128, 156, 157–58, 160
"I Can't Get Started," 137
"I Can't Make You Love Me," 258
"ICHN," 170
"I Cover the Waterfront," 228
"Idaho," 142
"I Didn't Know What Time It Was," 68
"I Don't Want to Be Kissed," 64
"I'd Rather Drink Muddy Water," 229
"I Fall in Love Too Easily," 185
If Bix Had Played Gershwin (Hyman), 227
"If Ever I Would Leave You," 186–87
"If I Could Be with You (One Hour Tonight)," 23
"If I Need Someone," 175
"If I Were a Bell," 200, 241
"If This Isn't Love," 253
"If You Went Away," 243
"I Get Along Without You Very Well," 233
"I Got It Bad," 170, 221
"I Got Rhythm," 85, 86, 94, 127, 241
"'I Got Rhythm' Variations," 41
"I Just Can't See for Lookin'," 143
"I Know That You Know," 28
"I'll Be Seeing You," 249
"I'll Keep Loving You," 253
"I'll Know," 237–38
"I'll Remember April," 38, 120, 228
"I'll Take Romance," 112
"I Loves You Porgy," 100
"I Love You," 96, 120
"I'm a Fool to Want You," 193
Images (Barron, K.), 81
I'm All for You (Jones, H., and Lovato), 74
"I'm Getting Sentimental Over You," 96
"I'm Glad There Is You," 66, 69
"I'm Gonna Laugh You Right Out of My Life," 191, 193–94
"I'm Lost," 59
"Impressions," 64
improvisation, 90, 124, 128, 230
"Improvisation 1," 111
"Improvisation 2," 111
Improvising Artists (IA), 115–16
"In a Little Spanish Town," 228
"In Appreciation," 127
"In a Sentimental Mood," 158, 164
"Infant Eyes," 170
"Infinite Flow, The," 155
Inner Urge (Henderson, J.), 124, 207
In Search Of (Jamal), 65
"Insensatez," 185
interplay, 9, 16, 22, 62, 184–85, 222, 233
interpretation, 124, 208–9
"In the Ghetto," 209
"In the Hall of the Mountain King," 145
"In the Land of Oo-Bla-Dee," 43–44
"Introspection," 51
"Intro/Waltz for Debby," 101
"In Your Own Sweet Way," 60, 96
Irby, Sherman, 67
"I Remember You," 245
"Iron Man," 223
Irwin, Dennis, 169
"I Said It and I'm Glad," 243
"I Saw Her Standing There," 175
"Ishmael," 160
"I Should Care," 46, 112
"Is It Really the Same?," 193

"Island in the Sun," 146
"It Could Happen to You," 203
"IT Department, The," 255
"It Might as Well Be Spring," 39
"It Never Entered My Mind," 163
"It's a Raggy Waltz," 61, 193
It's Magic (Jamal), 63
"It's Magic" (song), 91–92
"It's Only a Paper Moon," 211–12
"I've Got a Crush on You," 85–86
"I've Got You Under My Skin," 212
Iverson, Ethan, 222–24
"I Walk with Music," 233
"I Was Doing All Right," 243
"I Wish I Knew How It Would Feel to Be Free," 107, 109
"I Won't Dance," 249
Iyer, Vijay, 121–22, 124–25, *125*

"J. J.," 91
"Jabulani (Joy)," 158
Jackson, Milt, 32, 62, 140, 214, 215, 216, 217, 218
Jackson, Munyungo, 172
Jackson, Noah, 163, 164
Jacobsen, Eric, 247
"Ja-Da," 242
Jamal, Ahmad: biographical information, 64; death, 69, 253; as influence, 67, 191, 252; performances, 63, *64*, 65–67, 68–69; performance style, 63–64, 99; recordings, 63, 68; songs of, 124; style comparisons, 86, 248, 253; style descriptions, 63, 64–65, 67, 68
Jumbo Caribe (Barron, K.), 80
James, "Blackie," 141
James, Harry, 21, 240
"Janeology," 185
Jarrett, Keith, 190–94
Jazz Discography, The (Lord), 30, 38, 39, 80
Jazz Epistles, 159
Jazz from the Kennedy Center (radio show), 109
Jazz Live (radio show), 109
Jazz Masters Award, 109
Jazz Messengers, 104, 105, 171
Jazzmobile, 107, 131
Jazztet, 110
Jeffries, Herb, 17
"Jelly, Jelly," 18
"Jelly Roll Blues," 1
"Jerusalem," 190
"Jitterbug Waltz," 7, 227
Jobim, Antonio Carlos, 178, 185, 186, 201, 206
John Coltrane Quartet, 72, 111
"Johnny One Note," 68
John Pizzarelli Trio, 254
Johnson, Budd, 16, 17
Johnson, James P., 3, 6, 15, 23, 65
Johnson, Marc, 98
Johnson, Martin, 175
Johnson, Pete, 20, 21, 22
Jones, Elvin, 16, 72, 73, 124
Jones, Hank, xvi, 71–77, 78, 80, 118, 120–21
Jones, Philly Joe, 95
Jones, Quincy, 109, 172
Jones, Randy, 62
Jones, Sean, 67, 198, 199
Jones, Slick, 5, 6
Jones, Thad, 72, 73, 74, 200
Jones, Willie, III, 120, 169
Jordan, Louis, 139–40, 141
Jordan, Sheila, 251
"Joshua," 200
Journey, The (Ibrahim), 158
Joyous Encounter (Jones, H., and Lovato), 74
Juju (Shorter), 170
"Jump," 236
"Jump for Joy," 250
"Jumping with Symphony Sid," 104
"Just You, Just Me," 46

Kahn, Roger Wolfe, 87
Kaminsky, Max, 226
Karn, Michael, 254
Karnik, Aayushi, 171, 172
Katz, Dick, 121
Kay, Alex, 101
Kay, Connie, 214, 215, 217–18
Keenan, Norman, 19, 22, 23
"Keepin' Out of Mischief Now," 6
Keepnews, Orrin, 48, 99

Keezer, Geoffrey, 171–73
Keith Jarrett Trio, 190–92
Kellaway, Roger, 241–42
Kemp, Hal, 60
Kendrick, Rodney, 157
Kenton, Stan, 25, 153
Kern, Jerome, 249
"Kerry Dancers, The," 133
Kessel, Barney, 32, 34
Keys, Amy, 197, 198
Khepera (Weston), 151
Kids: Duets Live at Dizzy's Club Coca-Cola (Jones, H., and Lovato), 76, 77
Kind of Blue (Davis, M.), 48, 49, 98, 101, 103, 241
"Kinds of Love," 207
Kinds of Love (Rosnes), 207
King, David, 222–24
King, Pee Wee, 192
King, Teddi, 59
King and I (Rosenthal), 204
King Cole Trio, 8, 23–26, 31, 33–35, 90, 211–13, 243
King Cole Trio, The, 211, 212
King Cole Trio Volume One, The, 211
"King Porter Stomp," 2
Kirby, John, 72
Kirk, Andy, 43, 72
Kitchell, Sonya, 197
Kitchener, Lord, 140
"Kitch's Bebop Calypso," 140
Knights, The, 247–49
Koenigswarter, Pannonica de, 46, 78
"Ko-Ko," 94
Konitz, Lee, 61, 89, 90, 103
Kossi, Kristina, 201
Kostas, Vasilis, 146
Krachy, Charles, 91
Krall, Diana, 32
"Krotao - Crystal Clear," 163
Krupa, Gene, 72
Kuprel, Trevor, 66

LaBarbera, Joe, 98
Lacy, Steve, 50–51
"Lady Is a Tramp, The," 239
"Lady Luck," 74
"Lady Who Swings the Band, The," 43
LaFaro, Scott, 96, 98, 99, 173
Lage, Julian, 185
Lambert, Hendricks & Ross, 242
"Lamp is Low, The," 59
Lampkin, Chuck, 68
"La Muralla (Glass Walls)," 147
Lane, Burton, 8, 237, 253
"Lark, A," 184
"Last Night When We Were Young," 192
"La Strada," 127, 130
Latin Tinge, The, 104, 105
LaTouche, John, 77
Laubich, Arnold, 28
"Laugh, Cool Clown," 24
"Lazy Afternoon," 77, 155
Leali, Brad, 167
"Lean Baby," 32
"Lean on Me," 170
Lee, Brandon, 249
Lee, Julian, 255, 256
Legendary OKEH & Epic Sessions, The, 64
"Lennie's Blues," 90
"Leo," 248
Leonhart, Jay, 99, 142, 241–42
Lerner, Alan Jay, 237
"Lester Left Town," 221
L'Etoile, 231
"Let Our Garden Grow," 222, 224
"Let's Call the Whole Thing Off," 142
"Let's Call This," 51
Levant, Oscar, 40–42, 84
Levy, John, 57
Lewis, Chris, 170
Lewis, Herbie, 113
Lewis, Jerry Lee, 175
Lewis, John: collaborations, 62; ensembles of, 138, 213–19; as influence, 23, 199, 248; performances, *213,* 213–19; quartet ensembles, 213–19; style comparisons, 91, 206
Lewis, Meade Lux, 175
Lewis Nash, 81
"Liebestod," 41
"Liebesträume," 39
"Life Is Good," 243
Life of a Song, The (Allen, G.), 126

"Life on Mars," 176, 223
"Like Someone in Love," 78
"Like Sonny," 103
Lion, Alfred, 113
Lionel Hampton Jazz Festivals, 71, 74
Liston, Melba, 152
"Little Joe from Chicago," 43
"Little Lulu," 98
"Little Max (Parfait), A," 13
"Little Niles," 149
"Little Rascal on a Rock," 74
Little Richard, 175
"Little Sunflower," 105
Live at Yoshi's (Miller, M.), 200, 201
"Live from Emmet's Place" (live stream), 251, 253
Live from @exuberance (Thompson, I. J.), 256
"Liver of Life," 123
"Living Time," 65
"Liza," 83, 84, 228
Locke, Eddie, 228
Locke, Joe, 58
Loesser, Frank, 200
"Lohengrin," 137
"Lollipops and Roses," 68
Lombardo, Guy, 67
London Flat, London Sharp (Brubeck, D.), 63
London House Sessions, The (Peterson, O.), 32, 33, 253
"Lonely Town," 236
"Lonesome Road, The," 239
"Longest Blues in the World, The," 227
"Longravity," 105
Long Yellow Road (Akiyoshi), 139
Looking Out (Tyner and Santana), 111
Look Out for #1 (Brothers Johnson), 172
"Look Up," 144
Lord, Tom, 30, 38, 39, 80
"Lords of the West Indies," 140
Lost Chords, 122–23
Lovano, Joe, 73, 74–75, 76, 77, 120
"Love for Sale," 206
"Love in the Cemetery," 141
"Love Is Here to Stay," 85
Love Notes (Alexander, M.), 144–46
"Lover Man," 137, 229
"Love Supreme, A," 209
Lucas, Al, 84, 85–86
"Lucky to Be Me," 65
"Lullaby of Birdland," 30, 57, 58
"Lulu's Back in Town," 6
Lundy, Carmen, 127

Mabern, Harold, 73, 256
MacDowell, Al, 123
Mackrel, Dennis, 73, 241
"Mack the Knife," 142
Mad Hatter, The (Corea), 181
"Mad Hatter Rhapsody, The," 181
"Maiden Voyage," 133, 198, 202
"Make Me a Pallet on the Floor," 131
Malek, Farayi, 146
Malone, Russell, 120
Maltby, Richard, 245
"Mambo Carmel," 38
"Mambo Inn," 59
Mandel, Johnny, 96, 98, 189
"Mandy," 8–9
"Manha De Carnival," 139
Manhattan Transfer, 242
"Man I Love, The," 25, 39, 85, 87, 106
Manilow, Barry, 243
"Mannenberg Revisited," 161
Mantilla, Ray, 104, 105
Many Open Minds of Roger Kellaway, The (Kellaway), 241
"Mara," 189
"March of the Toys," 51
"Maria," 236
"Marie LaVeau," 81
Marley, Bob, 141, 142, 145
Marsalis, Wynton, 1, 2, 65, 67, 146, 169, 180, 221–22
Marsh, Warne, 89, 90, 91
Martin, Lois, 190
Martino, Pat, 111, 143, 144
"Mary Lou's Mass," 44
Mary Lou's Mass (Williams, M.L.), 127
Masekela, Hugh, 159
"M*A*S*H* Theme (Suicide Is Painless)," 96
Master Class on 32 Jazz, 73

"Master of the Game," 199
Matador (Green, G., and Tyner), 111
Mating Call, 75
"Maxwell's Silver Hammer," 175
May, Earl, 78
"Maybe I'm to Blame," 17
Maye, Marilyn, 203, 244, 245
Mays, Bill, 106
M-Base, 128
McBride, Christian, 207, 254, 255
McDonas, Thollem, 121
McDonough, John, 34
McFerrin, Bobby, 178–80
McIntosh, Tom, 203
McKibbon, Al, 59
McLean, Jackie, 206
McLean, Mark, 244
McPartland, Marian, 57, 73, 100, 109
McPherson, Eric, 186
"Meditations," 160
"Medu," 166
Mehldau, Brad, 173–76, 184–85
"Melchezedik," 126
"Melodrama," 66
Melton, James, 206
"Memories of You," 28
"Memphis Blues," 131
"Mercy, Mercy, Mercy," 221
"Merrily We Roll Along," 250
"Message from the Nile," 114
Meyer, Joseph, 87
"Midgets," 120
"Midnight Sun," 221
Mikkelborg, Palle, 101, 102
"Milano," 218
Miles Ahead (Jamal), 64
Miles Davis Quintet, 47, 97, 177
"Milestones," 100
Militello, Bobby, 62, 63
Miller, Bill, 239–40
Miller, Hal, 221
Miller, Johnny, 23, 212
Miller, Mulgrew, 200–201
"Mindif," 164
Mingus, Charles, 11, 12–13, 14, 138
"Minor Adjustments," 68
"Minor Moods," 68
Mintun, Peter, 229–32
"Mirror Image," 208
"Misterioso," 46, 81, 123, 137, 164, 182
"Mister Misterioso," 123
"Misty," 37, 39, 40
Mitchell, Blue, 143
Mitchell, Brian Stokes, 244
Mitchell, Joni, 197, 198, 209
Mitchell, Shedrick, 171, 172
"Miyako," 184
"Moanin'," 216
Mobius, 104
Mobley, Hank, 201
Modern Jazz Quartet (MJQ), 24, 199, 206, *213,* 213–19
Modern Windows Suite (Barron, B.), 80
"Modinha," 206
"Mona Lisa," 24
"Monday Date, A," 14
Money Jungle: Provacative in Blue (Carrington), 14
"Money Jungle," 12, 13
Money Jungle (Ellington), 11–14
Monk, Thelonious: associates, 109; biographical information, 45; Coltrane collaborations, 47–50; Ellington reaction to, 11; house pianist positions, 201; as influence, 76, 123, 143, 149, 153, 157, 160, 165, 256; influences on, 12, 16; Lacy playing music of, 50–52; mentors to, 247; performances, 78; recordings, 47–48, 52–53, 73, 182; reinterpretations of, 131, 146, 181, 182, 184, 185, 186, 190, 200; solo performance behaviors, 193; songs of, 81, 95, 137, 143, 145, 146, 164, 170, 171, 182, 184–85, 192, 200, 203, 208, 234, 250, 254, 255; style comparisons, 168; style descriptions, 45–46, 49, 50, 92, 113, 157; theme appropriation accusations, 44; tribute recordings, 93
"Monkey Mind," 188
Monk Legacy Septet, 51
"Monk's Dream," 51, 185, 200
"Monksiland," 50–51
"Monk's Mood," 49, 234
Monk's Music (Monk), 48

"Monopatia (Pathways)," 147
Montgomery, Buddy, 254
Montgomery, Wes, 57, 58–59, 60, 111, 144
"Mood Indigo," 237
Moody, James, 80
Moody and the Brass Figures (Moody), 80
Moody on Another Bag (Moody), 80
"Moody's Mood," 49
Mooney, Joe, 28
"Moon Love," 204
Moore, Alton, 4
Moore, Michael, 62, 95–96
Moore, Oscar, 23, 212, 228
Moore, Phil, 56–57
"Moose the Mooche," 94
Moran, Gayle, 181
Moran, Jason, 130–32, 133
Moreira, Airto, 177–78
Morell, Marty, 101
Morello, Joe, 60, 61
Morgan, "Calypso John," 141
Morgan, Lee, 104, 123, 169, 216
Morgan, Thomas, 218
Morgenstern, Dan, 9, 253
Morton, Jelly Roll, 1–3, 14, 146, 226
"Mosaic," 104
"Mosaic (of Beauty)," 258
Mosaic Select: McCoy Tyner, 112
Mosaic Select: Toshiko Akiyoshi, 139
Moten, Bennie, 19–20
Motherland (Pérez), 146
"Mother's Diaries," 139
Motian, Paul, 98, 99, 180–81, 218, 219
"Mountain, The," 161
"Move On," 165
Mr. Nostalgia, 229
Mr. Wilson and Mr. Gershwin (Wilson, T.), 83–86
"Mr. Jelly Lord," 146
Mraz, George, 73, 120
"M's Bedtime Blues," 172, 173
"M's Heart," 129
Mtume, 114
Mulligan, Gerry, 62, 107
"Mumbles," 14
Murray, David, 216
"Music Box Suite, The," 30
Music Makes Me (Zeitlin), 86
Music of Buddy Montgomery, The (Thompson, I. J.), 254
"Al-Musifir Blues," 147
"My Devotion," 79
Myers, Amina Claudine, 121
Myers, Marc, 108
My Fair Lady Loves Jazz (Taylor, B.), 109
"My Favorite Things," 111
"My Foolish Heart," 100, 119, 120
"My Funny Valentine," 39
"My Heart Belongs to Daddy," 168
"My Heart Stood Still," 78, 252
"My Melancholy Baby," 253
"My One and Only Love," 222, 250
"My Shining Hour," 250
"My Ship," 59, 106
"My Sweetie Went Away," 32

"Nagasuckle Rose," 56
Nahigian, Alan, 154
"Naima," 103, 170–71
Nakamura,Yasushi, 251
Nance, Ray, 11, 44
NARAS Lifetime Achievement Award, 32
"Narcissus," 28
"Nardis," 98
Nash, Lewis, 217, 219
Nash, Ted, 180
"National Anthem," 122
Nat King Cole Story, The (King Cole Trio), 212
"Nearest of You, The," 145
Nelson, Steve, 217, 218, 219
Newborn, Phineas, Jr., 209, 256
Newman, Fathead, 106
Newman, Jill, 120
"New Orleans Bump," 2
"New People, The," 156
"New Rhumba," 64
New York Seven, 167
New York Sketch Book (compilation), 139
"Nice Work If You Can Get It," 84–85
Nichols, Herbie, 170
"Night and Day," 40, 124–25, 212, 243
Night and the Music (Hersch), 182
Nighthawks, 231

"Nightingale Sang in Berkeley Square, A," 106
"Night Song," 139
"Nine Bar Tune," 250
"1979 Semi-Finalist," 224
Nkosi, Damani, 165
Noble, Ray, 94
"Nobody Else But Me," 173
"Nobody's Business," 141
"No Moon at All," 243
Noone, Jimmie, 15
Norris, Philip, 252, 253, 255
Norvo, Red, 239–40
"Nothing but D. Best," 59
"Not While I'm Around," 229
"Now He Tells Me," 25
"No Woman, No Cry," 141
"Now's the Time," 94, 201
"Nutty," 49

Oberlin, Karen, 244
O'Donnell, Bill, 202–3
"Of Dreams to Come," 133
"Off-Minor," 46
"Off the Beat," 60
Ogerman, Claus, 146
"O Grande Amor," 201
Oh, Linda May Han, 125
"Oh, What a Beautiful Morning," 73, 75
"Oh Freedom," 126
"Oh! Lady Be Good," 85
"Oh! Look at Me Now," 75
"Ohosnisixaeht," 118
"Ojos de Rojos [Red Eyes]," 105, 254
"Ol' Grand Dad," 9
Oliver, Joe "King," 1
"Olivia's Dream," 219
"Once in a While," 59
Once Upon a Time (Hines), 16
"One for E," 170
"One for Majid," 193
"One for My Baby," 239
"125th Street Congress," 221
One More: Music of Thad Jones (Jones, H.), 74
"One Note Samba," 243
"One O'Clock Jump," 21
"Only the Lonely," 192
On the Road (Kerouac), 55
"On the Street Where You Live," 39
"Oop Bop Sh'Bam," 252
Open Book (Hersch), 190
"Opus No. Zero," 139
Orchid Room, 90
"Organ Grinder," 250
Origin (Alexander, J.), 258
Ormandy, Eugene, 41
"Ornate," 167
"Ornithology," 94
Ørsted Pederson, Niels-Henning, 102
Oscar Peterson: Black + White (documentary film), 35
Oscar Peterson Trio, *29*, 31–32, 33, 34
"Otto Make That Riff Staccato," 44
"Out of This World," 234
"Overjoyed," 125
"Over the Rainbow," 106
Owens, Brandon, 200

Page, Hot Lips, 72, 226
"Pages of Life," 242
Panama (Pérez), 146
Panama Suite (Pérez), 146
Panamonk (Pérez), 146
"Pandemic Jazz," 187
"Pannonica," 51, 190
Panzer, Marty, 243
"Papillon," 66
Parisian Thoroughfares (Powell), 95
Paris Sessions (Powell), 96–97
Parker, Charlie: associates, 108–9; band members, 47; biographical information, 29; as influence, 92–95, 226; mental hospital stays, 93; movement associations, 50; musicians working with, 72, 226; recordings, 73, 95; song introductions, 79; songs of, 73, 79, 92, 127, 133, 141, 185, 190, 201, 244; style comparisons, 93; style descriptions, 15, 18, 45, 46; tributes and homages to, 92–95, 140
Parker, Dorothy, 41
"Parker's Mood," 49
"Partita No. 1 in B-flat major," 42

"Passion Dance," 112
"Pastime Paradise," 170
"Pastoral," 189
Pastorious, Jaco, 220, 221
Paudras, Francis, 96
"Pauletta," 76
"Pavanne," 64
Payne, Sonny, 19, 23
"Peace," 170
"Peace on You," 155
"Peace Piece," 100
Peacock, Gary, 190, 191, 193
"Peacocks, The," 65, 96
"Pearls, The," 2
Pearson, Duke, 207
"Pelican, The," 81
Pelt, Jeremy, 104, 105, 167
Penthouse Serenade (Cole), 25–26
"People," 250, 253
People Time, 80
"People Will Say We're in Love," 204
Pepper, Art, 61
Peraza, Armando, 57
Peress, Maurice, 203
Pérez, Danilo, 146–47, *196*
"Perfidia," 105
performance behaviors, 190–92, 193, 222
performance models, 187
"Perfumed Forest Wet with Rain, The," 160
"Permanent Wave," 123
Perry, Harry, 56
Person, Houston, 106, 142, 251
Peterson, Fred, 30–31
Peterson, Oscar: arrangements for, 245; awards and honors, 32; collaborations, 24; documentary films on, 35–36; ensembles, *29,* 31–32, 33, 34; as influence, 143; influences on, 24, 31, 34, 35; performances, 33, 73; songs of, 207, 253; style comparisons, 24; style descriptions, 22, 29–31, 33, 92
Petrucciani, Michel, 98
Pettiford, Oscar, 32, 33, 35
"Pettiford's Tune" (*later* "Swingin' Till the Girls Come Home"), 32, 35
Philips, Pal, 242
Phillips, Flip, 72
"Physical Cities," 223, 224
"Piano Concerto in F," 41
Piano in the Foreground (Ellington), 13
Piano Jazz (radio show), 100, 109
Piano Jazz (Zinc Bar), 202–4
"Pianology," 17
"Piano Man," 17
pianos, as orchestra, 14, 111
Piano Style of Nat King Cole, The (Cole), 25, 26
"Piano Tune," 91
Picasso, Pablo, 46
"Pick Yourself Up," 59
Pietro, Dave, 139
Pinciotti, Anthony, 243
"Pisces," 248
"Pitter Patter Panther," 252
Pizzarelli, Bucky, 144, 228
Pizzarelli, John, 254, 256
"Planes," 243
Playdate (Keezer), 171–73
Plesser, Andy, 115
"Plus Belle Africaine, La," 14
"Poinciana," 64, 66, 68–69, 124, 248
Poole, Kyle, 251
Popkin, Lenny, 90
Porter, Cole, 96, 100, 120, 124, 146, 182, 186, 188, 193, 206, 232
Porter, Gene, 4
Porter, Lewis, 48
"Porter's Love Song to a Chambermaid, A," 6
Portrait in Jazz, 99
"Portrait of Tracy," 221
"Portraits and Dreams," 127
Portraits of Ellington (Weston), 151
Possibilities (Hancock), 197
Potter, Chris, 197, 207, 208
Powell, Bud: associates, 96; health, 96; as influence, 23, 56, 177, 184, 193; mentors to, 247; performances, 78; recordings, 92–95; songs of, 79, 192, 250, 253; style comparisons, 132–33; style descriptions, 92, 113
Power of the Spirit, The (Thompson, I. J.), 255–56

"Power of the Spirit," 256
"Prayer," 169
"Prayer, A," 254–55
Prelude in C-sharp minor, 39
"Preludes," 41
"Prelude to a Kiss," 78, 137
"preparing" pianos, 166
Presley, Elvis, 208–10
"Pretty-Eyed Baby," 43
Previn, Andre, 35
Priestley, Brian, 17, 18
Printmakers, The (Allen, G.), 128–30
"Printmakers," 129
Procrastinator, The (Morgan, L.), 169
Prog (Bad Plus), 223
"Prologue," 236
Prospect Park Bandshell, *116*
"Push-Ka-Pee She Pie (The Saga of Saga Boy)," 140
"Put on a Happy Face," 32, 234

"Queen of Hearts," 73
"Quiet Girl, A," 236
Quinerly, Reggie, 170
Quintet, The (Reed, E.), 167

Ra, Sun, 92, 115–18, *116*
Radiance (Jarrett), 192
Radio Sechaba (Dyer, B.), 165
Raghavan, Harish, 124
"Raise Four," 254, 255
Rantisi, Tareq, 146
"Rap #3," 229
Rascher, Sigurd, 75
Ratliff, Ben, 190–91
Ravel, Joseph Maurice, 41
Raye, Martha, 240
"Raymond's Blues," 104
Razaf, Andy, 6
Ready Take One (Garner), 38, 39–40
Real McCoy, The (Tyner), 112, 113
Rebirth (Childs), 199
Reddick, TJ, 255
"Redemption Song," 141, 145
"Red Top," 38
Reed, Eric, 73, 167–71, *168*
Reed, Rex, 244
Reflections: Steve Lacy Plays Thelonious Monk (Lacy), 50
"Reflections," 181
"Refuge," 172
Reid, Damion, 132
Reid, Vernon, 130
"Relaxin' at Camarillo," 93
"REM Blues," 13
"Remembering," 258
Remembering Miles (Davis, M.), 87
Return to Forever, 177. 178
reverse showmanship, 190–92, 193
Revolver (Beatles), 175
"Rhapsody," 90
Rhapsody in Blue: The Extraordinary Life of Oscar Levant, A (Levant, O.), 41
"Rhapsody in Blue," 40–41, 85
Rhapsody in Blue (biopic), 41
Rhapsody in Blue (Rosenthal), 204
Rhone, Calvin B., 170
"Rhythm" ("All God's Chillun Got Wings"), 79
Rhythms of the Heart (Barron, K.), 81
Ribot, Marc, 111, 112
Riddle, Nelson, 26, 33, 42, 240
Riggins, Karriem, 200
Riley, Ben, 51
Riley, Herlin, 141, 144
"Rise from Love," 147
"Rising, Falling," 189
River: The Joni Letters (Hancock), 197
"River," 197
Rivers, Sam, 185
Rizzo, Jilly, 142
Roach, Max, 11, 12, 13, 14, 60
"Road Song," 144
Roberts, Lucky, 3
Robin, Leo, 178
Robinson, Scott, 139
Rocco, Maurice, 175
Roche, Jerry, 90
"Rockin' in Rhythm," 252
Rodgers, Richard, 178, 204
Rodrigo, Joaquín, 145
Roger Kellaway Live at Mezzrow (Kellaway), 242
"Roll 'Em," 44

Rollins, Sonny: collaborations, 60; influences on, 141; musicians playing with, 60; performances, 48, 65; recordings, 99; song dedications to, 202; songs of, 169, 242; style comparisons, 139; style descriptions, 86, 186
Ron Carter Trio, 92
Roney, Antoine, 126
Roney, Wallace, 130, 132
Rooker, Bryon, 66
"Roots," 155
Rosengarden, Bobby, 73
Rosenthal, Ted, 142, 203–4
Rosenwinkel, Kurt, 173
Rosnes, Renee, 58, 59, 124, 204–8, *205*
Ross, Steve, 231
Rota, Nino, 127, 130
Rotondi, Jim, 139
"'Round Midnight," 46, 50, 137, 168, 258
Round Midnight (film), 96
Rouse, Charlie, 49, 50
Rowles, Jimmy, 65, 96
Rubinstein, Arthur, 29
Rudd, Roswell, 50, 51–52
Rueckert, Jochen, 188
"Run Joe," 140
"Running As Fast As You Can . . . TGTH," 128–29
Rushing, Jimmy, 24
Russ, Robert, 41
Russell, George, 65
Russell, Leon, 198
Russell, Miguel, 255, 256
Russell, Pee Wee, 16
"Russian Rag," 131

Sadownick, Daniel, 58, 59
"Sad Poet," 186
"Salt Peanuts," 94
"Salute to Garner," 30
"Sama Layuca," 112
Sample, Joe, 145
Sanders, Annette, 228, 229
Sando, Bill, 93–94
"San Francisco Holiday," 182, 184, 203
Santana, Carlos, 111
"Sarabande," 187
"Satchel Mouth Baby," 18
"Satin Doll," 40, 137, 252, 253
"Sati Suite," 188–89
Saxophone Colossus (Rollins), 99
Scene Changes, The (Powell), 94
Schaap, Phil, 94
Scheckter, Jane, 243, 244
Schneider, Maria, 1, 248
Schoenberg, Loren, 17, 47
Schumann, Robert, 41
Schuur, Dianne, 243
Schwartz, Arthur, 8, 65
Scofield, John, 111
"Scorpio," 358
Scott, Hazel, 27
Scott, Kendrick, 170, 171
Scott, Little Jimmy, 203
Scott, Tony, 99
"Scrapple for the Apple," 94
"Search for Peace," 170
Seasoned Wood (Walton), 103, 105–7
Seaton, Laura, 190
"Second Rhapsody for Piano and Orchestra," 41
"Second Time Around," 252
"Secret Beach, The," 185
Secret Recordings (Evans, B.), 181
Secret Sessions, The (Evans, B.), 95–98
Sedric, Gene, 5, 8
Seldes, Gilbert, 130
Sellick, Luke, 145
"Señor Blues," 254
"September in the Rain," 30, 57, 59
"Serenata," 105
Seven Lively Arts, The (Seldes), 130
"Seven Steps to Heaven," 200
Shakur, Hassan, 144
Shakur, Herman, 141
Shange, Ntozake, 74
Shaw, Artie, 73, 242
Shaw, Woody, 113, 250
"Shaw 'Nuff," 94, 97
Shearing, George, 29–30, 39, 55–59, *56*, 105, 253
Shelton, Anne, 81
Sheppard, Andy, 122
Shire, David, 245

Shorter, Wayne: bands and ensembles, 104, 114, 220–21; performances, 195–96; songs of, 87, 170, 184
"Should I," 67
Sickler, Don, 51, 105
"Sidewalk Blues," 2
Sidewinder, The (Morgan), 216
"Sidewinders in Paradise," 123
Silberstein, Yotam, 143
Silver, Horace, 129, 167, 170, 254
"Silver Bells," 145
Simone, Nina, 109
"Simple Pleasures," 104
"Simplicity," 59
Sims, Zoot, 48, 90, 97
Sinatra, Frank: clubs frequented by, 201; as influence, 143; pianists and conductors of, 24, 239; protégés of, 140, 142; song selling strategies, 174; songs of, 41, 208, 212
Sinatra, Frank, Jr., 239, 240
"Single Petal of a Rose," 160, 256
Singleton, Zutty, 4
Sissle, Noble, 131
"Sister Rosie," 158
"Skippy," 51, 164
"Sky and Sun," 117
"Sleep," 63
"Sleepin' Bee," 228
Sloane, Carol, 234
"Sly Mongoose," 94, 141
"Smashing Thirds," 4–5
"Smells Like Teen Spirit," 223
Smith, Bessie, 141
Smith, Derek, 228
Smith, Jabbo, 7
Smith, Janet, 161
Smith, Jimmy, 7
Smith, Sean, 58
Smith, Songai Sandra, 114
Smith, Stuff, 86
Smith, Willie "The Lion," 3, 24, 45, 109
"Smitty," 114
Snow, Valaida, 17
"Softly, as in a Morning Sunrise," 81
"So In Love," 182
Solal, Martial, 39, 135–37, *136*
"Solar," 100, 173
Soldier's Hymn (Reed, E.), 167
"Solitude," 13, 158, 188
"Somebody Loves Me," 83, 85
"Someday My Prince Will Come," 193, 208
"Some Other Spring," 79
"Some Other Time," 100
"Sometimes I'm Happy," 32, 33
Somewhere: The Songs of Leonard Bernstein (Charlap, B.), 232, 234–35
"Somewhere," 192
"Sonatine," 41
"Song for My Lady," 114
"Song for You, A," 198
"Song of the Vagabonds," 28
Songs From Home (Hersch), 187–88
Song Spirit (Benjamin), 162–63
"Song X," 224
"Sophisticated Lady," 237
Sorey, Tyshawn, 124, 125
"Soul Messenger," 256
"Soultrain," 75
"Sound-Lee," 90
South, Eddie, 109
"Spa Glass," 202
"Spain," 133, 177
"Speak Low," 142
"Special K," 167
"Spillin' the Tea," 252, 253
Spirit Song (Barron, K.), 79, 81
Spirit! The Power of Music (Weston), 151
"Spring Flower," 256
"Squeeze Me," 8, 21
"Squeeze Me (But Don't Tease Me)," 237
"Squeezin' the Blues," 57
St. Louis Blues (Ra), 115
"St. Louis Blues," 116, 131, 168
"St. Thomas," 202
Stalling, Carl, 23
"Standard Time" series, 178
"Stardust," 234
Stardust (Charlap, B.), 233
"Star Eyes," 79, 181
Starr, Kay, 24
"Stars and Stripes Forever," 28
"Stars Fell on Alabama," 194
"Star-Spangled Banner, The," 122

"Starting Here, Starting Now," 245
"State of the Nation," 165
Steinway pianos, red, xv–xvi, 118–21
"Stella by Starlight," 75
Stewart, Bill, 206
Stewart, Sandy, 235
Stewart, Slam, 4, 33
Stir It Up (Alexander, M.), 142
Stockenhausen, Karlheinz, 161
"Stone Cold Dead in the Market," 140
"Stop Start," 169
"Stormy Weather," 24
Storyteller, The (Weston), 151–52
"Straighten Up and Fly Right," 25, 145
"Straight No Chaser," 46, 192
"Strange Meadowlark," 60
"Stranger in Paradise," 59
Stratta, Ettore, 242
Stravelli, Gabrielle, 242
Strayhorn, Billy: band memberships, 44, 160; as influence, 76; songs of, 46, 96, 253, 254; style comparisons, 229; style descriptions, 163
"Street of Dreams," 237
Street of Dreams (Charlap, B.), 237
Strickland, Marcus, 167
"Strictly Instrumental," 9
Stritch, Billy, 242–43
"Stumbling," 104
"Stuttering," 186
Styne, Jule, 250, 253
Subject is Jazz, The (television program), 109
Suesse, Dana, 231
Sullivan, Joe, 3
"Sultry Serenade," 38
"Summer Night," 206, 207
"Summertime," 85, 86, 87
"Sunday," 244
Sunday at the Village Vanguard (Evans, B.), 99, 180
"Sunflower," 219
"Sun for Sunny," 202
"Sunken Cathedral," 59
"Sunny," 40
Sunset at Dawn (Barron, K.), 80
"Superwoman (Where Were You When I Needed You)," 244
Suspicious Activity (Bad Plus), 222
"Suspicious Minds," 209
Swallow, Steve, 122, 123
Swamp Sally (Barron, K.), 80
"Sweet and Lovely," 49, 104
"Sweet and Slow," 6
Sweet Basil, 159, 160, *205*
"Sweet Georgia Brown," 143
"Sweet Lorraine," 15, 23, 24, 28, 79
Swingadelic, 207
"Swinging on a Star," 245
"Swingin' Till the Girls Come Home," 32, 35
"Switch Blade," 13
"Swoop," 207–8
"Symphonic Raps," 252
"Symphony Sid," 227
Symposium of Swing, A (Waller, T.), 5

Tabackin, Lew, 138–39
Taborn, Craig, 121–22, 218
"Take Five," 60, 63
"Take the 'A' Train," 46, 241, 254, 255
"Tangerine," 68
"Tango Palace," 245
Tatum, Art: ensembles, 24, 27; as influence, 28, 29, 31, 34, 35, 108, 248, 256; influences on, 31; recordings, 27–29; style comparisons, 15; style descriptions, 27, 28–29
"Taurus," 248
Taylor, Art, 93, 94
Taylor, Billy, 5, 45, 107–9, *108*
Taylor, Cecil: performances, xvi, 43, 118, *119*, 119–20, 121–22; style comparisons, 13, 117–18; style descriptions, 92, 113, 119, 120, 161
Taylor, Kim, 109
Taylor Made Jazz, 109
"Tea for Two," 51, 79, 123, 137, 164, 252
Tea for Two (Fortner), 249
"Tenderly," 31
Tender Moments (Tyner), 113
"Tennessee Waltz, The," 192
Tenor Madness, 169
"Tenor Madness," 169
Terry, Clark, 14, 33, 73

"Thag's Dance," 253
"Thanks for the Memory," 39, 221
"That Face!," 240
"That Moaning Trombone," 131
"That Old Black Magic," 73, 245
Thelonious Alone in San Francisco (Monk), 182, 184
Thelonious (Hersch), 182, 184
Thelonious Monk Competition, 254
Thelonious Monk Quartet Featuring John Coltrane Live at the Five Spot Discovery, 47
Thelonious Monk Quartet with John Coltrane at Carnegie Hall, 47
"Thelonius," 170
"Theme, The," 201
"Theme for Malcolm," 169
"Them There Eyes," 229
"Then I'll Be Tired of You," 5, 8, 9, 65
These Are the Vistas (Bad Plus), 223
"These Foolish Things (Remind Me of You)," 90, 120, 256
"These Love Notes," 145
Thielemans, Toots, 57
Thigpen, Ed, 32, 33, 34
"Things Aint' What They Used to Be," 250
Things Unseen (Barron, K.), 79, 81
"Think of One," 168, 184–85
"Third Street Jump," 169
"This Happy Madness," 243
"This Is Always," 190, 244–45
Thompson, Isaiah J., 254–56
Thompson, Lucky, 72
Thornhill, Claude, 153
"Thoughts on Thoth," 117
"Three Bells, The," 175
3 (Ibrahim), 163–64
Three Keys, 23
"Three Little Words," 116–17
Three Peppers, 24
Three Suns, The, 94
"Three to Get Ready," 60
"Three Windows," 218
"Tiger Rag," 250
"Time After Time," 253
Time Again: Brubeck Revisited (Brubeck, D.), 60
Time Changes (Brubeck, D.), 61
"Time for Love, A," 189
Time for Tyner (Tyner), 113
Time Further Out (Brubeck, D.), 61
Time In (Brubeck, D.), 61–62
"Timeless Portraits and Dreams," 127
Timeless Portraits and Dreams (Allen, G.), 126, 130
"Time on My Hands," 252, 253
"Time Out," 30
Time Out (Brubeck, D.), 60
Time Signatures (Brubeck, D.), 60
Timmons, Bobby, 104, 216
"'Tis a Prayer," 258
"Tiya Mowa," 165
Tizol, Juan, 13, 151
"To a Wild Rose," 28, 39
"Tombeau de Couperin, Le," 42
"Tomorrow," 172
"Tomorrow (A Better You, Better Me)," 172
tone, 75–76
"Tones for Joan's Bones," 234
"Tonk," 229
"Too Marvelous for Words," 144, 145
Toshiko at Top of the Gate (Akiyoshi), 139
To the Stars (Corea), 177
To the Stars (Hubbard), 177
touch, 75–76
Town Hall, 44, 109, 138, 247
Tracy, Stan, 157
Traditional jazz, 89
"Trance-Mission," 164
"Träumerei," 41
Treasures: Solo, Trio & Orchestra Recordings from Denmark (1965–1969) (Evans, B.), 102
"Treasures," 102
"Tricotism," 33
Trio, The (Jones, H.), 73
Trio Rachmaninoff, 24
Tristano, Lennie, 4, 56, 89–92
Trucks, Derek, 111
"Trumpets No End," 44
"Try to Remember," 241
Turner, Emile, 203
Turner, Mark, 89, 91–92
"Turn Out the Stars," 96, 181

Turn Out the Stars (Evans, B.), 98
Turre, Steve, 104, 105, 107
Turrentine, Stanley, 67
Tuxedo Slickers, 159
"Tweedle Dee," 181
"Twelve More Bars to Go," 170
"20 Minutes After Three," 22
"Twilight Time," 94
"Twilight Waltz," 106
Tyner, McCoy: biographical information, 110–11; collaborations, 103, 112; performances, 73, *110,* 111–12; recordings, 110, 111, 113, 124; songs of, 170; style comparisons, 97, 125, 202, 208, 256; style descriptions, 110, 112–14

"Ugetsu," 104
"Ugly Beauty," 171
Uhuru Africa (Weston), 149, 152
Ultimate Adventure, The (Corea), 177
Underground (Hersch), 186
"Underground Memories," 106–7
Uneasy, 124
"Uneasy," 125
"Unknown Soldier," 221
"Until the Real Thing Comes Along," 7, 9
"Untitled Blues," 18
Uplife (Alexander, M.), 142–43
Upon Reflection (Jones, H.), 74
Uptown in Orbit (Cohen), 253

Valente, Gianni, 252
Valentin, Dave, 203
"Valentine," 189–90
"Valse Hot," 86
"Valse Sinestro," 123
Van Heusen, James, 107, 178, 240, 245
"Variation Twenty-Four," 170
Vaughan, Sarah, 15
"Very Special," 12, 13
"Very Thought of You, The," 77
"Vesti la giubba," 24, 28
"Vibration Blues," 113
Vijay Iyer Trio, 124–25
Viola, Al, 240
"Viper's Dog, The," 4
"Virgo," 249
"Vision," 114
"Voices of Spring," 39

Waits, Freddie, 113
Waits, Nasheet, 182, 184
Waldron, Mal, 153, 157
Waller, Maurice, 7
Waller, Thomas "Fats," 3–9, 20–21, 72, 131, 228
Walton, Cedar, 73, 103–7, 254
"Waltz for Darnelle," 200
"Waltz for Debby," 100, 101–2
"Waltz for Monk," 200
Waltz in C-sharp minor (Opus 64, No. 2), 28
"Waltz of the Flowers," 51–52
Ward, Carlos, 160
Wareika Hill (Alexander, M.), 145
"Warm Valley," 13, 22–23, 250
"Warna," 258
Warna (Alexander, J.), 258
"War No More," 202
Warren, Harry, 6, 206, 207, 244
Washington, Dinah, 7, 32, 220
Washington, Kenny, 58, 104, 203, 232, 234, 237, 254, 255
Washington, Peter, 105, 203, 206, 207, 208, 217, 232, 234
Watanabe, Mamiko, 203
Watanabe, Sadao, 138
Water form an Ancient Well (Ibrahim), 161
"Water from an Ancient Well," 164
"Water Is Wide, The," 187
Waters of March—The Brazilian Album (Stritch), 243
Waxman, Franz, 41
Wayne, Chuck, 57
"Way You Look Tonight, The," 63, 259
"Weather Bird," 15
Weather Report, 219–22
Webb, Jimmy, 174, 188
Webster, Ben, 72, 76, 109, 220, 248
"Wedding, The," 164
"Wednesday," 219
We Get Requests (Peterson, O.), 30
Weill, Kurt, 59, 142

Wein, George, xv, 118, 138, 227
Weir, Frank, 56
Weiss, George David, 58
"Well, You Needn't," 95
"We'll Be Together Again," 120
"Well Done," 127
Well-Tempered Clavier (Lewis, J.), 216
Wess, Frank, 76–77, 120, 233
"West End Blues," 15
Weston, Randy, 132, 149–53, *150,* 156, 157, 203, 254
"West Virginia Rose," 187
"What a Little Moonlight Can Do," 245
"What Am I Here For," 120
"What Are You Doing the Rest of Your Life?," 237
"What Is This Thing Called Love," 200, 237
"What's Your Story, Morning Glory," 44
Wheeler, Kenny, 187, 208
"When I Fall in Love," 192
"When I'm Sixty-Four," 188
"When Kayuba Dances," 130
"When Lights Are Low," 104
"When Love Comes to Town," 197
"When Your Lover Has Gone," 39
Where Did Everyone Go? (Cole), 23
"Where Have You Been?," 232
"Where or When," 38, 228
"Whirl," 186
"Whisperings," 65
White, Andrew, 114
Whitehead, Kevin, 50
Whittaker, Rodney, 206
"Who Cares?," 237
"Wichita Lineman," 188
Wiggins, Gerald, 144
Wilder, Joe, 228
"Wild Is the Wind," 63, 66
"Wild Man Blues," 2
"Wild Music," 40
Wilen, Barney, 97
Wiley, Lee, 85
Wilkins, Ernie, 65
Williams, Cootie, 46
Williams, David, 104, 105
Williams, Happy, 141
Williams, James, 73
Williams, Joe, 71, 208
Williams, John, 43
Williams, Leroy, 78
Williams, Mary Lou, 18, 43–45, 121, 127, 247
Williams, Tony, 220
"Willow Tree," 6–7
"Willow Weep for Me," 139
Wilmore, Larry, 112
Wilson, Cassandra, 128
Wilson, John S., 37–39
Wilson, Nancy, 59
Wilson, Shadow, 49
Wilson, Steve, 199, 206, 207, 208
Wilson, Teddy: associates, 84; career descriptions, 84; cartoon recordings, 84; as influence, 31, 72; influences on, 18, 83, 85; recordings, 83–86; students of, 226; style comparisons, 15, 23, 49; style descriptions, 27, 31, 84; television work, 72; trio ensembles, 84
Winds of Change, The (Childs), 198–99
"Winds of Change, The," 198–99
Winstone, Norma, 190
"Wish, A," 190
"With a Song in My Heart," 178
Withers, Bill, 170
"With Ev'ry Breath I Take," 243
With Respect to Nat (Peterson, O.), 34
Wolf, Warren, 219
Wong, David, 249
Woode, Jimmy, 160
Woods, Carol, 229
Woods, Guy, 250
Woodyard, Sam, 13
"Woody 'n' You," 237
Wopat, Tom, 244
World of Earl Hines, The (Hines), 15
"Worry Later" ("San Francisco Holiday"), 182, 184, 203
"Wouldn't It Be Loverly," 187
Wright, Eugene, 62
Wright, Laurie, 5
Written in the Stars (Charlap, B.), 232

"Yes and No," 170
"Yes Sir, That's My Baby," 141

"Yesterdays," 193
"You and the Night and the Music," 185
"You Belong to Me," 192
"You Can See," 67
You Don't Know Me (Cables), 118
"You Don't Know What Love Is," 119, 187, 258
"You Don't Learn That in School," 25
"You Know I Care," 207
"You Look Marvelous," 25
"You Made a Good Move," 77
Youmans, Vincent, 32, 252
Young, Lee, 24
Young, Lester, 24, 32, 33, 72, 96, 226, 242
Young, Victor, 120
"Young and Foolish," 173
"Young and Healthy," 28
"Young at Heart," 227
Young Lions, 232
"You're All the World to Me," 8, 237
"Your Feet's Too Big," 7–8
Your Mother Should Know: Brad Mehldau Plays The Beatles (Mehldau), 174–76
"Your Mother Should Know," 175
Yours for a Song—Here's to the Ladies (Mintun), 231
"You Taught My Heart to Sing," 112
"You Took Advantage of Me," 74
"You Won't Forget Me," 191

Zawinal, Joe, 219–22
Zeitlin, Denny, 86–87
Zenón, Miguel, 251
Zetterland, Monica, 100
"Zodiac Suite," 44
Zodiac Suite (Williams, M.L.), 247–48
Zorn, John, 23